Bordering on the Body

 W9-BXX-747

RACE AND AMERICAN CULTURE

General Editors:
Arnold Rampersad and Shelley Fisher Fishkin

Bordering on the Body

*The Racial Matrix
of Modern Fiction
and Culture*

Laura Doyle

New York   Oxford
OXFORD UNIVERSITY PRESS
1994

Oxford University Press

Oxford   New York   Toronto
Delhi   Bombay   Calcutta   Madras   Karachi
Kuala Lumpur   Singapore   Hong Kong   Tokyo
Nairobi   Dar es Salaam   Cape Town
Melbourne   Auckland   Madrid

and associated companies in
Berlin   Ibadan

Copyright © 1994 by Oxford University Press, Inc.

Published by Oxford University Press, Inc.,
200 Madison Avenue, New York, New York 10016

Oxford is a registered trademark of Oxford University Press

All rights reserved. No part of this publication may be reproduced,
stored in a retrieval system, or transmitted, in any form or by any means,
electronic, mechanical, photocopying, recording, or otherwise,
without the prior permission of Oxford University Press.

Library of Congress Cataloging-in-Publication Data
Doyle, Laura Anne.
Bordering on the body : the racial matrix of modern fiction and culture / Laura Doyle.
      p.   cm.—(Race and American culture)
Includes index.
ISBN 0-19-508654-6.
ISBN 0-19-508655-4 (pbk.)
1. American fiction—Afro-American authors—History and criticism.
2. American fiction—20th century—History and criticism.
3. English fiction—20th century—History and criticism.
4. Afro-Americans in literature.
5. Body, Human, in literature.
6. Modernism (Literature)
7. Mothers in literature.
8. Race in literature.
I. Title.   II. Series.
PS374.N4D65   1994
813'.509896073—dc20   94-5456

Since this page cannot accommodate all the credit lines, the following page
constitutes an extension of the copyright page.

9 8 7 6 5 4 3 2 1

Printed in the United States of America
on acid-free paper

Chapter 5 is reprinted from "Races and Chains:
The Sexuo-Racial Matrix in Ulysses," by Laura Doyle.
In *Joyce: The Return of the Repressed*, edited by Susan Stanford Friedman.
Copyright © 1993 by Cornell University.
Used by permission of the publisher, Cornell University Press.

An earlier version of chapter 6 first appeared as "'These Emotions of the Body':
Intercorporeal Narrative in *To the Lighthouse*," by Laura Doyle,
from *Twentieth-Century Literature* (vol. 40, no. 1).
Reprinted by permission of the publisher.

Permission to reprint material from the following is gratefully acknowledged:

Cane by Jean Toomer, reprinted by permission of Liveright Publishing Corporation.
Copyright 1923 by Boni & Liveright. Copyright renewed 1951 by Jean Toomer.

Ulysses by James Joyce. Copyright © 1934 and renewed 1962 by Lucia and George Joyce.
Reprinted by permission of Random House, Inc., and The Bodley Head.

Invisible Man by Ralph Ellison. Copyright © 1947, 1948, 1952 by Ralph Ellison.
Reprinted by permission of Random House, Inc.

Beloved by Toni Morrison. Permission granted by International Creative Management, Inc.
Copyright 1987 by Toni Morrison.

The Bluest Eye by Toni Morrison. Permission granted by International Creative Management, Inc.
Copyright 1970 by Toni Morrison.

To the Lighthouse by Virginia Woolf, copyright 1927 by Harcourt Brace & Company
and renewed 1954 by Leonard Woolf.
Reprinted by permission of Harcourt Brace & Company.

Three Guineas by Virginia Woolf, copyright 1938 by Harcourt Brace & Company
and renewed 1966 by Leonard Woolf.
Reprinted by permission of the publisher.

"Professions for Women" from *The Death of the Moth and Other Essays* by Virginia Woolf,
copyright 1942 by Harcourt Brace & Company and renewed 1970
by Marjorie T. Parsons, Executrix. Reprinted by permission of the publisher.

Melymbrosia by Virginia Woolf, reprinted by permission of Henry W. and Albert A. Berg Collection,
The New York Public Library, Astor, Lenox and Tilden Foundations.

For
Samuel and Leon

Preface

"Bordering on" means both "verging on" and "staking territory along." These joined meanings reflect my interest in the merging of aesthetics with politics—specifically in modern fiction's vertiginous encounter with the boundaried sexual and racial economy of Western culture. Experimental modern novels, I argue, return to the figure most closely associated with fleshly boundaries—the mother; they reveal a racial economy circumscribing her flesh-reproducing role; and they push narrative language to *its* outlying borders, to the verge where absence meets presence, visible touches invisible, thus exposing, and in some moments surpassing, the racial and gendered, linguistic and literary bordering of the flesh.

I speak of race in this book as a founding element of white as well as black traditions; and I speak of sexuality and race as structurally co-dependent in Western traditions, not merely intermingled by association nor intersecting in the bodies of the doubly—racially and sexually—oppressed. I offer a theory of racial patriarchy which articulates the necessary, mutual relation of race and gender formations. By encompassing a variety of white texts and traditions in a theory of race, and stressing the mutuality of sexual and racial economies across traditions, I necessarily forfeit detailed attention to those features that distinguish different racialized traditions from each other. That is, while I closely read the workings of what I call a racial–patriarchal economy within African-American texts, pointing to the means by which these texts slip the hold of that economy, my approach is not an Afrocentric one. Nor is my approach to the racial tropes in James Joyce's texts attentive to their Irish linguistic and literary maneuvers. Yet neither is my method Eurocentric. It benefits, rather, from the wealth of recent scholarship in anthropology, history, history of science, and cultural studies that cuts across these oppositions.

In fact, without entering into a long debate, I suggest that many modern innovations in theory have arisen exactly in and through dialogue with thinkers outside mainstream Anglo-European institutions and traditions. Without W. E. B. Du Bois's notion of double consciousness there would be no theory, I submit, of différance. Without Simone de Beauvoir's politicization of the notion of the Other, there would be no Foucaultian account of the hegemony of discourse. In a different vein and time, without strikes and riots there would be no Karl Marx; without suffragettes there would be no Freudian theory of sexuality to explain them away. It is not only that our theories are always already derived from white intellectual fathers, but also that "their" theories have always already enfolded the social acts and intellectual insights of mothers, daughters, workers, servers, and Others. As James Joyce once said of Ireland, "[I]n such a fabric it is useless to look for a thread that may have remained pure and virgin"—or that can be identified as original.[1] Our theories are never so "centric" in any direction, as opposing sides claim. When I intermingle, for instance, the tropes of slave narratives with the vocabulary of phenomenology in reading Toni Morrison's *Beloved*, I participate in this already crossed discursive history.

In articulating the racial and sexual politics of modern narrative forms, I draw heavily on the work of Maurice Merleau-Ponty. Given the current predominance of Lacanian notions of body and of language among feminist critics in particular, I find Merleau-Ponty's careful tracing of the "reversibility" of alterity a helpful corrective. As extended in the work of Julia Kristeva, Lacanian psychoanalytical theory does clarify the split between mothers and language, mothers and maturity, and mothers and author/ity which Western cultures consider proper. But all too often in the process, such theorists are seduced by the tragic drama and heart-breaking romance of such a split. Body and language *must* part, it seems, and body can only express its presence in an abject, semiotic supplication performed on hands and knees beneath the masterful text.

I suggest, by contrast, that such splitting is constitutive only of a historically specific and linguistically *challenged* heterosexual and racial social order; that this Lacanian drama of splitting is a social mirage which critics sometimes come to believe is fact; and that another phenomenology—one disregarded by deconstruction—offers modern critics the terms for narrating another story. I consider it telling, in this connection, that the deconstructive critique of phenomenology returns again and again to the transcendental (masculine) German phenomenologists such as Hegel, Husserl, and Heidegger but ignores the existential French (feminine) phenomenologists such as Sartre and Merleau-Ponty. An old racialized and gendered romance lives on here (as we shall see in chapter 2). More important, a whole generation of critics has followed it faithfully, overlooking thinkers who have moved the critique of transcendentalism in directions that both supplement and surpass the deconstructive critique. Among the latter, it is Merleau-Ponty whose work most informs this study, for his rethinking, or unthinking, of the divide between presence and absence, subject and object, speaks eloquently to modern fiction's experimental project.

One last methodological note. In integrating the materials of history and anthropology into my analyses, I diverge from the kind of new historicism that reads history and culture as discourse and uses historical/cultural tropes to read literary texts. I attempt a more balanced joining, or hybridization, of history and text, event and expression, act and word, in which neither term subsumes the other—an attempt also central to the fiction I analyze here. In the first three chapters of this book, I analyze directly the economics and cultural politics of modern racial and sexual history because it seems to me that to read history and culture *only* through the lens of discourse risks perpetuating the transcendentalist subsumption of sentience into speech, of things into words, which I seek, above all, to resist here. To presume that words and writing remove us from sentience replays an age-old drama of transcendence. We reenact this drama, often unintentionally, when we bracket bodies and objects as those things which words merely manipulate and displace; we do no justice to what is more fruitfully understood as the shifting, metamorphosing, *reversible* dialectic between writing and touching, resisting and speaking, remembering and forgetting, pausing, weeping, listening, repeating, and laughing.

Cambridge, Mass.   L.D.
February 1994

Acknowledgments

This book would not have been completed without the inspiration and support of many persons, communities, and institutions. Patricia Yaeger, Joseph Boone, Dale Bauer, Lillian Robinson, Barbara Johnson, Robert Kiely, and Nicholas Bromell all read the manuscript and gave me that combination of encouragement and incisive criticism which is indispensible to anyone who writes books. I am grateful for the gift of their friendship and intellectual fellowship. Nancy Stepan and Shari Benstock offered trenchant critiques that made me radically reorganize the book and improve it substantially. I thank them for their lucidity and directness. Vincent Cheng, Carol Batker, Werner Sollors, Karen Klein, Cynthia Smith, Alan Richardson, Calvin Bedient, and Toni Morrison all found time in their tight schedules to read individual chapters and give me the benefit of their intelligence. Hazel Carby urged me to press harder in thinking about motherhood and race. Not only her passing comments but the model of research and thought represented in her scholarship pushed me forward when I might otherwise have stopped short. Certainly any errors in the book are my own, but for its strengths, such as they are, I am indebted to these colleagues and friends.

I thank the American Council of Learned Societies for the fellowship which allowed me to take a year's leave to research the anthropological and historical dimensions of the book. Harvard University kindly relieved me of teaching duties and supplemented my fellowship support for the year. During that year I was also blessed to be an affiliate at the Five College Women's Studies Research Center at Mount Holyoke College. The quiet room with a view, the collegiality of the affiliates, the helpfulness of the colleges' library staff, and the intellectual support, in particular, of Gail Hornstein all made that year unforgettably precious.

It is impossible to specify each of the many mentors, thinkers, and communities that have served as a source of stimulation for the ideas presented in this book—the encircling, invisible medium of this now visible text. To my personal mentors (Kay Dodd, Bill Dodd, Michael Doyle, Debbie Doyle, Marion Stocking, Tom McBride, John Rosenwald, John Wyatt, Karen Klein, Helena Michie, Jim Merod, and Ruth Perry), to the scholars whose work I cite, and to the political activists who first pushed opened the institutional doors I and others now enter more freely I owe more than my thanks: they have made the conception of this book possible.

I am deeply grateful to Shelly Fisher Fishkin, Arnold Rampersad, and the editors at Oxford University Press for their belief in the project. Elizabeth Maguire and Henry Krawitz were endlessly helpful with the practical tasks of publishing this book. My heartfelt thanks go to Amanda Heller for her careful and patient copyediting. I especially want to thank Arnold Rampersad for his continuing support and encouragement, without which I might never have seen the light at the end of the long tunnel that led to this book.

The darkness of that tunnel sometimes called forth my darker side. For his imaginative, calming, and above all wonderfully distracting response to that underside I must again thank Nicholas Bromell. He called me back to the world of things which I often ironically forgot even while I wrote about it. And, finally, Samuel and Leon, for your sweetness, patience, love, and laughter, I dedicate this book to you.

Contents

Bordering on the Body

Introduction

It is startling to notice how many experimental modern novels begin with the figure of a mother. Recall William Faulkner's slow-walking, fully pregnant Lena Grove; Jean Toomer's Karintha crouching to give birth in the pine-fragrant woods; the opening and enveloping presence of Virginia Woolf's Mrs. Ramsay. Consider that Samuel Beckett's *Molloy* opens with the words "I am in my mother's room. I piss and shit in her pot," and Albert Camus's *Stranger* with the news that "Mother died today." Stephen Dedalus wrestles with the memory of his mother at the beginning of James Joyce's *Ulysses*. Nella Larsen's protagonist, Irene Redgrave, nearly faints on the first page of *Passing* as she searches for a gift for her son. Ralph Ellison's narrator dreams of a woman with a voice like his mother's in the "Prologue" to *Invisible Man*. Marcel Proust's protagonist begins the unraveling of his memories with the ritual good-night kiss from his mother. Ursa's hysterectomy constitutes the opening event of Gayl Jones's *Corregidora*, while the beginnings of Toni Morrison's novels, from *The Bluest Eye* to *Beloved*, habitually focus on scenes of troubled mothering. Across borders of nation, race, and sex, mother figures put in play the peculiarities—the very experimentality—of these modern novels.

Why all these mother-marked beginnings in experimental modern fiction? Many feminist critics have considered the meanings of mother figures in *women's* writing and art.[1] But how do we take into account the provocative confluence of men's fiction with women's through these maternal figures? What is the relation, for instance, between the process of "gynesis" in men's fiction, as identified by Alice Jardine, and the mother–daughter plot in women's fiction, as studied by Marianne Hirsch?[2] Moreover, how is it that the mother figure's influence cuts across two important modern literary traditions—the Harlem Renaissance and modernism—which we have come to treat separately? Much has been made of the question whether Jean Toomer, for example, is a Harlem Renaissance writer or a modernist one.[3] By examining the ground on which these traditions meet, a ground shadowed by the mother figure, this book throws the strictness of that opposition into question.

But I do not argue that a universal, race-transcending mother complex explains this common ground. On the contrary, if we look again at these literary mother figures, we see that the boundaries of race or ethnicity crucially constitute

3

their importance. Modern mother figures give birth to racial plots. Camus's story—of Meursault as "the stranger"—climaxes with his murder of an Arab, a crime which his police interrogators link to his callousness at his mother's funeral. Stephen Dedalus's disconnection from the rites associated with a mother likewise makes him a stranger in his own land and leads him to associate with the Jewish "foreigner" Leopold Bloom, who "so wants to be a mother."[4] In Doris Lessing's first novel, Martha Quest's recurring daydream turns from a rejection of both "fat and earthy" and "bitter and nagging" mothers to a vision of a four-gated city where "citizens moved, grave and beautiful, black and white and brown together."[5] Ursa's hysterectomy, the opening event of Gayl Jones's *Corregidora*, threatens and reconfigures her connection to her racial community and history—especially as embodied in her mother and grandmothers. Jean Toomer juxtaposes his sketch of Karintha, the young mother encircled by the gaze of her community's men, against that of Becky, the white mother of "Negro" sons from whom both white and black communities avert their gaze. In Beckett's novel the hunted Molloy is described by Moran as being "of dark colour . . . without being black."[6] And though the story of Mrs. Ramsay is less directly linked to race than these others, if we recognize the interconnection of race, empire, and world wars—which a reading of Woolf's *Three Guineas* tells us she herself recognized—we can begin to understand even the seemingly timeless and transcendent motherhood of Mrs. Ramsay as one that functions for the race.

In all of these texts the mother figure or role represents complications not just in the gender identities, then, but in the racial, ethnic, or national identities of the characters and narrators. One of the primary aims of this book is to show how these mother-entangled complications of identity determine the unorthodox narrative practices of experimental novels. The nonchronological, interruptive, or arabesque forms of modern experimental fiction reflect narrative efforts to disengage the mother from her function as sexual–racial matrix of group identity, while at the same time reintegrating the embodied individual and group past of which she represents the source. For, on the one hand, the racialized mother figure harbors a knowledge and a history rooted in the senses of a racially and sexually specific body. On the other, this figure carries out the dominant culture's subordination and use of that knowledge and history. In other words, the race or group mother is the point of access to a group history and bodily grounded identity, but she is also the cultural vehicle for fixing, ranking, and subduing groups and bodies. Twentieth-century narrative tells its way around, through, and past her in its determination to reconfigure the phenomenal self.

I unfold this literary project within a discursive and political history of the racialized maternal complex, or racial matrix, of modern Western culture. The race mother of modern fiction emerges here at the center of three concentric contexts. Most immediately, this figure shares a discursive and historical space with the early twentieth-century eugenics movement, which in its texts and its legitimized sterilization practices explicitly shaped the meaning of motherhood within the bounds of racial difference. Eugenics, in turn, develops out of a century-long reimagination of the culture–nature relationship which the racialized mother at once enables and threatens. Beginning with Romanticism, that is, and within the context of the transformation of an aristocratic racial order, the middle-class male intelligentsia put maternal nurturing at the heart of its ethics and aesthetics, in part to lay claim to a racialized folk heritage rooted in nature and soil. Nineteenth-century biology further racialized "mother nature," even deeming racial division her primal selective act. By the same token, however, Romanticism and nineteenth-century biology attributed a degree of power to the natural world that destabilized their metaphysical frameworks and their manipulations of the racial matrix. I interpret these eugenic, Romantic, and scientific discourses within the broadest context—and older political economy—of "racial patriarchy." In the first three chapters of this book I develop all of these contexts in detail before turning, in the fourth through eighth chapters, to the mother figures and narrative forms by which modern writers unsettle the racial matrix of Western culture. Here I will outline the contexts, beginning with the theoretical framework of racial patriarchy.

In racial or, more generally, kinship patriarchy, sexual and ancestral economies work together inextricably by way of the kin-bordered arrangement of women's mothering. ("Kinship patriarchy," in my usage, is a general term under which are subsumed the specific instances of what can be called ethnic, national, or racial patriarchy. In this study I regularly use the more specific term "racial patriarchy" because race is usually the operative term for my subject and authors.) In these economies, mothers reproduce bodies not in a social vacuum but for either a dominant or a subordinate group; the boundaries dividing dominant and subordinate groups coincide with racial or ethnic boundaries.

Many societies in fact manifest such a coincidence of class and racial or ethnic boundaries. Nearly all slave societies show this correlation. Historians of slavery point out that slave populations are most often (75 percent of the time, by Orlando Patterson's calculation) displaced populations, imported from outside and, above all, not "kin" to the ruling and free populations.[7] More generally, at least in Western nations, "dividing lines of race and class [have] coincided and deepened each other," according to V. G. Kiernan, as have class and nationality, so that we find "Croat peasants under Magyar landlords, Czech under German, Irish under English."[8] In order to clarify the function of the mother figure in modern fiction, in chapter 1 I theorize the way in which patriarchal institutions work to reproduce these boundaries of class and race through their controlled circulation of women in marriage. This interdependence of racial and patriarchal practices compels me to speak of "racial patriarchy."

Moreover, insofar as dominant groups in racial patriarchies—including, historically, most Western nations—normally monopolize education and better-paid intellectual labor while delegating physical labor to subordinate groups, mothers in racial patriarchies sort bodies not only according to racial hierarchies but also according to a metaphysical dichotomy between mind and body, all the while remaining aligned with the body. Because of the mother's alignment with the body and her function as reproducer of the group as a social body, the mother comes to signify, often ambivalently, a bodily and collective past. The narrative maneuvers of modern novels reposition the mother to use her as a point of access to a history while decoding the forces that use her as vehicle of domination. They aim to unhinge the mother from her pivotal role as a reproducer of borders (both metaphysical and racial). They seek to represent a bodily order and knowledge that elude the hold of social hierarchies on the material world, a hold maintained, in part, through control of the mother.

Although an understanding of the broader economic structure of racial patriarchy throws considerable light on the maneuvers of modern experimental fiction, attention to particular modern formations of racial patriarchy in Anglo-European and American cultures brings into focus the more culture-specific literary history that shadows this fiction. In chapter 2 I argue that the emergence of an aesthetic that places a racialized maternal figure at its center originates in Anglo-European Romanticism in the context of an emergent domestic racialism. Romanticism's preoccupation with a maternal Nature is well known, but the racialization of this maternal "ground" for the transcendental aims of Romantic poetry has until recently been overlooked. Some studies, such as those by Alan Richardson and Mary Jacobus, have begun to reveal the embeddedness of Romantic literature in colonial assumptions and fears about race; others have noted the importance of nationalism to Romanticism.[9] In chapter 2 I focus instead on the presence of a domestic racialism among Romantic writers such as Sir Walter Scott and William Wordsworth, which intermingles with their gendered poetic practices to produce a blossoming racial–patriarchal aesthetic. Romanticism bequeathes this aesthetic to modern authors, one in which the subsumption of a gendered material world makes possible a race-heroic, poetic transcendence. But many of these modern authors—especially the women and members of subordinate groups—transform or deconstruct this Romantic aesthetic of transcendence. The act of doing so, I argue, constitutes their modernity.

Throughout the nineteenth century, scientific descriptions of the material world proliferated, at once codifying and complicating the project to manipulate its resources, including the bodies of women and non-European peoples. Scholars have amply documented the proliferation of medical texts on motherhood and women which supported the enclosure of middle-class women and the complementary nineteenth-century ideologies of the angel in the house and the black mammy. Likewise, historians have charted the intensification of race consciousness and the growth of so-called race theory from the early nineteenth to the early twentieth centuries. But little work has been done to link these two developments.[10] Though I do not attempt to treat these discourses exhaustively, I analyze those points of overlap most pertinent to the role of the mother figure in modern fiction.

In chapter 3 I focus, first of all, on those theories within nineteenth-century science which correlate sexual–racial hierarchies with metaphysical hierarchies and thus help to define the function of the race or group mother. While seeming to privilege the organic world, biological theories from phrenology to evolution insidiously turn that domain against itself, using it to give evidence of the supremacy of mind and of the race and sex supposedly most skilled in the arts of the mind (including, in a circularly self-authorizing move, the scientific arts). This impulse to master the body from within its own borders dramatically culminated in the early twentieth-century movement of eugenics. Eugenics fostered a widespread public discourse on the race mother which conceived of her as instrumental to achieving a high "national intelligence" and adequate "national strength" in a competitive and imperialistic political world—an agenda aptly summed up by one writer's observation that "marriage has become evolved and developed as a social institution because of its services to race culture."[11]

But these biological discourses of race, sex, and motherhood had their underside, which I bring to the surface in the second half of chapter 3. For these discourses attribute new active powers to nature and the body even while they aim to contain and master those powers. As Terry Eagleton points out, "To lend fresh significance to bodily powers and drives . . . if only for the purpose of colonizing them more efficiently, is always to risk foregrounding and intensifying them beyond one's control."[12] This is one of the effects of nineteenth-century biology, which thereby precipitated the texts of early twentieth-century phenomenology and modern experimental fiction (as well as a variety of other writings that redescribe the sexual and racial body, such as those of W. E. B. Du Bois and Charlotte Perkins Gilman). Even eugenics, in its explicit discussion of reproduction and marriage, opened important points of entry for modern fiction's representations of what I call, echoing Merleau-Ponty, the intercorporeal body.

I distinguish three general tendencies in modern experimental novels—or three structural strategies for negotiating with the race mother—which may be termed "late Romantic," "interruptive," and "intercorporeal." As exemplified in James Joyce's *Ulysses* and Jean Toomer's *Cane* (chapters 4 and 5) but also manifest in William Faulkner's novels, the late-Romantic text laments or mocks racial patriarchy's subsumption of "pure" mother figures and instead foregrounds race-transgressive mother figures. This strategy, however, results in a recuperative narrative structure which returns to a symbolic mother figure and depends on her for the text's final moment of transcendence. The interruptive novel—represented here by Ralph Ellison's *Invisible Man* (chapter 7) but also typical of Samuel Beckett, Jean Rhys, Doris Lessing, and Gayl Jones—repeatedly excises the racialized mother figure and, along with her, an entire history and set of memories embedded in the protagonist's body. The text's excisions and the protagonist's disembodiment together create a gap-ridden narrative structure that exposes but also, to some extent, repeats racial patriarchy's alienation of embodiment. The intercorporeal novel—analyzed here through Virginia Woolf's *To the Lighthouse* and Toni Morrison's *Beloved* (chapters 6 and 8) but also characteristic of Colette, Zora Neale Hurston, and Isak Dinesen—begins from a narrative position within the racialized mother's body and then moves outward through the objects of a material world which the mother inhabits in common with others. This movement of the narrative voice through the object world unfolds the autonomous powers of that world while it also creates a centripetal narrative structure which gestures toward non–mother-centered positions of embodiment.

It is important to add, by way of qualification, that all of these texts mix narrative strategies of recuperation, interruption, and intercorporeality as they deconstruct and reconstruct their protagonists' relations to materiality and to the race mother. More important, they all point toward intercorporeality as the outer limit of narrative possibilities—that radical collapse of the mind/body and discourse/body divisions which are both suffered and upheld by the racial–patriarchal mother. The possibility of representing intercorporeality appears most slim in interruptive novels. And yet even these novels hint—at their "lower frequencies"[13]—that they have excised the alternatively possible in their defense against the bodily oppressive.

To some extent I privilege intercorporeal forms of representation. I do so, however, not in order to generate an ideal by which all other texts may be judged but rather to foreground and rigorously establish in the world of representation a possibility often obscured, denigrated, or, among strict deconstructionists, even denied. I aim to bring to light the deeper political and philosophical radicalism of what is often misunderstood, in covertly gendered readings, as modernism's sentimental, naïve aesthetic.

In sum, the story I tell is that eugenics and modern fiction together entered a well-developed discourse on the powers of racially and sexually different bodies, initiated at the end of the eighteenth century partly in conjunction with Romanticism and increasingly articulated in nineteenth-century science. Through representations of the racialized mother, experimental novelists in effect vie with Romantic and scientific (specifically, eugenic) discourses over the right to name—to dematernalize and deracialize—the body in the material world. They expose the function of the racialized mother who upholds a body-oppressive system, often capitalizing on the recognition, contradictorily implicit in these deterministic systems, of the ordering and code-eluding power of the body in the material world, sometimes even structuring their narratives around that power.

Thus, the contemporaneous development, on the one hand, of eugenics and, on the other hand, of the Harlem Renaissance and modernism—with their common focus on racialized mother figures—emerges as no mere coincidence. To set the stage they shared, I turn immediately to eugenics in the first part of chapter 1. I then pull back in that chapter and the two succeeding chapters to describe the racial–patriarchal history which calls forth the twentieth-century dialogues among eugenics, modern phenomenology, and experimental modern fiction.

1

Of Race and Woman: Eugenics, Motherhood, and Racial Patriarchy

The era of the Harlem Renaissance and of modernism was also the era of eugenics. Together yet differently, all of these movements take up the claim that "race and woman must not be left to their own devices."[1] Jean Toomer, Nella Larsen, Virginia Woolf, James Joyce, William Faulkner, and others published their race-inflected, mother-initiated novels at a time when eugenicists such as Charles Davenport and Harry Laughlin in the United States and Caleb Saleeby and Karl Pearson in England were making race an issue in public discussions of motherhood.[2] The preoccupation of eugenics with a racially proper motherhood surfaces explicitly and comically in several literary texts. In *Ulysses*, as Mina Purefoy gives birth, Stephen Dedalus and his friends debate the eugenic question of what kind of motherhood "is most beneficial to the race . . . in securing the survival of the fittest."[3] As an undergraduate at Princeton, F. Scott Fitzgerald penned his parodic ditty "Love or Eugenics," in which he asks his classmates, "Men, which would you like to come and pour your tea. / Kisses that set your heart aflame, / or love from a prophylactic dame?"[4]

These parodies of eugenics are the superficial reflections of a much more profound relation between eugenics and the experiments of modern fiction. To discover that relation we must turn our full attention to eugenics and then to the racial–patriarchal economy and history which give rise to eugenics.

THE "RACE CULTURE" OF EUGENICS

The history and tenets of eugenics are familiar to some scholars of modern fiction, though not to many. I offer in the first section of this chapter an overview of eugenics, drawing liberally on the work of historians of the movement, so as to establish the dramatic force of its ideological and historical presence in the early twentieth century. I show, in particular, how eugenics' explicit political agenda began to lay bare the crucial intersection of ideologies of race and sex at the site of motherhood.

Eugenics held that "racial degeneration" in Western nations threatened what the contemporary political writer Benjamin Kidd called "the struggle of the Western races for the larger inheritance of the future."[5] According to eugenicists, only racially responsible reproduction could reverse this trend and ensure success in the global economic struggle. Even in Britain, where class was an important element of eugenic theories (Leonard Darwin suggested that the level of a worker's wages should correspond to his "innate qualities"),[6] the unproductive classes were perceived, above all, as a threat to the Anglo-Saxon "race" as a whole. It was claimed that "whether apparent or not there is going on a ceaseless racial struggle for dominance that no number of platitudes about brotherly love will obviate."[7] A "residuum" of paupers, alcoholics, and moral degenerates was thought to weaken Britain's racial competitiveness. Karl Pearson at the Eugenics Laboratory at University College in England therefore spoke of "the imperative importance of humans doing for themselves what they do for cattle, if they wish to raise the mediocrity of the race."[8] Pearson urged "that all sympathy and charity shall be organised and guided into paths where they will promote racial efficiency, and not lead us straight towards national shipwreck."[9] Such a national struggle honored—or burdened—the procreative woman of the "higher races" with a special responsibility: reproduction for the race and, in turn, for the nation. Eugenics thus makes sharply visible the group agenda that informs ideologies of motherhood—an agenda expressed, as we will see, in other times and places, and sometimes involving ethnicity rather than race, but governed by an identical logic.

As spelled out by its founding thinker, Francis Galton, eugenics rested on the principle that mental and moral characteristics are inherited just as physical characteristics are inherited. In particular, intelligence for many eugenicists was a fixed trait, like hair or skin color, on which environmental influences such as nutrition and education have little effect. As Henry Goddard asserted in his Vanuxem Lectures at Princeton University in 1919, the "grade of intelligence or mental level for each individual is determined by the kind of chromosomes that come together . . . [and] is but little affected by any later influence. . . . Any attempt at social adjustment which fails to take into account the determining character of the intelligence and its unalterable grade in each individual is illogical and inefficient."[10] Understanding intelligence as genetically determined, many eugenicists rejected social support of the "feebleminded" as a "dysgenic prac-tice," characterizing as misguided the idea that improved sanitary conditions and educational opportunities could improve cognition.

Since intelligence was genetically coded, they reasoned, it must cluster in families, and more broadly in "stocks," and finally in "races." Well-publicized studies by David Heron and Karl Pearson at the Eugenics Laboratory gathered data on "endless pedigrees demonstrating how 'general degeneracy' runs in stocks, epilepsy, insanity, alcoholism, and mental defect being practically interchangeable."[11] What followed from this "fact" politically was that the healthiest, most competitive nations were those in which the genetically intelligent and their offspring outnumbered the genetically "degenerate." Scientific and social eugenics movements called for increased procreation among the "fit" members of society and decreased procreation among the "unfit."

This thesis had many implications which could be construed quite differently by different groups and persons. For some social radicals who embraced eugenics, it meant that marriages should be contracted on a rational basis, with partners choosing each other for their genetic qualities of appearance as well as character and intelligence. George Bernard Shaw argued that no class barriers should stand in the way of good eugenic matches. In commenting on *Man and Superman* he expresses the hope that the "objection of a countess to a navvy or of a duke to a charwoman" would give way to the laws of "natural selection."[12] Fabian adherents of a "socialist-imperialism," such as Sidney Webb and Julian Huxley, proposed that socialistic and scientific care of the domestic "stock" offered the best path to imperialist strength. Meanwhile, advocates of birth control such as Margaret Sanger felt that the eugenic aim of restricting the lower-class birthrate coincided with the desire of working women to have fewer children. Although prominent eugenicists such as Leonard Darwin considered birth control "racially devastating," Sanger embraced eugenics as a rationale for the availability of birth control devices and information. Others who favored sex education affirmed the eugenicists' claim that "men and women alike would be better equipped for race regeneration the more they knew about family and health."[13]

Thus, many reformist proposals were advanced in the name of eugenics, but they usually won their legitimacy by appealing to the cause of "race regeneration." Several influential social scientists, most especially W. E. B. Du Bois and Franz Boas, spoke openly against racialism of all kinds throughout this period.[14] Yet the wide appeal of the eugenics platform and vocabulary, even among other social reformers, indicates how embedded an ideology racialism had become.

Meanwhile, what the historian David Kevles calls "mainline eugenics" cared comparatively little for sexual, social, or reproductive reforms. With few exceptions (notably Hermann J. Muller and Lancelot Hogben, among others), the more professional, better-funded, more scientific eugenics circles embraced no progressive reform programs. On the contrary, the research carried out by mainstream eugenics significantly bolstered the prevailing social distinctions drawn between persons on the bases of race, sex, and class. In so doing eugenics was only adhering to practices and trends of thought that were well established in the biological sciences. Nearly every major biologist of the nineteenth century spoke of the "higher races" and the "lower races" and of men's evolutionary advances over women—including, of course, Galton, who considered "energy" as "an attribute of the higher races" and found "as a rule that men have more delicate powers of discrimination than women."[15]

The emphasis on differential intelligence among human groups was inspired by Galton's work and by the rediscovery of Mendel's theory of inheritance in 1899; but the accompanying sense of mission and urgency was fed by the "discovery" of what researchers called the "differential birthrate." Throughout the late nineteenth and early twentieth centuries, scientists and demographers presented data "proving" not only that the mentally and physically—or genetically—unfit were clustered in the "lower" classes and races, but also that (especially before World War I) these "lower" classes and races gave birth to two or three times as many children as the middle and upper classes: "There is not the slightest doubt that the decline [in the birthrate] is chiefly incident in—indeed one may say practically confined to—the best and most fit elements of the community, whilst the loafers, the incompetent, the insane and feebleminded, continue to breed with unabated and unrestrained vigor."[16] Such findings caused serious alarm among public officials. The cry went up in Europe and the United States that "national intelligence is falling disastrously." That is, "the birth rate is falling much more rapidly amongst those social classes in which intelligence is relatively high than it is in those in which it is relatively low."[17] Commentators in England bemoaned the "undue multiplication of lower types,"[18] for instance, "the careless, squalid, unaspiring Irishman" who "multiplies like rabbits."[19] Sidney Webb expanded the point:

> In Great Britain at this moment, when half or perhaps two-thirds of all married people are regulating their families, children are being freely born to the Irish Roman Catholics and the Polish, Russian, and German Jews, on the one hand, and the thriftless and irresponsible . . . on the other. . . . This can hardly result in anything but national deterioration; or, as an alternative, in this country gradually falling to the Irish and the Jews. Finally there are signs that even these races are becoming influenced. The ultimate future of these islands may be to the Chinese![20]

In his book *The Fight for Our National Intelligence* (1937), Dr. Raymond Cattell predicted with similar alarm that if such demographic trends continued, Britain would eventually be divided into "two distinct intelligence groups, as distinct socially as most Indian castes and more distinct biologically than most races."[21] Recklessly reproducing itself, the less intelligent "caste" would crowd out the higher, more intelligent "caste." And so, as C. H. Pearson predicted, "we shall awake to find ourselves elbowed and hustled, and perhaps even thrust aside, by peoples whom we looked down upon as servile."[22] With such predictions, eugenics helped to inspire a kind of racial panic among the professional middle classes of Western nations.

Even apart from these alarming predictions about the future, the growth of the poor and "lower" classes or races was already putting a worrisome drag on the national budget, for increasing amounts of money were required to fuel the social welfare system of institutions housing or serving the poor and the feebleminded. Taken together, the expanding social budget and the diluted gene pool were thought to be dramatically weakening Britain for its role in the "titanic struggle at the heart of Europe"[23]—the battle for control of resources in Africa and elsewhere. Many writers explicitly compared "dysgenic" trends in Britain to those characterizing other empires just before they collapsed. Raymond B. Cattell likened the crisis to that which had brought on "the decline of early Eastern civilizations, of Greece and Rome," which, he argued, "was primarily due to a biological withering of those strains of the population bearing high mental capacity."[24] By the lights of eugenics, the human foundations of empire were racial foundations, and these were shrinking or deteriorating.

In the United States eugenicists were less concerned with empire and the "unfit types" sustained by modern medicine and social welfare than with the tide of "genetically inferior" new immigrants and, as always, the "differential intelligence" of whites and blacks. As the numbers of immigrants rose into the millions in 1913 and 1914,[25] a wide range of interest groups, from politicians to labor unions to social workers, called for restrictions on immigration. What eugenics added to this program was a biological—more precisely a racial—justification. It also offered the criterion of differential intelligence for selecting "fit" from "unfit" immigrants: "The same arguments which induce us to segregate criminals and feebleminded and thus prevent their breeding," Prescott Hall wrote in 1910, "apply to excluding from our borders individuals whose multiplying here is likely to lower the average of our people." The president of the National Institute of Immigration hinted that the exclusions would have to be far-reaching since "we have bred more than sixty millions of the finest people the world has ever seen. Today there is to surpass us, none. Therefore any race that we admit to our body social is certain to be more or less inferior." Studies were duly undertaken, such as that by the sociologist Edward A. Ross in 1912, to gather data on the new immigrants. Ross's "data" led him to consider most new immigrant "races" inferior—including Slavs, Irish, Jews, and southern Italians—noting, for example, that the last generally had "low foreheads, open mouths, weak chins." Since "Such people lack the power to take rational care of themselves," the state—its mental institutions, orphanages, jails, social workers, and police—would be forced to shoulder the caretaking burden.[26] Ross was among those who believed that such a burden must be minimized by immigration restrictions that would block the entrance of "unfit" races. Although Carl Degler's consideration of figures such as Ross, who moved toward this racialist position, offers a needed corrective to the tendency to overlook dissenting voices and shifting positions in the early twentieth-century debate on biological determinism, Ross's case at the same time indicates how the general atmosphere made it difficult for even a fair-minded researcher to avoid a racialist vocabulary.[27]

Perhaps most influential on the question of immigration was Harry Laughlin, a protégé of the prominent eugenicist and biologist Charles Davenport and one-time superintendent of the Eugenics Records Office at Cold Spring Harbor on Long Island. In the 1920s, when Congress was considering a new immigration act, Laughlin presented the evidence gathered from his "biological investigation." In his written congressional testimony, "Analysis of America's Melting Pot," he concluded: "Making all logical allowances for environmental conditions, which may be unfavorable to the immigrant, the recent immigrants, as a whole, present a higher percentage of inborn socially inadequate qualities than do the older stocks."[28] Although other prominent scientists, such as H. S. Jennings, publicly challenged Laughlin's evidence, congressional committee members mostly ignored Jennings and instead sought, cited, and praised Laughlin's "expertise." In April 1924 Congress overwhelmingly passed the Immigration Act, one of the provisions of which required that immigrants take an intelligence test. President Calvin Coolidge openly endorsed the law, saying: "The Nordics propagate themselves successfully. With other races, the outcome shows deterioration on both sides. Quality of mind and body suggests that observance of ethnic law is as great a necessity to a nation as imigration law."[29] Immigration restriction thus assumed the status of a law of nature.

Eugenics, of course, also gave renewed expression to white racism in the United States. Legislative battles were largely unnecessary since twenty-eight states already banned marriage between Caucasians and Negroes and the remaining states suffered little threat of "miscegenation" (suppressed by lynching and segregation). Nonetheless, some eugenicists did argue that such laws needed to be "greatly extended if the higher races are to be maintained."[30] Apart from the question of law, prominent eugenically minded scientists such as Edward East of Harvard and Charles Davenport used the authority of genetics to reconfirm the wisdom of black-white segregation. Davenport claimed that "miscegenation commonly spells disharmony" in that "a hybridized people are a badly put together people and a dissatisfied, restless, ineffective people."[31] In *The Passing of the Great Race*—a book which the journal *Science* pronounced "of solid merit" and which "in the field of anthropology . . . has followed the latest authorities"—Madison Grant insists: "Whether we like to admit it or not, the result of the mixture of two races, in the long run, gives us a race reverting to the more ancient, generalized, and lower type. . . . The cross between a white man and a negro is a negro . . . and the cross between any of the three European races and a Jew is a Jew."[32] Numerous studies were published, especially using the increasingly widespread Binet intelligence test, to demonstrate a "racial difference in intelligence" between whites and blacks.[33] The much-discussed *Study of American Intelligence* (published in 1923 by the psychologist Carl Brigham, a World War I army tester), confirmed what whites needed to hear—"that blacks accounted for a disproportionately large fraction of the 'feebleminded.'"[34]

This last claim sheds light on the racism hidden in the eugenically driven sterilization laws enacted by thirty states between 1907 and 1931; under these laws over sixty thousand sterilizations of the "insane" and "feebleminded" were performed by the late 1950s.[35] Often led by doctors and superintendents of public mental institutions, but additionally authorized by scientific researchers such as Harry Laughlin, the push for sterilization of the insane and feebleminded rested on eugenic arguments. In the famous case of *Buck v. Bell*, Justice Oliver Wendell Holmes supported the decision to sterilize the seventeen-year-old Carrie Buck on the grounds that "in order to prevent our being swamped with incompetence" it is "better for all the world, if instead of waiting for their imbecility, society can prevent those who are manifestly unfit from continuing their kind."[36]

Yet since most sterilization laws applied only to the residents of public institutions, they affected mainly the poorer members of society. In states where the poor were largely black, Native American, or immigrant, sterilization was performed on disproportionate numbers of "non-Nordic" persons. Finally, because persons of non-Nordic races were scientifically held to be more often feebleminded than whites, they were also more likely to be committed to mental institutions, where the likelihood of their being sterilized was also higher, as the records of these institutions show:

> In Virginia, the overwhelming majority of those sterilized were poor; perhaps as many as half of them were black. In California [where by the 1950s over twenty thousand persons had been sterilized, two-thirds of them deemed insane], more than half the insane males sterilized were unskilled or semiskilled laborers. The foreign-born were more likely to be admitted to state institutions and to be sterilized once there. While they accounted for about a fifth of the California population in 1930, they represented at least a third of the group compelled to undergo the sterilization procedure.[37]

Sterilization practices thus covertly worked in accord with the racial agenda of eugenics.

It can be argued that sterilization laws reflected sexual as well as racial bias, giving further indication of the interdependence between racial and sexual agendas in modern Western economies. One of the main signs of behavior taken to indicate feeblemindedness was sexual waywardness. In California, of the approximately two thousand feebleminded persons sterilized between 1909 and 1930, three fourths had been admitted as sexual delinquents.[38] Overall just as many men were sterilized as women, and in some states more,[39] but in general feeblemindedness was more often believed to correspond with sexual deviancy in women than in men. Eugenicists "gave a good deal of attention to the sexual behavior of the 'feebleminded'" with the consensus that feebleminded women, in particular, were prone to debauchery and illegitimacy. The trustees of the New York State Custodial Asylum for Feeble-minded Women argued, typically, that retarded women required special care because they were "easily yielding to lust."[40] By the same token, sexual licentiousness could be considered further evidence of feeblemindedness. A report published by an institution for "epileptics and feebleminded" in Virginia ranked sexual infractions first among the crimes committed by feebleminded women who had been sterilized and third among men. In California a 1929 report showed that three out of four women sterilized had been deemed "sexually delinquent" on admission—which, as in the case of Carrie Buck, often meant merely that they had given birth out of wedlock.[41] (Lena Grove, William Faulkner's slow-witted unmarried mother in *Light in August*, seems to fit the eugenicists' "wayward" type.)

Interestingly, the justification for such practices, as in nearly all eugenical proposals, derives from metaphysical assumptions about the human being which privilege intelligence, in Henry Goddard's words, as "the chief determiner of human conduct."[42] (Here and elsewhere I use the term *metaphysics* in the narrow sense, not as a general discipline that scrutinizes the relations of matter and spirit but as a value system that subordinates matter to spirit.)[43] As one leading social worker averred, "The weaker the *Intellect* . . . the greater appears to be the strength of the reproductive faculties. It is as though where the higher faculties have dwindled the lower, or merely animal, take command."[44] Sexual deviancy itself counted as evidence of low intelligence and, therefore, racial unfitness. In accord with this logic, "sexual offenses or moral degeneracy figured explicitly in the grounds for sterilization found in almost half the state statutes then [1932] on the books."[45] Indicative of the way the bias against women's mental capacities dovetailed with these metaphysical assumptions about sexuality was Charles Davenport's characterization of "wayward" girls in particular as "feebly inhibited," a condition which he considered "innate." He concluded that the genetic condition

17

"resulted not only in sexual licentiousness but also in violent outbreaks of temper and derivative crimes."[46] (One cannot help but wonder why the girls might have displayed "violent outbreaks of temper" in Davenport's presence).

Clearly, the metaphysical and gender hierarchies encoded in sterilization practices supported its racial discourse. Sterilization programs implicitly outlined racial boundaries and terms for the sexuality of *all* women. If a woman was "non-Nordic," the eugenics discourse in effect pointed to the scientifically proven inferiority of her race to justify policing her sexuality and devaluing her motherhood. If the woman was white, any hint of "sexual deviancy" on her part (that is, sex outside marriage) indicated her unfitness to be a mother, while the policing of "good" women's sexuality could be cast as protection *of* them *for* the race. Thus, women's sexuality and motherhood inescapably took on a racial meaning in the early twentieth century.

Sterilization laws represent the main strategy for what Dr. Caleb Saleeby called "negative eugenics"—the inhibition of procreation among the unfit. Negative eugenics succeeded first and most dramatically in the United States. At first explicitly imitating the American laws, Nazi Germany eventually surpassed them with its far-reaching compulsory sterilization law of 1933, leading one American scientist to lament that "the Germans are beating us at our own game."[47] No sterilization law was ever passed in Britain, although eugenicists made concerted efforts in the 1930s to have one considered.

A "positive eugenics," by contrast, was embraced in both Britain and the United States. Advocates of positive eugenics supported legislation that required venereal disease testing for marriage certificates and other such reformist measures, but in the end the movement amounted mainly to a propaganda campaign to encourage procreation among the "fit"—in other words, a policing campaign directed at middle-class "Nordic" women's motherhood and marital status. Positive eugenics proliferated. Articles appeared in popular and scholarly publications ranging from *Cosmopolitan* to the *Yale Review* to *Biometrika;* eugenic "facts" and exhortations were written into biology and health textbooks. In the 1920s the American Eugenics Society boasted that over 350 colleges and universities offered courses dealing with the subject.[48] Positive eugenics addressed itself to both men and women, but it laid its heaviest stress on the importance of motherhood for the "fit."

According to many commentators, the problem of the differential birthrate which supposedly threatened the strength of Western nations stemmed from the new freedom of middle-class white women. In his popular textbook *Genetics and Eugenics,* the geneticist W. E. Castle ferrets out two root causes of "dysgenic" trends: "(1) late marriages, shortening the reproductive period and (2) voluntary limitation of the number of children."[49] In other words, by deciding to delay marriage or to use birth control, some middle-class women were threatening the economic dominance of the ruling races. If these choices were a threat, women's decision not to marry at all would clearly constitute a crisis. F. P. Armitage decried the debilitating "elimination from the ranks of motherhood of those hundreds of thousands of specially selected women who choose to remain unmarried rather than give up their professions."[50] His inflated numbers suggest the sense of crisis he felt. William Withers Moore might well have said "I told you so" to these panic-stricken early twentieth-century spokespersons. He had anticipated the problem in his 1887 presidential address to the British Medical Association, predicting that women's intellectual competition with men, although perhaps feasible in itself, would "hinder those who would have been the best mothers from being mothers at all" so that "the human race will have lost those who should have been her sons."[51] According to contemporary observers, Moore's prediction had come true (and is still being identified as a threat to the social fabric).[52]

In the discourse of positive eugenics, idealized notions of race culture reserved a special place for racially fit, procreative women. In his popular (if not strictly scientific) book *Parenthood and Race Culture,* in a chapter titled "The Supremacy of Motherhood," Saleeby links maternal supremacy to racial supremacy. Through physical and psychic nurturance of the baby (which Saleeby investigates with scientific thoroughness) the mother performs "a great function for society and for the race." In her role as mother, "Woman is Nature's supreme instrument of the future"—that is, the future of the race. Schools, Saleeby argues, must teach "the boy and girl . . . that the racial instinct exists for the highest of ends" and that "to be manly is to be master of this instinct." If "Woman" is the instrument of the racial instinct and man the master, it follows that man must master woman as the instrument of his "highest ends." This he does through the institution of marriage, for "marriage has become evolved and established as a social institution because of its services to race-culture."[53] Here we have what amounts to a cult of racialized motherhood following on the heels of the nineteenth-century cult of true womanhood.

Saleeby proposes, finally, that "the modern physiology and psychology of sex must be harnessed to the service of Eugenics."[54] That is, the cult of racialized motherhood required that the "science" of sexuality be "harnessed" to the latest "science" of race. And harnessed it was, both in theory and in institutional practice. Prominent practitioners of the emergent science of "sexology," including the relatively liberal Havelock Ellis, considered racial improvement one of their more laudable potential contributions to society.[55] Ellis called for "an enlightened culture of motherhood" in which women's sexual choices and desire were allowed expression for the good of the race. Ellis's stance, it must be noted, evolved throughout his long career and was always complex; he may well be considered one of those figures of the late nineteenth and early twentieth centuries (Charlotte Perkins Gilman is another) who attempted to "transvaluate," in the words of Nancy Stepan and Sander Gilman, the dominant positions of racial and sexual science.[56] His writing does enlarge the space for articulating women's sexuality while at the same time lending itself to a policing of female sexuality by invoking the racial agenda that motherhood may serve.

Meanwhile others began, less ambiguously, to undertake a "psychoanalysis of Social Melancholia," according to Raymond Cattell a disease supposedly occurring with "high frequency [among] the unmarried and childless in modern society." Invoking the newly powerful authority of Sigmund Freud, Cattell speculated that the disease stems from "mental energy being tied up too extensively in other fields to leave the individual adequate drives for interest in children." The "self-assertive instinct" and the "desire to rise socially" cause a dysgenic tendency and an excessive "restriction of the family." Cattell admirably carried out Saleeby's agenda by correlating race problems with gender deviations and spelling out corresponding racial and gender requirements.[57]

Oddly enough, no one attempted to explain how working-class women managed to have enough energy to produce those disastrously large families even though they labored all day, week after week. On the contrary, these theories of instinct were being spun to encourage procreation among middle-class women, while government agencies were enacting laws to discourage procreation among the "subcultural," the "feebleminded," and the "wayward" by institutionalizing and sterilizing them.

The scope and the claims of the eugenics movement entangled any public discussion of motherhood and sexuality in the questions of race and nation. As evidence that eugenics was succeeding in its propagandistic aims, Karl Pearson boasted to Francis Galton in 1907, "I hear the most respectable middle-class matrons saying if children are weakly, 'Ah, that was not a eugenical marriage.'"[58] On the other side of the ocean the undergraduate F. Scott Fitzgerald would soon write his parodic "Love or Eugenics." The hand of eugenics reached far and, for some, cut deep.

The hand moved, too, with the motions of a racial–patriarchal body politic. The pressure on women to reproduce classes within boundaries defined by blood has a history that is not restricted to modern Western cultures. A historical and cross-cultural consideration of the racial–patriarchal economy reveals the absolute interdependence of ideologies of race and sex. I will now analyze that interdependence, for it determines the significance of modern fiction's racialized mother figures and its experimental narration.

Toward a Theory of Kinship Patriarchy

All too often literary critics understand the relation between race and sex as either a rhetorical one in which tropes of race and sex substitute for and mingle with one another or an analogical one in which racial and sexual hierarchies mirror and compound one another.[59] Valid as these understandings are, they leave untheorized the shared structural underpinnings of race and sex. My formulations shift attention away from the psychoanalytical models that inform most analyses of the first kind and from the political models that use the second approach.[60] I draw instead on anthropological theories, vocabularies, and evidence to highlight the inextricability of racial and sexual practices. As Louise Lamphere points out, cross-cultural studies of anthropology can work to offset (though by no means overthrow) the middle-class and Eurocentric biases of feminist and cultural theory in ways that psychoanalytical and merely compounded models cannot.[61]

I undertake this cross-cultural, economic, and structural analysis of race and sex because an adequate account of the racialized mother figure in modern fiction requires it. It is useful, if not essential, for the critic of modern fiction to understand what has often been obscured: that hierarchies of race and gender *require* one another as co-originating and co-dependent forms of oppression rather than merely parallel, compounded, or intersecting forms; and that these co-dependent structures of race and sex converge especially on the mother, who reproduces racial boundaries in her function as subservient procreator. Substituting race for nationalism in Anne McClintock's observation, I suggest that we need to understand not only "gender as a category constitutive of [racism] itself," but also race as a category constitutive of sexism in itself.[62] I develop here a description of kinship patriarchy, of which I consider modern Western racial patriarchy one instance (race mythologies being a subset of kinship mythologies, which also include ethnicity, nationality, clan, and tribe). I have chosen to retain the term *patriarchy*, despite its limits, because of its easy recognizability and its neatness as a noun (as compared with the more accurate but less convenient *gender hierarchy*).[63]

The manipulations of narrative and mother figures in the novels I discuss have led me also to emphasize kinship patriarchy as an inherently metaphysical social formation—one that rests on the metaphysical distinction between a ruling "head" and a laboring "body" and one that genders and racializes or ethnicizes this distinction. Members of the kin group (or, in our case, the race group) and the sex affiliated with the privileged "brainwork" of the society, as one eugenicist calls it, accrue the wealth, power, and schooling that allow them to control those who do the "handwork" of the society.[64] To understand why modern authors represent "intercorporeal" or body-grounded fictional worlds, we must understand how metaphysical values (that is, values of mind over body) determine the meaning and position of the mother in modern racial patriarchy.

It is crucial to recognize two issues at the outset of this discussion of kinship patriarchy: the fictional or ideological dimension of kin group identities and boundaries and the contested nature of kinship studies within feminist anthropology. Concerning the first point, as Igor Kopytoff expresses it, frequently "the *idiom* of kinship relations provides a *metaphor* for political relations."[65] Although kinship-based hierarchies are usually founded to some degree on actual blood relationships, they also tend to take on a mythical life and authority which allow ample room for practices such as adoption or substitution of kin categories when social or economic interests require it. Among the Bedouin, for whom patrilineal cousin marriage is the cultural ideal and patrilineal ties are strongest, it may happen that "even if cousins are more directly related through some maternal link, their relationship will be described in terms of the paternal one."[66]

In some cultures kin substitutions and redefinitions go beyond the incidental to form a whole subcategory of kinship. The practice of adoption as a kinship-building strategy in Oceania is considered by some to be "comparable in complexity and importance to marriage as a domain in kinship studies" for this part of the world.[67] The widespread Christian practice of designating godparents operates as a fictive kin arrangement, a backup inheritance structure fictionalized as spiritual kinship.[68] More broadly, in feudal Europe both a rhetoric of kinship and kinship-modeled inheritance practices shaped relations between peasants and their overlords.[69]

Given these instances of kin substitutions, some anthropologists have gone so far as to question the vocabulary of kinship altogether, asserting that kinship is only a Western and Eurocentric anthropologist's fiction, not a universal genetic or political reality.[70] I concur, however, with Jane Collier, Sylvia Yanagisako, Harold Scheffler, and others who point out that, while kinship has been an ideologically overdetermined category in anthropological studies, it remains a tenable one if kinship analyses are sufficiently balanced with attention to other culture-specific patterns and identities.[71] The sometimes arbitrary, contradictory, or symbolic constructions of kin group boundaries indicate that these boundaries represent cultural rather than natural selections (and in this sense fit Benedict Anderson's model of "imagined communities"). That the peoples of Oceania "adopt" children or the Bedouin invoke patrilineal descent for marrying cousins demonstrates that mythologies of blood kinship operate influentially, even if actual blood connections are absent. At the least, the evidence of Western eugenics and a wide range of other cultural practices justifies using kinship as an *analytical* category to illuminate political structures and discourses. (Note that this debate parallels those over the term *race* as well as those over the categories man and woman. To adopt these terms in a critical context is not to adopt their essentialist implications.)[72]

The vocabulary and study of kinship has been contested within anthropology for another reason. Second-wave feminist anthropologists have until recently dissociated themselves from kinship studies because of the way these have tended to reify women's reproductive function in culture. Women were studied, that is, *only* in terms of their sexual and reproductive kinship functions. Feminist anthropology has worked to dislodge the dominance of this gendered methodology, studying women's same-sex relations, speech performances, and a range of other behaviors not directly related to kinship roles. But, having succeeded to some degree, many feminist anthropologists have felt free to return to kinship considerations, in part to recover the ways in which the qualifier not *directly* related leaves room for the more indirect and subtle but important relationships between gender and kinship. These scholars seek "to renew the intellectual promise of kinship and gender studies by reconstituting them as a single whole."[73]

My methods and aims here do not strictly coincide with those of the feminist kinship scholars. My own theory of racial patriarchy focuses attention primarily on women's reproductive roles in kinship structures, risking a delimitation of the field along dangerously familiar lines. But focusing on reproduction still has its analytical place if undertaken critically. In fact, an interpretation of experimental modern narratives and of the discourse of eugenics with which they enter into dialogue calls for such a focus. This call should come as no surprise since these literary and scientific discourses emerge from the same culture that gave rise to those earlier kinship studies fixated on women's reproductive role. (In effect, my theory of kinship patriarchy serves to explain not only the relation between modern fiction and eugenics but also the conditions under which the early male-biased kinship anthropology developed.) I undertake here a critique of the underlying logic of the kin–patriarchal ideologies of eugenics (and by extension early kinship studies), which reductively assume and depend on the reproductive function of women.

Kinship anthropologists have variously examined the way community bonds and boundaries are mythologized as kinship or blood boundaries. When a race, an ethnic group, or a nation claims to have its origin in ancestral blood relationships, it makes use of kinship mythologies. Meanwhile, feminist anthropologists have studied the foundational importance to the community economy of the "traffic in women," as Gayle Rubin calls it in her extension of Claude Lévi-Stauss's work,[74] but which, to avoid some of the narrowing implications of Rubin's phrase, may be more broadly characterized as a circulation of women. In order to clarify the interdependent economy of racial boundaries and patriarchal institutions, my theory of kinship patriarchy brings together these insights into kinship myth-ologies on the one hand and the circulation of women on the other as community-building strategies. My stress on community economy draws as well on the evidence of Marxist anthropologists that such cultural arrangements are economic arrangements.[75]

Broadly speaking, kinship anthropologists specify two kinds, or directions, of circulation of women in marriage: inside the kin group (endogamy) or outside it (exogamy). These frequently correlate, as Jack Goody in particular persuasively argues, with two contrasting sets of material circumstances.[76] In brief, the in-group marriage of women in endogamous communities often serves to protect the dominant kin group's possession of scarce resources of land or capital; the out-group marriage of women in exogamous communities usually serves to extend the dominant kin group's possession of scarce human resources, especially where land is abundant.

In other words, the in-marrying of women restricts control over material resources to the dominant kin group, while out-marrying enlarges that group's control over labor resources. The range of the circulation of women thus takes shape in relation to the community's needs and strengths. Aristocratic societies of western Europe and Britain, for example, followed endogamous marriage prac-tices by which they monopolized land resources for a relatively small kin group whose members had "noble blood." Although modern middle-class mobility in the West has tended to blur endogamous marriage boundaries, racial miscegena-tion laws in the United States and, more generally, eugenic attempts to prohibit marriage between the "fit" and "unfit"—terms with a racial subtext—indicate lingering endogamous values among Americans, British, and Europeans. Like earlier, more rigid endogamous codes, these practices reflect the group's desire to monopolize land and capital resources. Thus, at the turn of the century in the United States and Britain, the middle classes (identifying themselves as represen-tatives of an Anglo-Saxon or Nordic race) embraced an endogamous, eugenical platform in order to participate successfully in, to quote Benjamin Kidd, "the struggle of the western races for the larger inheritance of the future."[77]

That resources are at stake in the drawing of kinship boundaries finds confir-mation in the way these group (including ethnic or racial) boundaries can fold into class boundaries. The exogamous Kpelle of Liberia, as studied by Caroline Bledsoe and William Murphy, provide an example of this overlap of kin and class boundaries which contrasts with, and thus helps to improve our perspective on, Western systems.[78] Traditionally among the Kpelle important or wealthy new-comers are integrated into the community by being given land and a wife, usually a sister of the powerful chief in that territory. The sons who are born of such a union owe allegiance, goods, and life-risking activities (in ritual or in war) to the

24

chief who bestowed the woman in marriage. Such arrangements extend the reach of powerful men not only laterally, to include people who will produce more goods and protection, but also hierarchically, by creating or enlarging a kinship group that is subordinate to the ruling group. The subordinate group of men may be considered members of the larger kin group, but they are still a subordinate blood line within the kin group. Through control of the mother/sister, or by way of "matrilateral" ties, powerful men arrange both the horizontal and hierarchical dimensions of the overall group's structure. Anthropologists note that such ties commonly serve as "a vehicle for hierarchical relations" by defining "the very unequal relations between [locally dominant lineages] and subordinate, captured, conquered, poor, or immigrant people."[79] Male–female kin-defined relations, in this case of brothers and sisters, structure and in turn are structured by male–male kin-defined relations. One set of relations supports the other through the carefully kin-specified circulation of women.

The aristocracies of medieval and Renaissance Europe developed similar stratifications through kin distinctions and marriage practices, but they did so within an endogamous system. These aristocracies enforced practices of in-marriage to create kin-based classes that were eventually perceived as *racially* different (a point to be developed in chapter 2). Within this system the law of primogeniture served to stratify the sons born to aristocratic women. Eldest sons inherited the ancestral property and perpetuated the main aristocratic "line" through carefully arranged marriages with noblewomen. Younger sons either did not marry—thus being excluded from the project of governing and of reproducing the nobility—or they married women who were not of the highest nobility. These younger sons and their wives constituted and then reproduced a subordinate class of clergy, administrators, and military men.[80] In this scheme, as in the Kpelle chiefdoms, women serve as functionaries reproducing class and race. With the rise of a middle class in Europe, the dominant kin group changed, but middle-class women were encouraged to continue performing the traditional boundary-reproducing functions.

In these societies, then, three elements—circulation of women in marriage, circumscription of kinship (of which race is a specific kind), and class stratification—constitute a triangular interdependent dynamic in the formation of kinship patriarchies. These boundaries both reinforce and require one another. A dominant group must control marriage in order to define and mythologize kin boundaries in a way that serves their needs as rulers. At the same time, the dominant group needs those kin boundaries, elevated to the status of group mythology, to secure women's adherence to predominant marriage practices. Kinship or racial mythologies, as the eugenicists demonstrate, contrive allegiances that encourage or demand women's group "loyalty."

This is how kinship patriarchy operates for dominant kin groups. But for subordinate kin groups marriage is commonly circumscribed by taboos on "miscegenation," and access to resources is thus blocked or diminished. That is, subjugated kinship groups fail to gain or preserve their access to resources because they do not make the rules that control the circulation of women in marriage. Insofar as kinship boundaries established through marriage define an elite group, restrictive marriage or inheritance laws institutionalize the denial of resources to subjugated groups. In other words, even as marriage enhances group identity and group wealth, loss of control over marriage inhibits group wealth and group identity.

Even more to the point, the dominant kin group's presumption of access to women of the subordinate group also disrupts the formation of identity and the accumulation of resources by the subjugated group. This presumption finds expression not only practically—whether through rape or harassment or restriction of job opportunities—but also symbolically, in cultural discourse and aesthetics. As has been amply documented by feminist critics, dominant-group women serve the aesthetic and myth-making practices of dominant-group men, as muses, virgins, whores, or metaphors for nature. Through such practices, dominant-group men create and disseminate images of women that mirror and reinforce the actual circulation of women. But whereas among neighboring kin–patriarchal cultures foreign men are free to create images of "their own" women, in a stratified kinship culture men of the dominant kin group control the mainstream images of subordinate-group women as well. They thus deprive subordinate-group men not only of the power to circulate women freely and gain material resources but also of the power to disseminate images of "their" women so as to develop their own cultural traditions and resources. So it is in the discourse of eugenics: a dominant group (the middle class as self-appointed representative of a nation and a race) elaborates an ideology to control the meaning of middle-class women's reproductivity (through a cult of racialized motherhood) and of subordinate women's reproductivity (through denigrating categories such as "wayward" or "feebleminded" and the attendant practice of sterilization).

It is under such conditions that Kabnis in *Cane* and Stephen Dedalus in *Ulysses* struggle to regain access to culture-making activities and symbolic traditions by redefining relations to kin group mothers. In the United States white men's enforced access to black women and their concurrent manipulation of the social mythologies of black womanhood appear to give white men, as Ralph Ellison's narrator in *Invisible Man* protests on behalf of black men, "a treacherous and fluid knowledge of our being imbibed at our source and now regurgitated foul upon us."[81] Like the white men who steal Sethe's milk in Toni Morrison's

Beloved, dominant-group men drink the milk that would nourish the cultural expressions of subordinate-group men. As Halle dramatizes, this theft renders the men emotionally numb and strikes them symbolically deaf and dumb. Meanwhile the theft of literal and metaphorical milk leaves the women to create a "told story" out of nothing but their own scarred and sequestered bodies. In fact, all women who would be artists, whether they belong to dominant or subordinate kin groups, must struggle to de-symbolize themselves, which they often begin to do by withdrawing, either voluntarily or involuntarily, from the marriage circuit. Witness Colette (for instance, in the autobiographical *Break of Day*), Sula, Lily Briscoe, or Ursa Corregidora.

Not just psychologically but politically and aesthetically, then, the logic of kinship patriarchy turns a man against his kin source and leaves a woman to her own resources. The underlying problem, of course, begins when kinship patriarchy defines the mother *as* kin source.

In sum, within the kin–patriarchal (or, more specific to this study and the modern West, the racial–patriarchal) economy, the racial group mother plays a central, highly stressed role. In the race-bounded economy the mother is a maker and marker of boundaries, a generator of liminality, both vertically and horizontally. She is forced across a border, or she is prohibited from crossing a border; in either case her function is to reproduce, through offspring, the life of that border. One might say that in exogamous communities mothering women serve as a cultural advance guard, sent out to fortify extended group boundaries; and that in endogamous communities, such as those which the modern eugenicists sought to fortify, mothering women are a defensive border guard who are themselves tightly policed and selected for their sexual, class, and ethnic or racial purity, so that they may stand strong against contamination.

Women are both marginal and central, then, as feminists have often noted.[82] In particular, their marginality constructs patriarchy's center not only by creating an ideological Other, and not only by forming a class of supportive reproductive women. Under kinship patriarchy women are both central and marginal in that they serve the central role of creating the group's margins. At the symbolic level the figure of the mother reproduces a racialized cultural discourse. She becomes an instrument in the formulation of crucial categories of difference: fit or unfit, black or white, Nordic or Mediterranean, wayward or eugenic. Paradoxically, despite her crucial and central function as generator of liminality and difference, the mother herself remains a borderline figure. Her doubleness, even as it secures cultural boundaries, also vexes them. This paradox intensifies in her role as a reproducer of vertical or metaphysical distinctions between ruling "heads" and serving "bodies."

Reproducing Racial–Patriarchal Metaphysics

Most eugenicists uncritically adopted the assumption, spelled out by Henry God-dard, that "the chief determiner of human conduct is the unitary mental process we call intelligence." The widespread use of intelligence tests to identify feeble-mindedness and therein unfitness for reproduction reflects a scale of value in which, as we saw, the "higher faculties" of the intellect normally assume prece-dence and power over "the lower, or merely animal."[83] The ubiquitous term *feebleminded* itself makes "mind" the treasured, scrutinized object. Likewise, the hysteria about a declining "national intelligence" places intellect at the center of the drama.

The eugenicists' privileging of intelligence of course serves the self-interest of middle-class professionals, whose claim to power rests partly on their "higher" education and "higher" intelligence. But, more deeply, this celebration of intel-ligence continues an old ideological practice whereby metaphysical assump-tions—of spirit over matter, idea over thing, mind over body—function to uphold social divisions between master and slave, owner and worker, light-skinned and dark, man and woman. Aristotle was neither the first nor the last "father" of an ideological tradition to whom it has seemed self-evident that "the rule of soul over body is like a master's rule, while the rule of intelligence over desire is like a statesman's or a king's."[84]

Kinship patriarchies, the evidence suggests, have made full use of this meta-physics of political and labor divisions; and because hierarchical political divisions are kin-inflected in kinship patriarchy, its metaphysics also becomes kin-inflected (or, in the case of modern Western racial patriarchy, racialized). That is, under kinship patriarchy dominant kin groups associate themselves with mind or spirit and associate subordinate groups with body or matter. The conflated kin and metaphysical distinctions in turn justify a division of power and labor by which "handworkers" serve "brainworkers."[85] This metaphysical division further de-termines the function of the dominant-group mother: she sorts bodies not only into kin and non-kin but also into brainworkers and handworkers—or, to para-phrase Robert Penn Warren, "metaphysical" and nonmetaphysical "breeds."[86]

Slavery is an institution that manifests all these features of kinship patriarchy—a racialized division of labor upheld by metaphysical metaphors and sustained by control over women's reproduction. Slavery exaggerates but also confirms and clarifies the interconnections among these practices. Through an account of slavery, then, we can further explain the engagement of African American modernist writers with racialized mother figures and metaphysical assumptions. At the same time, we can see how ideologies of slavery prefigure and prepare the way for the cult of racialized motherhood typical of modern eugenics, which white modernist writers participate in and critique to varying degrees. Thus, in the shared kin–patriarchal discourses of slavery and of eugenics we see the framework that bridges these two (up until now) distinct and disparate modernisms.

In the section of the *Politics* titled "Slavery as Part of a Universal Natural Pattern," Aristotle explicitly bases his claim that "by nature some are free, others slaves" on the metaphysical principle that "it is both natural and expedient for the body to be ruled by the soul, and for the emotional part of our natures to be ruled by the mind, the part which possesses reason."[87] Democritus makes a metaphor of this analogy between slave and body when he advises the "heads" of Greek households to employ slaves "like the limbs of their bodies, each with a different purpose."[88] Other traditions have done the same. In the ancient Hebrew writings of the Mishnah, the sages "liken the slave to the master's body, specifically his hand . . . since the actions performed by both the master's body and the slave ultimately stem from the master's decision of will."[89] When the ancient Chinese signified "slave" with the characters for "hand" and "woman," they partook of this analogy while at the same time indicating the gendering of metaphysical distinctions.[90] In all of these formulations a metaphysical hierarchy of head over body provides a metaphor and rationale for a hierarchy of labor and power. Although in slave societies not all handworkers are slaves nor all slaves handworkers, on a discursive level the distinction between master and slave often figures as a simple one between head and body.

Equally often kin group differences enforce this same division between master and slave. As historians of slavery have amply shown, throughout history slavery has most frequently developed along ethnic, racial, or kin lines. If females were the first slaves, as Gerda Lerner and others note, they were usually Other females, won, kidnapped, or bought from rival tribes or kin groups.[91] Although eventually most of the gender divisions defining chattel slavery dissolved, ethnic or kin group identities continued to distinguish slave from free.[92] In many cases the slave is by law not kin to the master group. The Old Testament, for instance, decrees that one Hebrew may become the indentured servant of another, but never a slave. When the indentured servant has served his time, "he shall go out from you, he and his children with him and go back to his own family and return to the possession of his fathers" (Lev. 25:41). By contrast, "you may buy your male and female slaves from among the nations that are round about you . . . and they may be your property. You may bequeath them to your sons after you, to inherit as a possession forever" (Lev. 25:44–46).

According to the eminent historian of ancient slavery M. I. Finley, the slave is by definition, and probably by strategy, an "outsider" cut off from his or her own kin.[93] In Greece slaves were imported, in the words of another historian of Greek slavery, "almost without exception from outside the state. Indeed, on principle, they were supposed to be barbarians, that is to say nonGreek [*sic*] speakers."[94] This practice undergirds Aristotle's statement that "non-Greek and slave are by nature identical."[95] Likewise in Rome most slaves were foreigners imported from conquered communities. In our own society the word *slave* has its root in *sclavus*, or "Slavic," following the medieval practice of capturing and selling Slavic peoples as slaves.[96] The very word *slave* carries an ethnic connotation.

In his monumental study *Slavery and Social Death*, Orlando Patterson amasses evidence from a number of slave societies to substantiate the pattern of the slave as outsider. Patterson estimates (based on George Peter Murdoch's survey of 538 world cultures) that in 75.4 percent of slave societies masters and slaves were perceived as being of different ethnic groups, and 21 percent of these considered themselves of different races. In all of these cases slaves were subjugated and rendered helpless in large part by being removed from their native lands, institutions, and customs (including, I would add, their gender positions and roles). Patterson therefore considers "natal alienation" one of the key principles underlying slavery, engendering what he calls the "social death" of slaves.[97] The French anthropologist Henri Lévy-Bruhl has gone so far as to claim that what he calls "endoservitude," or in-group enslavement, cannot succeed.[98] While Lévy-Bruhl may overstate the case (for instance, some Hindu societies practiced endoservitude), certainly exoservitude is the rule.[99]

As in kinship patriarchy generally, an extra burden falls on the mother in a slave society. Especially given the fact that birth is the main source of slaves,[100] the mother plays a particularly functional role in the reproduction of the divisions between master and slave, a role which special inheritance laws often reinforce. That is, patrilineal inheritance laws frequently become matrilineal in the case of slaves, a legal practice which ensures that no dominant-group property is forfeited when masters impregnate their slaves. The matrilineal slave rule within an otherwise patrilineal system constitues what Orlando Patterson calls the Roman pattern. It is found in some parts of the Asian world and in most historical slave societies in the West, including the United States.[101] Within such systems the mother sorts persons not only by race but also by status as slave or free.

African American slavery follows both the Roman pattern of inheritance and the general slave-society pattern of kin difference (in this case mythologized as racial) between master and slave. At the same time, metaphysical assumptions (again, in the narrow sense, of mind over body) permeate descriptions of the racial differences that supposedly distinguish the white master group from the African-descended slave, as documented by Winthrop Jordan, Ronald Tataki, and others.[102] In the seventeenth and eighteenth centuries these metaphysical assumptions found implicit and piecemeal expression, as when Linnaeus suggested that the African is governed not by reason but "by caprice," or when Edward Long insisted that in the African the "passions rage without any controul." White observers and practitioners of slavery in the American colonies also partook of an implicit metaphysics of race when they concluded that Africans were merely "brutes" whose nature was suited to bear the floggings and labor of slavery, and whose "sufferings are not attended with shame or pain beyond the present moment."[103]

By the early nineteenth century, Romantic thinkers had begun to give systematic expression to a metaphysics of race, explicitly invoking it to support the practice of African American slavery. Hegel elaborates his scheme of racial hierarchy within a grand metaphysical account of "world-historical" cultures—of which Africa has never been one because in the African "the Knowledge of an absolute being, an Other and a Higher than his individual self, is entirely wanting." In fact, for the African, "slavery is itself a phase of advance" from his or her former "merely isolated sensual existence."[104] As in Aristotle's formulation, the non-kin slave is a mere body, fit to serve those races who "by nature" work with their heads and live in the world of spirit. Schelling echoes Hegel when he suggests that Africans "[border] on the animal" and that slavery provides "the only means of salvation for this race of humans abandoned to the most terrible barbarism," their only hope of "elevation toward the divine."[105] This metaphysics of race and slavery found both lingering and increasing expression after abolition, when ideology took over the where the laws and institutions of slavery had left off. Near the end of the nineteenth century, Sir Richard Burton proclaimed that "the world still wants a black hand" since "enormous tropical regions yet await the clearing and draining operations by the lower races." He pronounced Africans "inferior to the active-minded and objective . . . Europeans" and suggested that their "stagnation of mind" naturally suited them for this role.[106]

The twentieth-century discourse of eugenics preserved the labor-sorting legacy of a kin–patriarchal metaphysics generally and of American slavery specifically. Eugenics carried out an agenda in which the "mind" was measured, races were rated in "intelligence tests," and their "fitness" for education, professional work, and privileged motherhood was publicly determined. These findings were used to justify the clustering of blacks in manual labor and the lack of support for equal education, and they figured in judgments on interracial marriage. In the United States eugenics thus perpetuated the interplay of racialized labor, metaphysics, and motherhood first configured in the institution of slavery.

In England the monopoly over professional work is most often understood as a class monopoly. But the eugenicists tried to insinuate racial difference into class competition by speaking of "types" and "blood." In an article titled "Positive Eugenics" (1917) the statistician and geneticist A. R. Fisher urged the Eugenics Education Society to "put itself in direct and sympathetic touch with the special aspirations of professional bodies," for eugenics could well enhance a professions' "power to select its own members, rigorously to exclude all inferior types, who would both lower the standard of living and the level of professional status." He argued that professions generally must seek to limit the entry of "new blood," which was, "on the whole, inferior to the professional families of long standing."[107] Clearly, the eugenical vocabulary of "inferior types," "selection," and "new blood" could serve to privilege and limit the membership in the same professional classes to which the eugenical spokespersons belonged.

Karl Pearson likewise invokes the idea of eugenic selection to explain the middle classes' special claim to brain-work and intelligence: "The middle class in England, which stands there for intellectual culture and brain-work, is the product of generations of selection from other classes and of in-marriage." He goes on to claim that "[working-class] county council scholars are on the average not up to the mean middle-class intelligence." Therefore "it is cruel, it serves no social purpose, to drag men of only moderate intellectual power from the hand-working to the brain-working group."[108] The tight intertwining of professional concerns and eugenic theories in these statements prompts one historian to conclude that "eugenics can be seen as, initially, the practice and experience of the intellectual aristocracy read onto nature."[109] This intellectual aristocracy was also a racial–patriarchal aristocracy which invoked the "natural" differences of race to uphold its monopoly on professional work and higher wages.

On both sides of the Atlantic the competition for the brainwork positions was also a gender competition, and the vocabulary of metaphysics therefore merged with that of gender for this reason as well as for the reason that motherhood supports racial–patriarchal labor divisions. As feminist historians have documented, scientists and other professional men faced increasing competition from women in the nineteenth century. James Hunt founded the Anthropological Society of London in part becuse the Ethnological Society had voted "to render its meetings fashionable and popular by the admission of ladies." In disgust he decided to establish "a really scientific society . . . which might become worthy of a great nation."[110] Hunt's decision gives us a glimpse of the very real threat of professional competition that helped to condition scientific theories and institutions. This threat lurks behind Galton's use of the metaphysical criterion of "powers of discrimination" to justify a gendered labor force, as well as behind Saleeby's and Cattell's insistence on women's supreme fitness for the unpaid "handwork" of mothering.[111] Such gendering of metaphysical qualities makes it difficult, according to the historian Donald MacKenzie, "to avoid the suspicion

32

that one of the social interests sustaining 'positive eugenics' may have been that of professional men in having women—especially the growing number of women professionals—return to their traditional roles and stop 'shirking' mother-hood."[112] Thus, the metaphysical vocabulary of eugenics helped to enforce labor hierarchies not only of race but of gender, while gender roles in turn served to reproduce racial hierarchies.

And yet the insistence on women's fitness only for handwork destabilizes the mother's membership in the dominant kin group. The dominant-group mother must above all be a member in good standing of the brainworking class; she must be a kin-group or racial "insider" (a requirement that throws some light on the racial agenda underlying the nineteenth-century spiritualization of mother-hood).[113] But she herself, in order to reproduce that insider group, must remain a handworker; she must not stray into the work of the mind which would make her unfit for her procreative labor—as the eugenicists repeatedly insisted. Thus, she becomes a handworker dangerously lurking within, and yet necessary to, the ranks of the brainworkers. To a man of the dominant kin group, perhaps especially if he senses this contradiction, the mother is a threat not only because she can potentially transgress a kin group border, but also because she *necessarily* transgresses the mind-body border. In social terms her body is the instrument of his group membership and his cultural productions, as we will see in analyzing the Romantic aesthetic; but her body at the same time recalls his own embodiment, from which he must dissociate himself as a member of the brainworking race, class, and sex.

For members of the subordinate-race, and to some extent also for women generally, the handworking racial mother likewise provokes ambivalence, but for different reasons. The son of the subordinate race or the daughter of either group may feel a solidarity with the racial mother. But she is also the instrument and embodiment of their oppression. A dominant man has some means for controlling the mother as an instrument of his group membership and as his vehicle of access to brainwork, but for the subordinate-group man or for any woman the mother is the instrument by which others—dominant men—*deny* his or her access to brain-work. The racialized embodiment they inherit from her not only unsettles them, it disables them. For the subordinate-group member in particular, the mother's handwork both as mother and as manual or domestic laborer doubly ensures his or her future in the world of handwork and want. As a result, modern protagonists such as Ralph Ellison's invisible narrator, Jean Toomer's Kabnis, and Doris Lessing's Martha Quest attempt to de-mother and disembody themselves—despite the fact that this strategy cuts them off from a history and set of memories embedded in the body. Disembodiment seems preferable to mastered embodiment. For these authors, moreover, the representation of disembodiment or "social death" foregrounds a condition in need of recognition. To appreciate fully the project of modern novelists who focus on the racial mother, we first need to encounter the Romantic aesthetic they both inherited and deconstructed. For at the end of the eighteenth century, male Romantic artists—understanding themselves both as brainworkers and as male members of a newly dominant kin group—forged a transcendental aesthetic which carefully negotiates the racial, sexual, and metaphysical hazards embodied in the mother figure.

2

Romanticism and the Race Aesthetic: Scott and Wordsworth

In his final journal entry at the conclusion of *A Portrait of the Artist as a Young Man*, Stephen Dedalus commits himself to "father artificer," and hopes by this allegiance to "forge in the smithy of my soul the uncreated conscience of my race."[1] In the context of the charged racial discourse of Joyce's day, a discourse that urged certain "races" to take their future in hand and forge their eugenic progress, Stephen's aesthetic ambition emerges as race-specific, undertaken for the Irish race, not the human race. Moreover, his appeal to "father artificer" invokes a gendered metaphysics, as does his desire to transform the "sluggish matter of the earth [into] a new soaring imperishable being" (429). Stephen's perception of women as merely a passive element, "sluggish matter" transformed by men into immortal, transcendent art, also forecloses his sexually charged encounter with the girl on the beach, from whom he "turned away . . . suddenly" to thoughts of his art; her "image had passed into his soul forever," serving "the holy silence of his ecstasy" (429, 432). Joyce thus represents Stephen's aesthetic (with some critical distance, as I will argue later) as both racial–patriarchal and metaphysical, for it enfolds yet subordinates the feminized world of matter in the production of a transcendent and masculine race culture.

Stephen's aesthetic ambitions take flight decisively at the moment when he withdraws his respect for the mother's bodily labor. He answers his friend Cranly, who asks whether a mother—as bodily origin—is "the only true thing in life," with a resounding "no." His artistic ambitions are more "real." The question arises when Stephen discusses with Cranly his refusal to attend Easter Mass. Cranly insists that "whatever else is unsure in this stinking dunghill of a world a mother's love is not. Your mother brings you into the world, carries you first in her body. . . . Whatever she feels, it, at least, must be real. What are our ideas or ambitions? Play" (512). Cranly chides Stephen specifically for denigrating the mothering body in relation to mind or "ideas." But Stephen silently objects. He cherishes an autonomy realized by "mind." And so he comes to his crucial decision about Cranly and about his vocation as an artist: "Cranly had spoken of a mother's love. He felt then the sufferings of women, the weaknesses of their bodies and souls: and would shield them with a strong and resolute arm and bow his mind to them. Away then: it is time to go" (516). As in the earlier scene on the beach, Stephen's response to the mortal reality of women is to turn away toward "imperishable" art. This imperishable art is a racial art founded on an aesthetic of transcendence which Stephen inherits from Romanticism.

ROMANTICISM AND RACE RECONSIDERED

Race lies at the heart of Romanticism. In saying so I join contemporary scholars who have begun to measure the stresses of slavery and colonialism as they fall on Romantic writing.[2] Pursuing the hints thrown out by Martin Bernal in *Black Athena*, however, I read Romanticism not within colonial racial discourses, which distinguish Anglo-European from Indian or African, but rather within a racial dynamic *internal* to Anglo-European cultures.[3] What one may call "domestic" race distinctions—between Gaul and Frank, Celt and Norman, Norman and Frank—not only shape Romantic thought but also form the seedbed for colonial racial thought. These domestic, *intra*national racial divisions electrify the rhetoric of revolution in France and England and energize the transcendent Romantic aesthetic that Joyce and others challenge, including its folk, feminine, and con-queror mythologies.

Scholars of Romanticism have charted male poets' "colonisation of the feminine," to borrow Alan Richardson's phrase. Among the Romantic poets, as Richardson points out, the appropriation of a feminized sensibility may be detected in Keats' "negative capability," Shelley's greatly good man who "put[s] himself in the place of another,"[4] and Wordsworth's advice to the poet "to confound and identify his own feelings with those of his subjects."[5] In Romantic poems mother figures frequently stand in as sources for the poet's other-tolerant, other-sensitive feminine aspect.[6] Wordsworth in particular wrote many poems that could be called studies of mother figures, such as "The Sailor's Mother," "The Emigrant Mother" "The Complaint of a Forsaken Indian Woman," "The Matron of Jedborough and Her Husband," and "Her Eyes Are Wild." As is well known, in his more autobiographical poems, Wordsworth's developing poet "imbibes" sensibility at the breast of a feminized Nature or a nature-equated mother. In *The Prelude* the infant poet "drinks in the feelings of his mother's eye"; the poem insists that "he whose soul has risen / Up to the height of feeling intellect . . . his heart be tender as a nursing mother's heart."[7] Maternal sensibility forms the nurturing ground of the poet's rise to literary, expressive power.

Less documented is the nationalization, and especially the racialization, of the nurturing sources subsumed within the Romantic poet's vision. As Marlon Ross and Anne Janowitz point out, in Romanticism mother nature is also a nationalized nature—in the form of "Albion," "English ground," "Cumberland wilds," or the "Oak of Guernica."[8] I propose that behind the attention to a national "ground" or "soil" lies a racial politics and history which feeds the essentializing impulse of this rhetoric. In the racial history that inspires Romanticism we discover a cultural matrix that still resists dismantling and reconstruction. More narrowly, we find a previously concealed link between Modernism, the Harlem Renaissance, and Romanticism.

Domestic English and European myths of racial hierarchy have their origins in the medieval Anglo-European history of the conqueror—that figure Wordsworth, Byron, and others recreate as the poet of Imagination.[9] That is, with the weakening of the Roman Empire and the increase in raids from the north in and after the middle centuries of the first millennium (circa A.D. 400–500), the populations of France, England, Spain, and Germany all found themselves subdued and brought under the rule of new foreign warriors. Conquerors were mythologized, especially in periods of upheaval, as outsiders, strangers, non-kin invaders who installed themselves as kings, violated aristocratic lineages, and ruled over "native" populations. Meanwhile the conquering aristocrats fashioned themselves as "noble" races fit to rule over "common" races. For instance after Charlemagne's defeat of the Gauls in what then became France, the Salic Law began by celebrating the Franks as an "illustrious race, founded by God himself, strong in arms, steadfast in alliance, noble and sound in body."[10] Such claims indicate that in the class structures of premodern European states, as historian V. G. Kiernan observes, "dividing lines of race and class coincided and deepened each other."[11] In these states we find racialized labor hierarchies that are reproduced through stratified marriage practices. In short, we find racial patriarchies.

Especially as the growth of colonies, the expansion of trade, the rise of manufacturing industries, and other far-reaching political and economic changes disrupted agricultural practices and created laboring and middle classes that challenged these strict divisions between nobleman and commoner, the ruling classes more insistently invoked ethnic or racial difference as the legitimizing basis for their power.[12] Celebrating the Franks as by nature "free and completely equal and independent," the Comte Henri de Boulainvilliers of France remarked in the mid-eighteenth century that "after their conquest of the Gauls, [the Franks] were the only recognized nobles, the only people recognized as lords and masters."[13] Nor surprisingly, given the system of aristocratic patronage of intellectuals, eighteenth-century French historians such as Loyseau, echoed these racialized oppositions between noble and peasant: "The victorious Franks were of noble birth; the vanquished Gauls were of common stock."[14] Montesquieu attributed many French virtues to "these [German] ancestors of ours," such as their sensitivity in matters of honor and their modes of government, attributions that provoked skeptical responses from other writers. Voltaire wondered incredulously: "Who tells you that you are descended in a direct line from the Franks? . . . There is not a single great family in France which can produce . . . the least presumption of being descended from a Frankish founder."[15]

As the events leading to the French Revolution unfolded, these legendary blood divisions came readily to hand—on both sides. Indeed, many contemporary observers understood the revolution as a racial or ethnic conflict as much as a class war. In April 1793 Catherine II of Russia wrote with concern to one of the Grimm brothers: "Do you not see what is happening in France? The Gauls are driving out the Franks."[16] At the same time, supporters of the revolution saw a way to turn such formulations to advantage. One of the French founders of racial history and racial science, Augustin Thierry, used the revolution to support the claims of the new science even as he used racial science to bolster his view of the revolution. He pointed to "recent studies in physiology" which "show that the physical and moral constitution of nations depends far more on their descent from certain primitive ancestors than on the influence of climate."[17] Drawing on this scientific formulation of racial difference, Thierry proclaimed that in France "there are two enemy camps" on the same soil, and "whatever may have been the mixture of the two primitive races, their spirit of unending contradiction has survived to this day." Thierry spells out the connection between race and class underlying the revolutionary events in France: "We are the sons of the men of the Third Estate. This Third Estate issued from the communes which were the sanctuary of the serfs. The serfs were those who were vanquished in the conquest . . . so we are led to the extreme conclusion of a conquest which has to be erased."[18]

In sum, in revolutionary France the noble and peasant classes were understood by prominent thinkers to derive from different races. According to newly emergent cultural myths, the invading race had conquered the indigenous race, reducing them to serfs. In this context the rise of the middle and educated classes in France was often celebrated as the return to power of an unjustly subjugated race. This domestic racialism inspired, in turn, a Romantic reconceptualization of European racial patriarchy.

The events and especially the rhetoric of racialized class revolution in France echoed what had developed earlier in England. William the Conqueror's invasion of England in 1066 provided the key event for modern English history and ideology. William bequeathed his French Norman blood to the aristocracy of England, as did the Franks for aristocratic France and the Visigoths for aristocratic Spain: "It was characteristic of the British families who could do so to point with pride to a family tree which reached back to William the Conqueror."[19] And yet the claims of such families came under attack from the poorer classes, just as they did later in France. Like the French Revolution, the Puritan Revolution and the dismantling of the monarchy in England may be understood, and were frequently mythologized by contemporaries, as class *and* racial revolutions—notwithstanding the fact that the English dismantling of the aristocracy was more gradual than the French.[20]

In England racial oppositions between classes were strategically invoked from the seventeenth century on to explain and mythologize the processes of class reconfiguration. In the middle seventeenth century, through popular movements such as the Levellers and the Diggers, whose known adherents had Saxon rather than Norman family names, the non-noble middle class, freeholders, and peasants agitated for equality and even in some cases a kind of communism. Their Puritan and egalitarian ideals were derived from Scripture but also from an idealized notion of the Anglo-Saxon past. Anonymous pamphleteers cursed that "outlandish Norman Bastard" William the Conqueror as a brute who had introduced French laws—written in French—by which the "poor miserable people" might be "cheated, undone and destroyed."[21] One leading writer, John Hare, advocated "depriving William of his title of 'the Conqueror,' abolishing his laws, and expurgating the English language of all words of French origin."[22] The prolific pamphleteer Gerard Winstanley integrated the Leveller theory of the "Norman yoke" into his theological views, concluding that "the last enslaving conquest which the enemy got over Israel was the Norman over England . . . killing the poor enslaved English Israelites."[23] Such statements and politics have led Christopher Hill to highlight the notion of the "Norman yoke" as a force throughout seventeenth-century English history.[24] While we may not wish to make this "yoke" the dominant framework for understanding English history, we must nonetheless acknowledge that in England, as in revolutionary France, "at the root of this class confrontation there was a cultural confrontation which was *perceived* as a conflict between different bloods."[25]

The Puritan Revolution paved the way for the continued disempowerment in eighteenth-century England of what was often represented as the French–Norman aristocracy, which occurred in concert with the popularization of the idea of the Germanic Saxon origin of the English people. Bolingbroke, Jonathan Swift, and David Hume, among others, all traced the more egalitarian or parliamentary concept of government to the pre-Norman "great councils" of the Saxon kings, who, Swift tells us, "first introduced them into this island from the same original with the other Gothic forms of government in most parts of Europe."[26] In Hume's words, the Anglo-Saxons' "manners and customs were wholly German," and they displayed a "fierce and bold liberty" (unlike the "abject" Celtic Britons) which "gave rise to those mutual jealousies and animosities between them and the Normans."[27] Hume's account reflects the rise of a domestic racial ideology which, at the end of the eighteenth century, was supported by events in revolutionary France and in independence-seeking Scotland.

Thus were political claims debated within a vocabulary of race and ancestry. In the wake of Karl Marx's class analysis of revolution, twentieth-century scholars tend to be deaf to this vocabulary, translating it into class terms. Although a class critique remains valid, a *strictly* Marxist analysis can obscure the racial dimensions of Anglo-European discursive history. We need to recognize the racial themes in this history in order to appreciate the continuity of race as a paradigm in European ideology. For the modern cultivation of racial ideologies in the West derives not only from the desire to justify enslavement of Africans or rule over Indians abroad but also from the wish to naturalize and legitimize class revolution at home. This convergence of motives accounts for the intense proliferation of racial ideologies in the nineteenth century.

This point sheds light on the confusing conflation of race and nationality among writers from Kant to Darwin to the eugenicists. Once the purportedly native races regained power, it made sense that they would equate themselves with whole nations, speaking of the American or the British race. With the revolutions in England and France, the rhetoric of chosen races which had once served the aristocracy came to naturalize the rise to power of the "common races"—culminating in the mid-nineteenth century in a science of race which placed those once common races at the top of a "racial chain of being" and at the forefront of a national mission.[28]

Wordsworth, Scott, and others write in the period of transformation of this racial rhetoric, manipulating it to legitimize their literary innovations. That is to say, Romantic writers cultivate poetic authority for their innovative projects in part by affiliating with and mythologizing a revolutionary folk race. In so doing they make their accession to discursive authority heroic as well as natural. If Harold Bloom is right about male Romantic writers' Oedipal struggle with their poetic fathers, I would suggest that culturally resonant racial *affi/i*ations arm them in that struggle.

The novels of Sir Walter Scott provide the most obvious example of the relation between Romantic literature and this intranational racial sensibility. In *Ivanhoe,* set in the medieval era of Norman French dominance, Scott embellishes the myth of the proud but conquered Anglo-Saxons as the original English people. His romanticization of this conquered aristocracy reflects exactly that ideological "hybridity" noted by Antonio Gramsci.[29] For Scott, in effect, ennobles the new generation of nonaristocratic, self-consciously Anglo-Saxon champions of culture.[30]

As the narrator relates in the opening pages of *Ivanhoe*, "four generations had not sufficed to blend the hostile blood of the Normans and Anglo-Saxons, or to unite, by common language and mutual interests, two hostile races."[31] Scott's reference to blood that refused to blend gives early literary expression to the emergent biological theories of race mentioned by Thierry (accounting for Thierry's admiration for Scott), and also obliquely alludes to marriage as the instrument of union. Scott's narrator goes on to celebrate the "milder and more free spirit of the Saxons," at the same time claiming a special masculinity for this race (and perhaps for his own writing) in admiring the "far more manly and expressive Anglo-Saxon" language (9). Finally, he reminds his readers that "the great national distinctions betwixt [the Saxons] and their conquerors . . . continued down to the reign of Edward the Third, to keep open the wounds which the Conquest had inflicted, and to maintain a line of separation betwixt the descendants of the victor Normans and the vanquished Saxons" (10). If, as some have claimed, Scott initiated the tradition of the proletarian or historical novel, we should also note that racial mythologies envelop both Scott's characters and the generic tradition he founded.[32] Meanwhile, those critics who stress Scott's royalist politics might attend to the way his racialized aristocratic sentiments worked contradictorily to foster the emergent discursive authority of middle-class (that is, nonaristocratic) intellectuals. In romanticizing the Anglo-Saxon citizen as a historically wronged aristocrat, he authorized himself and other writers as the rightful inheritors of British literary culture.

A sexual plot structures Scott's racial story. His narrative plays out the dynamic by which the loss of aristocratic power is effected in part through the loss of gender prerogatives, for the curtailment of gender privileges both symbolizes and partly enforces that loss of power by preventing the conquered from constructing a kin group elite through the monopolized circulation of women. Scott's narrator bemoans this disinheritance of a racial elite: "The whole race of Saxon princes and nobles had been extirpated or disinherited . . . nor were the numbers great who possessed land in the country of their fathers, even as proprietors of the second or of yet inferior classes" (9). Cedric the Saxon figures in the novel as one of the few worthy carriers of Saxon tradition and power; and clearly one of the main sources of his power is his beautiful surrogate daughter Rowena, "whom he cherishes with the most jealous care" (28). (Her surrogate condition may well symbolize his disinherited place in the culture, thus intensifying his jealousy.) Cedric has made himself the guardian of this woman, whose hand is repeatedly sought by others and around whom much of the drama of the tale revolves.

Control over the body of Rowena powerfully assuages Cedric's sense of injury, even driving him irrationally to disinherit his son, who carelessly "lift[ed] his eyes in the way of affection towards his [Cedric's] beauty"—Rowena (28). Cedric's loss of racial–patriarchal power leads him to cling to Rowena as instrument of that power.

Rowena's instrumental in-group sexuality is juxtaposed against the powerfully attractive yet taboo out-group sexuality of Rebecca, "the Jewess." It is Rebecca who attracts the men in the novel, including the hero, more than Rowena; but by the end the hero is a group hero in large part because he resists his desire for Rebecca and stays true to the woman of his own kin group. Scott's tale thus traces both gender and racial disruptions (including some attempts at cross-racial rape) to the conquering of England by the "bastard" William of Normandy; and he celebrates racial solidarity and in-group marriage as the means for restoring order. Because of the absolute interdependence of kin group and gender privileges, the Saxons' group renewal requires the restoration of its racialized gender arrangements.[33]

Scott's text illustrates how racialized cultural productions, including novels such as this one, depend on the manipulation of the marriageable and racialized bodies of women. His popular story employs Rowena as a precious sign of a renewed Anglo-Saxon future even as the emergent, self-racializing class of culture bearers to which Scott belongs needs its feminine tropes of reproduction for its discursive present and future. Twentieth-century inheritors of Romantic literary culture would take up and question this racialized and gendered narrative practice.

WORDSWORTH, THE FEMININE, AND THE FOLK

Like Scott, William Wordsworth makes symbolic use of the reproductive woman in the process of reconfiguring a racial inheritance for his culture, but he does so at the level of tropes rather than of characters. He allies himself with a maternalized and racialized materiality while using countertropes of gender and race to extricate himself from full equation with that "otherness"—so as to forge in the smithy of his soul a transcendent race poetry. For Wordsworth, the world of nature belongs especially to the yeomanry, to those who work the ground: the wood-gathering, grain-binding "solitary reaper" or "farmer of Tilsbury Vale." Laboring men and women, by proximity to and equation with the soil, embody a racial folk heritage with which Wordsworth affiliates himself. Moreover Wordsworth's yeomanry is complicatedly gendered—at once manly and maternal. He handles this complication so as to authenticate his own hybrid sensibility and unfold an aesthetic in which the masculine transcends the maternal, the poet subsumes the people.

Despite Wordsworth's shifting politics, it is noteworthy that throughout his most productive years, from the letter to the Bishop of Llandaff (1793) and the "Preface" to the *Lyrical Ballads* (1798) to his essay on the Convention of Cintra (1809), one idea remains constant: that of the soil-laboring "people" as a nation's foundational spiritual, linguistic, and material resource. His trope for this grounding position is that of a plant or tree. In the "Preface" to the *Lyrical Ballads* Wordsworth explains that he has chosen characters from "humble and rustic" life as his subject because "in that condition, the essential passions of the heart find a better soil in which they can find their maturity, are less under restraint and speak a plainer and more emphatic language" (*SP*, 282). Elsewhere he carries this fusion of laborer and soil even further, suggesting that the laborer is "in his person attached, by stronger roots, to the soil of which he is the growth" (*SP*, 230).

Similarly, in his public letter protesting the extension of train lines into the Lake District, Wordsworth tells of a "magnificent tree" on one of the properties threatened by the railway. When advised to fell the tree for profit, the yeoman who owns it exclaims, "Fell it . . . I would rather fall on my knees and worship it" (*SP*, 76). Wordsworth hopes that his reader will enter into the "strength of the feeling" and remarks that the "attachment which many of the yeomanry feel to their small inheritances can scarcely be over-rated" (*SP*, 77). The tree symbolizes the yeoman's attachment to his inheritance and to the soil of which it and he are the "growth."

These soil and tree metaphors take on more than local significance in the light of an emerging, if still infant, science of national or racial character. Although thinkers and scientists such as Thierry were beginning to explore the genetic transmission of racial characteristics, the predominant secular explanation in this period was still the climatic theory, namely, that racial features were shaped by the soil and climate of a country. Wordsworth expresses his own version of this belief in answer to John Wilson's inquiry about "the influence of natural objects in forming the character of nations." Wordsworth explains that insofar as the terrain and flora and fauna of a country "must have been not the nourishers merely but the fathers of [the people's] passions, they will make themselves felt powerfully in forming the character of the people, so as to produce a uniformity or national character" (*SP*, 309).

In his essay on the Convention of Cintra, Wordsworth follows contemporary practice in racializing and essentializing this national character: he speaks of the "genius" of the "present race" in Spain; he refers to the French as "a people prone and disposed to war" and "presumptuous by nature"; and he reiterates the familiar notion of the "indeed indisputable and immeasurable superiority of one nation over another" (*SP*, 183). His poems of this period likewise essentialize national character, deeming Switzerland and England the voice "of the mountains" and "of the sea," respectively (725).[34] These poems naturalize national character especially through images of trees: "Such men of old / Were England's native growth; and, throughout Spain, / . . . forests of such remain" (823). Wordsworth elaborates his tree metaphor, moreover, through its familial and patriarchal connotations. Nations are vast family trees, and some national trees are more "thrusting," more manly, than others. Again, as in racial patriarchy generally, the best nations or races are the most masculine ones.[35] In his essay protesting the French invasion of Spain, Wordsworth invokes his tree metaphor, maintaining that while some "inferior" nations are rightly "grafted" (*SP*, 225) onto "superior" ones, "the Peninsula cannot be protected but by itself: it is too large a tree . . . for a station among underwoods: it must have power to toss its branches in the wind, and lift a bold forehead to the sun" (*SP*, 226).

Throughout the essay Wordsworth continues to employ a racial–patriarchal rhetoric of ancestry, families, and inheritance in his descriptions of European nations, also folding in words evocative of the gender values underlying this system. He specifically implies that the French were perpetrating in Spain what the Germans had done in France and the French in turn had threatened to do in Germany: the subjugation of a kinship structure of inheritance. "Perdition to the Tyrant who would wantonly cut off an *independent* Nation from its inheritance in past ages: turning the tombs and burial-places of the *Forefathers* into dreaded objects of sorrow, or of shame and reproach for the Children!" (*SP*, 231; emphasis added) In poems on the Napoleonic invasions Wordsworth laments the loss of "the Land we from our fathers had in trust" ("The Feelings of the Tyrolese") and of "captive chieftans" ("Is There a Power"). He gives these invasions and subjugations a sexual connotation by using words such as "ruined," further evoking the national–racial shame of his countrymen, as when he asserts that "the man, who in this age feels no regret for the ruined honour of other Nations, must be in poor sympathy for the honour of his own Country" (*SP*, 232). The man who suffers the invasion of his or another (manly) country, and—in racial–patriarchal terms—permits the subjugation of its kinship traditions thereby allows the "ruin" of the nation's women (who no longer can perform their nation-serving reproductive role) and of the nation itself. Wordsworth refers obliquely to England's conquered past, and his vocabulary recalls the story of that history as told by Scott.

Most important for his poetic practice, within his account of contemporary history Wordsworth celebrates the laborer as the basis of a stable racial–patriarchal order. In the poems and the essays Wordsworth insists that the man who shows no respect for "ancient rites" which are the basis of "ancient liberty" (837, 839) "neither has—nor can have—a social regard for the lesser communities which Country includes" (*SP*, 232). Wordsworth considers these "lesser communities" the heart of a nation's identity and strength, insisting that "from *within* proceeds a nation's health" (839). In "Cintra" he uses an elaborate metaphor to express his idea that, in a nation, "the outermost and all-embracing circle of benevolence has inward concentric circles . . . from which [the larger circles] proceeded and which sustains the whole" (*SP*, 246). As we shall see, these "lesser communities" sustain the project of Wordsworth's poetry just as they "sustain the whole" of nations.

In "Cintra" Wordsworth indicates the sustaining function of his alliance with "lesser communities" when he openly affiliates philosophers and citizens with "peasants." In making his point that a nation's dignity is upheld most feelingly and righteously by the people of the middle and lower ranks, he points to Germany. Rest assured, he tells the reader, that Germany, "with its citizens, its peasants, its philosophers," and "in spite of the . . . fetters of . . . degenerate nobility," will "not lie quiet under the weight of injuries which has been heaped upon it" (247). The grouping of philosophers with peasants is telling: it hints at the usefulness for the emergent political identities of educated men of a rhetorical alliance with an idealized and, in Wordsworth's case, racialized peasantry. Wordsworth's argument that nations will find their prowess in non-noble hearts both legitimizes his own claim to serving as national visionary and more subtly gestures toward his appropriation of the laborer to empower his own position as thinker and poet. Wordsworth's poetic theories and practice make explicit use of this alliance.

In the "Advertisement" to the *Lyrical Ballads* Wordsworth announces his aim to "adapt" the "language of conversation in the middle and lower classes" to the forms of poetry (278). The "Preface" to the *Lyrical Ballads* continues to emphasize that the poems are written in the "real language of men" (a phrase that appears at least ten times), and that therefore "personifications of abstract ideas rarely occur . . . and are utterly rejected" along with "gaudiness and inane phraseology" (281). He refuses to "elevate the style" of his poetry simply to gain the ear of an aristocratic audience (284). And he unflinchingly acknowledges that his use of "such materials . . . has necessarily cut me off from a large portion of phrases and figures of speech which from father to son have long been regarded as the common inheritance of Poets" (285). Wordsworth here acknowledges that his poetic choices are inherently political ones that partly forfeit his high-cultural "patrimony."

What Harold Bloom might read as Oedipal posturing in this passage I interpret as racial refashioning. In casting off the male poet's traditional heritage,

Wordsworth was ingeniously positioning himself to benefit from a "lower" and powerfully emergent racialized myth of cultural paternity. I doubt that this strategy was a calculated one. We might trace it to causes as personal as the fact that Wordsworth was an orphan and as public as the larger culture's employment of similar appropriations. But in any case, it was an appropriation and a substitution fostered by the class and racial revolutions of Europe rather than constituting, in itself, a revolution.

To appropriate the inheritance of the "lesser communities," however, required strategies that would at the same time separate and distinguish Wordsworth from his humble allies. In the "Preface" and other poetical statements, Wordsworth places himself in a betwixt position that gives him access to the resources of the lesser communities even while it assumes his difference from them. He speaks of the necessity for poets and their critics to "descend lower into cottages and fields and among children" (*SP*, 311) in order to develop or understand a poetry "not for Poets alone, but for men" (*SP*, 292). His verb "descend" indicates that the poets to whom he speaks, while not of the aristocracy, are also not of the lower and middle classes, where they must seek their poetic subjects. Whatever mixture of sentiment and expedience this advice reflects, it implicitly expresses the poet's difference from both the noble and the laboring classes. He is a man neither of the land in the aristocratic sense nor of the soil in the laboring sense. He speaks in this equivocal position "for" (does this mean "to" or "on behalf of" or "for the pleasure of"?) "men" (does this mean "all men" or those laboring men who use the "real language of men"?).

Likewise, in his letter to the Bishop of Llandaff, Wordsworth denounces the system of nobility and criticizes "the necessity of dissimulation which we have established by regulations which oblige us to address as our superiors, indeed as our masters, men whom we cannot but internally despise" (155). In this letter Wordsworth locates the cause of social ills in the nobility whom "we" despise (a position he would later modify). But at the same time he is party to the "we" who "established by regulations" this system of subordination. Again we see evidence of the hybrid nature of ideologies in reformist England. Wordsworth may be understood here as manipulating that hybridity, and its racial subtext, to advantage.

Wordsworth, in short, needs his difference from his rustic subjects as much as he needs his alliance with them. The identity gains him access to his soil-bound subjects, but it is the difference that allows him to speak for rather than as one of them. Thus, Wordsworth's poems often celebrate laborers in a way that clearly marks his difference. In "The Solitary Reaper" Wordsworth celebrates and imitates the song of the laborer, but he asks despairingly, "Will no one tell me what she sings?" (657). He admires her song but acknowledges that he cannot grasp it.

46

He *may* sing—and sing in a way that makes us attend more closely to the laborer—as he intends. His project is to some extent reformist and successful: to call attention to the voice of labor. But until he too "cuts and binds the grain," as he recognizes, he will not understand what he celebrates. Yet this very failure to understand is the subject of Wordsworth's poem. He makes poignant poetry of the gap between him and his soil-laboring subject, even as the subject may well be making song of the same gap.

The poet is economically dependent, then, as both a citizen and a poet, on the laborer about whom he writes. The peasant reaps grain not only for the nation to which the poet (more comfortably than the peasant) belongs, but also for the poetry which is the poet's labor and his bread. Wordsworth needs the impasse between himself and the laborer, for out of it, in a double sense, he makes his poetry. Such a condition is tenuous, however. Wordsworth must himself labor to avoid collapsing into his soil-bound and feminized subject, or else he will never make the transition into a poetry written for men of the educated class. This is where a rhetoric of gender alleviates Wordsworth's difficulty, just as racial patriarchy in general employs women's mothering to hold in place its racial stratifications. Gender steps in to fill, articulate, and maintain this gap between Wordsworth and his racialized subjects.

In both his poetry and his essays Wordsworth manipulates the gender of his rustic subjects, introducing feminine subjects and metaphors of nature which he then subsumes into masculine subjects and metaphors. Thus, in the *Lyrical Ballads* Wordsworth writes many tenderhearted poems about children and hillocks, but in his "Preface" he characterizes his poetic topics as "manly." Similarly, in his letter to John Wilson, when Wordsworth describes the flora and fauna and landscapes of a country as "not the nourishers merely but the fathers of the [people's] passions," he quickly subordinates a conventionally maternal metaphor of nurturing to a paternal metaphor of fathering. In other words, the logic of the subservient maternal helps Wordsworth to subsume into a transcendent poetry the soil-bound essence of his subjects. Wordsworth's gendered rhetoric effects his appropriation of a racialized rustic subject matter and cultural inheritance.

This use of a gender-inflected racial inheritance finds full expression in the Cintra essay. The "people," while necessarily affiliated with a maternalized soil, merge into that which is "manly" to serve their function in Wordsworth's masculine poetic and cultural vision. In his argument for the centrality of soil-bound laborers to a nation's power, Wordsworth's peroration opens with a paternal invocation and climaxes with another bold, thrusting tree image of the people; but in between lies a pair of maternal "nesting" tropes.

Wordsworth holds that nations, like Christian individuals, should strive to be perfect, quoting Scripture to make his point: "even as your father, which is in

Heaven, is perfect" (246). For Wordsworth as for Hegel the trajectory of nations is clearly metaphysical and its ideal is patriarchal. Yet Wordsworth grounds this paternal metaphysical ideal in a sentient maternal origin: "These principles, that love to soar in the pure region, are connected with the groundnest in which they were fostered and from which they take their flight" (246). Wordsworth moves from this first nesting metaphor to another at the climactic moment of his essay on the character of nations:

> The outermost and all-embracing circle of benevolence has inward concentric circles, which, like those of the spider's web, are bound together by links, and rest upon each other; making one frame, capable of one tremor; circles narrower and narrower, closer and closer, as they lie more near to the centre of self *from which they proceeded, and which sustains the whole.* . . . The higher mode of being does not exclude, but necessarily includes, the lower; the intellect does not exclude, but necessarily includes, the sentient; the sentient, the animal; and the animal, the vital—to its lowest degrees (246; emphasis added)

Though it recalls, to some degree, the hierarchical concept of the chain of being, Wordsworth's description of the structure of nations is notably bottom-centered. The sentient—and the "lesser communities" tilling the soil in the world of the sentient—form the "necessary" and maternalized web-spun center of nations, the "within" which "sustains the whole." Yet, having said so, Wordsworth quickly recuperates the top-oriented, paternal values with which he began the passage. He calls again on his thrusting tree metaphor to ascend upward toward the "pure regions" of sky: "Wisdom is the hidden root which thrusts forth the stalk of prudence; and these uniting feed and uphold 'the bright consummate flower'—National Happiness—the end, the conspicuous crown, and ornament of the whole" (246). Wordsworth celebrates the origins of soil and race by troping them as maternal, but equivocally subordinates that origin to a paternal end.

In these rhetorical moves, as in racial patriarchy generally, the "nesting" mother function is simultaneously central and marginal, necessary and inadequate—used but subsumed in cultural ideals and functions. When we recall that Wordsworth, like others, identifies the nation as an expression of a physically nourished "uniformity or national character," this parallel suggests that his rhetorical manipulation of maternal tropes freshly articulates the racial–patriarchal manipulation of maternal bodies in the service of a paternal and uniform race group culture.

In Wordsworth's poems about peasant men, such as "The Last of the Flock" and "The Brothers," he crosses and confounds masculine and feminine constructions in order to reap the benefits of both while escaping the cultural devaluations that might be effected by his sympathetic construction of the men. Lower-class laboring men are simultaneously feminized and "manly." Tears fall freely from their eyes, most copiously when they are forced to part from the hillocks or trees or sheep they have nurtured, like the yeoman and his magnificent tree. The sheep in "The Last of the Flock," for example, are as "dear" to the shepherd "as [his] own children" (297)—the children for whom he has had to kill the sheep in order to buy food. When the poet meets the weeping shepherd "on English ground" (295), the shepherd is taking his last sheep to market. He is brave yet feeling. He stands as an emblem of sensibility in English rustic manhood and thus validates the poet's own claim to this mixture of gendered qualities and to an alliance with the laboring people of the English soil. Likewise, the father in "The Brothers" is "two fathers in one father"—or, rather, mother and father in one: "If tears, / . . . And hauntings from the infirmity of love, / Are aught of what makes up a mother's heart, / This old Man . . . / Was half a mother to [his sons]" (408)—who are "the last of all their race" (404). These men of the earth, in Wordsworth's rendering, have internalized the mother's function through their involvement in labors of the soil and the hearth. And yet, as Wordsworth would also have it, their speech and their sensibilities become more manly or doubly fatherly, as a result.

Traditional readings of Wordsworth sometimes have suggested that he constructs an androgynous subject in these poems. Yet we should note Wordsworth's appropriations of feminine values into a masculine teleology. Moreover, Wordsworth partially aims to disarm, rather than doubly empower, his rustic male subjects by ambiguously gendering them. For, even as Wordsworth borrows these men's feminized manhood to express his poetic sensibility, he strives to reserve the most manly and most metaphysical "making"—of reason and order—for himself.

In the "Preface" to the *Lyrical Ballads*, although Wordsworth throws poetic tradition to the winds and embraces his new manly subject, he carefully measures his embrace. That is, he gauges his relation to his subject through meter, which is, as he acknowledges, the one traditional poetic feature he retains. Since, as Wordsworth writes, in a poetry of manly passion and language "there is some danger that the excitement may be carried beyond its proper bounds," he uses meter for the purpose of "tempering and restraining the passion" (296). In doing so he trusts that "a dissimilitude will be produced altogether sufficient for the gratification of a rational mind" (287). Wordsworth may not be addressing the aristocracy, but he clearly hopes to gratify the higher, or restraining, powers of rationality—powers monopolized by the intellectual class he addresses.

Thus, even though Wordsworth minimizes the differences between poetry and prose, suggestively using a biological metaphor to argue that "the same human blood circulates through the veins of them both" (287), he nonetheless always reinstates reason, meter, and thought as the means of limiting these blood mixtures and bodily passions that would transgress literary bounds. Not surprisingly, then, we find on second look that the oft-quoted phrase from the "Preface" that "good poetry is the spontaneous overflow of powerful feeling" receives immediate qualification in the same sentence: "though this be true, Poems to which any value can be attached were never produced . . . but by a man who . . . had also thought long and deeply. For our continued influxes of feeling are modified and directed by our thoughts" (283). Insofar as long and deep thought is the prerogative of the educated class, Wordsworth subordinates the soil-bound and therefore partially feminized labor of the yeoman to the educated man's labor of thinking. He immerses the supposedly manly laborer in an inchoate "flux" of feeling which gets "directed" by the poet's thought. Thus Wordsworth's local subsumptions of feminine/soil metaphors into masculine/ tree metaphors form part of a poetic practice wherein feminized, feeling laborers become the subservient subjects, in a double sense, of the masculine, race-representative poet.

Wordsworth achieves his ultimate subsumption of a feminized racial inheritance into a masculine poetic self-image in his identification of the visionary poet with "Hannibal among the Alps," or, in other words, with the conqueror figure. In *The Contours of Masculine Desire and the Rise of Women's Poetry* Marlon Ross documents the widespread presence of a "conquering" trope in English Romantic poetry.[36] He specifically considers the gender politics of the visionary conqueror poet, a politics in which a feminized materiality is "colonized" and put in the service of a masculine will to poetic power over feminine materiality. As Ross shows, much Romantic poetry deifies the thinker-poet whose visions transform and conquer the world, as when Byron speaks of the poetic soul which "preys upon high adventure" and harbors a "lust to shine or rule" (*Childe Harold's Pilgrimage,* canto 3, sts. 42–43). Wordsworth imagines the visionary poet as "Hannibal among the Alps" whose poetic subjects "change in their constitution, from [his] touch" (*SP,* 383). Nineteenth-century readers echo this conqueror-poet myth, as in the case of a critic who in 1818 identified Scott, Wordsworth, and Byron as the "three great master-spirits of our own day . . . who may indeed be said to rule, each by a legitimate sovereignty, over separate and powerful provinces in the kingdom of the Mind."[37]

I suggest that Wordsworth's (and others') trope of conquering came readily to hand in the wake of the revolutions occurring in Europe in the seventeenth and eighteenth centuries, in which the old conquerors were finally ousted by a new breed of intellectual conquerors. The Romantic self-image of the conqueror partakes of Thierry's scenario, wherein the subjugated native race becomes the new visionary and conquering race. Wordsworth argues in his "Supplementary Essay" in 1815 that the poet who aims to "[widen] the sphere of human sensibility" (*SP*, 410) must undertake the "breaking of the bonds of custom" (*SP*, 408). Meanwhile, like the dominant conqueror, the poet practices "the application of powers to objects on which they had not been exercised, or the *employment of them* in such a manner as to produce effects hitherto unknown" (*SP*, 410; emphasis added). Wordsworth most reveals the agenda of conquest which the national and the poetic projects have in common when he asks, in reference to the expanding and transforming effects of a poetry of "Imagination": "What is all this but an advance, or a conquest, made by the soul of the poet?" (*SP*, 410).

Not gender alone, then, but the *combination* of gender assumptions and a contemporary nationalism that invoked a racialized past leads Wordsworth to an image of the Romantic poet as conqueror. Wordsworth's later poems featuring conqueror-shepherd figures fully play out a drama in which an avenger who combines a feminine, soil-inspired sensibility with a masculine warring spirit returns from "homefelt pleasures" to vindicate his "race." In "Song at the Feast of Brougham Castle upon the Restoration of Lord Clifford, the Shepherd, to the Estates and Honours of His Ancestors," the shepherd Clifford exacts revenge for past injustices to his "race." One day recompense "on the blood of Clifford calls":

> Happy day, and mighty hour,
> When our Shepherd, in his power,
> Mailed and horsed, with lance and sword,
> To his ancestors restored
> Like a re-appearing Star,
> Like a glory from afar,
> First shall head the flock of war!
>
> (730)

This shepherd-avenger succeeds in part because his cause is the cause of the soil itself: "Earth helped him with the cry of blood":

> Loud voice the Land has uttered forth,
> We loudest in the faithful north:
> Our fields rejoice, our mountains ring,
> Our streams proclaim a welcoming . . .
>
> (727)

After his bloody battle, sanctioned by the maternal Earth, Clifford returns to a gentle life in Earth's embrace where "the Shepherd-lord was honoured more and more" (730). Similarly, in "Character of the Happy Warrior" we meet a warrior "whose master-bias leans / To homefelt pleasures and to gentle scenes"; and yet "if he be called upon to face / Some awful moment" in war, he is "happy as a lover" (661).

Out of such materials Wordsworth formulates his late myth of the poet who, through immersion in (and subsumption of) a maternalized Nature, transforms warring impulses into a reasoned poetry. In "The Recluse" it becomes clear that Wordsworth's picture of the warrior as a man who harbors a sensitivity to nature enables him to cast the nature-sensitive poet as a man who harbors, without contradiction, the soul of a warrior—and thus quietly carries on the conqueror legacy. At the end of "The Recluse" the poet recalls himself as an "innocent Little-one" who, despite his "tender moods," very much felt "motions of savage instinct." We read that "deep pools, tall trees, black chasms and dizzy crags, / And tottering towers" were challenges that "urged" the child-poet to "daring feat[s]" (716). These "savage" impulses remain alive in the adult. In a passage that recalls Hegel's primordial battle for subjectivity in any meeting between two self-conscious individuals who "prove themselves and each other through a life-and-death struggle,"[38] the recluse-poet writes: "To this hour I cannot read a tale of two Vessels matched in deadly fight / And fighting to the death, but I am pleased / More than a wise man ought to be. I wish / Fret, burn, and struggle, and in soul am there" (716). As the poet enters adulthood, however, "Reason" transforms his thirst for battle into a quest for truth. The voice of reason assures the poet he need not fear "a want of aspirations" or "foes / To wrestle with, and victory to complete . . . the undaunted quest" for these shall survive "though changed their office." The poet thus bids "farewell to the warrior's schemes." Instead, the poet's "Voice shall speak . . . On Man, on Nature, and on Human Life / Musing in Solitude" (717). "The Recluse" narrates the poet's transformation from weapon-wielding conqueror to word-wielding visionary.

The Romantic poet's transformation can be read as an allegory of that other transformation which was fully under way by the beginning of the nineteenth century in the West: the rise of an educated professional class in place of an aristocratic military class—protecting what Edmund Burke deemed "this new-conquering empire of light and reason."[39] Herbert Spencer later summarized this history in his observation that "the duty to work has taken the place of the duty to fight." In Spencer's account, "the ancient ideal [of] conquest by man over man" which accomplished the "spread of the strongest races" (i.e., middle-class Anglo-Saxons) was giving way in the mid-nineteenth century to the "modern ideal," which dictated that men pursue, through science, the "conquest of the earth."[40] Thus do scientists carry on the internalization of the conqueror legacy which, as we see in Wordsworth, the Romantic writers initiated.[41]

Accordingly, in their nineteenth-century explorations of the "lesser materials" of the natural world, scientists would echo Wordsworth's imagery of Alps, advances, and conquests. (Charles Darwin, for example, favors an imagery of summits, atop of which sit "Reason" and the "higher" races: and T. H. Huxley names man "that great Alps and Andes of the living world.")[42] In fact, by the middle of the nineteenth century, scientists would openly rival the poet's ability to enter into and integrate a feminized and racialized materiality only to subsume and subordinate it.

But nineteenth-century science would also inherit the tension or contradiction that issues from this subsumption of a materiality which is at first celebrated. Both the poets and the scientists sense and cautiously circle the irony teetering in the balance. They must "descend" into the world of soil, cottages, and children; they must privilege, study, listen to, even submit to the feminized and other-racialized material world in order to build their visionary fortresses firmly upon it. To gain the metaphysical—or to become an elite in a secular world—they must trek through the blood and mess of the physical. To conquer the natural world with words rather than weapons, they must observe it closely. But they must not lose themselves in it. Like Lord Byron's Don Juan, they cultivate intimacy with feminine, other-kin bodies, but only to prove superiority, difference, and autonomy.

I have shown how Wordsworth struggles rhetorically with this predicament. By way of a teleology of masculine transcendence, a containment of "passion" within meter, and an image of the poet of "Imagination" as "Hannibal among the Alps," Wordsworth resists the rhetorical feminization and racialization of himself which immersion in a rhetorically feminized and racialized soil or Earth might effect. His rhetorical negotiations with an ideologically freighted materiality help to prepare the way for a contradictory metaphysics in Western biological discourse in which materiality is at once celebrated and cannibalized, as we will now see. Wordsworth's poetry of transcendence reaches forward through this nineteenth-century biological science to the eugenical metaphysics of intelligence and to the challenge to such metaphysics posed by experimental modern novelists.

3

Reimagining Materiality after Romanticism: Science, Phenomenology, and Narrative

The world of soil and trees which had enchanted Wordsworth, and of which he fashioned himself suckled child, warring champion, and poetical master, increasingly absorbed the interest of nineteenth-century British and American intellectuals. Study of the biological order of things, in particular, became a widespread activity among educated men—a "gentleman's pursuit"—and an authorizing discourse for philosophy, psychology, sociology, and politics.[1] The evidential status of organic materiality increased, the detailing of its powers proliferated, and the challenge of harnessing those powers (in significant part through the written word) loomed large, promising social and intellectual riches.

Although much of this chapter corroborates Michel Foucault's argument that the nineteenth-century naming of materiality, specifically the body, amounted to discursive containment of its powers, I also argue that the drive for containment succeeded only in part.[2] The telos of nineteenth-century descriptions of materiality is clearly one of domination and enclosure, especially along racial-patriarchal lines of gender, race, class, and nation; but not all of the discourse's descriptive moments serve that end. Vocal dissenters to biological determinism eventually used scientific methodologies to resist it,[3] and even the initiating authors of determinism generated conceptions of the material realm that potentially challenged their own framing arguments. To colonize the world of matter, rational or scientific thought "must achieve hegemony in collusion with the senses it subdues, rather than trampling roughshod over them," as Terry Eagleton says of rationalist aesthetic theory.[4] In this process of collusion certain moments and notions in the biological discourse open up the possibility of more horizontal conceptions of the relations not only among things and bodies but also between writing and materiality—conceptions latent in Hegelian phenomenology, later foregrounded in twentieth-century phenomenology, and, finally, imaginatively rendered in experimental twentieth-century novels. As a first step in understanding the multivalent complexity of late eighteenth-, nineteenth-, and twentieth-century discourses of materiality, we need to consider the competitive atmosphere in which they developed.

RIVALS FOR THE HAND OF NATURE

Border disputes and territorial jealousies structured the intellectual professions in Wordsworth's day no less than in ours. Ideas themselves, then and now, take the shape they do at least in part because of this context of competition, which is in significant part gendered and racialized. It is therefore no surprise that professional competition among nineteenth-century educated men influenced the formulation of notions about materiality, especially hierarchical notions bearing on race and sex. In particular, a gendered rhetoric of male intimacy with and cultural production through a feminine Nature found expression within this competitive context. The import of this rhetoric emerges especially clearly when it is considered as part of the professional competition among the Romantics and nineteenth-century thinkers in general.

Scientists in the nineteenth century promoted the principle that the study of biology must form the starting point for all knowledge. "We must acknowledge," wrote J. G. Spurzheim in 1832, "that without a sound physiology of the nervous system, there can be neither psychology nor any species of philosophy."[5] By the end of the century Karl Pearson could claim with confident authority that "there is no way to gain a knowledge of the universe except through the gateway of science."[6] Philosophers, politicians, poets, and novelists all responded to the claim of science to primary knowledge—some enthusiastically, some grudgingly, some jealously—and their responses further inscribed the hierarchical construction of materiality.

Although most histories have persuasively identified the middle years of the century as the period when science emerged as *the* hegemonic discourse,[7] preparatory territorial skirmishes and maneuvers can be detected among intellectuals at the end of the eighteenth century. Hegel explicitly refers to science as the discipline that provoked his analysis of the "phenomenology of spirit." In fact, *The Phenomenology of Spirit* begins with a long preface, "On Scientific Cognition," in which Hegel spells out his aim to "help bring philosophy closer to the form of Science."[8] Although Hegel openly bows here to the methods of science, he subtly shifts his terms so as to reenlist science in the service of metaphysics. He disabuses the reader of the idea that science deals only with materiality or appearances and metaphysics only with abstraction or spirit. He aims to merge science with metaphysics by pursuing a "Science of the *experience* which consciousness goes through."[9] Completing this simultaneous effort to raise metaphysics to the level of a science and to bring science into the service of metaphysics, Hegel pronounces that "the Spirit that . . . knows itself as Spirit, is *Science.*"[10] By claiming Spirit as, paradoxically, the essential "Substance" of human self-consciousness, Hegel is able to conclude that the truest and highest science is that which studies the substance and the experience of this self-consciousness, namely, the phenomenology of spirit. By this means he appropriates the radical, emergent "pure" sciences to the traditional realm of metaphysical philosophy and works to disarm this new scientific rival, some of whose adherents were directly challenging "the metaphysical notions of the schools."[11]

Wordsworth likewise felt compelled to position his visionary poeticization of nature's powers in relation to the scientific codification of nature's laws. The uncertainty of his position emerges in the "Preface" to the *Lyrical Ballads*, where he claims that "poetry is the first and last of all knowledge." He then turns to science: "If the labours of Men of science should ever create any material revolution . . . the Poet . . . will be ready to follow the steps of the Man of science, not only in those general indirect effects, but he will be at his side, carrying sensation into the midst of the objects of science itself."[12] Wordsworth predicates his comments with an "if" so as to put in question the reality of the "material revolution" which science was in fact at that moment creating. He briefly acknowledges that the "Man" of science might lead the poet, who would be "ready to follow" the scientist's new advances into the material world. But quickly, in this hypothetical scenario, Wordsworth places the poet "at [the] side" of the scientist; and by the end of the passage the poet has already entered and transformed—through "sensation"—the realm of objects which science only gazes upon. Wordsworth goes on to condescend to science, holding out the promise of a *possible* place for it "as a dear and genuine inmate" of an implicitly patriarchal "household of man."[13] He positions the poet as the caretaking father of the cultural "household," generously allowing the scientist-son a room within that house. Shelley likewise uses an implicitly gendered rhetoric when he argues that science needs poetry to achieve "full and good dominion": "The cultivation of those sciences which have enlarged the limits of the empire of man over the external world has, for want of the poetical faculty, proportionally circumscribed those of the internal world."[14]

But the Romantic poets' competitive references to science belie their anxieties about its new influence. When Wordsworth insists that the "business of poetry" is "as permanent as pure science,"[15] he reminds us that science is the new standard by which the staying power of all intellectual "business" will be judged. Poetry's discursive project of extending dominion over the material world now faces a healthy challenge in the form of science. Although their business is the same, and the heroic rhetoric of Romanticism would be put to good use by scientists, science would turn that rhetoric against poetry in order to defend its superior claim on the material world.

By midcentury, in fact, science could announce its "dominion" over poetry as a practice that described the material world in the name of transcendence. In a speech before the Royal Academy of Art, T. H. Huxley spells out the reversal of poetry's fortune, using an explicitly gendered language wherein men of science and men of poetry vie over access to (and rhetorically assume the powers of) a reproductive feminine Nature. Huxley chastises those in his audience who might view science, this "new birth of our times," as a "sort of monster rising out of the sea of modern thought with the purpose of devouring the Andromeda of art."[16] Science appears here as a kind of monstrous mother which uses its reproductive powers to an unnatural degree by threatening to devour all others who might claim the power to give birth. At the same time, in a mixing of gendered metaphors typical of nineteenth-century discourse,[17] science is figured as a masculine threat of rape to the vulnerable, feminized Andromeda of art. While ostensibly rejecting the idea of science as a menacing male dragon, Huxley nonetheless continues his empowering metaphor, going so far as to issue a warning to the defenders of art, personified by Perseus: "I hope Perseus will think better of [trying] conclusions with the scientific dragon . . . first, for his own sake, because the creature is hard of head, strong of jaw, [and has] a great capacity for going over and through whatever comes in his way."[18] Science is an indomitable dragon conquering not only nature but also those who would pursue "her" in competition with "him." Having flashed the teeth of science in the face of a chivalric Perseus of art, Huxley then, without skipping a beat, contradictorily claims chivalry for the dragon of science, confessing that it is after all "very debonair and gentle." He maintains the chivalric rhetoric, using it to feminize and maternalize art most thoroughly: "As for Andromeda, he has the tenderest respect for that lady, and desires nothing more than to see her happily settled and annually producing a flock of such charming children as those we see about us."[19] Note that when science finally proclaims dominion over poetry and the material world, it does so through metaphors of a subdued maternalism. In a manner reminiscent of Wordsworth's poetic practice Huxley draws heavily on the imagery of a circumscribed, feminized reproduction to construct science's activities of cultural production. Such constructions are also always implicitly racial, national, and class-related, since the circumscription of motherhood, whether metaphorical or literal, serves to fortify these boundaries, as we have seen.[20]

Science likewise usurps Romantic poetry's tropes of labor in staking its claim to name the feminized material world. Aligning the scientist with the manual laborer in his essay "Technical Education," Huxley compares the scientist to a cobbler: both have direct "contact with tangible facts."[21] Through such comparisons Huxley pursues the same alliance claimed by Wordsworth. We saw that Wordsworth found ways to participate, through his poetry, in the sensibility of the feeling yet manly yeoman, pointing to his own poetic sensibility as that which gave him an intimacy with nature akin to the peasant's. Huxley as spokesperson for science similarly claims to share the laborer's intimate contact with nature, that is, with tangible facts.[22] But Huxley argues for the scientist's superior knowledge of nature, again by gendering the contest. He privileges laborer and scientist together, over and against the poet, who merely tries to woo "Mother Nature" with "honeyed words." Unfortunately for the poet, Nature has shown herself to be "serenely obdurate" to his courtship, while the "craftsman" (of which the scientist is one) can exercise "greater power over nature" by his hands-on "contact" with her.[23]

Associating themselves with the laborer, the poet and the popular scientist meanwhile slyly employ him as a useful rhetorical pawn in their cultural competition with each other for the "office" of mythmaking about materiality, of cultural production organized around the world of reproduction. Seeming to offer themselves as his equals, these writers fashion the laborer as an empowering metaphor for the disciplines of educated men. They thereby reestablish educated men as a class that controls the meaning and values of the working person's labor, capitalizing on the empowering masculinity of the laborer while placing him in a subordinate and feminized position in relation to their authority.

Just as educated men vie rhetorically with one another and with the laborer for "intimate" knowledge of a feminized Nature, they similarly keep women's very real threat of competition in check by employing women, especially mothers, as mere metaphors for nature.[24] The verbal drawing of boundaries and staking of claims in these discourses depends on and maintains the image of feminized reproductive materiality. It inscribes discursively those same gendered roles of cultural production and reproduction performed socially and physically by men and women. The discourse conforms, as we will now see more fully, to that racial–patriarchal logic in which a feminized, border-perpetuating reproduction serves a male-privileging and racialized cultural expression.

NATURE AS AUTHOR OF RACE AND GENDER

In the course of the nineteenth century, gendered metaphors for nature became increasingly complex, contradictory, and problematic.[25] Huxley's maneuvers give us one glimpse of this complexity. I suggest that new conceptions of matter further intensified these complications. One of the key insights of science into materiality concerned its "active" nature, its structuring power. Spurzheim wrote:

"Nowadays matter is considered as active . . . and as exercising some influence in the universe," which put, as he pointed out, "the doctrine of souls . . . in the most inextricable difficulties."[26] Or, as Herbert Spencer later observed, physical scientists began to perceive "dead matter" to be "everywhere alive."[27] Less and less were bodies conceived of as moving only when inhabited by a soul. The mechanical eighteenth-century conception of matter's motion gave way in the nineteenth century to a more organic imagery of webs, drives, and interdependencies.[28] As we shall see later in this chapter, the notion of matter as dynamic and interdependent found especially rich and influential, if metaphysically framed, expression in the thought of Hegel and Charles Darwin.

But perhaps in part because of the destabilizing potential of this reconception of materiality—its potential to attribute activeness to a feminized Nature—the framing values of this discourse were insistently hierarchical and antagonistic along lines of gender and race. (Christopher Herbert's analysis in *Culture and Anomie* of nineteenth-century "metaphors of social organization" as containers for the "boundless scope of human desire" provides an interesting parallel to this point.)[29] In the nineteenth century the disciplines of phrenology, physiology, anthropology, and biology all privileged material proofs and powers and yet contradictorily recuperated the metaphysics of racial patriarchy, in which the hierarchy of spirit over matter legitimizes hierarchies of race and sex.

Phrenology was one of the first biological sciences to adapt a metaphysics of race and sex to the emerging materialist methodologies of science, and so to establish materialism as a tool of the ascendant cultural discourse of educated men. Historians have documented the initiating role of phrenology in the development of the sexual and racial sciences.[30] Here I supplement their accounts by drawing special attention to the innovative, and implicitly contradictory, biological metaphysics of phrenology.

Phrenology, though it easily degenerated into quackery in practice, was nonetheless a significant advance for biological science insofar as it privileged the human brain as the site at which the metaphysical might be understood to merge into (and therefore be measurable by means of) the physical. In their focus on the brain and skull phrenologists successfully negotiated the double demands of materialism and metaphysics. Given the middle-class desire to shift the center of power downward toward the material world and into the hands of the conquered but rising classes or "races" without altogether sacrificing mind-privileging hierarchies of power, phrenology offered a perfect solution in its approach to the brain.

As summarized by George Combe in 1841, the tenets of phrenology were simple: "that the brain is the organ of the mind; that different parts of it are connected with different faculties; and that the size of the organ exerts an influence on the power of manifestation."[31] Phrenologists identified thirty-five "organs" of the brain which controlled key mental traits, ranging from "propensities" such as "secretiveness" and "combativeness" to "perceptive" functions such as "time," "tune," and "language." Using the principles outlined by Francis Gall, Combe, and others, phrenology purported to be "a system of Philosophy of the Human Mind."[32]

Phrenologists claimed that their science joined and reconciled the work of anatomists, metaphysicians, and physicians. Anatomists and physiologists, according to Combe, had mounted exhibitions of sections of the brain, but as "connected with nothing."[33] Metaphysicians from "the days of Aristotle to the present" had discoursed on the "faculties of mind," but without any reference to "material systems." And, finally, physicians had overlooked the brain when they located the "passions and affections" in other bodily organs and products, especially the stomach and the fluids. Idiots, for instance, lack affections, but they have complete "abdominal viscera"; therefore the source of the problem must lie elsewhere.[34] Phrenologists, by contrast, integrated all of these concerns and, in the words of Spurzheim, held that "the brain is the sole organ both of the feelings and of the intellectual faculties."[35]

In asserting the phrenological principle that "the size of the organ exerts an influence on the power of manifestation," phrenology rendered the mental and emotional—in a word, metaphysical—capacities not only observable but measurable. This localization of emotional and moral as well as intellectual qualities in the brain and the equation of size with power enabled phrenologists to classify human types according to the size of different parts of the brain. This meant that now the metaphysical essence of individuals and groups could be differentiated and measured in terms of the brain or the skull. In this way phrenologists collapsed the old separation between personality and soul—between differences in individual character (according, for instance, to heat and cold or bodily fluids) and the underlying cosmic similarity of all souls, regardless of personality type. The new equation of sensibility, brain, and spirit made the very spiritual essence of persons accessible to classificaton. No longer would it be held that, although a person or a people might be phlegmatic or sanguine, their souls were equivalent in the eyes of God. Scientists now implied that persons, and nations, differed in their very essence—which could be physically categorized, measured, and of course hierarchically ordered.

Thus it is that phrenology marks the beginning of biological attempts to locate the differential "capacities" (a word conveniently straddling quantitative and qualitative values) in the brains of men and women, the Negro and the white, the Irish and the English, the criminal and the law-abiding. Interestingly, a supposed "organ" for mothering came in for special attention from phrenologists. Combe suggests, for example, that a larger "philoprogenitive" organ can be found in women in general, and a smaller one in "25 out of 29" infanticides.[36] The isolation of such an organ, especially if thought to be detectable through the skull shape, could obviously become a very powerful weapon in the hands of men who faced competition from women, for now competitive women could be cast as biological deviants.[37]

More explicitly, Gall, Spurzheim, Combe, and other phrenologists openly offered the phrenological method as a social tool in distinguishing national or racial types. Spurzheim wrote:

> It is of great importance to consider the heads of different nations. . . . Though all observations of this kind are very defective, they are yet rather for than against the physiology of the brain. The foreheads of negroes, for instance, are very narrow, their talents of music and mathematics are also in general very limited. . . . According to Blumenbach the heads of the Kalmucks are depressed from above, and very large sideward above the organ which gives the disposition to covet. It is also admitted that this nation is inclined to steal, etc.[38]

Such "data," Spurzheim suggests, can help to establish the rightness of social hierarchies: phrenological studies may "exercise a great influence on the welfare of nations, in indicating clearly the differences between natural and arbitrary nobility, and in fanning the relations between individuals to each other in general, and *between those who govern and those who are governed in particular.*"[39] This new biological metaphysics thus offered itself as a means for reinstating and recodifying the old political metaphysics wherein some persons' bodies "naturally" serve other persons' governing heads. Along the same lines, Combe recommended that the state might study the heads of prospective emigrants to the colonies to sort out "atrocious and incorrigible characters" from more productive and docile types.[40]

Not only did such claims rearticulate old hierarchies but, more important for my purposes, they also worked to secure the scientists' place in them. By foregrounding the social applications of their science, they could put themselves in a position to "exercise a great influence" on the welfare of nations and, in turn, on the welfare and status of their profession. So once again we see how the inscription of a racialized and gendered discourse of the body supports the newly ascendant intellectual productions of its authors. An implicit metaphysics of writer over body and materiality drives this discourse. In their representations of racialized mother figures, twentieth-century writers would grapple with the hierarchy wherein the reproductive, racialized body serves to sustain discursive or "mental" creations.

Despite phrenology's demise, Victorian writers extended its central principles, namely, that the brain is the organ of the mind, that human emotional and mental capacities merge in the brain, and that these capacities can be analyzed and measured in physical terms and by physical means. Dissecting and measuring the brain directly (rather than externally, by means of the skull) and also studying the nervous system more fully, scientists penned volumes such as *The Senses and the Intellect, Principles of Mental Physiology, Mind and Body, or The Philosophy of Health,* and *Physiology and Pathology of the Mind.*[41] Writers conceived of "physiological psychology," "transcendental anatomy," "transcendental physiology," and "psycho-synergic traits."[42] The apparent (and politically volatile) dissolution of the mind/body distinction in these writings was counteracted by their careful, scientific reinscription of racial and sexual ranks.

At midcentury Robert Knox heralded the arrival of a full-fledged racial science in *The Races of Man* (1850), stating as "simply a fact" that "human character, individual or national, is traceable solely to the nature of that race to which the individual or nation belongs. . . . Race is everything: literature, science, art, in a word, civilization, depend on it."[43] He goes on to establish a biological hierarchy of races, arguing for instance that members of colored races have half the nerves of whites (10), and that, despite some evidence of larger Negro skulls, he feels "disposed to think that there must be some physical, and consequently a psychological inferiority" in Negroes (157). Knox's reference to his "disposition" to find inferiority tells all; but he constructs that disposition within the scientist's logic of "physical, therefore metaphysical" in such a way as to downplay the subjective and political determinants of his "disposition."

Knox applies the principle that "physical changes must precede the moral" (81) when he reasons that, since he sees "no symptoms" of physical changes in Celts or Jews, he can conclude that their low intellectual and moral character will never improve. Their fixed physical traits indicate that the Celts, who "[do] not understand what we Saxons mean by independence" (21), "never could be made to comprehend the meaning of the word liberty" (26). "We" should therefore not be surprised that "there was never any Celtic literature, nor science, nor arts" (218).

Knox was among those who understood the French Revolution as a racial uprising—an unfortunate one, since it was the conquered Celtic French who led it. The Celtic Frenchman, he writes, demonstrates "furious fanaticism; a love of war and disorder." This creature is "restless, treacherous, uncertain: look at Ireland" (26). And so in France, "never was the destruction of a dynasty more complete" (26). Lest he be taken for a friend of the aristocracy, however, Knox quickly adds, "As a Saxon, I abhor all dynasties, monarchies, and bayonet governments, but the latter seems to be the only one suitable for Celtic man" (27). Knox's equivocal qualifying statement dramatizes the straddling act required of the educated-class champions of liberty: political hierarchy must be dismantled—to a point.

Similarly wielding the principle of "physical structure" to deny the presence of metaphysical or artistic qualities in other races, Knox attempts to counter Benjamin Disraeli's celebration of Jewish character (itself caught up in the racial discourse of the era): "In the long list of names of distinguished persons whom Mr. Disraeli has described as of Jewish descent, I have not met with a single Jewish trait in their countenances, so far as I can discover; *and therefore, they are not Jews, nor of Jewish origin*" (140). The principle of physical structure shifts here into one of physical *appearance*, creating a malleable standard which overrides all other evidence, whether physical, metaphysical, or commonsensical. Above all, for Knox, the "new element of mind" brought into play by the "Saxon" race, of which Knox considered himself a specimen, may be read in their bodies—for the "Saxons are a tall, powerful, athletic race of men; the strongest, as a race, on the face of the earth. . . . They may almost be considered the only absolutely fair race on the face of the globe" (43).

Knox was a bit of a renegade in the scientific community partly because his formulations were so flagrantly antagonistic and absolute. And yet most nineteenth-century scientific writers, as Nancy Stepan, George Stocking, and others have documented, expressed the same views, if with more rhetorical tact and intellectual subtlety. Charles Darwin approvingly quotes John Beddoe, author of *The Races of Britain*, who asserts that when "a race attains its maximum of physical development, it rises highest in energy and moral vigour."[44] Francis Galton echoes this formulation when he identifies "energy" as an "attribute of the higher races" and reiterates that "the very foundation and outcome of the human mind is dependent on race."[45] Darwin folds this principle into his observation that the European races "immeasurably surpass their former savage progenitors, and stand at the summit of civilization."[46] (Note the typically Romantic "summit" image.)

Darwin, in fact, fully underwrites the "physical dependence for metaphysical transcendence" account of human labor arrangements. He maintains that "the presence of a body of well-instructed men, who have not to labour . . . cannot be overestimated; as all high intellectual work is carried on by them and on such work, material progress of all kinds mainly depends."[47] Here it is the intellectual, not the laboring class, who effects even the "material progress" of civilization. Even as the body is made to bear testimony to the metaphysical superiority of particular races, so laboring-class bodies serve intellectual-class minds.

By the early twentieth century these metaphysical encomiums would—as was only scientifically appropriate—be brought down to earth in flat statements that, for example, "the Negro is *organically* incapable . . . of being educated to the same level of intelligence as the European."[48] Even into the twentieth century, scientific-minded professionals clung to physical size as the measure of meta-physical or mental capacities. One social scientist especially concerned with the "oriental threat" iterates the principle that "the taller the race the larger the brain tends to be" so as to argue that Japanese "superiority" over the Chinese."is due to the fact that in the two diameters of the head . . . they out-measure the Chinese at every age."[49] Such measurements support this author's warning that the Japanese constitute a threat to Western hegemony. Here we see again that racial distinctions derive from a concern with control over material resources and power.

With gender the implications of the size and strength standards are predict-able. As was noted in chapter 1, Galton played a formative role in establishing a correlation between gender and biologically grounded metaphysical hierarchies. In *Hereditary Genius* he catalogues the parentage of "great" people of the English nation in support of his idea that "genius" is hereditary. (His book has an implicit racial–nationalist agenda as well). As Flavia Alaya points out, his "system of selection [is] rigorously heroic, in the Carlylean sense," so that "the geniuses in his pantheon were almost exclusively men."[50] Military commanders constitute one of the largest categories of Galton's "men of genius."

Galton further reveals his adherence to the principle that "might makes mind" when he asserts that he had originally intended to "make memoranda of the physical gifts of my heroes" since so often men of achievement are "massive, vigorous, capable-looking animals" who present "a feast" to the observer's eye.[51] Such a correlation between "massive" size and "genius" clearly puts women at a disadvantage. This implicit judgment on women's innate limitations of mind finds further expression in Galton's claim that no environmental conditions can inhibit true genius, which "if hindered or thwarted, will fret and strive until the hin-drance is overcome."[52] Later researchers would spell out what Galton left un-stated, namely, that "if there had been in women a really great ability . . . it would have shown itself in overcoming the difficulties opposed to it."[53]

When Darwin, himself influenced by the work of his cousin Francis Galton, refers to the "greater size, strength, courage, pugnacity, and energy of man, in comparison with women," we can extrapolate the implications for men's "men-tal" qualities. But we needn't bother. Darwin does the work for us: in the same paragraph he states as a given the "greater intellectual vigour and power of invention in man"—in comparison, that is, with women.[54] The word "vigour," a favorite among Victorian intellectuals, who linked strong physical qualities to strong mental qualities,[55] particularly indicates Darwin's connection to the mas-culinist model in which greater size, strength, and energy mean better intellectual and moral "fiber." Darwin does assign women "powers of intuition . . . and perhaps of imitation" superior to those of men; but he qualifies his generosity by pointing out that these are "characteristics of the lower races, and therefore of a past and lower state of civilization."[56]

This last statement by Darwin brings me to one final scientific theory particularly pertinent to this analysis: paedomorphism. Emerging at the end of the nineteenth century, paedomorphism aligned all women with the "lower races" by suggesting that both embodied the childhood of humanity. (The theory also provides one of the many examples of a discourse that erases the presence of subordinate-race women by speaking of "lower races and women," as if these other races included no women.) Certain races and the female sex represent, in this theory, "older" evolutionary forms beyond which other "younger" races and the male sex have evolved. Thus, in 1904 G. Stanley Hall suggests that "woman's body is phyletically older and more primitive, while man's is more modern, variable, less conservative"; at about the same time Benjamin Kidd asserts that the "tropical" races "represent the same stage in the history of the [human] race that the child does in the history . . . of the individual."[57]

Galton, too, adheres to the idea that "as the years go by," both in the child and the race as a whole, "the higher races continue to progress, while the lower ones gradually stop."[58] Carl Vogt spells out, in a tellingly circular formulation, the paedomorphic correlation between white women and darker races, emphasizing the supposed inferiority of intellect in both. Drawing on the familiar brain and skull data, Vogt concludes, on the one hand, that "the grown-up Negro partakes, as regards his intellectual faculties, of the nature of the child, the female, the senile White," while, on the other hand, "the type of the female skull approaches, in many respects, that of the infant, and in a still greater degree that of the lower races."[59]

Such statements explicitly served to legitimize relations between, as Spurzheim had put it, "those who govern and those who are governed," especially along racial and gender lines. Josiah Strong explains that the "lower" races need the governance of the higher, for "an undeveloped race, which is incapable of self-government" is simply like "an undeveloped child who is incapable of self-government."[60] Similarly, woman's conservative, slow-moving nature fits her for serving rather than leading roles in the workplace: "Women assistants, for example, are as a rule more conscientious than men but they display less initiative."[61] Paedomorphic arguments asserting an "anthropological relationship," as Otto Weininger calls it, between women and "lower races" thus clearly reinforce a racialized and gendered metaphysical division of labor. They further confirm the affiliation of gender and racial boundaries in the metaphysical order of racial patriarchy. They implicitly reflect the way in which dominant-class women's procreative "handwork" encourages an alignment of all women with "other" races, both the men and women of which are confined entirely to hand-work.

Paedomorphism represents a scientific attempt to rationalize and delimit the boundary-making and boundary-crossing position of dominant-race women. It constitutes an effort on the part of science to handle the contradiction inherited from Wordsworth, and inherent to racial patriarchy more generally, whereby the bodies of dominant-group women, because of their physical labor and the mothering function of reproducing boundaries, become associated with vulnerable racial borders and with subordinate, body-laboring races—an affiliation that could undercut the security of men within those racial boundaries. Paedomorphism makes use of this association between all women and subordinate races, turning it into a full-blown theory so as to defuse the threat. That is, paedomorphism uses this association to draw a racial line between dominant men and the women who give birth to them; it makes women's location *at* the racial border and their potential for slipping *over* it proof of dominant-race men's metaphysical difference between them. At the same time, it turns the threat around and points it toward dominant-group women by holding out a reminder that women can be disaffiliated from the dominant group through their association with lower races.

For my purposes, as with phrenology and other racial and sexual scientific theories, paedomorphism represents above all a cultural discourse—quite a well-received one in its time—of the body. In such theories the racialization and gendering of the body works *discursively* to make the intellectual class ascendant in the same way that such differentiated bodies work *physically* to do the same. Nineteenth-century biology thus not only repeats but also extends the contradictory Romantic attachment to Nature—its embrace which subjugates. In effect, scientists continued the Romantic project as outlined in Friedrich Schiller's "On the Aesthetic Education of Man," in which "the autonomy of reason is already opened up within the domain of sense itself, the dominion of sensation already broken within its own frontiers." That is, as Schiller later rephrases his point, artists "play the war against Matter into the very territory of Matter itself." Such artists "show greater respect for Nature through a nobler confidence in her willingness to obey them."[62] Victorian scientists similarly enter the feminized territory of the body to dominate the body and its territory.

By the same token, these artistic and scientific discourses curve their speech along the arcs traced out by bodies and things in the world. While both scientists and Romanticists such as Schiller recognize that matter is dynamic, interactive, even counteractive, they falsely separate its dynamism from the dynamics of writing and representing. They elide the fact that their own writing bodies partake of that world of matter and that, moreover, they can describe matter only because they partake of it. Schiller can "observe" and "play the war against" matter only because he himself—his very ability to hear and look and record—belongs to matter. His writing gives him access to matter even as his writing is a form and product of it. Thus in inscribing the body, these writers play into its (inscribing) hands, despite their rhetoric of autonomy and mastery.

Attempting to make room for the possibility of resistance to the domination Schiller describes, Terry Eagleton suggests that "there is something in the body which can revolt against the power which inscribes it"; he reads the aesthetic as the site of "the body's long inarticulate rebellion against the tyranny of the theoretical."[63] But, in my view, resistance to this Romantic and Victorian project of tyranny over the world of matter and bodies comes not in the form of "inarticulate" bodies—indeed, not strictly in the form of bodies (conceived as mute) at all. In critiquing Schiller, Eagleton implicitly assumes, like Schiller, a radical break between inscription and embodiment, theory and matter. What both Schiller and Eagleton overlook is the subjectivity of bodies, the articulateness inherent in the physical, the inextricability of sentience and speech which itself allows "the dominion of sensation" to be "broken within its own frontiers"—because the frontiers of sensation encompass those of speech and writing.

Hence, although one of the formidable accomplishments of nineteenth-century thought was to authorize the dominance of mind through bodily proofs and a materialist discourse, this task nonetheless contradictorily necessitated an "intimacy," to borrow Huxley's word, with the body and its material realm. The insistent nineteenth-century repetition of images of science "unveiling" a half-clothed Nature, astutely studied by Londa Schiebinger and Ludmilla Jordanova, represents the attempt to control this tenuous balance between intimacy with and invasive power over Nature, especially an active Nature.[64] It will not, then, surprise us to find a more enmeshed and mutual conception of materiality partly unveiled in nineteenth-century thought and then more openly articulated in twentieth-century phenomenology.

THE UNDERCURRENT OF THE INTERCORPOREAL

In the *Origin of Species* Darwin remarks that "we see beautiful adaptations everywhere and in every part of the organic world."[65] He asks, "How have all those exquisite adaptations of one part of the organization to another part, and to the conditions of life, and of one organic being to another being, been perfected?" Darwin's "exquisite adaptations" actually anticipate Maurice Merleau-Ponty's notion of the "intercorporeal," which I take to describe an other-enmeshed shape, structure, and sensibility in living things. But in Darwin's writing this notion of co-adaptation vies for position with his notion of natural selection.

67

Darwin answers his question about the source of "beautiful co-adaptations" with the competitive principle of natural selection: "All these results . . . follow from the struggle for life" (51). He argues that variations and adaptations develop "if they be in any degree profitable to the individuals of a species" (52) in those individuals' competition with other individuals. His account reduces the other-coordinated movements of living things to an oppositional jockeying for advantage and position. Like other thinkers of his time, he deftly masculinizes the "active" principle which scientists had located in matter by characterizing it as competitive, as driven by a battle impulse.

Indeed, Darwin denies the possibility of any pure helpfulness in the organic world, purging this newly active Nature of its feminine associations: "As in the case of corporal structure, and conformably to my theory, the instinct of each species is good for itself, but has never, as far as we can judge, been produced for the exclusive good of others" (186). Darwin reviews in detail an example of a creature "apparently performing an action for the sole good of another"—that of aphides "voluntarily yielding . . . their sweet excretion to ants." Darwin's observations of this exchange uncovers, by his own admission, no evidence of any "profit" to the aphides; yet he nonetheless concludes that the aphides' excretions must be self-serving. He can only offer the explanation that "as the excretion is extremely viscid, it is no doubt a convenience to the aphides to have it removed" (186). Apart from avoiding the issue of whether this "convenience" really amounts to a "profit," Darwin begs the question of why the aphides produce the "sweet excretion" in the first place. For a scientist so attuned to the subtle operations of the natural world, this oversight is noteworthy.

Darwin nonetheless closes his paragraph with an intensified restatement of his theory: "Although there is no evidence that any animal performs an action for the exclusive good of another species, yet each tries to take advantage of the instincts of the others, as each takes advantage of the weaker bodily structure of other species" (186). Oddly, Darwin begins his absolute reiteration of the competitive principle with an "although" which at first seems to promise a qualification of his theory; the very syntax of Darwin's sentences reflects the awkward maneuvers necessary to his unqualified argument.

Darwin's words "exclusive good," moreover, set up an either/or framework that leaves no room for the in-between possibility that an action might "profit" both species without harming either. Always the game is zero-sum. Likewise, all the relatedness and every co-adaptation among species serves the order of competition: "The structure of every organic being is related, in the most essential yet often hidden manner, to that of all the other organic beings, with which it comes into competition for food or residence, or from which it has to escape, or on which it preys" (61). As we have seen, Darwin furthermore explains sexual and racial hierarchies as the result of this naturalized competition.

But many of Darwin's examples can be unhinged from his framework and may in another context be understood to name the noncompetitive interminglings of the world, at which his concept of co-adaptation hints. A few Darwin scholars have emphasized this obverse side of this thought; several early twentieth-century commentators even argued that Darwin creates a paradigm for a cooperative socialist world.[66] In my reading Darwin himself always remains a contradictory thinker, celebrating but battling the disorder, the alternative order, and the discourse-encroaching order he finds in matter. Here I use his descriptions, as I will later allude to Hegel's, to suggest the presence of a potentially disruptive undercurrent in nineteenth-century thought, or a threshold at which the descriptions of materiality move beyond the battle-inflected language and the mastering telos and edge toward a different dynamic model.

Such is the case with both the notion of co-adaptation and the manner in which Darwin expresses it. In choosing examples of co-adaptation, Darwin often purposely selects unglamorous creatures in order to emphasize how this principle reaches into and structures the most homely corners of the material world:

> We see these beautiful co-adaptations most plainly in the woodpecker and the mistletoe; and only a little less plainly in the humblest parasite which clings to the hairs of a quadruped or feathers of a bird; in the structure of a beetle which dives through the water; in the plumed seed which is wafted by the gentlest breeze; in short we see beautiful adaptations everywhere and in every part of the organic world. (51)

Darwin emphasizes that this principle of co-adaptation operates "everywhere" in every thing; in doing so he *nearly* bestows on it a status equal to the principle of competition. But he never does do so; competition remains the first principle or the force generating all co-adaptations.

And yet, here and throughout his writing, Darwin's proliferation of examples and his embracing, iterative syntax function to emulate the generous, inclusive reach of the principle of co-adaptation. The description of one creature always involves the description of another, or of a plant or rock formation which the creature inhabits, making his prose circuitous and difficult. One co-adapted thing leads to another, and Darwin's discussions follow this lead. My point here concurs loosely with Gillian Beer's emphasis on the way Darwin's prose mirrors and is even sometimes overcome by the fertility and abundance he sees in nature.[67] I specifically read this tendency in his prose as a function of his interest in the principle of co-adaptation, that is, as an expression of a structural and generative relatedness among things, a relatedness that is in play, I would add, between books such as Darwin's and the organic bodies they describe. In this sense Darwin's book itself manifests the potential for a collapse of metaphysical, book-over-body distinctions.

In his examples of co-adaptation Darwin focuses our attention on an organic symbiosis of both activity and structure. In his view the co-adaptation of the structures of living things engenders their symbiosis of activity. In focusing on "the structure of a beetle which dives through the water," Darwin draws our attention to the fact that the beetle's curved shape tells the story not only of its diving habits but also of the liquid resistance of water; its shape "means" water. The liquidity of water at the same time "means" the mobility of living things such as beetles. Water is a fluid net simultaneously feeding insects, holding those insects for the beetles, and buoyantly embracing the diving beetles. The "meaning" of an organism's bodily structure is simply its implicit reference to the physical environment that sustains it. The "meaning" of the collectively constituted organic environment is simply its structure's implicit reference to the organisms that survive in it. (In this context, Jacques Derrida's notion of différance might be used to describe the infinite interreferentiality of things as well as words, of things in relation to words, not in a one-to-one correspondence or a meaning-erasing slippage, but in a shifting, mutually displacing and replacing exchange.)

One hundred years after Darwin published the *Origin of Species*, Maurice Merleau-Ponty meditates on the co-adapted, referential structure of the body, although he omits the rhetoric of competition. In defining intercorporeality Merleau-Ponty traces the "horizons of the flesh" in contact with the world. Writing in the wake of the cataclysmic genocide of Jews and of two world wars, he chooses a scene of stroking for his study of co-adaptation, as if in an attempt to calm or heal a war-riven body:

> How does it happen that I give to my hands, in particular, that degree, that rate, and that direction of movement that are capable of making me feel the textures of the sleek and the rough? Between the exploration and what it will teach me, between my movements and what I touch, there must exist some . . . kinship. . . . This can only happen if my hand, while it is felt from within, is also accessible from without, itself tangible . . . if it takes its place among the things it touches, is in a sense one of them, opens finally upon a tangible being of which it is also a part.[68]

Merleau-Ponty's description of the way our hands "open" upon a tangible being of which they are a part emphasizes that hands inherently beckon to the phenomenal world as the phenomenal world invites the touch of hands—as the water lies open to the beetle's curved shape. Rather than originating in an autonomous and intangible consciousness, epistemology is here embedded in the very structures of physicality we share with the world. Thus does Merleau-Ponty argue that "the

70

thickness of my body, far from rivaling that of the world, is on the contrary the sole means I have to go unto the heart of things" (*VI*, 135). Following Husserl and Heidegger, he further blurs the division between being and body, spirit and matter, self and world that so infiltrates Western thought. He takes up and disputes, in fact, an assumption originally preserved within phenomenology itself. That is, Merleau-Ponty's descriptions emerge from the tradition of dialectical phenomenology initiated by Hegel at the end of the eighteenth century; but Merleau-Ponty extracts this dialectic of interdependent bodies from the transcendental logic of Hegelian phenomenology in the same way one must extract Darwin's principle of co-adaptation from the competitive ethos of nineteenth-century biology.[69]

As is well known, Hegel formulated with great subtlety the notion of an interdependent intersubjectivity between self and Other, or "lord" and "bondsman." He furthermore theorized a notion of matter that placed it in active relation to the world of the "Universal Spirit." With these formulations he participated in, not to mention played a role in initiating, the nineteenth-century focus on an active organic world and a "transcendental anatomy" or embodied subjectivity. He fed, in other words, that potentially (and eventually) disruptive undercurrent of nineteenth-century thought. Yet he also shared his contemporaries' metaphysical and competitive assumptions and their impulse to contain or rechannel that undercurrent.[70]

In his later work entitled *The Philosophy of History* Hegel elaborates the historical implications of his phenomenology, distinguishing himself as one of the first nineteenth-century thinkers to build a racial hierarchy on the basis of his insights into an active materiality, or "phenomenology." For Hegel, as we know, the history of nations repeats the metaphysical and forceful dialectic that operates, in his account, between individuals and between matter and Spirit. Just as individual enslavement issues from a "life-and-death struggle" wherein one consciousness supersedes another, and just as matter and Spirit become manifest in the fluctuations of what he calls "force" so too does the metaphysical freedom of "world-historical" cultures issue from a struggle among nations which ends in the enslavement of one by the other. Such is the case for the African, in whom "the Knowledge of an absolute being, an Other and a Higher than his individual self, is entirely wanting." And so the European enslaves him. For the Chinese, similarly, "the sea is only the limit, the ceasing of land," whereas for the European, "the sea gives [him] the idea of the infinite"—as well as inviting him not only "to conquest, and to piratical plunder, but also to honest gain and commerce."[71] The two economies—racial and metaphysical (not to mention capitalistic)—go hand in hand for Hegel as for many who follow him. In sum, Hegel submits both matter and the human subject to a "higher," spiritualized,

71

subjugating force, and he rationalizes the racialized enslavement of some humans by others by invoking this same metaphysical hierarchy.

At the same time, Hegel breaks ground for thinkers who challenge such metaphysical and social hierarchies by recognizing both materiality and the intersubjective body as nuanced, active elements in the world which form the inscape of the world of Spirit and, by extension, of discourse. He thus helps to initiate an interactive description of the body and matter which infiltrates the larger culture and comes historically, if unintentionally, to authorize new narratives. These narratives dislodge the race mother's anchoring of traditional metaphysics and explore an unmothered materiality so that, as Christopher Herbert says of nineteenth-century anthropologies of "savage" cultures, "a strategically introduced idea seems to have generated unforeseen circumstances."[72]

UNBORDERING THE BODY

Edmund Husserl, Martin Heidegger, and Maurice Merleau-Ponty are among the twentieth-century phenomenologists who take up and further disseminate Hegel's insights but at the same time distance themselves from the scientific and mastering conception of materiality. In accepting mathematical and scientific accounts of the universe as the most accurate forms of description, Husserl argues, "We take for *true being* what is actually a *method.*"[73] Emphasizing an "intercorporeal" knowing and grasping of the world which precedes rational description, Merleau-Ponty reiterates that "we must begin by re-awakening the basic experience of the world of which science is the second-order expression."[74]

Their comments reflect the degree to which science had come, by the early twentieth century, to monopolize descriptions of materiality, a monopoly these thinkers resist in part by returning to and extending the intersubjective phenomenology of Hegel. While Merleau-Ponty here speaks of "re-awakening the basic experience of the world," in effect he simply offers *another* "second order expression," but one that questions the necessity of an either-or oppositionality and theorizes another kind of dialectic in the world. This alternative account may never be verifiable as the "true" description, but it nevertheless takes on a presence in the world, *as* description, that can challenge the monopoly of an oppositional and hierarchical discourse.

I turn particularly to Merleau-Ponty at this point and in this study generally because his descriptions seem to me to position themselves more fully in the "in-between of self and other," to borrow Hélène Cixous's phrase,[75] than the descriptions of either Husserl or Heidegger, the other two phenomenologists most attentive to the subject as body. Husserl does speak of the "kinesthetically functioning living body" which "holds sway" in the world and which provides the only means by which one can "understand another physical body in which another 'I' is embodied and holds sway."[76] Thus he further foregrounds the role of the body in that intersubjective dialectic outlined by Hegel.

For Heidegger, even more centrally than for Husserl, Being is always *Dasein*, is always "being *there.*" In other words, Being is always already situated in the phenomenal world. Heidegger further collapses the hierarchical mind/body division and the corollary self/Other opposition when he insists that in perceiving the world *Dasein* "does not somehow first get out of an inner sphere in which it has been proximally encapsulated, but its primary kind of Being is such that it is always 'outside' alongside entities which it encounters and which belong to a world already discovered"; or, again, "Knowing is grounded beforehand in a 'Being-already-alongside-the-world.'"[77] Heidegger distinguishes his account from Hegel's and even Husserl's when he refuses to read the seeable, "ready-to-hand" body as the point of necessary vulnerability for a consciousness already there—the weak point, in effect, of consciousness. The body's physical situatedness is "essentially constitutive for *Dasein*'s Being."[78]

And yet both Husserl's and Heidegger's preoccupation with *a* "Being" in the world reflects—and here I would agree with Jacques Derrida—their residual orientation within an "economy of the same," or within a paradigm concerned with an individual, if embodied, consciousness.[79] Not only do Merleau-Ponty's more microscopic tracings of the "flesh in contact with the world" make rich use of the minutely precise language that characterizes Darwin's attention to co-adaptation and so invoke the fertile undercurrent of the biological tradition, but also his narrative position at the meeting points of one thing and another in the world gives him more access to their paradoxical interplay of dependence and transcendence, of sameness and difference, of a "reversibility" between them. Most important, this narrative location in the space of intercorporeal reversibility approximates and illuminates the stance of the narrators of several experimental twentieth-century novels—that space from which they dismantle the boundary-reproducing role of the race mother.

Merleau-Ponty's early conception of what he eventually names intercorporeality resonates strongly with Darwin's notion of co-adaptation, a resonance enhanced by his occasional use of biological terms such as "organism." In his earlier discussions of "dialectical relations" he focuses on a "circular process" by which "the organism itself measures the actions of things upon it and itself delimits its milieu."[80] He imagines, like Darwin, a constantly adjusted and finely co-adapted economy of phenomena and consequently considers that "there is in human existence no unconditioned possession, and yet no fortuitous attribute" (*PP*, 193   ). Evoking the evolutionary imagery of tool-grasping apes, he suggests that the history of human behavior is "the transformation of contingency into necessity by the act of a renewed grasp" (*PP*, 199). But Merleau-Ponty does not finally focus on the visible effects, the products, or the telos (racial or otherwise) of this intercorporeal economy. Phenomena provide no bedrock on which true description can fix itself or from which it can generate a determinate narrative trajectory of transcendence. He attends instead to the dynamic contingency, the indeterminacy, and what he calls the "reversibility" of intercorporeality.

Initiating his challenge to the division between for-itself and in-itself, or subject and object, he points out that no quality or thing exists "in itself." In the intercorporeal world all qualities—of the thing and of the perceiver—are inter-determinate. Consider, for instance, that "the blue of a carpet would never be the same blue were it not a woolly blue" (*PP*, 317). On the contrary, "it is impossible completely to describe the colour of the carpet without saying that it *is* a carpet, made of wool, and without implying in this colour a certain tactile value, a certain weight, a certain resistance to sound" (*PP*, 323). The borders among the qualities of the thing (color, shape, texture) and between the thing and the surround of space it inhabits are never directly accessible. The intercorporeal subject witnesses the intermingling of those intertwined qualities of the thing both within and against the intertwining of that thing with other things, with "certain" other tactile values, weights, and resistances to sound.

Perception does not, then, involve a singular, for-itself subject that views while existing "alongside" a single, in-itself object with distinct, extractable qualities. For perception cannot light on an object free of the context of other objects. Perception hovers at the threshold between the blue carpet and all the infinitely adjacent things whose coexistence with the carpet "defines" it and constitutes it—including the thing we call space. We can never see space without the things that inhabit it and can never see the things without the spaces they inhabit. The "in-itself" thus exists not in itself but only as part of the terrain of space and of other things which connects intercorporeal perception to it. Perception and object cannot be strictly distinguished and bordered

But what, after all, is this perception? For Merleau-Ponty the perceiving subject is, like the thing, never singular. But in contrast to Jacques Derrida, for whom decentered perception derives from the nonpresence of the subject to herself or himself (the always-logos-mediated or deferred access to the world of the body), for Merleau-Ponty it is on the contrary the subject's embodiment that makes him or her doubled and decentered—although not necessarily disoriented and at a loss. Because "I start from outside myself and open to the world" (*PP*, 457), I come to myself from outside myself, through that body through which others come to me.

It is important to emphasize, as Merleau-Ponty does, that intercorporeal self-presence "is not coincidence, fusion with . . . it is separation," and the condition of this self-presence *"is* presence to a differentiated world" (*VI*, 191). The difference of oneself from others *in body* which also generates one's vision of and difference from oneself is an enabling condition—perhaps *the* enabling condition. The self-presence of embodiment is, for Merleau-Ponty, "the foundation of space and time" (*VI*, 191). Seeing and touching ourselves, we inhabit the spatial and temporal openings that make up the finite spatiotemporal world. Thus again space and time are not constructs generated by a subject to organize the world of inert objects; our embeddedness in the world of objects gives us a place within its temporal and spatial differentiations.

It is from within space and time, and within the openings of space and time, that what Merleau-Ponty calls the reversibility of the flesh has its space of unfolding. It is in the "intertwining of my body with the visible things" (*VI*, 49) that I *receive* what comes to me. My flesh is reversible: "My eyes which see, my hands which touch, can also be seen and touched" so that "in this sense they see and touch the visible, the tangible, from within" (*VI*, 123). The depth of my body gives me access to the depth of things, and these reiterate the depth of the world in which they take their place.

This reversibility and the depth it traverses, again, rests on a "dehiscence," an *écart* or separation between things (*VI*, 123). That is, for me to be present to myself in this way and to receive things into my hands, I must be differentiated from the world, radically transcendent of it in my embodiment, as its things are likewise radically transcendent of me in their embodiment. This transcendence, however, is not a surpassing; it is what returns things to one another. In their difference lies their identity, for difference would not have any value unless against a common ground of phenomenal being. As Merleau-Ponty says in disagreeing with Hegel's absolutely oppositional conception of intersubjectivity: "For the struggle ever to begin, and for each consciousness to be capable of suspecting the alien presences which it negates, all must necessarily have some common ground" (*PP*, 355). The Other's or other thing's transcendence of me is also what gives the Other to me, often pleasurably, through the material embeddedness we have in common. The shared concreteness of things creates a "fold" wherein things both touch and diverge from one another. "The immediate is at the horizon and . . . it is only by remaining at a distance that it remains itself" (*VI*, 123). As we shall see, modern authors explore a similarly understood intercorporeality wherein difference and distance—horizontally rather than vertically or hierarchically conceived—form the conditions of encounter and speech.

The invisible medium of space is especially crucial to this horizontal intercorporeality. Space is not an opening to be collapsed in all directions except the one created by the gaze of a "lordly" subject. Nor is space an open wound, the injury inflicted by that supposedly primordial, infantile loss (expressed, for Freud, in the "fort-da" game) which in turn can only be closed willfully, violently, in the masculine act of appropriating the Other to oneself. The transparent space between things constitutes them, offers them the place where together they inhabit the visible and the invisible. Even as the flesh is reversible and ecstatic, so the world of visible things folds back on the atmosphere of the invisible. In this sense do Toni Morrison and Virginia Woolf, in particular, carefully depict the spaces between the bodies and things of their fictional worlds. As with the "Clearing" in which Baby Suggs preaches in *Beloved,* that space and the things occupying it must be honored if the subject-body is to displace and undo its dominated position.

UNMOTHERING THE MASTER NARRATIVE

To reimagine materiality in this way radically disrupts the function of the mother within the metaphysics of racial patriarchy. The ideology of mind over body, as we have seen, keeps the mother in her contained place as bodily reproducer of racialized bodies which themselves then take their fixed places in the mind–body social and labor hierarchy. But if one collapses the distinction between mind and body, between subject and object, one begins to bankrupt the function of the race mother, for one begins to withdraw the capital invested in her differentiating body.

The disruption of the race mother's position by a phenomenology of intercorporeality emerges more clearly when we consider her originary structural role in the master narratives of transcendence. The imagery of the mother's racialized corporeal reproduction generates, as we have seen, an economy of cultural production. The primary human development narratives of Western culture have further reinforced the mother's position as originary but left behind within this racial–patriarchal economy.

Traditional stories of human development in the West, whether Christian, Hegelian, Darwinian, or Freudian, have told a metaphysical tale of spiritual or mental transcendence of the material.[81] In the Christian and the Romantic-Hegelian stories we struggle in body, gaining incrementally wisdom that would be unavailable to us without bodies, but all for the purpose of a final beatific transcendence of body into the heavenly world of impalpable souls, of imperishable art, or of the Universal. Bodies house the Spirit, they manifest Force, but they do not constitute the essence of either. They *serve* the will of Spirit.

In the Darwinian story bodies struggle murderously with one another and with things; many bodies die so that the most metaphysical, civilized, reasoning bodies may live on in dominance. For Darwin Reason stands at the summit of human faculties, and the most reasoning humans stand at the summit of civilization. Darwin argues clearly that in a "civilized" society mind needs to be freed from bodily labor in order to effect material progress: "The presence of a body of well-instructed men, who have not to labour . . . cannot be overestimated; as all high intellectual work is carried on by them and on such work, material progress of all kinds mainly depends."[82] Thus, the body both serves the mind through labor and depends on the mind for its own material progress. The evolutionary story of human development is the story of progress away from body and toward mind, a progress that is partly material but is nonetheless effected by mind.

Sigmund Freud explicitly aims to be to psychology what Darwin was to biology.[83] Like Darwin and the phrenologists before him, Freud aims to ground the mind in the body, as Stan Draenos has fully analyzed in *Freud's Odyssey*.[84] Freud explores the somatic manifestations of emotional and psychological disturbances. But Freud's work, like that of his predecessors, is equivocal and ambivalent about the bodily powers it identifies.[85] In *Civilization and Its Discontents* and *Totem and Taboo*, Freud maintains the hierarchy of races according to their deployment of "reason" versus body, and, as Herbert Marcuse, Leo Bersani, and others have noted, he confirms the necessity for repressing the body's "drives."[86] In Freud's story the infant begins as merely a bundle of drives—for food, warmth, and so on—lacking the concept of differentiation from others that comes with the practice of egoistic rationality. The development of individuals in "civilization" requires the ego and superego, which help to contain drives, by sublimation or repression, for the sake of achieving order, maturity, and rationality. Freud's story of both the individual and the culture maintains the metaphysical movement away from groundedness in the body. Even recent theorists rethinking the body have difficulty resisting this deeply embedded narrative.[87] I no doubt have sometimes unwittingly reiterated it in this volume.

But we need to seek out more energetically and read more carefully other evidence. Here again Merleau-Ponty is helpful. Drawing on the work of Henri Wallon, in *The Primacy of Perception* he tells an alternative developmental story, one that highlights the primary, co-adaptive powers of the body which are present from infancy rather than developed only conceptually in a trajectory of transcendence. He directly reorganizes the narrative of human development and offers leverage for a removal of the border-reproducing mother.

Merleau-Ponty takes up Wallon's idea that the infant is "turned toward others" rather than turned inward, and folds it into his evolving philosophy of the intercorporeality of subject and object. Wallon argues that the very young child does think, but thinks "syncretically."[88] This syncretic thinking is akin to what Carol Gilligan describes as characteristic of women making moral choices and also to what Sara Ruddick has called "maternal thinking."[89]. The syncretic thinker organizes objects, concepts, and others not logically but within the context of the human relationships in which he or she encounters them. Merleau-Ponty likewise suggests that the child's early sense of fusion with others is not merely a confusion to be sorted out and transcended but rather the basis for the adult experience in which "the consciousness I have of my body is not the consciousness of an isolated mass; it is a postural schema. It is the perception of my body's position in relation to the vertical, the horizontal, and certain other axes of important coordinates of its environment."[90] In other words, the child, far from blindly sending signals of need with no awareness of others, emits a sort of radar, constantly reading the bodies of others and adjusting his or her body accordingly.

As in the adult, the child's "postural schema" is not necessarily "conscious," but it is ceaselessly operative. Consider James Ramsay in *To the Lighthouse*, attuned to his mother's own (largely bodily) attunement to his father, or Claudia in *The Bluest Eye,* who detects a high-pitched note in her mother's song. These fictional scenes highlight the "postural" radar capacities of young children, "that great clan which cannot keep this feeling separate from that."[91]

The work of the psychologist Daniel Stern likewise specifies (in ways I will only sketch briefly here) the workings of this receptivity in the infant. He further challenges the assumption of unreceptive, blindly embodied egocentrism in the child—that assumption which underlies the story of the development of a reasoning consciousness whose job it is to control and order the body's irrational demands. Stern's and others' experiments demonstrate, for instance, that if simultaneously shown two films accompanied by a soundtrack that is synchronized with only one of the films, infants of two and three months tend to look at the film that is in synch with the soundtrack. This finding implies that infants perceive the correlation between sound and sight and attend to that correlation. By grouping such correlations in the external world, according to Stern, infants can identify the differences between one person or thing and another.[92]

This means that the child's initial sense of order—the child's knowledge—comes not through a set of imposed cultural images, whether given by a mirror or by an encoded language or by an adult authority, but from its own sentient powers of correlating material phenomena in the world, including those issuing from its own body—from, that is, its "intercorporeality." The infant's sense of separateness is not forced in from outside but is generated through the discrete correlations, or lack of correlations, among the phenomena of the material world. Objective knowledge starts, in other words, with the infant's knowledge of itself as an object separate from other objects. The mother's supposed developmental function of guarding the body *before* it becomes fully organized mentally is unveiled as simply the job of hierarchical mind-over-body socialization in which her subordinate and differentiated position as reproducer (but not producer) plays the key reinforcing part. In the intercorporeal story, however, mothers do not merely protect helpless bodies and then discipline them within the limits decreed by language, including the law that leaves mothers and bodies "behind"; rather, parents and children move together in a world of shifting reversibility, continually emplacing, displacing, reorienting one another.

In this nontranscendental narrative of the intercorporeal body, the functions of language also become potentially more diverse, less oppositional, and less helpless in the face of hegemonic discourses. Language need not be understood solely as a function of Lacan's phallic Law, Darwin's Reason, or any other metaphysical construct.[93] Early verbalization is not simply a rambling, non-referential babble, distinct from intentional adult language and inspired only by bodily sensations of gas or satiety. Nor is it an unstructured semiotic flow which, as in Julia Kristeva's conception, survives only as a disruptive presence in phallic speech.[94] Infants' speech or sound-making is a series of questions put to the world and to others in the world. It is of a piece with all of our adult questions. Infant speech, like adult speech, works as a kind of lever to unfix and resettle positionality. Language and hearing are intercorporeal instruments of co-adaptation.

Thus, speech operates in a way similar to gesture, which, in Merleau-Ponty's words, "brings about a certain polarization as it sketches out in space a comport-ment . . . that modifies the sense of the whole world for those present."[95] Like the appearance of a body, our sound-making initiates an exchange that opens the meaning of space and begins to readjust the orientations of self, object, and Other within that space. Mikhail Bakhtin has fully theorized this palpable exchange-ability of speech, and William Andrews has shown how speech and dialogue operate to unfix and reauthorize the slave's physical positionality in the master's world.[96] Likewise, in modern fiction, for the similar purpose of generating a palpable but frequently unrecognized subjecthood, speech often takes on the status of a negotiable or sharable object, a thing that is heard or seen, in addition to its function as a vehicle of particular meanings. As, for instance, with the airplane writing in Woolf's *Mrs. Dalloway* or the "moo cow" rhyme in Joyce's *Portrait of the Artist,* seen words or spoken sounds in modern texts often take their import more from their shared externality or felt materiality than from the partic-ular meanings they spell out. Their meaning is in part their palpability, for the palpability of words or sounds makes them sharable with others. The palpability of sounds "means" sharability. Meanwhile, the pitch or volume or length of the sounds rearranges or clarifies the positions of subjects in relation to one another.

Like the things of the world, then, speech and objects share a reversibility that stems from their common materiality and can coterminously support the kinship of body and body or body and world. In this light, as Merleau-Ponty argues, "the musical idea, the literary idea . . . would not be better known to us if we had no body and no sensibility; it is then they would be inaccessible to us" (*VI*, 149). Such a formulation takes us a long way from the Wordsworthian idea that meter serves to regulate the folk passions and the Victorian assumption that the musical and literary arts prosper to the degree that a civilization surpasses its "primitive," sensuous, and maternal beginnings.

The notion of the intercorporeal body thus counters the metaphysical assumptions of Western aesthetics and disrupts the maternal matrix of those aesthetics.[97] As we shall now see, experimental modern novelists put this intercorporeal revision of aesthetics and of the mother's role in those aesthetics into narrative practice.

4

Swan Song for the Race Mother: Late-Romantic Narrative in *Cane*

At the beginning of the twentieth century, alongside the descriptions of being and materiality offered by Western phenomenology, complicated and sometimes convoluted representations of the race mother began to appear in literary texts, mostly, though not exclusively, among writers whose group membership (in terms of either race or gender or both) associated them with the body rather than the mind, with "handwork" rather than "brainwork." These writers reconfigured narrative so as to open a horizon of mutual access between language and the body, or handwork and brainwork, as Husserl and his followers worked to do in extending and revising the Hegelian story of intersubjectivity. Yet to do so, especially for women artists and for artists of a subordinate race, particularly in the era of eugenics, required a recasting or a casting off of the protagonist's identity as determined by the race mother and a reshaping of the narrative trajectory which she originates.

For this reason Jean Toomer's collection *Cane* abandons progressive plotting and organizes narration spatially, tracing instead the liminal positionality of the mother figure and her sons. *Cane* makes a narrative locale of the spaces between white and black, inside and outside, mother and man.[1] It wedges its narration inside those border zones and imagines within them chiasmatic figures—of dusky daylight, pale-skinned Negroes, unmaternal mothers, and ambiguously first- and third-person narrators. In particular, the text discovers in its marginal spaces and liminal times mother figures who resist the role of reproducing racial, sexual, and metaphysical borders. Sometimes the narrative intimately enters these border spaces to discover these figures, as when we crouch among the pine trees on the opening page of *Cane* and witness Karintha soundlessly giving birth; in other stories it only invokes them, as with the border-line shack "between the railroad and the road" to which Becky's racial mixing has exiled her.

It is through such women and at these borders that the text accumulates its suggestions of a regenerative intercorporeality, including a close affiliation of song and text with embodiment. *Cane,* however, problematically equates the intercorporeality and the "flesh-notes" of song embedded in its marginal spaces with mother figures and with women generally. It depends on mother figures, in effect, to open up and sustain those other spaces and the intercorporeal voices which inspire its lyricism. In this way *Cane* perpetuates the Romantic gendering of materiality and remains caught in the reductive inscriptions of motherhood and embodiment which are deemed acceptable by racial patriarchy. In this way *Cane,* along with *Ulysses* (and *The Sound and the Fury* and *Light in August*), pursues a late-Romantic aesthetic practice.

And yet Toomer's use of first-person, self-revealing narrative voices and his tortured, ironic portraits of artist-characters who cherish Romantic visions of art, such as Dan Moore and Kabnis, indicate his self-consciousness about the problems of this aesthetic practice for a subordinate-race artist. Toomer's portraits of such artists cut very close to the bone of his own problematic representations of mothering and storytelling.

BREAKING INTO THE BORDERS

Especially in the first southern section of *Cane,* women move, ghostlike, within male boundaries, encircled by the group gaze of competing men. The sketches in the first and second sections of the book repeatedly expose the dynamics of male ownership of women's sexuality. They represent the economy in which women are items of exchange and in which boundaries of race serve to regulate the exchange of women—boundaries which mothering women in turn reproduce. More specifically, many of the sketches and poems explore the way in which competition both within and between communities of men, often racially constituted, impels the quest for sexual control of women.

Cane thus illuminates the larger racial setting for the "homosocial" dynamic (to borrow Eve Sedgwick's term) between men.[2] In the triangle man–woman–man, as Lévi-Strauss observed, the heterosexual relation for a man often emerges not as the end but as the means to a relationship with another man or men. Heterosexuality becomes secondary to the homosocial intercourse it makes possible, and, as Sedgwick points out, poetry making (or storytelling) is one important form of that intercourse. In racial patriarchy this homosocial bonding occurs within and across racial communities, through the women who help to define racial boundaries and identities. The homosocial "traffic" in women along racial channels generates racial communities; and similarly the storytelling "traffic" in *images* of women founds racialized literary traditions.

Karintha, the woman at the center of *Cane*'s opening sketch, epitomizes the encircled, gazed-on condition of women in these traditions. We learn in the opening lines of *Cane* that Karintha's skin is "like dusk on the eastern horizon."[3] The image serves to describe the mellow tones of Karintha's brown skin, but at the same time it compares Karintha to that part of the sky which reflects light—the eastern horizon—not from which light originates. Karintha's body absorbs light and value from without, as it absorbs the gaze and intentions of the men who desire her.

The sketch stresses that, in early girlhood, the gazed-on Karintha provides the basis for an implicit conversation and competition between young men and old: "Old men rode her hobby-horse upon their knees. Young men danced with her at frolics when they should have been dancing with their grown-up girls. God grant us youth, secretly prayed the old men. The young fellows counted the time to pass before she would be old enough to mate them" (1). The seesaw of the sentences between the desires of the old men and those of the young recreates the seesaw of competition between the men which positions Karintha as a fulcrum in their relations to one another. Karintha both joins the men in a common desire for her and opposes them as competitors in that desire. In a way analogous to the competition of nineteenth-century intellectuals for discursive intimacy with "Nature," the men in this story orient themselves toward one another *through* Karintha. This dynamic urges the men to "ripen a growing thing too soon"; the narrator explicitly criticizes the outcome for Karintha: "This interest of the male could mean no good to her" (1).

Indeed, like several other women represented in *Cane*, Karintha exiles her sexuality in the face of a sexualizing, proprietary male community. As an adult Karintha lives alienated from her community, from her body, and from the child created by the body which her community has invaded and usurped for its own "interests." Although she "indulges [the men] when she is in the mood for it . . . she has contempt for them" (2). The more aloof Karintha becomes, the more the men seek her out. Men continually bring her gifts and money; but, the text reasons, "Karintha is a woman and she has had a child" (2).

More specifically, Karintha has had *their* child, the men's child, which she lets fall from herself, in the text's rendering, like an unwanted, unsuccessfully connected limb: in the forest "a child fell out of her womb onto a bed of pine-needles" (2). She returns from the forest without the child, but allows the child to return to the community in the form of the smoky pine-dust air the people breathe and the pine-infused water they drink, for Karintha leaves the infant's body to smolder in the sawdust pile so that "weeks after Karintha returned home the smoke was so heavy you tasted it in the water" (2). Karintha sets up a cycle of return, setting in play the principle of "what goes around comes around." Or, in the terms favored by contemporary theory, Karintha initiates the "return of the repressed." The text lends her the covert agency to do so.

Like Karintha, Becky is a mothering woman invisible to and yet constituted by, and constituting of, a communal gaze. Whereas in "Karintha" the text identifies the gender conditions of alienated mothering, the story "Becky" explicitly refers to the racial oppositions that help to enlarge and sustain these conditions. Becky, "the white woman with two Negro sons," becomes literally invisible to both the black and the white communities as a result of her taboo cross-racial mothering: "No one ever saw her" (5). Yet the sketch tells the story of how the two communities nonetheless orient themselves toward her in their active segregation of her. Together the communities covertly help Becky to survive, but in a physical space outside the borders of each and invisible to each: "The railroad boss said not to say he said it, but she could live, if she wanted to, on the narrow strip of land between the railroad and the road. . . . Folks from the town took turns, unknown, of course, to each other, in bringing corn and meat and sweet potatoes." In short, "White folks and black folks built her cabin, fed her and her growing baby, prayed secretly to God who'd put his cross upon her and cast her out" (5). The sketch traces Becky's outcast position and motherly alienation to the communities' delineation of racial borders.

As with the seesaw sentences in "Karintha," Toomer neatly employs a syntax of oppositions embedded in parallelisms which express the oppositional logic of racial borders. First, the sketch characterizes the white community's response to Becky's Negro son: "Who gave it to her? Damn buck nigger, said the white folks' mouths. She wouldnt tell. Common, God–forsaken, insane white shameless wench, said the white folks' mouths" (5). Then it characterizes the black community's response: "Who gave it to her? Low-down nigger with no self-respect, said the black folks' mouths. She wouldnt tell. Poor Catholic, poor-white crazy woman, said the black folks' mouths" (5). While using different idioms of denigration, the white and black communities speak parallel languages which together "cast her out" (5). Through this common not-seeing of Becky, the white and the black communities defensively protect their own race–group boundaries from confusion and further violation.

In "Becky" and "Karintha," then, *Cane* depicts the racial boundaries and homosocial conditions underlying women's silenced and alienated mothering. In several other sketches as well, the detached women of the titles either are mothers or are associated with mothering, caught within the community gaze (even if it is half averted). Spied on by the narrator and his friends in their boyhood, Avey, for instance, eventually reminds the self-absorbed first-person narrator of "a cow" whose maternal gestures provoke his indignation ("she laid me in her lap as if I

84

were a child" [44]). Esther, in another sketch, has pale skin, neither white nor black, which seems to express her ghostly suspension in a socially removed fantasy world. In this nowhere world she imagines herself as a mother-savior (she fantasizes rescuing a baby from a fire and then "she loves it frantically" [22]) until, by the time she is twenty-seven, "her mind is a pink meshbag filled with baby toes" (24). Similarly, Fern's "body was tortured with something it could not let out" (17), and that "something" may be, if Fern is like Esther, a thwarted or distorted maternal impulse. Certainly Fern occupies the same position of enclosure within male boundaries as the other women (who are also expected to reproduce those male racial boundaries). The implicated first-person narrator in "Fern" appeals to his male readers, explicitly including both black and white, to help him explain Fern—"your thoughts can help me" (16)—and he closes by giving Fern's full name and inviting the men to see her for themselves. Among these subordinate-race, miscegenational, or biracially gazed-on women, mothering is a forced, thwarted, or displaced act.

The text of *Cane* partly counteracts these conditions, however, by foregrounding the women's experience. That is, these women may inhabit the communities' margins, but they form the text's narrative center. Moreover, they inspire the text's imagistic core. Although Becky remains silent and invisible, her subjectivity appears to find expression in the same whispering pine trees that encircle Karintha's story. "O pines, whisper to Jesus" forms a refrain in Becky's story. The minor variations of the whispered refrain suggest that it expresses Becky's point of view, such as when we learn that the townspeople bring not only food but "even sometimes snuff . . . O thank y Jesus" (5). Later, just before Becky's house collapses on top of her, the refrain intensifies: "Pines shout to Jesus!" (6). On this day of collapse, as on the day of Karintha's childless return, the pine smell hangs in the "listless and heavy" air, "stale and sticky, like the smell of food that makes you sick" (6). Like Karintha, Becky lives nowhere, but her presence is everywhere, soaking the very atmosphere the community breathes. In "Carma," again, there is the melancholy, elegiac imagery of pine trees: "Smoke curls up" to form a "marvelous web spun by the spider sawdust pile" (10). The pine smoke rises high just as the proud Carma rides high on her wagon at the sketch's opening: "Curls up and spreads itself pine-high above the branch, a single silver band along the eastern valley" (10).

By virtue of their exceeding the community's narrow bounds, the women must live in an exiled kinship with the pine trees and the smoke-laden skies, a natural and intercorporeal world that returns the repressed feminine into the community unbeknownst to the community. The code-surpassing embodiment of these women draws attention to the body's kinship with a phenomenal world that surpasses and ill suits human, political categories for it. But for these mothers shadowed by the racial–patriarchal legacy of slavery, this intercorporeal connection to the phenomenal world is a burden as much as a kind of freedom. Their position at the edge of a cultural domain gives them a carnal knowledge that serves to push them further outside community and into marginality.

Yet in rendering and valuing an intercorporeality lived by "wayward" subordinate-race mothers, Toomer challenges the racial, gender, and metaphysical judgments of eugenics and the culture at large. The enfolding of pine smoke images or pine-spoken refrains into the narrative prose represents the enfolding of these women's alienated points of view into the communities' stories. By floating heavy, languorous pine smoke over its sketches, *Cane* fills the atmosphere of the southern black community with sad but inspired and elegiac maternal airs. In the process *Cane* displays its access to and inclusion of an embodied maternal subjectivity which homosocially organized, subordinate-race communities overlook, misconstrue, or evade.

Many of the poems in the collection closely depict this uncoded and alienated dimension of embodied subjectivity. The poems embroider what the sketches frame. Both "Face" and "Portrait in Georgia" undertake this task by revising the body-cataloguing blazon poem,[4] the first by deromanticizing the female experience of embodiment, and the second by highlighting the racial conditions of embodiment. "Face" characterizes a woman according to her individual body parts, in the tradition of the blazon, but it implicitly critiques that tradition by reading the woman's experience of pain, rather than the male viewer's perception of beauty, in the woman's body:

> Hair—
> silver-gray,
> like streams of stars,
> Brows—
> recurved canoes
> quivered by the ripples blown by pain,
> Her eyes—
> mists of tears
> condensing on the flesh below
> And her channeled muscles
> are cluster grapes of sorrow
> purple in the evening sun
> nearly ripe for worms.
>
> (8)

Here the fusion of the woman's features with natural phenomena, verging on decomposition, serves to reveal her subjectivity as inscribed in her body, and not merely to inscribe poetically her effect as a body on the subjectivity of a male poet. Unlike the idealized virgin in a Petrarchan blazon, this woman has gray hair, her body quivers with pain rather than desire or duplicity, and her fate is death rather than love. Directly following the "Becky" sketch, and describing a body which, like Becky's, is left to deteriorate in the "evening sun," this poem also alludes indirectly to the "outcast" context or racialized setting for this undignified death.

"Portrait in Georgia" more explicitly enacts a racialized rewriting of the blazon poem. The celebrated features of a white woman's body typical of the blazon—"Hair," "Eyes," "Lips," "Breath"—become equated with the lynched and burned body parts of a black person. The female whiteness frequently idealized in Renaissance blazons here appears "white as the ash of black flesh after flame" (27). This revision of the blazon turns up the underside of the idealized celebration of the white woman's body: the denigration and destruction of the racialized body of the "outsider." That is, the poem mimics the logic in which the possessive privileging of dominant-race women serves implicitly to reinforce racial hierarchies which subordinate non-kin bodies. "Portrait in Georgia" and "Face" expose the interrelated sexual and racial–patriarchal foundations of the blazon tradition of poetry by depicting the pained embodiment of the racial Other.

The poem "Cotton Song" continues, from another angle, the revisionary construction of subordinate-race embodiment as it sounds a call to heal the body and move it—through labor—to freedom. It openly offers another "face" of embodiment, one that can "roll away" from the oppressor's hold; and it authorizes its call to "roll away" through a nonmetaphysical account of "God": "God's body's got a soul, / Bodies like to roll the soul, / Cant blame God if we dont roll, / Come, brother, roll, roll" (9). Imagining God as embodied, and attributing to the body the power and desire to "roll the soul," the poem celebrates an alternative tradition of spirit–body relations that might substitute for the passive, objectified embodiment created by Western racial patriarchy.[5] This is an objectification in which blazon poems traditionally participate.[6] Whereas hierarchies of race and sex often construct the laboring body as an abject body, this poem employs a double entendre that mingles labor and freedom: the call to "roll away" the cotton bales implicitly also calls the laborers to "roll away" *from* the cotton bales, away from the plantation and from forced labor: "Shackles fall upon the Judgment day / But lets not wait for it" (9).

Moreover, such poem–songs work as covert yet concrete instruments of bodily freedom—that is, as songs sung to set in motion those many slaves' plans to "roll away," to escape their slavery. Songs clearly had these various concrete valences in the slave world.[7] They functioned in the face of imprisonment to effect escape in several senses. That is, songs make audible not only the dialectic of body with voice within a community but also the reversible intertwining of enslavement and mastery. For, while the songs' rhythms facilitate work done for the master, that very act of facilitation constitutes the fold, the opening, and the act in which slave subjects, together, find and manifest a measure of self-determination. By embedding these songs in his text, Toomer recuperates their linguistic power to open up an ontological space of freedom for the subjugated subject and community.

IN SEARCH OF VIRGIN LIPS

And yet two related problems arise within the text's reconceptualization of body and spirit, slave song and freedom. A residual gender opposition intrudes to rupture the fold in which slave songs might touch and tap a realm of freedom for the whole community—in this text as they once did in history. Women are affiliated with embodiment and men with the speech that will embrace embodiment; in order to maintain this division, the text implicitly repeats the metaphysical movement which privileges speech over embodiment and undercuts its own radical challenge to traditional metaphysics.

Although often celebratory in tone, the conflation of women with nature and embodiment serves at crucial moments to silence women or to demonize those subordinate-race women who challenge men's hold on them. In other words, celebration of women's embodiment of nature all too easily shades into incrimination of women's potential embodiment of transgression. Those women most capable of singing or speaking for themselves are exactly those in whom the female affiliation with nature appears as dangerous. In "Carma," for instance, the woman of the title initially impresses the narrator as a kind of freedom rider "driving the wagon home" (10). The dignified Carma inspires his comment that "God has left the Moses-people for the nigger" (10). The text then turns parenthetical for a long paragraph which climaxes in an equation of women with a predatory nature. At first the parenthetical passage continues the ennobling imagery: "The sun is hammered to a band of gold. Pine-needles, like mazda, are brilliantly aglow" (10). The text seems to imply that, despite their alienated circumstances, such women "glow" with an empowering energy akin to nature's. But then women *become* nature in a way that strips them of agency: "From far away, a sad strong song. Pungent and composite the smell of farmyards is the fragrance of the woman. She does not sing; her body is a song" (10). Although her song is "strong," the singing woman is no longer an agent interacting with nature to remanifest the repressed, as in "Karintha." She has become instead an instrument of nature, *its* song—which suddenly turns African, and then beastly:

88

She is in the forest, dancing. Torches flare . . juju men, greegree, witch-doctors . . torches go out . . . The dixie Pike has grown from a goat path in Africa.

Night
Foxie, the bitch, slicks back her ears and barks at the rising moon.
(10)

The metaphor of woman as nature slips unsettlingly into that of woman as natural and sexual predator. Woman–singer becomes woman–conjuror becomes woman–bitch. Just after this parenthetical passage we hear how Carma's husband is "in the gang. And it's her fault he got there" (11). It remains unclear, in a sketch that also asks, "Should she not take others, this Carma?" who is at fault and to whom we should attribute these judgments of fault or of right—to the narrator or to the community. The text, as we shall see, remains ironic and ambiguous in judging Carma. We can nonetheless observe that this sketch celebrating racial and sexual boundary breaking in the figure of a woman also climaxes rhetorically in a reinscription of oppositional boundaries wherein women are bitches matched against juju men.

In "Blood-Burning Moon" Toomer intensifies the sinister kinship between women and nature even as he dramatizes the interracial conditions which particularly force into being this intensified, contradictory mythology of women. Here the black woman Louisa desires both the white man Bob Stone and the black man Tom Burwell, both of whom desire her. The text develops Louisa's double desire simply and frankly, from her viewpoint: "[A] warm glow . . . came into her mind at the thought of" Bob, while Tom "held her to factory town more firmly than he thought" (28). This conflict of attraction might be trivial except that it crosses racial boundaries and in part grows out of them: "[Tom's] blackness balanced, and pulled against, the white of Stone, when she thought of them" (28). As reflected in her race-inflected double desire, Louisa's attraction engages and unsettles the entire machinery of the racial and homosocial containment of women's sexuality. The firing up of this machinery of sexual-racial containment ends in the death of Tom.

Race also shapes the desire of Tom and Bob. "She's my gal," Tom insists, against insinuations about Bob and Louisa, thinking to himself that the giver of Louisa's silk stockings "better not be" the white man, Stone (30). Meanwhile, Bob admits to himself that "it was because she was nigger that he went to her" (32). Yet the text begins and ends with Louisa, and with the imagery of the "evil face of the moon" associated with her. She is cast as the pivotal inciting figure between communities in a way that seems to take for granted the men's racialized attitudes of ownership toward her. As in the "Becky" sketch, the story is not about the *men's* sexuality as transgressing race. In the text's rendering, which allows

Louisa to float "indolently" atop this turbulent race-inflected current of desire, it is Louisa's race-transgressive desire that betrays her racially subordinate community and leads to the death of a black man. Whereas Karintha's repressed desire returns as haunting and enticing pine smoke, Louisa' uncontained desire returns with a vengeanace through the influence of a "blood-burning moon" to which she sings.

The nature-affiliating representations of women's desire differ, then, according to how active and vocal a role the woman plays and how severely she disrupts the racial–patriarchal containment of her desire. The racially subordinate woman's desire, when clearly circumscribed by men and repressed, as in "Karintha," emanates languorously from a silent space outside the community in a smoky, whispering wind. When enacted by a dominant-race woman, like Becky, the potential threat of such desire is negated by the casting out of the woman from the dominant group and her nonacceptance by the subordinate group. Therefore, again in this second case the disempowered woman's desire finds expression in whispering winds that float in lazily from outside the community. But when a racially subordinate woman, such as Louisa, acts on her race-entangled and transgressive desire, its expression in nature takes on an "evil" aspect. Her transgressions can call down punishment on the whole community.

The danger of Louisa's transgressive desire is real: in the end Tom gets burned at the stake. Her desire threatens the community's self-protective economy, which is structured both sexually and racially. That her desire threatens an entire economy is suggested by the fact that the "evil" stands in the very "door" of the black community's spatial and economic center—the factory. But when we place Louisa's story alongside Carma's, as the common imagery of rising moons and witchery encourages us to do, we can also see that an in-group ownership of women by men creates the conditions of danger. Carma crosses no racial boundaries. She is simply said to have "had others" (11), which drives her man, Bane, to a violence that lands him on the chain gang. Very likely the harshness of Bane's punishment, as well as the violence of his response, derives in part from the larger racist conditions encircling black communities. But Carma's story nonetheless shows Bane invested in the ownership of a woman's sexuality, and therefore to some degree jockeying for a masculine place in the racial–patriarchal order. It is in part that possessive jockeying that results in violence, as it does in Louisa's story—and, as we shall see, in Ralph Ellison's *Invisible Man.* But the men's possessiveness is not the cause most emphasized in either "Carma" or "Blood-Burning Moon."

As we consider how women's, rather than men's, transgressive or alienated sexuality generates these plots, it is instructive to compare them to the sketch

"Bona and Paul," which focuses its account of a racially transgressive relationship through the character of the subordinate-race man. In that story Paul pursues, as Louisa does with Bob, a cross-racial relationship with a white person, Bona, but his moment of hesitation (unlike Louisa's) preserves rather than destroys a community bond. Furthermore, that bond is a male homosocial bond, not a heterosocial or heterosexual one: "Paul leaves Bona and darts back so quickly he doesn't give the door-man a chance to open. He swings in. Stops. Before the huge bulk of the Negro" (78. Paul attempts to explain to the black doorman that his out-group relationship with Bona does not negate his in-group relationship with him. Although Paul's claim that the two are not mutually exclusive seems proven wrong by Bona's absence on his return to the spot where he left her, he has managed symbolically to affirm a homosocial bond through his communication with the doorman. What becomes clear in the contrast between Louisa's and Paul's stories is that the threat of most concern is the potential interruption of a male homosocial order, whether that order explicitly rests on containing the ownership of in-group women, as in Louisa's story, or whether it simply involves male–male friendship, as in Paul's story.

Thus, the gradations from haunting to threatening and from affiliative to radically reductive in *Cane*'s imagery of women's bodies can be correlated with the degree to which female characters challenge the masculine order of the black community. So long as black women repress and resent but never revolt, the text allows a haunting, sympathetic, nature-affiliated portrayal of their sexual and maternal suffering. But once black women actively transgress or subvert the black male homosocial order which encloses their sexuality, the text moves toward a threatening and unsympathetic, nature-reductive portrayal of their sexual conflicts. For the white community it is the cross-racial relationships of black *men* that most threaten the racial–patriarchal economy; but for the black community it is the cross-racial relationships of black *women* as constructed in Toomer's book which threaten the economic and social stability—in other words, the homosocial base—of the black community.

We need to scrutinize even the sympathetic imagery that affiliates women's embodiment and desire with nature in light of this homosocial logic in the text. And we need to interpret these sympathetic and negative portrayals of women's desire not as two alternatives but as points on a continuum that connects them to each other and always leaves open the possibility of slippage from one to the other. Much of the imagery that seems to use nature as material ground and manifestation of women's oppressed or thwarted embodiment on second look paradoxically achieves its expressive power by displacing women's desire onto nature. In this sense the text repeats the racial–patriarchal use of women's bodies for a male cultural gain; and it limits its own entry into the "in-between" of intercorporeality, which, in turn, stops the text short of that fuller narrative intercorporeality explored by Morrison and Woolf.

When we reconsider, for instance, the elegiac refrain in "Karintha," we may note that, while it focuses the reader's attention on Karintha's predicament as male group object, it also constructs its poetry out of this woman's predicament in a way that is reminiscent of Wordsworth's "Solitary Reaper." Just as the inaccessibility of the reaper's beautiful song to Wordsworth increases the pathos of his poem, so too does Karintha's Other-reflecting beauty intensify the lyricism of Toomer's sketch: "Her skin is like dusk on the eastern horizon, / O cant you see it, O cant you see it" (1). The fact that "you" can't see "it" because of its reflective rather than active status adds to the seductive poignancy of Karintha's beauty, for the text as well as for the sketch's community of men.[8] Furthermore, by remaining this side of Karintha's beauty, the text can only allude to images of intercorporeality through Karintha without sustaining a narrative and lyricism which fully accommodate black women's phenomenal experience of intercorporeality.

Moreover, the call to free expression and embodiment in "Cotton Song," like that in "Georgia Dusk" and "Harvest Song," addresses the "brothers," not the sisters. "Cotton Song" ends with a call to "come, brother, roll, roll!" (9); "Harvest Song" climaxes with the cry "Eoho, my brothers! (69); and "Georgia Dusk" addresses "the men" who feast and sing "with vestiges of pomp, / Race memories of king and caravan": "O singers, resinous and soft your songs" (13). These calls to brothers beckon the men to embrace an unalienated embodiment, and to vocalize a song or speech integrating that embodiment—but the bodies to be claimed are female or feminized while body-expressive speech belongs to the men. "Cotton Song" summons the brothers to a physical labor adapted to song, which liberates rather than shackles the body.[9] Similarly, both "Song of the Son" and "Georgia Dusk" celebrate the possibility of a song inspired by the land itself; and the land is that same pine-permeated landscape associated with women. "Song of the Son" beseeches the speaker's male ancestors to "pour o pour that parting soul in song, / O pour it in the sawdust glow of night, / Into the velvet pine-smoke air to-night" (12). Pouring their "seed" into the female pine smoky air, *men* bear songs: "One seed becomes / An everlasting song, a singing tree" (12). Similarly, "Georgia Dusk" urges the men to sing their "soft and resinous songs / Above the sacred whisper of the pines, / Give virgin lips to cornfield concubines" (13). The poem acknowledges the "concubine" condition of the land and, implicitly, of the women whose alienation is textually embedded in the land. But it invites the men, not the women, to "give virgin lips" to that condition, to purify it of sexual subjugation and so "bring dreams of Christ to dusk cane-lipped throngs" (13). In short, such poems urge the men to create, through song and text, their own romantic myth of "their" women's embodiment. It is in this male introjection of a feminine material nature which empowers the man—as speaker, as a male member of a subordinate race, and as custodian of materiality—that Toomer's text reenacts the racial–patriarchal legacy of Romanticism.[10]

The relationship between the first and second parts of *Cane* partially continues this Romantic use of woman as bearer of men's embodiment and as instrument of men's group speech and membership. As the text moves from the South to the North, it portrays the alienation of northern black men as a condition of their and "their" women's further disconnection from a female-grounded, naturalized embodiment, an alienation which the text traces in part to the sharper class divisions among northern blacks. Among educated and therefore (the text implies) less embodied blacks, the voice of song generated from women's bodies in the first part becomes fainter. Fewer poems and refrains appear both between and within the sketches, and characters who hear tinny northern bands wish for a chorus singing "Deep River."

In "Box Seat" it is the woman, Muriel, who has diminished her embodiment by her association with polite northern society, epitomized in Mrs. Pribby. Dan longs to reinspire Muriel's "lips, flesh-notes of a forgotten song," and therein "stir the root-life of a withered people" (56). Although Muriel's "animalism" is still "unconquered by zoo-restrictions and keeper-taboos" (59), in the end she "flinches back" (66) from "Dan's impulse to direct her" (59). In "Theater" the uneducated woman Dorris remains fully embodied, but her educated admirer, John, resists involvement with her. Dorris is a dancer who rehearses on stage with her company while John, the manager's brother, watches from a seat in the theater. When Dorris performs, "glorious songs are the muscles of her flesh" and "her singing is of canebrake loves" (53). Dorris thus preserves in her dance that southern female embodiment which the narrators in the first part of the collection call on their brothers to imitate and express.

At first John answers this call. Dorris's dancing body becomes a room John and Dorris share: "The walls press in, singing. Flesh of a throbbing body, they press close to John and Dorris. . . . John's heart beats tensely against her dancing body" (53). But a mind–body split in the educated or "dictie" John makes him turn defensive, afraid to sustain this closeness to the body-constituted world of Dorris.[11] Early on, he vacillates about the possibility of "touching" Dorris:

> Here's right: get her to herself—(Christ, but how she'd bore you after the first five minutes)—not if you get her right she wouldnt. Touch her, I mean. To herself—in some room perhaps. Some cheap, dingy room. Hell no. Cant be done. But the point is, brother John, it can be done. Get her to herself some-

where, anywhere. Go down in yourself—and she'd be calling you all sorts of asses while you were in the process of going down. (52)

John's fear of the vulnerability that accompanies going "down in" himself—through Dorris—leads him to disparage her potential to keep him interested. As a further defense his "mind" intrudes and inserts a fantasy that rewrites the encounter. After a moment of total involvement in Dorris's expressive dance, suddenly "mind pulls him upward into dream"—a dream that takes place not in a cheap room but among "leaves powdered by a million satin slippers" and in which, at the climactic moment, "John reaches for a manuscript of his, and reads" (53). Making Dorris a character in his powdery script, John mediates his encounter with her dancing body.

The text implies that John substitutes mind and text for an intercorporeal embodiment in which he would "touch her . . . to herself." Consequently, when Dorris finishes her dance and looks at John, "his whole face is in shadow. She seeks for her dance in it. She finds it a dead thing in the shadow which is his dream" (53). John's "dictie" education helps him write and think his way into a place where he is safe from bodies which otherwise might make him "go down" in himself. John thus carries on a long tradition wherein movement into the educated class means distance from and containment of other bodies by way of texts.[12]

In this sketch, as in others in the second part, *Cane* exposes this body-displacing tradition of texts while also retaining the assumption that women live the essential embodiment alienated by this tradition. In that sense *Cane* joins the body-displacing tradition by keeping its own distance, as male text, from female embodiment. In other words, it perpetuates the myth of woman as origin and source of embodiment when it uses a woman's body as the symbol of what the educated northerner's texts deny and repress. By attributing embodiment to women and authorship to men, *Cane* thus reinscribes the function of the embodied woman as material instrument of men's culture. It affirms the racial–patriarchal aesthetic myth, which we saw operating in Romanticism, of female content and male form, with form as the governing metaphysical mechanism. *Cane* eschews metaphysical hierarchies without, however, withdrawing from the gendered oppositions that inflect those hierarchies.

BETWEEN THE BODY AND THE BOYS

In two respects, however, Toomer obliquely critiques this feminine aesthetic mythology, namely, through his ironic use of first-person narration and through his partly critical presentation of such artist–characters as John, Dan, and especially Kabnis. Throughout *Cane* Toomer increasingly exposes in his first-person narrators an equivocal mixture of identification with women and a will to appropriate them for cultural—specifically textual—production. He shows such men engaged, no less than the men they criticize, in a racial–patriarchal competition for control of women. Furthermore, as implicit storytellers themselves (and in "Avey" explicitly so) the first-person narrators can be associated with the artist–characters, who likewise attempt intimacy with women and who further display an equivocal mixture of desires toward them.

Four of the twelve sketches in *Cane* use a first-person narrator: "Becky," "Carma," "Fern," and "Avey." In "Becky" the first-person narrator speaks anonymously for the first two thirds of the story. The story mostly refers only to "she" and "them" without mention of a witnessing "I." But an "I" enters explicitly at the moment Becky's chimney collapses, when, it turns out, the narrator happens to be passing in a wagon with his friend Barlo. Just after the chimney collapses, Barlo and the narrator enter the house, hear a groan, and flee. "After that," the narrator tells us, "I remember nothing . . . that is, until I reached town and folks crowded around to get the true word of it" (7). By his own account the narrator becomes a storyteller *because* he has witnessed the death of Becky, which exlains why he becomes an "I" in the text only at this moment of her death. He tells the story of her death for the community, and he repeats that function for the text of *Cane*.

But notice that the "until" in the narrator's sentence casts irony on his phrase "the true word of it"; it is not until "folks crowd round" that the narrator remembers "the true word of it." And yet the narrator has actually fled from knowledge of the "true word" of Becky's death. Although in telling her death to the community he becomes a recollector and storyteller, in actually witnessing her death he momentarily becomes an amnesiac who cannot speak. Just before the chimney falls, he tells us that he experienced an "uncanny eclipse! fear closed my mind" (6). He witnesses the event of Becky's death, then, with a fearful "closed" mind. Thus it is the community's *desire* for a tale about Becky's death that prompts the narrator to create one, and thereby to become a storyteller.

What do we make of the fact that this narrator who fabricates a word about Becky at the demand of her rejecting community is the very same narrator who speaks the text's "true word" of Becky? Is the text's "true word," like the narrator's, equally a cover for an underlying fear of Becky that serves to displace her own account? It seems that in creating a narrator who begins by speaking about a racial–patriarchal community but ends by speaking to and for that community, the text traces the way a story that seems to be written from outside can hardly resist reenclosure inside the community.

The same doubleness of narrative positioning appears in "Carma." As in

"Becky" we see a narrator and a text teetering on the border between the inside and the outside of the community, in this case specified as a male circle of viewers. The narrator confesses that Carma's story *"as I have told it* is the crudest melodrama" (11; emphasis added). He herein emphasizes, even more self-consciously than Becky's narrator, that his story is a "told" thing, made according to cultural formulas for crude melodrama. He implies that Carma's story might be told otherwise. But he does not do so. He admits to indulging his culture's predilection for racial–patriarchal melodrama. He simultaneously points out the limits of and engages in such melodrama.

But this narrator also posits a relationship with the woman of the title which allows us to see more precisely, as the expanding presence of the first-person narrators throughout the text increasingly allows us to see, the competitive homo-social impulses behind such equivocal storytelling. Early in the sketch as the narrator watches the manly, bound-for-freedom Carma "driving the wagon home," he stands with a group of men around a stove. As she rides away, he "leave[s] the men around the stove to follow her with my eyes down the red dust road" (10). The narrator's literal departure from the group of men symbolizes the initiation of his narrative distance from them; he "follows" her to tell her full tale. But for whose sake? Carma's? Ours? His? Theirs?

As the narrator watches, Carma looks back toward him, and he comments: "Maybe she feels my gaze, perhaps she expects it. Anyway, she turns. The sun, which has been slanting over her shoulder, shoots primitive rockets into her mangrove-gloomed, yellow flower face" (10). The first sentence here invites two opposed readings of Carma's backward look. In one the narrator stands out as special among the men; he communicates so effectively with Carma that she "feels" and returns his gaze. In the other the narrator is one among many ogling men whose gaze Carma "expects"; her look carries a sneer. The narrator imagines "primitive rockets" directed, like his gaze, toward her face, which seems to suggest that his interest is as sexual as the other men's. Furthermore, the narra-tor's highly figurative, sun-filled description of Carma as seen from the outside occupies the space in which we might have received a more precise description of her look, one that would clarify its meaning.

Hence, although the narrator separates himself from the community of men supposedly in order to give an insider's sympathetic attention to Carma, the text hints that he is in fact not so different from the community of men. His interest is sexual, his language veilingly metaphorical; and its very metaphoricity keeps him one crucial step short of an "in-between" positionality. He keeps one foot in the men's circle. This description of his special moment with Carma thus reenacts the doubleness by which the narrator distances himself from the oversimplifying codes and positions of melodrama even as he practices them.

This equivocation in the narrator's position casts new light on the slippage, in the parenthetical section of this story, from the sympathetic pine-smoke allusions to classical moon, bitch, and witch imagery, from victim rhetoric to revenge rhetoric. That is, the narrator's attribution of witchery to Carma may reflect his own "interest" in her sexuality: he slips into identification with Bane's view of Carma as femme fatale because he also desires to ride the sun's "primitive rockets" into her "yellow flower face." Our narrator's interest, initially suggested in his connection to the "men around the stove," eventually finds expression in an imagery which makes Carma a dangerous player in an old racial–patriarchal drama.

The first-person narrators of "Fern" and "Avey" actively step forward into their stories and more fully display this double will to empower and overpower the women of the title. The narrator of "Fern" speaks explicitly as a man addressing other men about women:

> I ask you, friend (it makes no difference if you sit in the Pullman or the Jim Crow as the train crosses her road), what thoughts would come to you—that is, after you'd finished with the thoughts that leap into men's minds at the sight of a pretty woman who will not deny them; what thoughts would come to you, had you seen her in a quick flash, keen and intuitively, as she sat here on her porch when your train thundered by? (16)

With statements like this one (or "As you know, men are apt to idolize or fear that which they cannot understand, especially if it be a woman" [14]), the narrator frames the story as a conversation among men but one in which men admit to the shortcomings of their perceptions of women. The narrator playfully encourages his male audience to let down their guard and confess what mystifies or threatens them in women. He describes men's relation to Fern in a way that recalls men's relation to Karintha: "[Men] were everlastingly bringing her their bodies" even though they "got no joy from it" and then "they felt bound to her . . . felt as though it would take them a lifetime to fulfill an obligation they could find no name for. They became attached to her, and hungered after finding the barest trace of what she might desire . . . they would do some fine thing for her" (14). The narrator, in short, describes that by now familiar male pursuit of borderline-inhabiting women.

But this narrator, unlike the "Karintha" narrator, implicates himself in this enigmatic quest early on when he speaks in the first person: "Why, after you noticed [the down on her upper lip] you sought her eyes, I cannot tell you" (14). Clearly he is one who has felt her charms and sought her eyes. In fact, he explicitly equates himself with the other men when he says, "I too had my dreams: something I would do for her" (15). He appeals to the male audience to go beyond their first sexual thoughts "at the sight of a pretty woman" because "your thoughts can help me, and I would like to know" (16). Here he reveals that this letting down of one's guard is actually one more strategic move in the attempt to get "inside" a woman.

In his climactic moment of intimacy with Fern, this narrator, like the one in "Becky," claims "forgetfulness" and takes no responsibility for her alienation:

> From force of habit, I suppose, I held Fern in my arms—that is, without at first noticing it. Then my mind came back to her. Her eyes, unusually weird and open, held me. Held God. He flowed in as I've seen the countryside flow in. Seen men. I must have done something—what, I dont know, in the confusion of my emotion. She sprang up. Rushed some distance from me. . . . Her body was tortured with something it could not let out. (17)

The narrator leaves blank the place where he touches Fern, leaves "unreadable" his relation to her, making it uncertain whether his relation is one of liberatory breakthrough or patriarchal reenclosure. Thus it seems that this narrrator, too, blocks our insight into Fern as much as he assists it. Although he makes poignant Fern's convulsive response to his approaches, he fails to name exactly or to acknowledge his part in her "tortured" response. He falls silent about himself at the crucial moment. In the end, he puts Fern right back into a male audience's questing hands: "And, friend, you? She is still living. . . . Her name, against the chance that you might happen down that way, is Fernie May Rosen" (17).

Even more explicitly than the earlier stories, this story displays the male narrator's collusive veiling of the very woman he supposedly attempts to reveal. The narrator openly states his similarity to other men, and he speaks directly to an audience of men—though he just hints that he might be different because he has "talk" to offer. All these confessions pose as frankness and as an attempt to get beyond the first sexual thoughts that "leap into men's minds." But in the end this narrator seems to act out these first thoughts "from force of habit"—or, rather, a habit of force—as much as other men.

Like the "Fern" and "Carma" narrators, the "Avey" narrator first becomes aware of his heterosexual desire in a scene of homosocial competition, in this case a boyhood competition with a more sexually forward rival named Ned. His youthful "love" for Avey is "brought home" to him when "I turned hot as bare pavements in the summertime at Ned's boast" (42) about Avey (that he could have Avey if the narrator and the other "little niggers" weren't always around). Ned clearly gives heat to the narrator's feeling for Avey. Our narrator at once distinguishes (in metaphorical language) his more noble desires from those of Ned ("something deep in me responded to . . . the young trees that whinnied like colts impatient to be let free" [42]), while at the same time his desire issues from an encounter with Ned.

In his young manhood the narrator achieves an occasional and unsatisfactory intimacy with Avey—unsatisfactory in that according to him it is tender rather than passionate, maternal rather than sexual. At the same time Avey's "indifference to things"—supposedly in this case job-related things—"began to pique me" (44). He goes on: "There was no excuse for a healthy girl taking life so easy. Hell! she was no better than a cow" (44). The narrator's judgment here finds an echo several lines later in Ned's assessment that "she was no better than a whore" (45). This echo again links the narrator to Ned (whom he has recently "hunted" so as to catch "his opinion of her") and also suggests that the narrator's anger about Avey's "indifference" is actually anger about her sexual indifference to him (or her cowlike kindness to him).

In their final encounter the narrator takes Avey to a place where he always goes "when I want the simple beauty of another's soul" (45). This narrator, like the one in "Fern," offers the woman not his body but his "talk." And this talk exposes the first-person narrator's equivocality more fully and unintentionally than that of any other narrator we have met so far:

> I traced my development from the early days up to the present time, the phase in which I could understand her. I described her own nature and temperament. Told how they needed a larger life for their expression. How incapable Washington was of understanding that need. . . . I pointed out that in lieu of proper channels, her emotions had overflowed into paths that dissipated them. I talked, beautifully I thought, about an art that would be born, an art that would open the way for women the likes of her. I asked her to hope, and build up an inner life against the coming of that day. I recited some of my own things to her. I sang, with a strange quiver in my voice, a promise-song. And then I began to wonder why her hand had not once returned a single pressure. My old-time feeling about her laziness came back. I spoke sharply. My policeman friend passed by. I said hello to him. As he went away, I began to visualize certain possibilities. An immediate and urgent passion swept over me. Then I looked at Avey. Her heavy eyes were closed. Her breathing was as faint and regular as a child's in slumber. (46)

The narrator indicts himself from the moment he pretends to explain Avey's "own nature and temperament" to her. But when he confesses that he has actually penned "an art that would open the way for women the likes of her" which he recites to Avey, this narrator may also indict the other narrators, whose art has very much striven to depict the alienation of women "the likes of" Avey.[13] Most whimsically, we can imagine this narrator reciting "Becky" or "Karintha" to Avey. How does she respond? She sleeps the sleep of boredom and deeper despondence—or maternal exhaustion.

Meanwhile, our narrator's relation to Avey once again occurs within the context of his relation to another man, in this case a man of the law. The narrator's passion resurfaces in the presence of the policeman, although it is unclear whether the "certain possibilities" that give rise to "an immediate and urgent passion" in him have the policeman as their object or their catalyst (46). In fact, this ambiguity lets us feel momentarily the shared roots of these two possible roles for the other man—that is, both involve a male bonding formed over the "sleeping" body of a woman (in a scene recalling those invocations of woman's dead body studied by Elisabeth Bronfen).[14] Earlier, when the narrator explains to the policeman that he has come to this place "to find the truth that people bury in their hearts," the narrator emphasizes that "I look deep in his eyes when I say these things, and he believes me" (46). Luckily the policeman believes our narrator, for Avey couldn't care less, and the reader now must doubt him thoroughly. After holding Avey in his lap for hours, the narrator "found my policeman friend and talked to *him*. We both came up, and bent over her" (46; emphasis added). They both bend over Avey, as perhaps the reader, in reading the earlier sketches, has "bent" with the narrator "over" Karintha or Becky or Carma.

I would argue that this sketch, positioned more than halfway through the book, leaves the reader implicated in the narrators' textual use of women when it is too late to claim innocence—but, as a consequence, with heightened knowledge of our own, and perhaps Toomer's, complicity. The "promise-song" that the narrator sings here finds an echo in the closing "birth-song" of the book and should make the reader think twice before accepting the hopeful swing of that closing song. The book's ending instead should make us hark back to this moment in "Avey," and to other similar moments in "Carma" or "Fern" where such "promise-songs" issue from the male narrator's text-making of and through women.

The self-interest of the male operating in the narrators is also detectable in the collection's artist–characters, to a degree that suggests Toomer's critical distance from these characters as well as his self-consciousness about his own textual and rhetorical conflict of interests. In "Theater," as we saw, John invokes his fantasy manuscript to (re)direct the movements of Dorris's body. Although her body generates the content of his "manuscript," John's involvement in the manuscript actually blocks out Dorris herself. Dorris's body compares in this way to Karintha's, Carma's, Becky's, Fern's, and Esther's, overshadowed, like theirs, by a "manuscript," or by a rhetoric of pinesmoke, moon rockets, and mangroves.

It is important to note that the reader experiences this encounter between John and Dorris predominantly from Dorris's point of view. While the narrative voice reveals a knowledge of Dorris as well as of John which both of them lack of themselves, what it tells us about Dorris favors her over John. For example, "Her own glowing is too rich a thing to let her feel the slimness of his diluted passion" (51). Like John, Dorris at first calculates how she might best take advantage of her admirer's desire ("I'd get a pair of silk stockings out of it" [52]), but at a certain point she "forgets her tricks. She dances" (52). Unfortunately for her, this letting go of tricks intensifies John's need for a defense, that is, it prompts the substitution of his manuscript for her authentic body. Although this sketch, like the earlier sketches, generates a feminized, essentializing imagery of embodiment through Dorris (an imagery uncomplicated by the kind of knowledge Dorris's friend Mame seems to possess), at the same time it critiques the male onlooker and in so doing implicitly critiques the text's similarly positioned first-person narrators as well as the text's own depictions.

"Box-Seat" also introduces a degree of narrative distance from its artist–character, Dan Moore. More heroically than John in "Theater," yet in a way that prefigures Kabnis and parallels other late-Romantic male artists such as Stephen Dedalus, Dan imagines himself a bearer of something akin to what Stephen calls the "conscience" of his "race": "Something vibrant from the earth sends a rumble to him. That rumble comes from the earth's deep core. It is the mutter of powerful underground races. . . . The next world-savior is coming up that way" (57). But Dan needs Muriel to realize his vision. Like the first-person narrator in "Avey," Dan imagines that "my talking to you will make you aware of your power" (59–60). Dan urges Muriel to commit herself to his heroic group cause: "Say that you have tried to make them create . . . or say that you will. . . . Say that you will love, that you will give yourself in love—" (60). But Muriel (and Toomer through Muriel) interrupts Dan to ask, "To you, Dan?" (60), cutting through his heroic mythology to his underlying self-interest.

In reaction, Dan's mode of embodiment shifts transparently from the heroic to the aggressive: "Dan's consciousness crudely swerves into his passions. They flare up in his eyes. . . . Dan's fingers and arms are fire to melt and bars to wrench and force and pry" (60). Dan momentarily "slips to his knees before" Muriel, but when she continues to repel his appeal, "Dan tightens his grip . . . grabs her wrists. Wedges in between her arms" (60). Muriel astutely asks, "What are you killing?" and Dan gives an unknowing racial–patriarchal, even eugenics-inflected answer, "Whats weak in both of us and a whole litter of Pribbys," closing with the threat: "For once in your life youre going to face whats real, by God" (60). Attempting to fight the body-subjugating order of his racial–patriarchal society, Dan unwittingly reinstates it over Muriel. Adopting a conqueror's logic, he attempts to reduce the real to the "forced." But Muriel understands how she becomes a necessary sacrifice in Dan's heroic vision; she thinks to herself, "He'd rape!" (62).

In "Theater" and "Box Seat" the women characters affiliated with embodiment, like Louisa, live their role simply and naively; but the men championing embodiment entertain heroic visions of themselves as group "saviors" of its legacy. The men would build new racialized myths of embodiment, but unfortunately they would do so unreflectingly, like their dominators, on the serving bodies of women. Although Dan's driving desire in "Box Seat" seems to contrast with John's diluted desire in "Theater," both men inflate their desire to accommodate a myth of heroic expression which inherently damages women. In its narration of these men's desires *Cane* intentionally opens a space of critical distance from them and from their appropriations of women's bodies.

At the same time, the text itself repeats that appropriation by generating its own imagery of embodiment through women. These narrators and characters begin to unveil the workings of Toomer's intimate representations of women— for his text, too, lays claim to a superior intimacy with women, a knowledge of what most men, as the "Karintha" narrator boasts, "will die not having found . . . out" (2). By creating a text out of that knowledge, it beats other men at their own competition for the female as cultural resource. In this light it may be that the "Becky" narrator's sudden first-person appearance as storyteller and Becky's simultaneous disappearance into death symbolically enact Toomer's own production of an imagery of female embodiment which after all silences, contains, and displaces women's bodily desire.

This storytelling practice launched at the site of female death conforms to that aesthetic practice deconstructed by Elisabeth Bronfen in her subtle study *Over Her Dead Body*. *Cane* narrates the racial terms of that aesthetic, which I seek to clarify. My analysis differs more deeply from Bronfen's, however, in that whereas she argues that the image of woman as death figures forth the inherent and inevitable split between (masculine) language and (feminine) body, I doubt the inevitability of that split and therefore stress the sociopolitical determinants of such an imagery. In my view political rather than linguistic-ontological forces encourage the rupture between writing and embodiment and engender this storytelling over the dead or sleeping woman's body.

I likewise foreground sociopolitical determinants in explaining the fact that Toomer critiques his own aesthetic practice. This remarkable self-consciousness and self-exposure stem in part from Toomer's awareness of the inevitable failure of a Romantic aesthetic for a racially subordinate man, whose "own" women cannot, after all, win him literary transcendence in a "bull-necked" racial–patriarchal world. It is only apt that Toomer closes his book with a stark dramatization of this failure in "Kabnis."

Swan Song at Dawn

In light of this last point it is significant that, increasingly from beginning to end, *Cane* deepens the reader's involvement in the male narrators' points of view. We progress from the invisible narrator of "Karintha" to the chatty narrator of "Fern" to the thoroughly involved narrator of "Avey." Correspondingly, in other stories we increase our intimacy with the male characters, from Barlo to Tom Burwell to Dan Moore to Paul—and finally to Kabnis. More and more we experience events from inside the men's perspective. While this gradual movement into the male point of view serves the project of exposing the men's appropriative desire, it also reflects the text's deepest concern: with men and with their encounter with a racial–patriarchal aesthetic.[15] In this critical yet fascinated attention to the alienated male artist of the race, *Cane* compares with *Ulysses*. In fact, one critic has considered *Cane*'s closing story Toomer's "portrait of the African-American artist as a young man."[16] I suggest that these artist–characters, Stephen and Kabnis, share sexual–racial as well as aesthetic dilemmas. Although Kabnis's dilemmas are more acute to the degree that the legacy of racial–patriarchal slavery is a more extreme form of subjugation, both texts burrow deeply into the angst of the male subordinate-race artist.

At the opening of "Kabnis" the title character hears the wind-carried songs of the mothers of the black community. They have floated into this last story all the way from "Karintha." As Kabnis lies in bed, the cracks between the boards of his cabin "are the lips the night winds use for whispering. Night winds in Georgia are vagrant poets, whispering" (81). Kabnis feels the "weird chill of their song":

> White-man's land.
> Niggers, sing.
> Burn, bear black children
> Till poor rivers bring
> Rest, and sweet glory
> In Camp Ground.
>
> (81)

The alienation of Karintha, who bore and burned a black child, and whose story is recalled in the imagery of whispering winds, here haunts the black male poet. Like earlier artist–characters, Kabnis is drawn to the songs of his race's alienated mothers. Like Dan Moore or the "Avey" narrator, Kabnis longs to "become the face of the south . . . my song being the lips of its soul" (61). He would speak the sorrow of women's nature-embedded, overburdened, intercorporeal bodies. Yet he also shrinks from the mothering female body. Listening to this song, Kabnis finally slips beneath his covers, "seeking release" (81). Like the earlier narrators and characters, he runs into resistance to his project; but in this case, where no particular woman is his object, it becomes clear that the resistance originates in the artist's own dis-position as much as in that of the women he might seek.

In Kabnis's story the text exposes why the male artist–characters of the black community cannot succeed in the Romantic project of subsuming mother figures into their art: the black mother cannot neatly serve as the black man's basis for cultural reproduction because of her prior historical reproductive function for the white man's culture and the white man's concurrent monopoly over the cultural discourses that negatively mythologize black women. White men have thus usurped black men's means for building their own racial–patriarchal economy and culture.[17] Nonetheless the text, as we shall see, ultimately attempts this subsumption.

Under his sheets Kabnis self-consciously moves into a dream world, like some of the other narrators, announcing that "Ralph Kabnis is a dream" (81). As John did in "Theater," Kabnis attempts to rewrite the story of his relation to a black woman. He would make that woman the inspiration for a dream from which she, as an agent, is absent. He would give birth to himself in a world of dreams rather than issue from a woman carrying so many burdens—burdens which he inherits. He would redream this vexed and diminished cultural inheritance descended through the mother.

But his dream gets interrupted by the real presence of a "she-bitch" in the form of a hen that begins to scratch and cackle in the attached shed. That Kabnis's home is actually part of the hen coop of "old Chromo in the big house" (82) suggests that, much as he would make the mother a serving inspiration in the male artist's culture, as the black son of an appropriated mother he instead becomes the feminized occupant of a "hens'" house. In this position, Kabnis resents the mother's disruptive effect on his dream. He wishes, as he says, that her "cackle would choke" her, and "choke every *mother's son* of them in this God-forsaken hole" (82); emphasis added). Kabnis wishes for the death of both the black mother and her humiliated boy–child, implicitly including his own death. Irritated to the point of hysteria, he finally bursts into the shed, grabs the "she-bitch," and steps outside to wring her neck. Just before he does so, the pine-infiltrated night evokes for him a song of the black mother's racial boundary position—that position which forestalls the black artist–character's use of her in his cultural production:

> With his fingers about her neck, he thrusts open the outside door and steps out into the serene loveliness of Georgian autumn moonlight. Some distance off, down in the valley, a band of pine-smoke, silvered gauze, drifts steadily. The half-moon is a white child that sleeps upon the tree-tops of the forest. White winds croon its sleep song:
>
> > rock a-by baby
> > Black mother sways, holding a white child on her bosom.
> > when the bough bends . .
> > Her breath hums through the pine cones.

> cradle will fall . .
> Teat moon-children at your breasts,
> down will come baby . .
> Black mother.

> Kabnis whirls the chicken by its neck, and throws the head away. Picks up the
> hopping warm body, warm, sticky, and hides it in a clump of bushes. (82)

Just as the condition of a black mother forced to hold a white baby rends the
relation of black children to black mothers, so this song of the black mother splits
open the lines of the lullaby. The black male artist cannot subdue his race mother
for his group's homosocial purposes because the culture she would generate and
reproduce has been displaced by the dominance of white culture. The black
mother is subdued and represented by non-kin rather than kin men. In an act of
spite Kabnis thus splits the hen, symbol of the mother, rending her head from her
body, and leaving a body which involuntarily lives on. In trying to return to the
cabin, however, "he totters as a man would who for the first time uses artificial
limbs. As a completely artificial man would" (83). In splitting the mother figure,
as imaged in the hen, Kabnis splits and cripples his own body, and his art,
ultimately making him as unfit for working in Halsey's smithy as he is for becoming "the face of the South" (81).

At the same time, having coopted the black male artist's mother figure, depriving him of the possibility of becoming "her lips," the dominant white culture
excludes and disparages the black male artist's "dream." In this context Kabnis's
aim to become the "face of the South" by dreaming new dreams runs smack up
against the wall of racial–patriarchal force: Kabnis realizes that the dreams of
subordinate-race poets "are faces with large eyes and weak chins and broad
brows that get smashed by the fists of square faces. The body of the world is bull-
necked" (91). When "the body of the world" is a racial conqueror's bullying, or
bull-necked, body, the racially subordinate man who redreams the world can
become that bully's casualty.

In response to the physical and implicitly economic reality of a competitive
world, Kabnis strives for a masculinized art, despite its inspiration by vagrant
poet–mothers—or rather *because* of that feminine source. Like Stephen Dedalus,
Kabnis feels cowed by a masculine world of "fists" and wishes to make an art that
will resist its threat: "If I could develop that in words. Give what I know a bull-
neck and a heaving body, all would go well with me, wouldn't it sweetheart?" (81).
Only by making the masculine, "bull-necked" self the foundation of that speech
and art—as we have seen the first-person narrators attempt to do—can the male
artist hope to protect himself internally, against the threat of being emotionally
engulfed by the mother's suffering, and externally, against the threat of physical
and social indignity conferred by a dominating kin–patriarchal male community.

Kabnis herein lives the predicament endemic to the attempt of the racially subordinate man to create his own Romantic tradition of mother-grounded texts. The voices of race mothers are his art, yet they disrupt his art with their reminders of their borderline position and his disempowered relation to them. Therefore, when Kabnis hears (with "mingled fear, contempt, and pity") the voices of the women praying in church, he suggests the church men "should see to it they are stopped or put out when they get so bad the preacher has to stop his sermon for them" (89). In other words, subordinate men's speech, by being disempowered, exists on a par with subordinate women's speech—so much so that the women's speech can actually rival or drown out the men's expression. Kabnis insists that women's humiliating rivalry of expression be silenced or "put out." Such a putting beyond the bounds of sympathy or hearing has been precisely the fate of those female title characters whose expressions of desire rival the men's control of desire. Karintha, Carma, and Louisa stand apart and alone, threats to the very narrative and rhetorical order centered on them.

As in the earlier stories, however, the woman's repressed voice returns with a vengeance, this time leaving Kabnis running around like a chicken with its head cut off. The climax of the story of Mame Lamkins coincides with a climactic woman's shout from the church and the crash of a rock through Halsey's window which sends Kabnis running. Layman has been telling how the pregnant Mame Lamkins was killed in the street a year before for hiding her husband from some white men. Not only did the white men kill her but one of them "took an ripped her belly open, an the kid fell out. It was living; but a nigger baby aint supposed t live. So he jabbed his knife in it an stuck it in a tree" (90). This account dramatizing white racist sentiment emphasizes the larger white context that intensifies the alienation of a black mother such as Karintha, whose predicament haunted Kabnis in the opening scene and returns to haunt him here. Kabnis identifies with the baby in Mame Lamkins's story, as suggested by his later wish that "some lynchin white man ud stick his knife through [my soul] an pin it to a tree" (110). But the "impotent pain" of that identification sends him running (102).

In contrast to Kabnis, who flees, symbolically, at the climax of this story of plundered motherhood, the man named Lewis has sought out information about exactly such stories. In fact, the note on the rock that breaks the window is intended for him: Lewis's "pokin round" into things "that werent fer notin down" (90) has turned some of the community against him. For Lewis is a man who would speak the silenced stories of the black community, who would look into rather than avoid or sexualize "eyes that loved without a trace of fear" (4) as he does with Carrie K.[18] In this sense Lewis would seem to represent the text's self-consciousness about the "interest of the male" and the community's alienating use of women as mothers.

Yet even Lewis works to recuperate a Romantic vision of those mothers, especially for the men descended from them. In the scene in Kabnis's cabin, in which Lewis first appears, Lewis turns his gaze toward Kabnis, offering a non-competitive homosocial invitation:

> His eyes turn to Kabnis. In the instant of their shifting, a vision of the life they are to meet. Kabnis, a promise of soil-soaked beauty; uprooted, thinning out. Suspended a few feet above the soil whose touch would resurrect him. Arm's length removed from him whose will to help. . . . There is a swift intuitive interchange of consciousness. Kabnis has a sudden need to rush into the arms of this man. His eyes call, "Brother." (96)

Lewis has succeeded in provoking from Kabnis the response that the speakers in "Harvest Song" and "Cotton Song" desire from the black "brothers" they address. Like those earlier speakers, Lewis also calls his brother Kabnis to "a promise of soil-soaked beauty," which, within the mythology of the entire text, arises from a soil-soaked woman. Lewis inspires in Kabnis a homosocial "vision of the life they are to meet" on this soil.

Kabnis, however, like the text, cannot sustain this vision. His consciousness of its contradictions turns his hopeful sense of promise into a mockery of promise.[19] "And then a savage, cynical twist-about within him mocks his impulse and strengthens him to repulse Lewis. His lips curl cruelly. His eyes laugh. They are glittering needles, stitching. With a throbbing ache they draw Lewis to. Lewis brusquely wheels on Hanby" (96). Once more Kabnis embraces and then repulses the Romantic vision of a gendered, soil-soaked artistry, even when, as in this case, it is offered as the basis for a homosocial bond. Kabnis rejects the vision not, however, for women's sake, but rather because he feels a black man's visionary art will only expose him as a usurped and unmanned "bastard son." Such an artist's "beautiful words" quickly become "misshapen, split-gut, tortured, twisted words" (110). The white meddling with the black community deprives black men of the "virgin" or undefiled materials for a mythology of mothers, which in turn interferes with black men's aesthetic vision-making.

The closing story of *Cane* repeats its title character's vacillation between embrace and rejection of a homosocial vision grounded in a mythology of mothers. At the end of "Kabnis" Carrie K's virgin mother "lips murmur, 'Jesus, come'" (118). Carrie's call echoes Becky's, but we should remember that it is above all the text's call, attributed to women such as Becky and Carrie K and then borrowed back from them to form a literary text.

In some of its details the sketch seems to mark the limits of this borrowing of an enclosed feminine voice. As Carrie K kneels in supplication to Jesus at the feet of Father John, "light streaks through the *iron-barred* cellar window. Within its soft circle, the figures of Carrie and Father John" (116; emphasis added). Kabnis has earlier characterized this iron-barred room as "just like th place they used t stow away th worn-out no-count niggers" (113). Carrie's supplication fixes her as impotently in that barred place as Father John's silence fixes him.

And yet a "soft circle" of light surrounds them. They take on "pregnant" iconic meaning in that light, as does the text in its next and closing paragraph. At its close the narrative moves outside its barred space and at the same time more deeply into the soft halo of light:

> Outside, the sun arises from its cradle in the tree-tops of the forest. Shadows of pines are dreams the sun shakes from its eyes. The sun arises. Gold-glowing child, it steps into the sky and sends a birth-song slanting down gray dust streets and sleepy windows of the southern town. (116)

In this passage we find continued, even brought to a climax, the text's suffusing imagery which embeds women in nature and casts the "son," here metaphorically named the "sun," as the expression of both that imagery and women. If women are pine trees, and are the men's source of embodied speech, then appropriately those trees that at first "cradle" the sun/son become "dreams" which the sun/son "shakes from" his eyes when he "arises," leaving in his wake a "birth-song" for the town. In short, this passage writes the full allegory for what Dan Moore and the "Avey" narrator and Kabnis have dreamed: that the mother will cradle *them*, not others, and then give place to *their* lyrical visions of a "root-life"; that the mother will enable them to make her literal "birth-songs" their cultural "birth-songs"—as the mother figure does in the dominant culture.

But the imagery of the cradle in the treetop, recalling the earlier split lullaby heard by Kabnis, quietly topples this reborn mythology; the wind does not just whisper, it blows, and down comes baby, cradle and all. *Cane* has repeatedly represented that toppling, as when Becky's house falls on her, or when songs become flames at the shoes of Tom Burwell. At the same time it has exposed the "interest" of those who narrate that mythology—such as the narrator in "Avey," who sings a "promise-song" after self-asbsorbedly describing "her own nature and temperament" to Avey (46). Here the text reveals how "the interest of the male" in this mythology unconsciously colludes with racial patriarchy, for patriarchy's racial boundaries reflect this same male "interest." Jean Toomer needs the support of this "promise-song" mythology for his book no less than his narrators need it for their self-uplifting visions. But he never wrote another book-length work, characterizing *Cane* as a "swan-song."[20] As it does for Kabnis, the mythology he needs tortures and cripplies his art-making as much as it serves it.

Toomer's embrace of his African American identity culminated in the completion of *Cane*. But shortly afterward he withdrew from identification with black Americans and even at one point denied certain knowledge of his African American ancestors.[21] He eventually refused to have his work collected in African American anthologies, instead wanting to be identified as one of the new breed of Americans made up of many races. There is validity in Toomer's denial of a predominantly African ancestry and insight in his resistance to the idea that any African blood makes one "black" rather than "white." His denials, like his book, challenge the ideological function of such oppositions, even if they overlook the political necessity for group solidarity in the face of such oppositions.

Yet perhaps the paradoxical gender allegiances Toomer faced in writing *Cane* also underlie his subsequent dissociation from black culture. Identification with black culture sustained his art, as many critics have noted, and yet could not sustain his late-Romantic interest in art—as the artist–characters in *Cane* attest. The gender difficulties he faced, as a subordinate-race artist who sought to adopt a transcendental Romantic aesthetic, caused him subsequently to cast off that racial identity and to seek a new race-transcendent myth for his art, as he does in his long poem "Blue Meridien."

In *Cane,* then, the desire to build an art on behalf of black women, especially mothers, with other black men entangles Toomer in the companion desire to own, in many senses, black women in homosocial competition with other black men. This desire to own black women by naming them is itself undercut with ambivalence about black women's power and sexuality, which threatens to become disempowering both because of the dominant culture's displacement of black women's culture-building function and because of their own desire, which threatens to displace the black male artist's desire. Toomer's pursuit of a revised Romantic vision for black culture brought him face to face with his own allegiance to the racial–patriarchal terms of such visions. Thus, in *Cane* Toomer writes what may be accurately called a late-Romantic text which questions its own racial–patriarchal loyalties. James Joyce's *Ulysses,* written about another mother-ambivalent son, displays a similar mingling of contradictory allegiances.

5

The Parodic Purge, the Maternal Return: Late-Romantic Narrative in *Ulysses*

What has race to do with this most canonical of modernist texts? With its legendary "obscenity" and baroque narrative? Its sexual scenes and language have provoked excellent readings of the role of gender in the novel. But until very recently race has remained an invisible or reductively read signifier in *Ulysses*. Even more invisible is the entangled affair of race and gender in this text, which for many epitomizes literary modernism. If *Ulysses* is a representative and important modernist work, then race and gender may well occupy the heart of modernism as they do the heart of this novel.

In Nighttown Leopold Bloom comically urges Cissy Caffrey, "Speak, woman, sacred lifegiver!"[1] He would have her intervene in the scuffle between her companion, Private Carr, and Bloom's companion, Stephen Dedalus, who has insulted the king of England and now faces the fist of Carr. Contributing to the comic inflation of mundane incidents so characteristic of *Ulysses*, Bloom calls on Cissy, as "the link between nations and generations" (15.4648), the maternal paragon, to smooth over this blood feud as she smoothed over her younger brothers' sand castle fight on the beach. Such scenes in *Ulysses* parodically invoke that racial–patriarchal eugenic discourse in which feuds over race or nationality and claims on "sacred" motherhood mingle. Through the comic motif of the Gold Cup horse race, through Stephen's vexed meditations on his mother, and through his farcical and heretical account of Shakespeare Joyce exposes the competitive interests underlying these intertwined myths, while his parodically epic and eclectically allusive text reflects his awareness of their old and wide expression. In addition to tracing the historical coupling of these myths, the novel teases out their racialized and gendered metaphysics and simultaneously pushes narrative toward a representation of intercorporeality that challenges this metaphysics. The spatial organization of the narrative (in which cross-racial and cross-sexual characters repeatedly cross paths) violates the values of a purist sexual–racial mythology and reveals a counteragency in intersecting bodies.

Joyce's text sets in counterpoint to purist notions an intercorporeal narrative structure that is at the same time parodic, a doubleness that hints at Joyce's cautious embrace of intercorporeal alternatives. Finally, however, even after much unraveling and unveiling of bodily mythologies, *Ulysses*, like *Cane*, nonetheless remains attached by a single strong thread to the racialized mother figure, for Joyce remains invested in the dominant aesthetic tradition she serves. Joyce leaves his book, with all its parodic racial, sexual, and narrative misfirings, to be swept up and redeemed by the mother figure's overworked body.

A RACE-CONSCIOUS JOYCE

In texts by white authors the problematic, constitutive dimension of race often escapes notice.[2] Until quite recently the issue of race in Joyce's fiction, when it was considered at all, either called forth questionable pronouncements about Joyce's "racial inheritance" (such as Harry Levin's conclusion that "from first to last, [Joyce's] underlying impulses were those of his racial endowment: humor, imagination, eloquence, belligerence")[3] or was narrowed to the question of whether Joyce's representations of Jews are positive or negative, complex or stereotypical. But Joyce, like Toomer, reflected openly and sometimes controversially on the deeper questions of racial identity, including Irish racial identity. He both embraced and denied what he considered Irish in himself, and, like Toomer, he both integrated and questioned the term *race* in his fiction.

Scholars such as Marilyn Reizbaum, Ira Nadel, and Vincent Cheng have begun to notice and bring to bear on Joyce's texts his critical awareness of the early twentieth-century discourse of race.[4] Reizbaum has established that Joyce owned a sizable library of books on contemporary racial theory.[5] In one of these books, Otto Weininger's *Sex and Character* (1903), Joyce would have discovered a noteworthy case of that explicit paedomorphic coupling of racial and sexual mythologies which had been propagated since the nineteenth century. (Arguing that "some peoples" have "a greater share of womanishness" than others, Weininger, a Jew himself, suggests that Jews, like women, are selfish and deceitful, and show a "want of depth." He bemoans the modern age because it is "not only the most Jewish but the most feminine.")[6] Disagreeing with Richard Ellman and others who consider Joyce to be under the anti-Semitic influence of books such as Weininger's, Reizbaum argues that in *Ulysses* Joyce borrows Weininger's notions in order to parody them.[7] I agree with Reizbaum that Joyce's representations in *Ulysses*—for example, of Leopold Bloom, the "new womanly man" who advocates intermarriage between races—critically parody such gendered racialism (though sometimes with double-edged irony). I would add that the racialism

Joyce parodies extends beyond anti-Semitism to include the Irish-English racial discourse as well as, through textual allusions, a black–white racial discourse.

This interpretation of the subversion of racial–patriarchal mythologies in *Ulysses* finds support in Joyce's nonfiction. In his lecture "Ireland, Isle of Saints and Sages," he rejects racial categories and racial purist accounts of history, insisting instead on the fertility and inevitability of racial mixture. Joyce points to Ireland's complicated history of invasions and migrations, holding up the country as a "vast fabric, in which the most diverse elements are mingled," and concluding that "in such a fabric it is useless to look for a thread that may have remained pure and virgin."[8] Joyce's adjectives "pure" and "virgin" call attention to the sexual mythology entwined with the racial mythologies he debunks here. In the conclusion of his lecture Joyce's antiracialism leads him to question "the purpose of bitter invectives against the English despoiler" (173). In *Ulysses* he implicitly questions invectives against both the English and the Jewish "invaders" and, in addition, exposes these invectives' masculinist interests.

As with most of his characters and materials, Joyce's parodic distance serves willfully to separate him from those cultural inheritances he once embraced—and perhaps cannot be expected to have let go altogether. For as a young man Joyce did, at least briefly, embrace racialism. In a youthful internalization of the pervasive racial discourse of his day, Joyce wrote an early college essay titled "Force," in which he defends the virtues and naturalness of subjugation, including that of one race by another.[9] The young Joyce points to "man's" subjugation of the earth for farming, to his subjugation of the animals and jungles to make way for civilization, and to the subjugation of the "lower races of the world" by the "higher," adding that "among the human families the white man is the predestined conqueror" (20). Joyce even goes on to reiterate the metaphysical assumptions of contemporary racialists, wherein physical superiority, expressed in the use of physical "force," necessarily issues in and illustrates metaphysical superiority. All of these kinds of physical subjugation, Joyce ultimately argues, prepare the ground for man's "subjugation of his own mental faculties" in the service of high art and culture (22).

As an adult Joyce critically interrogated both the metaphysics and the racism of this discourse of subjugation and force. If the ruminations of Stephen Dedalus are any indication of Joyce's reflections, we may speculate that Joyce's increasing consciousness of the Irish as themselves members of a subjugated race—Robert Knox's unruly and illiterate Celts—may have contributed to this change of view. In *Ulysses* Joyce not only parodies racialism but also creates the very "chaotic mazes" and "huge shapelessness" against which the young Joyce in "Force" warns "unsubdued" artists (22). At the same time, his treatment of Molly Bloom shows some lingering attachment to an aesthetic that employs the mother as its racialized instrument of transcendence.

A DAY AT THE "RACE RACES"

A prototype of Molly Bloom, Cissy Caffrey serves early in the novel as a touchstone of Leopold Bloom's, and the novel's, transgressiveness. In her first appearance Cissy Caffrey saunters along the contested borders of racial, sexual, and maternal identity. Watching her on the beach, Gerty MacDowell and Bloom, respectively, identify her as a "tomboy" (13.480) and as "the dark one with mop head and nigger mouth" (13.898). Thus Cissy crosses to the "other" side of norms of both girlishness and whiteness. The two violations seem to go hand in hand, cast in comic contrast to the idealized qualities of the ever-feminine and ever-so-white Gerty ("her face almost spiritual in its ivorylike purity" [13.87]).

Furthermore, in the very movements of her body Cissy flouts proper sexual and racial boundaries. While Gerty flirts secretly with Bloom (the "dark-eyed . . . foreigner" on the rocks [13.415, 416]), Cissy strides uninhibitedly over to him to ask the time. Similarly, Gerty feels repulsed by the noisy children and irritated by their interruptions of her blossoming sexual fantasies; Cissy easily mixes sexuality and maternality, seemingly scolding and caressing and diapering her brothers all at once. Her language, which Gerty admires but rejects for herself, speaks crassly and boyishly of bodily things. Cissy's cluster of qualities makes her a titillating transgressor of the culture's idealized, purified mythology. For Bloom, the foreigner, her intermingling of sexual, maternal, and racial qualities renders her especially worthy of the role as "link between nations and generations" (15.4648).

Yet in "Nighttown" Cissy senses her own precariousness as she stands on the charged borderlines of sex and race. She responds to Bloom's appeal for intervention with "alarm." She "seizes" Private Carr's sleeve and insists, "Amn't I with you? Amn't I your girl? Cissy's your girl" (15.465). Cissy chooses in this scene not to get caught in the cross fire over men's blood feuds or the superiority of their respective races. She sides with the one in power, though she later attempts inconspicuously (and unsuccessfully) to deter him from smacking Stephen in the mouth. Cissy abdicates the racially and sexually mixed throne on which Bloom has placed her, evading the humiliations to which Bloom, in his Nighttown ascent (or descent) to that throne, has just been subjected. Cissy knows that Bloom's ideals of open intercourse between nations and generations are eccentric and Bloom himself is marginal; he has been labeled, as we shall see, a "a bloody dark horse" (12.1558) in the race among races.

Moreover, Cissy seems to know that a woman in her position has even more to fear than a man in Bloom's. For women who mix sexually with "other" races initiate, according to long-standing racial–patriarchal mythologies invoked repeatedly in *Ulysses*, that entrance of "strangers" into a nation, thus spelling its destruction. Helen of Troy epitomizes the woman who betrays "her" nation to another; many a nation has succumbed to such betrayal, as several men in *Ulysses* emphasize. In explaining the downfall of their race and nation, Deasy and others repeatedly return to this model of history. They deplore the disruption by women of the national and racial boundaries which women should protect and reproduce, never cross of their own will. The schoolmaster Deasy bemoans that "england is in the hands of the jews. . . . Wherever they gather they eat up a nation's vital strength" (2.346–50). He traces the presence of such strangers to the sins of "woman," alluding to the biblical sexual–racial mythology of Eve and Cain[10] and citing famous historical cases of women's racial–patriarchal sins: "A woman brought sin into the world. For a woman who was no better than she should be, Helen, the runaway wife of Menelaus, ten years the Greeks made war on Troy. A faithless wife first brought strangers to our shore here, MacMurrough's wife and her leman, O'Rourke, prince of Breffini. A woman brought Parnell low too" (2.390–94). Women bring whole nations "low" in allowing sexual infection by "strangers."

Within this logic the woman who violates group borders is designated, first of all, sexually deviant—a prostitute. In the lyrics of the song that shadows both Stephen's conversation with Deasy and the Nighttown scuffle between Stephen and Carr, "The harlot's cry from street to street/Shall weave old England's windingsheet" (2.356; 15.4641). The promiscuous woman who treacherously weaves the windingsheet of "old England" is stigmatized further as a racial other, a practice *Ulysses* mimics by casting the "harlots" of Nighttown as of African descent: Zoe identifies herself as black (15.1333), and both Florry and Zoe are called "jujuby women" (15.4123).[11] Joyce's "weaving" of this song about the harlot's winding-sheet throughout these scenes mocks the racial–patriarchal logic by which women who cross sexual borders (like the eugenicists' "wayward" women) become other-racialized. He reveals sex and race as entwined at the heart of nationhood.

In the course of the novel this argument about women's determining role in national destinies and downfalls weaves its own winding-sheet, parodied from so many angles that finally the manifest destiny of the sexual–racial argument itself meets its downfall. The notorious citizen mouths it in "Cyclops," the chapter of blindness and bad vision: "A dishonoured wife . . . that's what's the cause of all our misfortunes. . . . The adultress and her paramour brought the Saxon robbers here. . . . The strangers . . ." (12.1156–58). In addition to Joyce's demystification of such accounts of Irish history in his lecture "Isle of Saints," here his epic-parodying narration makes laughable the heroic (yet defensive) rhetoric of such attitudes: "he said and then lifted he in his rude great brawny strengthy hands the medher of dark strong foamy ale, and uttering his tribal slogan, Lamb Dearg Abu, he drank to the undoing of his foes, a race of mighty valorous heroes" (12.1210–13). Joyce comically accumulates heroic adjectives and so parodies what we might call the jargon of racial–patriarchal warrior myths—"tribal," "mighty race," "brawny strengthy," "heroes." The word "slogan" particularly hints at the critique implicit in the parody.

But even more telling is the narrational turn in the next paragraph to the Gold Cup, the horse race won by Throwaway—"a rank outsider" (12.1219), says Lenehan—and lost by Sceptre, the unfortunate (phallic) betting choice of Lenehan and all his mates. Joyce's frequent strategic interjection of the topic of horse races, particularly the winning of the Gold Cup by a "dark horse outsider" and the loss of it by Sceptre, suggests its importance to the men's sexual–racial posturing throughout June 16, 1904. As Vincent Cheng has noted, references to horse races surface repeatedly in the men's conversations and serve to reveal an undercurrent of warriorism in their talk.[12] In "Nestor," we learn that pictures of horses stand "in homage" on Deasy's walls; and as Stephen listens to both Deasy's ranting and the boys' hockey game outside, he imagines increasingly bloody and chaotic horse races, climaxing in an image of "jousts, slush and uproar of battle . . . a shout of spear spikes baited with men's bloodied guts" (2.314–18). Stephen tries to imagine himself "among them" but is ridiculed by a voice that laughs, "you mean that knockkneed mother's darling who seems to be slightly crawsick?" (2.320). Stephen falls short of the eugenic standards of a masculine warrior race; he therefore several times derides the sexual–racial discourse by which eugenic ideals are buttressed and protected.

In "Oxen of the Sun," however, Joyce shows Stephen participating in, at least passively, the same eugenic discourse that makes him appear feminine and racially inadequate. In their pseudoscientific discussion at the Maternity Hospital of ideal childbearing conditions, the young men explicitly invoke eugenic Darwinist terminology. They consider motherhood and childbearing in terms of "the future of a race" and what is most "beneficial to the race . . . in securing the survival of the fittest" (14.832; 14.1284–85). With this juxtaposition of Stephen's doubts about his masculine fitness for the "race" and his involvement in his peers' discussion, the text indicates again how racialist spoutings often harbor anxiety about masculine and racial belonging. At the same time, by making this conversation echo the Darwinian pronouncements of contemporary politicians

115

and scientists, Joyce hints that the same gender and group anxiety feeds that larger public discourse. Strengthening this connection, Joyce intermingles the boys' discussion not only with an anti-Semitic diabribe against Bloom (who has chastised the young men for their "frigid genius") but also with an account of the Gold Cup horse race, on which both Madden and the younger Lenehan have lost, owing to the "dark horse Throwaway" (14.1132). Through association with Bloom especially, this horse race becomes a parodic symbol of the "race races" so aggressively promoted by Joyce's political contemporaries.[13]

Bloom, himself a member of an "other" race within an other-racial Irish culture, is repeatedly affiliated with this Gold Cup "dark horse," this defeater of Sceptre. In "Cyclops," for instance, the false rumor that Bloom won money on Throwaway yet fails to buy a single round of drink ignites the race riot that so dramatically closes that section. The reader's knowledge of the falseness of the rumor exposes the scapegoating, self-defensive impulse of "race races." In addition, Bloom's recurring thoughts about the "throwaway" flyer announcing "Elijah is coming" associate him with the dark horse Throwaway, and the flyer links both Bloom and the horse to "outsider" Semites (8.13, 10.294, 10.1096).

In the "Nighttown" scene with Private Carr, which also climaxes with a nationalist race, Joyce's punning use of the word implies yet again how a competitive racial paradigm fires an aggressive nationalism. After the cry "Dublin's burning!" we learn in a long parenthetical description of brimstone and artillery and shrieks that "a chasm opens. . . . Tom Rochford, winner . . . arrives at the head of the *national* hurdle handicap and leaps into the void. He is followed by a *race* of runners and leapers. In wild attitudes they spring from the brink. Their bodies plunge" (15.4672–76; emphasis added). Especially given that characters such as the one-legged (phallically disabled?) sailor hold up the Irish as the "best jumpers and racers" (16.1017), the word "race" in the "Nighttown" catastrophe points in two directions—toward competitive running and toward a kin group mythology—collapsing these two meanings into the implication that the human races race one another, a race of races ending in catastrophe.

The fact that, in this scene, the "race of runners" is led by their hero and winner into "the void," and that the whole catastrophic moment is an imaginary inflation of a street scuffle, flaunts the idiocy of such racial mythology. But the insidious pervasiveness of this mythology—present not only among the younger and older men in *Ulysses* but also in, for example, the self-mythology of the white-skinned, blue-eyed Gerty as against the mop-headed Cissy—demonstrates that it is a force to be reckoned with on many levels and in many identities. In addition, that the "race race" climaxes when the runners' "bodies plunge" in "wild attitudes" into a void suggests that eugenic "racing," despite its aim of physical racial improvement, actually distorts and sacrifices the bodies of its runners to an

116

ideological void. An extended look at Stephen Dedalus's inner turmoil within this society illuminates more closely the debilitating effects of this ideology, including the metaphysics (in the sense of a mind–body hierarchy) underlying it.

STEPHEN'S MOTHER-TROUBLED METAPHYSICS

In the very same chapter in which Stephen participates in eugenic discussions of the future of the race, he elaborately mocks the idea that women's promiscuity invites strangers who bring about the downfall of the "original" race. Thus, there begins to be manifest in Stephen the split allegiances and the emotional ambivalence inherent in the position of subordinate-group men under racial patriarchy. Bawdily parodying the Bible, pagan myth, Shakespeare, scholarship, and himself all at once, he pronounces early in the "Oxen of the Sun" chapter:

> Bring a stranger within thy tower it will go hard but thou wilt have the secondbest bed. . . . Remember, Erin, thy generations and thy days of old, how thou settedst little by me and by my word and broughtedst in a stranger to my gates to commit forniication in my sight and to wax fat and kick like Jeshuram. Why hast thou done this abomination before me that thou didst spurn me for a merchant of jalaps and didst deny me to the Roman and the Indian of dark speech with whom thy daughters did lie luxuriously? Look forth, now, my people, upon the land of behest, even from Horeb and from Nebo and from Pisgah. (14.365–76)

Here Stephen mimics the Old Testament rhetoric as one source for the belief that the promiscuous "miscegenation" of women ("thy daughters") destroys nations. Stephen's irreverent sexual puns, such as "it will go hard," and his loose intermingling (like Bloom's) of Erin and Palestine or Jews and Irish imitate this feminine promiscuity. His conflated references commit in language the "mixing" of values or referents that cross-national or cross-racial sexuality commits in body. His inflated language also implicitly deflates that mythology which grandly equates the Hebrews and the Irish as chosen, wronged peoples. His parody hints that such epic racial equations perpetuate the very racialism by which their adherents are victimized.

Stephen feels and expresses these ironies as a result of his emotional position as outsider who nonetheless seeks to gain a hearing in the inner circle of Irish insiders. Like Kabnis in *Cane*, as a male of a subordinate race Stephen sees through the gender and racial mythologies of racial patriarchy; and yet, again as an artist of a subordinate race, he seeks all the more urgently to find a defensible position within racial patriarchy and its mythologies. Throughout *Ulysses* Stephen identifies and is identified with "strangers" and with women, those welcomers of

117

strangers. At the same time he moves among those who reject strangers and defame women, and he himself sometimes openly defames or rejects women and Jews. In addition, Stephen shares the contradictory attitude of Romanticism and modern racial patriarchy toward the world of the body; this contradiction afflicts his attachments to art, to religion, and to his mother.

We saw in chapter 2 that in *A Portrait of the Artist as a Young Man* Stephen embraces the racialized Romantic aesthetic. In order to "forge the uncreated conscience of [his] race," he searches for the best means of folding the feminized world of physical phenomena into what he conceives of as the "father artificer's" spiritual energy of creation.[14] In the early twentieth century, to follow the father's secular yet transcendental aesthetic is indeed to "forge" a culture mined from the resources of something called "race." Like the founders of "positive eugenics," Stephen imagines he will use the feminized body to found and substantiate a powerful racialized world of masculine spirit or intelligence. Although by the end of *Portrait* Stephen has rejected the priesthood, he has sustained a gendered and racialized metaphysics. At the same time, however, he has inherited the contradictions of the ambivalent Romantic involvement in the feminized world of matter.

In *Ulysses* Stephen lets his conundrum surface; he allows the return of repressed contradictions and costs. He realizes that to live in his body, to watch his "woman's hand" (15.3678) hold a mirror for Buck Mulligan, to see the "white breast of the dim sea" (1.244), and smell sea breath, to do all of these things is to recall his mother and her birthing of him. He begins silently to acknowledge that his fearful sense of his own "feminine" characteristics (as a "knockkneed mother's darling" [2.320]) partly underlies his distaste for the idea of shielding women "with a strong and resolute arm" (*Portrait*, 516). First of all, he may not have such an arm. More important, he keeps returning to—or allowing the return of—the image of his mother's body, a return that forces him to consider his attachment to and dependence on things material and things feminine. In short, the charge that he killed his mother's body for "ideas" haunts him partly because he has a positive attachment to her body and partly because it hits the nail of his aesthetic problem on the head: it names the mother sacrifice required by his Romantic artistic ambitions, and yet that naming recalls the cultural obstacles which obstruct his enactment of that sacrifice.

The first of these obstacles is the contradiction in the relation to the mother figure, the felt tension between her nurturing of embodiment and her reproduction of the cultural denigration of embodiment, not least in the spectacle of her own colonized embodiment. Thus, when Stephen recalls his mother's body he inevitably also remembers, with irritation, her "bowing" of mind and body to the church and its metaphysics. She urges him on her deathbed, in her last gasp of bodily life, to accept the church, as she had earlier asked him to attend Easter Mass, that ceremony celebrating bodily resurrection in the pursuit of beatific divine transcendence. He refuses both of her pleas and in doing so denies his own "blood." But to accede to her would also have been to conform to a tradition that denies "blood." The doctrine of the Irish-Catholic church denies body and blood not only in its sexual prohibitions (which Stephen struggles with in *Portrait*) but also in its making a mere servant (racialized, as we shall see) of the embodying mother. So long as his mother believes in the Easter version of the spirit–body relation—the body dies for the spirit—and so long as she urges that view on Stephen, he cannot wholly reconnect with his own body which comes from her body. He stands caught between two mothers: one as bodily reproducer who gave birth to him and the other as cultural reproducer whose subordination helps to construct the subordination of the body, beginning with her own body and passing on to her children's. Stephen's body is on the rack, pulled in two directions.

Though Stephen in *Ulysses* becomes more conscious of his metaphysical dilemma as it is centered in his relation to his mother, he cannot readily find a substitute for the transcendental formula he espouses at the end of *Portrait*. Publicly he often parodies the old myth of racialized masculine transcendence. Privately he suffers both longing for and bitterness toward the mother who holds his body captive. Repeatedly he sets up an antagonism between mother figures and children. At the beach he sees two midwives carrying their medical bags and suspects them of carrying an aborted or unwanted baby whom they will dispose of in the sea (3.29–37). In the "Oxen of the Sun" chapter Stephen alone argues that in childbirth the infant's life should be saved before the mother's. His opinion would seem to have implications for his own situation, wherein he must sacrifice his subservient mother if he is to pursue his own aesthetic desires—though, as we have seen, this solution cannot succeed altogether. In his vision of his mother in Nighttown he as first gladly and without bitterness beseeches her to name that word which merges maternality and sexuality or transcendent and corporeal womanhood—love—but when she turns instead to prayer and damnation, his bitter alienation returns.

Among the newspapermen Stephen tells his mocking story of the two lifelong virgins who climb Nelson's (phallic) pillar but are too frightened to take in the view it affords them. By suggestively interspersing Stephen's tale of thwarted female sexuality with a paperboy's cries offering a "racing special!" (7.914), the text hints again at the connection between the mythology of "race races" and the constriction of female sexuality. When Stephen finishes his anecdote, the professor comments that Stephen reminds him of Antisthenes, who was the "son of a noble and a *bondwoman*" (7.1037; emphasis added). In other words, Antisthenes is a son descended from a male master and a female slave, from both dominant and subordinate kin groups. This divided heritage splits Antisthenes against himself so that (recall Kabnis) "none could tell if he were bitterer against others or himself" (7.1036–37).

Stephen is likewise split against himself, and as the result of a similarly troubled heritage. He sees his own mother as a bondswoman—her body in thrall to a paternalistic church—whose bondage he himself must serve out. His position makes him bitter toward himself and others, but in *Ulysses* it also makes him empathize with his mother's predicament.

Early in the "Telemachus" chapter through Stephen's memories we learn of Mary Dedalus's "secrets: old featherfans, tasselled dance cards, powdered with musk, a gaud of amber beads in her locked drawer. . . . Phantasmal mirth, folded away: muskperfumed" (1.255–63). That these baubles of Stephen's mother's adolescent sexuality are "folded away" or kept in "locked drawers"— and that he here dreams of them—may well indicate an Oedipal relationship. But what is an Oedipal relationship but the struggle with an artificial paternal law denying maternal sensuality, a law deeply baffling to children who have felt the mother's caresses and known her body as intimately as anyone? If fathers caressed and fed and cleaned as much as mothers, and the split between virginal motherly home and licentious fatherly polity were absent, children might not feel with such deep nostalgia that desire for the acknowledgment of the mother's desire. For when Stephen thinks of "the white breast of the dim sea" together with tasseled dance cards and phantasmal mirth, all folded away, his tone is not one of sexual lust for the mother but one of nostalgic sadness for her lost sensual past—sadness for her as much as for him. That Stephen returns to these images of his mother's past and recognizes how they are "folded away" suggests his sympathetic understanding of the limitations within which she lived her life.

The wider social conditions that set up these limits on the mother's life emerge more clearly in Stephen's thoughts about the milkwoman. Just as Mrs. Dedalus has her "secrets" and comes to Stephen decaying and "silent" in a dream, so the milkwoman enters this opening chapter "old and secret . . . maybe a messenger" (1.399–400). Stephen imagines her as "the lowly form of an immortal serving her conqueror and her gay betrayer" (1.405). After she demurs to the mocking Buck Mulligan and the condescending Haines, Stephen reflects that "she bows her old head to a voice that speaks to her loudly, her bonesetter, her medicineman: me she slights." He goes on, puzzled by, but resigned to, her deference "to the voice that will shrive and oil for the grave all there is of her but her woman's unclean loins, of man's flesh made not in God's likeness, the serpent's prey. And to the loud voice that now bids her be silent" (1.420–22). Stephen refers here to the Catholic practice of anointing a dying man's genitals but not a woman's, suggesting again that the milkwoman defers to a tradition that scorns her sexuality yet buys her milk. Racial as well as gender hierarchies have, since Eve, informed this Christian tradition which marks woman's procreative body as "impure," as the biblical allusions in "Oxen of the Sun" remind us.[15] Meanwhile, by characterizing the milkwoman as one who serves her "conqueror," Stephen invokes the more contemporary European racialism and merges it with the racialism inherent in the Judaeo-Christian tradition.

Stephen's equation of the loud voices of Haines and Mulligan with those of the church fathers, though neither Haines nor Mulligan is particularly reverent, also suggests that Stephen is thinking of his mother and her deference to "her conqueror and her gay betrayer" as well as of the milkwoman's. This link implies that Stephen understands his mother to have been "conquered" by a tradition that says man's flesh but not woman's is made in God's likeness; he recognizes that the muteness of what he earlier called his mother's "mute secret words" is enforced by the "loud voices" of the church fathers who "bid her be silent" (1.272; 1.422). Stephen thus sees beyond his mother's supplication and recognizes the conditions of racial paternalism which make her, like Cissy Caffrey, "serve her conqueror," or which make her "pray," as Cissy does in effect to Private Carr, for favor with the conqueror. An Irishwoman, in other words, is marked as impurely embodied not only by England but by the church, especially insofar as her sexual "otherness" becomes affiliated with a racial "otherness." Even without actually transgressing, she lives as an embodiment of potential racial and sexual transgression. To forestall her transgression, she is cast in the role of servant, both sexual and racial.

If Stephen's mother is a servant, Stephen is, as he calls himself just after this passage, "the server of a servant" (1.312), for he is flesh of her ungodly, impure flesh. Moreover, he too defers repeatedly to, or serves, the loud voices of Mulligan and Haines; if he could, he would be "among them," as he says in the horse racing fantasy quoted earlier. Like the women, he serves—in order to share the society of—his gay betrayers. Not surprisingly, then, he has his mother's face and his sister's eyes (10.865; 15.4949; 16.804). Likewise, his hands, which hold up the mirror by which the brash, manly Mulligan shaves his coarse, thick beard, are a "woman's hands" (15.3678).

Stephen's phrase "server of a servant" associates him, the Irish son of a church-serving mother, with the denigrated African "race" as well. This phrase places both his and his mother's servitude in the context of a parallel history of service codified along racial lines, for it alludes to the fate of Ham's son Canaan. Both early biblical interpreters and nineteenth-century racialists cast Ham, the cursed son of Noah, as the ancestor of the African peoples. (Significantly, the crime for which Ham and his son are cursed involves a sexual transgression in which Ham views the naked body of his racial–patriarchal father, Noah). At the same time, in nineteenth- and twentieth-century racial theory Africans and Irish were commonly considered affiliated "lower" races.[16] Through Stephen's self-characterization the text of *Ulysses* alludes to both biblical and contemporary scientific racial mythologies.

Even in the earliest pages of *Ulysses,* then, Stephen invokes and exposes the modern scheme whereby the Celts share this stigma with Africans; at the same time, by making the milkwoman and his mother originators of a line of conquerors' "servants," Stephen indicates the crucial role of the female reproducer in perpetuating this schema. By reference to modern Western culture's racial framework, the text associates Stephen, his mother, and the milkwoman with an other-racial sexuality, just as later on, Stephen, the "jewjesuit (9.1159), is said to practice "woman's reason. Jewgreek is greekjew. Extremes meet" (15.2097–98). In both cases Joyce hints at the interdependence of race and gender constructs. He makes clear how racial lines serve to mark another side by which sexuality that does not serve the claims of paternal lineage can be cast as "dark," "impure," "slavish." And he suggests how gender mythologies uphold the position of dominant-race men and limit or denigrate the resources of women and sub-ordinate-race men. *Ulysses* positions Stephen, his mother, and their conflicts with each other within this racial–patriarchal framework.

IMPLICATING SHAKESPEARE

In his critique of Shakespeare, Stephen more fully, if still cryptically, spells out the jealous racial and gender dynamics of Western culture. Using Shakespeare as an example, he suggests that the invisibility of men's paternity provokes anxiety—especially because property and power are at stake—which motivates a mythology of race. As we will see, his theory suggests that traceable physical characteristics of race, together with an *idea* of ethnic or racial integrity, can support the claims of an otherwise invisible fatherhood. For members of any dominant group, identifying and celebrating their shared characteristics may become an economically and politically driven need. When generalized within a kin group, this becomes a mythology of ethnicity or race. As we saw in chapter 2, the circulation of women in marriage serves to fortify or extend ethnic and racial boundaries, thereby defining and consolidating men's economic and political claims. Men can thus lay claim to a racial paternity, relieving the pressure on an otherwise ever-challenged individual paternity and legitimizing their control over property and resources, both through and including women.

In his critique of Shakespeare, Stephen establishes these racial mythologies as integral to the production of art. Renowned artists become spiritual "fathers of a race," using fictional women and sexual dramas to create an artistic economy the way dominant men use real women and sexual boundaries to create a political economy. Such "father artificers" are in the most enviable position because they can, through their art, lay claim to the body of every woman of the race and thus "play the part" of every man of the race. But as a result they not only suffer unceasingly the pressure of homosocial competition but also come starkly face to face with the contradictions of metaphysical aesthetics.

In his theorizing Stephen again compares Western culture's contradictory aesthetic metaphysics with its paradoxical Christian metaphysics. He also borrows, as he did in his identity as the "server of a servant," from the point of view of an African Other. He calls for authority on "Sabellius, the African, subtlest heresiarch of all the beasts in the field" (9.862). Sabellius claimed, in his own Christian complications of the relation of spirit and matter, that "the Father was Himself His Own Son" (9.863). Stephen takes a similarly heretical view of Shakespeare, identifying him not only with the put-upon hero Hamlet but with Hamlet's father, the vengeful ghost. Stephen suggests that as an artist, Shakespeare could be father, son, mother, and wife, which raises him above the role as "father of his own son merely" and allows him to make himself instead "the father of all his *race*" (9.868; emphasis added). Thus, an artistic father of a race of men (or of a corpus of cultural self-definitions around which members of the Anglo-Saxon "race" have rallied), Shakespeare seemingly transcends the limits of being one specific man.

But Stephen goes on to expose Shakespeare as a man sunk in racial–patriarchal jealousies, one who strives for transcendent racial paternity over and against those sexual and blood jealousies—as does Stephen at the end of *A Portrait.* Shakespeare therefore remains caught, Stephen argues, in the contradiction of having to borrow from that blood life to create his transcendent art. To support his account Stephen first of all applies the details of Shakespeare's own biography to the familial drama of *Hamlet.* He defends his approach by pointing out that Shakespeare drew on real historical details for his plays, and Stephen touches, significantly, on some episodes of gynophobia and anti-Semitism in his account:

> All events brought grist to his mill. Shylock chimes with the jewbaiting that followed the hanging and quartering of the queen's leech Lopez. . . . Hamlet and Macbeth with the coming to the throne of a Scotch philosophaster with a turn for witchroasting. The lost Armada is his jeer in Love's Labour Lost. His pageants, the histories, sail fullbellied on a tide of Mafeking enthusiasm (9.748–54)

Family life proved no lesser, and no less richly political, a source for Shakespeare's art, according to Stephen. The character Hamlet is Shakespeare's son Hamnet, and the vengeful ghost is Shakespeare himself speaking to his real son about the possible relationship of his real wife, Ann Hathaway, with his real brother Richard. Yet Stephen makes sure to deflate any sentimental sympathy for Shakespeare which this scenario might evoke when he establishes Shakespeare as a man of double standards who himself "dallied . . . between conjugal love . . . and scortatory love" during twenty years of marriage (9.631–32). He paints him as a rich man and a money-lender who "drew Shylock out of his own long pocket," and as "a man who holds [as] tightly to what he calls his rights over what he calls his debts [as he does] to what he calls his rights over her whom he calls his wife" (9.788–91). Furthermore, Stephen argues that, though Christians attribute avarice to Jews, Shakespeare was vulnerable to that "avarice of the emotions" in which "love given to one near in blood is covetously withheld from some stranger who, it may be, hungers for it" (9.781–82). Shakespeare aimed to ensure that "no sir smile neighbour shall covet his ox or his wife" (9.790). Stephen herein highlights the economic stakes in racial and sexual possession and heretically argues that such an economy produces the complicated "mortal" underpinnings of Shakespeare's "immortal" art.

Thus, Stephen challenges the view of Shakespeare as a universal "myriad-minded" man, exposing instead his petty entanglement in the blood jealousies endemic to the interdependent practices of racial division and patriarchal marriage. In doing so Stephen involves Shakespeare, and by implication other canonical artists, in the same metaphysical dilemma with which he struggles. Like him, such artists need the blood of life to create their art, as he needs the feminine "sluggish matter," but the point of their art, its advantage to them, is precisely to transcend that blood matter and transform it and themselves into masculine "impalpable, imperishable" beings, made immortal and dignified by association with a particular "race." In his most powerful moment among Irish insiders (the floor is his), then, Stephen ironically uncovers the control-seeking racialism and paternalism at the heart—and the height—of "universal" Western art.

Stephen's recognition of this contradiction indicates how he has shifted his position since the end of *A Portrait*. Perhaps his most penetrating insight is that traditional aesthetics lead not to a triumphantly transcendent art but to a covertly androgynous art (of which Romantic poetry such as Wordsworth's offers another example). When Stephen concludes that *Hamlet* "foretold" an "economy of heaven" in which "there are no more marriages, glorified man, an androgynous angel, being a wife unto himself" (9.105–52), he not only parodies Hamlet and Saint Matthew but also hints that Renaissance "kin" dramas such as *Hamlet* already point toward the Romantic aesthetic which subsumes the feminine and makes of the "glorified," supposedly "androgynous" poet "a wife unto himself." This parody may allude as well to the nineteenth-century discursive appropriation of tropes of procreation to a masculine ethos (see chapter 3) so that intellectual men may be "wives unto themselves."

And yet, although this parody serves as Stephen's means of purging himself of self- and other-alienating sexual–racial mythologies, the absence of any other kind of intersubjective performance by him suggests an inability to step outside those mythologies. His parodic pose fixes him within the kin–patriarchal world. We should remember, after all, that Stephen fabricates this entire deconstruction of Shakespeare, Christianity, and the transcendental racial aesthetic to win a hearing *inside* his culture—among the intellectuals of Dublin. To some extent the same is true for Joyce in an Anglo-European context: his epic-scale text and intricate web of learned allusions, while deflating Western traditions and rhetoric, also place him "among them" as a master of those traditions. Joyce's parodic use of allusion may be read, as I read the narrators' intimacy with female characters in *Cane,* as the double-edged strategy of a subordinate-race author within a homosocial cultural competition: each text uses the master's resources (women or learning) *against* the master's discourse but also to gain authority within the master's culture.

The next sections of this chapter, however, emphasize the opposite: Joyce's supplement to Stephen's strictly parodic pose. In them I argue that Joyce authors an alternative intercorporeal narrative practice in *Ulysses* which surpasses parodic performance.[17]

THE AESTHETIC OF INTERSECTION

We have seen that through Stephen, Joyce undertakes a parody of transcendent aesthetics and unfolds a psychological critique of the sexual–racial matrix of racial partriarchy, especially as that matrix debilitates the son's relation to the mother. Through the character of Leopold Bloom, Joyce delves into the daily intersubjective dialectics of a racial outsider, one who is at once excluded from, oriented toward, and essential to the dominant culture. In attending to the sensibility of his cross-gendered and cross-racial character, Joyce further interrogates the metaphysics of racial patriarchy; he takes a close look at the racialized human specimen pinned under the microscope of contemporary science. He sheds science's contradictory attention to and abhorrence of human physical structure, instead tracing the body's activities and powers with unflagging fidelity and linguistic enthusiasm. Through Bloom Joyce represents intercorporeality—or bodily situated, co-adaptive (rather than Hegelian and competitive) intersubjectivity, for

Bloom lives out rather felicitously the crass bodiliness with which nineteenth- and early twentieth-century racial theories frequently associated the Africans, Irish, and Jews. This bodiliness the text reveals as more than merely crass, verging instead at times on the exquisite and inspired.[18] At the same time, Joyce imitates and elaborates Bloom's embeddedness in the physical world by way of the underlying spatial structure of his novel.

To characterize Bloom as a man particularly attuned to bodily sensation is to state the obvious. His sensitivities, as rendered by Joyce, positively impinge on the reader. Joyce's narrator minutely records, even merges with, Bloom's physical sensibility. Just as Bloom in his imagination places himself close enough to other bodies to smell their smells and to feel their antennae twitching, so the narrative voice moves shoulder to shoulder alongside Bloom. In the first sentence we read about him the text relishes Bloom's own "relish" of "inner organs" (4.1), just as Molly, at the opposite end of the book, admires him for knowing "a lot of mixedup things about the body and the inside" (18.179–80). We might, in fact, wish Bloom somewhat *more* indifferent to the comings and goings of Nosey Flynn's nasal phlegm. But we accept these data so as also to delight in his delicate attention to intercorporeal sensation in small, quiet moments, such as when he remarks that on one of its turns the funeral carriage which he shares with Dedalus, Cunningham, and Power "united noiselessly their unresisting knees" (6.228).

It might be argued that this last observation belongs to the narrator rather than to Bloom. If it seems to belong to the narrator because it describes a sensation shared by several characters, I would point out that the narrator can speak of several characters at once precisely because their bodies touch, or unite, at this moment. As is also the case in texts by Virginia Woolf and Toni Morrison, the intercorporeal narrator in *Ulysses* synchronizes characters' perceptions through the material world they inhabit in common. The "break in the hedge" in *To the Lighthouse*, for example, joins both the perceptions of Lily and Mr. Bankes *and* the text's narration of Lily's and Mr. Bankes's perceptions. In varying degrees such narrators may themselves be said to occupy the interstices of the material world, recording characters' lives as they impinge constantly on that world or on one another through it.

In this way these authors usurp and dematernalize the mother figure's role as the materially embedded coordinator of bodies. Although in general I consider Woolf's vision of intercorporeality more profound than Joyce's (for reasons I discuss later), it is interesting to note that Joyce, more than Woolf, compares to Morrison insofar as he exploits the reversibility of the actual touch—in Joyce knees "unite" the way "his holding fingers are holding hers" in *Beloved*[19]—to gain access to the in-between of intersubjectivity. In this respect Joyce practices a very direct intercorporeal narration, whereas we can perhaps detect a reticence in

Woolf's narrator, who mediates the touch with objects or spaces such as openings in hedges.

In *Ulysses*, then, as in these other novels, intercorporeal perceptions like that of the unresisting knees belong to both narrator and characters. Like the narrator Bloom manages intersubjectivity through bodily signals, such as with the blind man ("Knows I'm a man. Voice" [8.1102]) or when he thinks in the pause that follows the lowering of Dignam's coffin, "If we were all suddenly somebody else" (6.836). That is, Bloom, like the narrator, pursues a desire to place himself inside others' bodies and thereby know their points of view. Accordingly, Bloom, like the narrator, dwells on the "meetings" of eyes, as with Mrs. Breen ("Look straight into her eyes. I believe in you. Trust me" [8.250]); and he appreciates the complex dynamics of watching oneself being watched, or watching oneself watch, as Kimberly Devlin has detailed in her analysis of Bloom's visually enacted sex with Gerty MacDowell.[20] In general, Bloom repeatedly espouses the value of "see[ing] ourselves as others see us" in a way that merges subjective with physical "seeing" (8.662; 13.1058). This self-presence of the reversible intercorporeal subject epitomized in Bloom creates a crucial opening through which Joyce's narrator enters the text and situates his characters together in space and time.

For Bloom—a person so sensitive to intercorporeality and the character most crucial to Joyce's narrative of intersecting bodies—his unintended yet seemingly fateful meetings with Blazes Boylan throughout the course of his day have a potent impact. Bloom marvels at his repeated near-collisions with his rival, especially when "just that moment I was thinking [of him]" (6.197). As this comment suggests, these meetings display for Bloom the affinity between the internal and the external, or thought and fact. It is because Bloom is so aware that his eyes which see and his hands which touch can "also be seen and touched" that he can "see and touch the visible, the tangible, from within."[21] That is, his sensitivity to his own bodily movements heightens his awareness of others' as well, especially those whose hands touch the same woman's body he touches. On the same day that Boylan and Bloom's wife will consummate their affair, Bloom sees Boylan from the funeral carriage, avoids him at the barroom of Miss Douce and Miss Kennedy, swerves out of his sight into the museum. In noticing and honoring the intersecting orbits of his body and another with common yet (according to convention) antagonistic interests, Bloom disinvests, at least partially, in the competitive and oppositional dynamic usually organized around a woman's body.

One can of course read Bloom's response to his sightings of Boylan quite differently: that is, one could suggest, as some critics have,[22] that Bloom is a weak man and that in sighting but avoiding Boylan, Bloom shrinks womanishly from a face-to-face encounter with his rival (as he does later with his sexual partners, Gerty and Molly). My reading, by contrast, stresses that, in avoiding Boylan,

Bloom takes wonder-struck note of unintended daily intersections of bodies and yet respects their separate trajectories, honoring encounters that convention would consider grounds for confrontation or even for a Hegelian life-and-death struggle.

In the treatment of Bloom in Nighttown the text seems to explore both readings of him—as the cowardly cuckold and pervert who engaged in sordid, unmanly encounters and as the sensitive champion of unscripted encounters. He is scourged as a ridiculous man of "Mongolian extraction" (15.954) who foolishly "so wants to be a mother" (15.1817). He is sat upon and spat upon as a grotesque "example of the new womanly man" (15.1798–99). But a dissenting faction also gains the floor and elects him the messianic mayor of Dublin, whose call for "mixed races and mixed marriage," for the "union of all jew, moslem, and gentile" so antithetical to Anglo-American eugenics (15.1618) meets with cries of approval. His advocacy of intersections or overlappings of the sexes and races thus wins him both admiration and condemnation. The envelope of parody encasing both of these views of Bloom and many others has left readers with few clues as to Joyce's view, a state of things which probably best fulfills Joyce's intentions.

Joyce does reveal his own earnestness to some degree, I would argue, insofar as he privileges structures of intercorporeal encounters in the same way Bloom does. We must at least acknowledge that Joyce's narrative, whether parody or not, imitates Bloom's attention to chance meetings. In tracing the paths of his characters, his narrative extends or enacts the structure of intersection epitomized in Bloom's experiences with Boylan. In the case of the criss-crossing paths of the two men it is significant that at one point Bloom nearly intersects with Boylan unaware: Boylan flirts with a shopgirl while Bloom peruses the books outside at a nearby bookstall. Both men are choosing presents at this moment for Molly Bloom (10.315). This coincidence appears as the text's special knowledge, revealed to the reader but unknown to the characters. In this coincidence we note that the text's knowledge is not only special—shared between us and the narrator—but also spatial, for the narrator can render this moment by virtue of his vantage point *between* the two characters. In constructing this near-intersection, the text works to evoke in the reader Bloom's own experience of and conviction about the wonder of spatialized, intercorporeal coincidence: the magnetic pull of two "opposite" bodies which have a shared ground or interest, a ground also occupied by the narrator (who may in the end betray his shared interest).

Consider, too, the text's attention to the flyer handed to Bloom which proclaims "Elijah is coming." Bloom throws it away but returns again and again to the possibility of Elijah's return. Likewise, the novel is studded with references by Stephen and other characters to Elijah or a Messiah. At the level of narrative structure the text reiterates Bloom's meandering yet pregnant pattern of intersections by following the course of the thrown-away flyer. Cast here and there by wind and water, it appears and reappears in the path of various characters; in registering these intersections of character and object, the narrative creates a framing structure for itself—a structure of intersection that parallels Bloom's drama of intersubjective encounter. The text furthermore weaves this flyer into its thematic critique of the sexual–racial mythology by repeatedly refering to it as a "crumpled throwaway" (10.294, 10.1096), thus associating it with the "dark" horse Throwaway who wins the Gold Cup.

In this way Joyce not only weaves intersections into the structure of his text (through Bloom) but also repeats that pattern of intersection in his own quite separate tracing of the path of a flyer whose meaning reverberates within, or intersects with, the thematics of the text. The text thus shares Bloom's fascination with chance, with signifying intercorporeal intersections, and with the way such encounters confound sexual and racial distinctions.

In organizing his narrative around the literally crossed paths of differently embodied characters—of Bloom and Stephen, or Bloom and Boylan, or Cissy and Bloom and Gerty, or Stephen and Molly—Joyce finds structural representation for his challenge to the path-segregating narratives of sexual–racial mythologies. (In this narrative feature, and in its close attention to the co-adjusted movements of bodies, *Ulysses* bears comparison to Faulkner's *Light in August*.)[23] I understand the pattern of chance intersections of characters' bodies in *Ulysses* as Joyce's rendering of the larger phenomenal setting that makes possible human-to-human intercorporeality. Because humans share space, in this case a city, they inevitably "meet." On the most primordial level those meetings, like that between the water and the beetle in Darwin, "mean" the shared phenomenality that makes the meetings possible. Although racial patriarchy—through, for instance, the discourse of eugenics—attempts to delimit such meetings along racial, gender, and class lines, in Joyce's text the characters' chance meetings disrupt or cross these same lines which would limit and codify their bodies' possibilities of encounter. In focusing on the feminine and Irish-Catholic Stephen and the feminine and Irish-Jewish Bloom, Joyce selects characters whose bodies "mean" those lines even while they also collapse and transgress them.

It is true that Joyce limits the possible meanings *beyond* cultural codes to which his characters' bodies and interactions point. By establishing intercorporeal encounters as chance, Joyce partly orients his representation of the phenomenal world toward comic and deflationary effects. The chanciness of his character's meetings injects into them an element of parody and comedy while at the same time it flattens out the influences of the phenomenal world. In this way Joyce's representations remain this side of what I would consider a fully intercorporeal narrative practice. His narrative stylization of intercorporeality may indicate the limits of his imagination at least as much as it reveals a mocking intention. Still, through the intersecting structure of his text and through his narrator's affiliation with Bloom, Joyce expresses his interest in the spatial conditionality which gives literal place to human encounter and expression.

Joyce displays his desire to transgress the racial–patriarchal segregation of persons above all by bringing together Stephen Dedalus and Leopold Bloom. By temporarily placing the son, Stephen, colonized but still relatively an "insider," in the motherly–fatherly, Jewish–Irish hands of the "outsider" Bloom, Joyce suggests that fatherhood must give up both its gender and its racial loyalties if the Stephens of the world are to find what they seek. If the final meeting of Stephen and Bloom represents the climax of intercorporeal encounter for both Bloom and the text, their early chance encounter at the door of the library forms a link in a chain of associations which helps us interpret the value of all of the novel's intersections. This chain suggests a dialectical philosophy of physical encounter that further encourages us to read Joyce's sytlized narrative structure of intersection as more than merely comic or parodic.

Foreshadowing their final prolonged interaction (ending at the doorway to Bloom's house), the paths of Stephen and Bloom cross so closely at the library door that Stephen must step aside to let Bloom pass. Stephen thinks of the word "portico" (9.1205), which recalls his prior analysis of the life of William Shakespeare and hints at those implications of intercorporeal intersection which most interest Joyce. That is, in answer to the characterization of Shakespeare's marriage as a mere error, Stephen had countered with the claim that such "errors" are, rather, "portals of discovery" (9.229). The mismatched joinings of Socrates and Xanthippe or Shakespeare and Ann Hathaway, Stephen insists, are in fact doorways into dialectic—a dialectic not unlike that which finally develops between the older Jewish Bloom and the younger Irish-Catholic Stephen. The meeting of differences, or even opposites, Stephen suggests, opens doors—as opposed to inducing a life-and-death struggle.

The late-night dialogue between Bloom and Stephen bears out this suggestion. In this dialogue the direct acknowledgment of differences between Stephen and Bloom continually opens into another question or comparison between them. When the text asks, "What two temperaments did they individually represent?" the answer implies just such a meeting of opposites: "The scientific. The artistic" (17.560). (Here Joyce, whether consciously or not, suggests a laying down of weapons in that centuries-old rivalry between art and science which we saw expressed by Wordsworth and Huxley in chapter 3.) And when the narrator asks, "Did he find four separating forces between his temporary guest and him?" the answer names the four socially "separating forces": "name, age, race, and creed"

(17.402–3). As the dialogue proceeds, suppressed affinities surface and cut through these "separating forces," such as Bloom's and Stephen's exploration of the similarities between the ancient Hebrew and Irish languages (17.731–60). Meanwhile, the text's mock-learned account of their discussion luxuriates in the balancing and sometimes oxymoronic language of dialectic, as their conversation reveals "similar differences," "counterproposals," "points of contact," "connecting link[s]" (17.893, 960, 745, 478). Such expressions of non-negating simultaneous difference override an oppositional logic of either/or, object or subject.

The phenomenology of such a dialectical meeting finds its most dense expression at the point where Bloom meditates on the racial difference between himself and Stephen. We learn that "neither [of them] openly allude[s] to their racial difference" (17.525) but that they interpret each other's thoughts about it: "He thought that he thought that he was a jew whereas he knew that he knew that he knew he was not" (17.530–31). In both halves of the sentence we begin with Bloom's perspective. Bloom thinks that Stephen thinks that Bloom is a Jew, whereas Bloom knows that Stephen knows that Bloom knows that Stephen is not. The "whereas" between the "thought" and the "knew" clauses implicitly contrasts the hiddenness of Jewishness and the public normality of Irishness and Catholicism. But the ambiguous use of "he" grammatically collapses the separation between the two men so that the reader must sort through the phrasing to reseparate them. In the meantime any such reader has considered at least one or two alternate ways of referencing the pronoun—alternatives that, even if ultimately rejected in favor of one that seems "right," subvert the strict separation of persons and types on which the racial–patriarchal system depends.

Roy Gottfried has demonstrated how midsentence shifts in syntax characterize Joyce's prose in *Ulysses*.[24] I suggest that these shifts in syntax particularly give rise to ambiguous pronoun references and to confusion about the subject of the sentence; together with shifts in person (i.e., mixing of first and third person) and "stacked" pronouns (as in the "he thought" example) this syntactical shifting conspires to undercut the stable orientation of the reader. We must change position as the prose slips from one pronoun to another, and our struggle for orientation reveals our dependence on categories and oppositions in determining the grammatical, the existential, and the racial subject. In this way Joyce's prose realizes the social and grammatical potential for confusion, convergence, collapse, recovering in the end into a reorientation with difference enfolded rather than expelled. Thus again the text contrives the linguistic as well as corporeal convergence of differences—*within* Cissy or Molly or Stephen, and *between* Bloom and Stephen or Molly—precisely to open "porticos" which allow egress from the purist, separatist mythologies of twentieth-century racial patriarchy.

THE RETURN HOME TO THE RACIAL MOTHER

The final "portico" of *Ulysses* leads into Molly's bedroom and, from there, out of the text. In Molly's room Bloom and Molly "unite noiselessly," but even more important, within herself Molly mingles sexual and racial differences. Molly is a mother, a married woman, she lives safely indoors. Yet she is sexual, both with other men and, in fantasy, toward women. Molly is also polyracial—Irish, Jewish, and possibly Spanish. She is "impure," then, both sexually and racially. Yet Joyce gives this "other" woman a voice. In fact, he gives her the last word.

In her final word Molly explicitly continues the text's subversion of racial and especially sexual mythologies, even extending that subversion to the positions of Stephen and Bloom. Previously agents of comic deflation, Bloom and Stephen become in Molly's monologue objects of deflation. At the same time Molly celebrates sensuality among and between women and men, delighting in its polymorphous bisexual flux. Molly's monologue extends the earlier chapters' racial–patriarchal critique and their intercorporeal vision, although it does so in a text that belongs most of all to the men.

Because many readers, feminist and otherwise, have considered Molly a flat or stereotyped female character,[25] I begin this last section by attending to the details of Molly's monologue which give her dimension—sharp edges and curving depths. Only in recognizing these dimensions of Molly can we appreciate her simultaneously critical, visionary, and conservative roles in the text's closure and at the same time avoid Bloom's errors in his understanding of Molly.

Of prime importance to Molly's subversion of racial and sexual mythologies is simply the fact that in Molly's monologue we learn *her* perspective on both the men who have commented on her and the racial and sexual heterogeneity she embodies. The "other" body speaks, copiously and critically. Molly's comments recast even the sympathetic, sensual Bloom. Though we have by now gathered that Bloom fantasizes freely about all sorts of inventions and schemes for moneymaking, we have not been aware of the degree to which he misrepresents his skills and plans. Molly recalls their near-shipwreck at Bray, Bloom having told the boatman he knew how to row when it was barely true. She remembers his plan to start "a musical academy on their first floor drawingroom with a brassplate or Bloom's private hotel he suggested," neither of which ever materializes, "like all the things he told father he was going to do" (18.980–83). At one point, when his latest scheme has failed and money is short, he suggests to Molly that she pose nude for a local painter (18.560). Molly feels she was a "born fool to believe all his blather" (18.1187), but she nonetheless admits that "he used to amuse me the things he said" (18.1185). Even more, she acknowledges her attraction to his oddity: "I kiss the feet of you senorita theres some sense in that didn't he kiss our halldoor yes he did what a madman nobody understands his cracked ideas but me" (18.1405–7). Bloom's kissing Molly's "halldoor," while referring to the Jewish practice of kissing the mezuzah, also hints that between them, too, intersecting differences open "portals of discovery."

In light of Molly's sympathetic yet frank account of Bloom's failings, Bloom's complaints about Molly's lack of intelligence (17.674–702) carry less of a punch. By juxtaposing Molly's criticism of Bloom against Bloom's criticism of Molly, Joyce sets up a comic mutuality between wife and husband. But even beyond their countering of Bloom's criticisms, Molly's comments and background on herself significantly revise our understanding of her. Through Bloom and other men we have received the impression of Molly mainly as a buxom, flirtatious, promiscuous woman with a good singing voice but no brains. Molly offers us fragments of her personal history that both explain and reshape this picture of her. Molly depicts herself as polycultural, a woman who has either inherited or inhabited several cultures—Jewish, Spanish, and Irish among them. This fact alone puts her at odds with the racial–patriarchal order. She explains her "harumscarum" personality ("I know I am a bit") as the result of having spoken different languages and lived in many places and on many streets ("and all the bits of streets Paradise ramp and Bedlam ramp and Rodgers ramp and Crutchetts ramp and the devils gap steps well small blame to me if I am a harumscarum" [18.1468–70]). In the course of her monologue Molly defensively speaks a little Spanish to show "I havent forgotten it all" (18.1472), but her larger point is that she is the put-upon victim, not the proud master, of polylingualism. Molly sees herself as having been uprooted repeatedly by men—whether by her father, by her husband, or by the threat of war. The resulting exotic background which attracts Bloom to her also leaves her uncommitted to and unschooled in the codes of any one culture, and positioned at one remove from the codes of all. She conflates the borders a mother is supposed to reproduce.

Molly points out specifically that her charged position within constructs of both motherhood and racialism at the time Bloom met her—a young, sexual Jewess tending her dying mother—was partly what drew him to her. ("I suppose on account of my being a Jewess looking after my mother" [18.1184]). Like Cissy Caffrey, Molly straddles borders of sexuality, maternality, and race in a way that challenges dominant mythologies—and excites Bloom. Molly's identity as sexually and racially "impure" daughter (and later mother) makes her a titillating touchstone for Bloom's wandering desires. But while Bloom finds excitement in Molly's sexual and racial multiplicity, he fails to see that this multiplicity underlies what he considers her "deficient mental development" (17.674–702). Bloom's incomprehension of Molly's personality in relation to her polyvalent history and his criterion of "mental development" reveals his contradictory attachment, like

Stephen's, to a gendered metaphysics. That is, even Bloom, the "new womanly man," easily reduces Molly to a body without a brain, overlooking the complicated racialized history that gives rise to her "different" sensibility. The text, however, avoids this habitual error; in her monologue Molly presents her own history. Furthermore, within the monologue the text establishes what Bloom considers Molly's lack of intelligence as a consciously taken anti-intellectual, antimetaphysical position on her part, which she adopts in resistance to the misogyny and racialism inherent in modern Western metaphysics.

Repeatedly Molly challenges traditional definitions of intelligence. For her, intelligence is the ability to read people, not books: "when I put my hat and gloves in the window to show I was going out not a notion what I meant arent they thick never understand what you say even youd want to print it up on a big poster for them . . . where does their great intelligence come in" (18.704–9). She contrasts her pleasure in "rivers and lakes and flowers and colours springing up even out of the ditches primroses and violets" to what men call knowledge, saying "I wouldnt give a snap of my two fingers for all their learning" (18.1562–65). As for intellectual atheists, she suggests, "why dont they go and create something"? (18.1565). Molly pits the resources of bodily gesture and palpable nature against the uses of explanatory languages and impalpable learning. Although her oversimplified reversal of the metaphysical position here may fail, finally, to dislodge its oppositions, we should remember to ask whether this simplistic turnabout is only Molly's or also the text's. As we shall see, there is cause for considering Molly's simplifications the text's simplification of Molly.

Meanwhile, other of Molly's observations cut nearer the heart of racial–patriarchal metaphysics. In the spirit of Stephen she pointedly attacks men's metaphysical pretensions as hypocritical. She remarks on the hidden sensual indulgence in priests' learned tracts, such as one about "a child born out of [a woman's] ear because her bumgut fell out" (18.489–90). And she considers the material ramifications for women of men's supposedly mind-inspired "inventions." Men's most clever invention, according to Molly, is simply "for him to get all the pleasure" (18.158), as in the design of women's restrictive clothing: "these clothes we have to wear whoever invented them expecting you to walk up Killney hill then for example at that picnic all staysed up you cant do a blessed thing in them" (18.627–29). Similarly, men have invented a sexual double standard: "they can pick and choose what they please a married woman or a fast widow or a girl . . . but were to be always chained up" (18.1388–91). Finally, again buttressed by a myth of men's intelligence and invention, men leave women with the unacknowledged work of raising children: "if someone gave them a touch of it themselves theyd know what I went through with Milly nobody would believe cutting her teeth too" (18.157–59); and later: "they wouldnt be in the world at all only for us they dont know what it is to be a woman and a mother" (18.1440). With these comments Molly hints that, through the mythology of transcendent intelligence, men both pursue bodily desires and avoid bodily drudgery, meanwhile denying women's desire and heaping them with labors. Molly takes a firm stand against such bondage, not least in laying her claim to the pleasures of sexuality. She insists: "theyre not going to be chaining me up" (18.1391).

Yet while Molly has successfully worked around the restrictions on her heterosexual liasons, her less-noticed attachments to women have suffered repeated sunderings at the hands of men. Joyce critics have made much of Molly's recollections of her various male lovers; but Molly also describes her sensual memories of women from whom she has been separated. These separations occur not just psychologically but physically as she or the other woman is moved from place to place by fathers or husbands or wars. She thinks of a former neighbor of hers and Bloom's, "a lovely woman magnificent head of hair down to her waist . . . 1st thing I did every morning to look across see her combing it . . . *pity I only got to know her the day before we left"* (18.477–81; emphasis added). Likewise she thinks longingly, and with much sensual detail, of her old friend Mrs. Hester Stanhope, who used to write calling her "dearest Doggerina" and telling how she has "just had a jolly warm bath" or how she "will always think of the lovely teas we had together scrumptious currant scones and rasberry wafers I adore" (18.612–21). It seems that because of the war Mrs. Stanhope left and "never came back" (18.667). When she left, Molly remembers, "she kissed me six or seven times didnt I cry yes I did or near it my lips were taittering when I said goodbye she had a Gorgeous wrap of some special kind of blue colour" (18.673–5).

This memory moves Molly to comment on her lonely and paternally determined state at that time, as a girl bereft of her own mother ("thats what I never had" [18.1442]): "after they went I was almost planning to run away mad out of it somewhere," for she knows that as a woman she won't be allowed simply to travel or live single: "were never easy where we are father or aunt or marriage waiting always waiting to guiiide him toooo me waiting" (18.677–79). This complaint against the male-controlled system of marriage flows directly into a complaint against the war: "their damn guns bursting and booming all over the shop especially the Queens birthday and throwing everything down in all directions" (18.679–80). That the worst bombing happens on the queen's birthday seems to Molly a particular insult, perhaps because of the way the war has separated her from her "queen," her friend and surrogate mother, Mrs. Stanhope. Thus the text indicates that war (over "race races") and marriage, two cornerstones of the racial–patriarchal order, intervene rudely between Molly and the women with whom she desires intimacy. That the text portrays Molly as wanting intimacy with women at all, rather than considering women simply as antagonists in a racial–patriarchal contest, further testifies to its transgression of the old mythologies.

Even as the text shows the destructive effects of men's dominance on women's intimacy, it manages also to suggest that the interplay of men's and women's "worlds" can potentially increase the pleasures in each, as in Molly's girlhood memory of her friend Hester: "we used to compare our hair mine was thicker than hers she showed me how to settle it at the back . . . we were like cousins what age was I then the night of the storm I slept in her bed she had her arms around me then we were fighting in the morning with the pillow what fun he was watching me whenever he got an opportunity at the band" (18.638–44). This passage perfectly demonstrates how the non-punctuation of Molly's prose makes possible a bisexual slippage from homosocial to heterosocial pleasures, how Joyce's method carries us toward such a slippage, and how Molly's personality delights in it. The text represents Molly's sexuality as capable of overriding conventional sexual oppositions.

We might even draw a parallel between Stephen's and Bloom's pleasure with each other over Molly in their parting scene, on the one hand, and Hester's and Molly's pleasure with each other in the context of a watching man, on the other. In the "Ithaca" chapter, after a light in Molly's room "attract[s] Bloom's who attract[s] Stephen's gaze" and leads Bloom to describe his attraction to Molly, the men become "silent, each contemplating the other in both mirrors of the reciprocal flesh of their hisnothis fellowfaces" (17.1183). Similarly, the male gaze woven into Molly's memory of Hester adds surprising texture to their intimacy. Of course, in both cases the men watch and the women are watched. Yet Joyce's arrangement does imply, again as Kimberly Devlin has shown in her reading of the Gerty scene, that the women are also watching: Molly implicitly "watches" the man who watches, and Molly is aware of, if not watching, the men who stand below, watching her. As in the sentence "he knew he knew he knew," Joyce uncovers layers of interrelated watching and reading of the other's readings. This intersubjective dynamic, made possible by the "reciprocal flesh" of the subjects, is a turn-on that overrides divisions between hetero- and homoerotic, pure and impure. It offers an alternative to Hegelian oppositionality. Such an intercorporeal dynamic thrives on the mutual differences of self and Other, men and women, dark-skinned and light. That these "reversible" bodies are oriented toward all other bodies yet each remains separate and different *in* body makes the body an exquisite merging of sameness and difference, an *écart* within the kinship of the flesh; and so the spaces *between* bodies become "portals" seductively open to the intersections *of* bodies.

This joyous, high-comic reading of *Ulysses* requires final qualification, however. The fact remains, first of all, that most of *Ulysses* lives inside the lighter-skinned men. African men and women, after all, serve mainly as tropes in *Ulysses*, an outer ring of associations used to define lighter-skinned characters as out-siders to the dominant light-skinned patriarchal order. And then Molly, in the context of the many pages that precede her, appear as most of all as a final lens through which to view Stephen and Bloom, as well as the vehicle for our exit from the parodic text. Joyce achieves his final intercorporeal vision *through* this mono-logue, through Molly. In a sense Molly is for the text what Cissy Caffrey is for Bloom: an exciting embodiment of boundary-crossing identity. In closing his text with such a figure, Joyce underwrites Molly's transgressive, intercorporeal body, but he also rides upon it.

Paradoxically, in shaping Molly's monologue as the final instrument of an intercorporeal intersubjectivity, Joyce must contain and delimit Molly's capacity for intercorporeality. Several features of Molly's monologue operate to set it apart from the rest of the text and to restrict its effects to those that serve the text's narrative end, in both senses. As we saw, one of the key mechanisms of intercor-poreality for the characters and for the text's narrative structure is the intersecting movements of persons and things. But consider the "blocked" spatial rendering of Molly: she never moves. On June 4 Molly never leaves her house—nor, virtually, her bed—because the text depends on, all of its previous intersections accumulate toward, her fixed presence there. Accordingly, Molly's closing "Yes-yesyes" nostalgiacally *recalls* a moment of face-to-face sexuality with Bloom; it does not surge *forward* into a renewed future with him. Molly's spatial fixedness clearly entails a temporal fixedness or nostalgia. And yet the text creates the sense of entering an affirmative future beyond the "nightmare of history" precisely through this temporal and spatial fixing of Molly's subjectivity.

The constriction of Molly's body and subjectivity continues at the level of narrative voice. As I noted earlier, the rest of the narrative is characterized by pronoun shifts that create a fluctuating relationship between the narrator, charac-ters, and reader. The narrator uses a third-person narration to occupy the space between characters and stress their movements in common, as with the men's "unresisting knees." He also stacks pronouns, as we saw in the dialogue between Stephen and Bloom, to disrupt the boundaries between characters. Finally, he sometimes omits pronouns so as to give the effect of first-person monologue when he especially wants to focus on a character's "self-presence" or internal functions, as when Bloom takes his trip to the outhouse. Yet why in Molly's monologue is the narrator restricted to the first person? Why the lack of complex narrative fluctuations and interventions here? If, as I have argued, the earlier third-person narration, in its position between bodies, usurps and thus de-genders what is traditionally the mother's function of coordinating intersubjective bodies, then in this last section the text apparently returns that function wholly to the mother figure. When the characters are male, the narrator plays the feminine function of narrating the "in-between of self and other"; but when, finally, the character is a female and a mother, the third-person narrator disappears and the mother figure assumes the mediating, embodying role. The undifferentiated univocality of Molly Bloom's voice reinforces her function as generator of *others'* differences and as instrument of Joyce's narrative ends.

Thus, the sudden separate singled-outness of Molly's compact closing monologue contains the energy of a reversal. That energy betrays, even as it struggles away from, an old attachment to the opposite viewpoint, to an ethic of sexual–racial subjugation. Joyce's aim in *Ulysses* is radical: to collapse the body-subjugating binarism of metaphysics by riding into rather than up and away from the physical. But his vehicle, the racialized mother, functions conventionally, despite her transgressions; she is a relic of the same metaphysical mythologies he critiques.

In short, Joyce above all desires to know his men, especially his Irish-Catholic men. As an inheritor of an "other" racial tradition, throughout most of the text Bloom serves Joyce's desire. It is through immersion in Bloom as a sensual "other" man that Joyce can reconstruct his bond to himself—that is, to himself in the person of Stephen, the fallen-away Catholic sensualist. The perspective of Molly, in whom the other sex and race are combined, completes the attempt. Her view allows him to get the final angle on these men who lead him to the most multiple, most intercorporeal man in himself. This transgressive self-embrace, instrumental as it is to the project of surpassing old racial and sexual mythologies, begs other texts to pick up where it leaves off—to risk a fuller, face-to-face embrace with and finally a liberating disengagement from the transgressive mother figure. Intercorporeal narratives answer this call most clearly.

6

Voyaging Beyond the Race Mother: *Melymbrosia* and *To the Lighthouse*

Beginning with her first novel, *The Voyage Out*, Virginia Woolf's fiction repeatedly opens in the presence of mother figures—Helen Ambrose, Mrs. Hilbery, Clarissa Dalloway, Mrs. Ramsay—and then maneuvers sinuously, in its very syntax, to draw the center of narration away from these figures. The novels, especially *To the Lighthouse*, move narration along the opening or dehiscence between mothers and others, finding in the space between them a horizon of access to another intercorporeal story. It is in this persistent positioning and back-and-forth movement of her narrator between self and mother, between mother and things, between things and humans that Woolf breaks up both the Romantic-transcendental plot which subsumes the mother figure in its movement away from her and the late-Romantic plot, which circles back in a final arc toward the mother figure, the effect of which is to reify rather than reconfigure the mother's position. In the process of recasting the mother figure and demystifying the Romantic mythology that envelops her, Woolf undertakes a revisionary phenomenology of intersubjectivity which anticipates the notions of Merleau-Ponty—which in turn can describe Woolf's fiction. Woolf engages and challenges that same Romantic narrative of transcendence which so permeated Victorian thought, and she joins with and surpasses emerging twentieth-century phenomenology in envisioning alternatives to it.

But in what sense are Woolf's mother figures racialized in her fiction, and in what way does her intercorporeal mode of narration challenge racial boundaries? Neither race nor eugenics figures as an explicit term in Woolf's fiction. No obviously mixed-race characters appear in her novels; in fact, very few non–Anglo-Saxons can be found in her work. To speak of Woolf in the context of a racialized modernism thus seems to strain common sense, or common notions of race.

At the outset of her career as a novelist—in *Melymbrosia*, her draft of *The Voyage Out*—Woolf carefully maps the relation between empire, race, motherhood, and representations of materiality in a way that clarifies both the racial–patriarchal meaning of mothers in her novels and the antitranscendental import of her narrative experimentation. In *Melymbrosia* and *To the Lighthouse* Woolf employs the trope of the voyage to signify on both the racial–colonial context delimiting her mother figures and the submerged intercorporeal counterjourneys undertaken by their daughters. At the same time, if we recall the implicit racialization of class difference in England, specifically in eugenics, and if we note that Woolf consistently gives her female working-class characters a foreign heritage (as with the German Mrs. Kilman and the Irish Mrs. McNab), we may approach these women as figures who throw into relief the kin boundaries that hold and are upheld by the dominant-race mother figures. But Woolf most explicitly critiques the national and racialized boundaries that condition the meaning of motherhood in her essay *Three Guineas*. Let us turn there first.

In *Three Guineas* Virginia Woolf proposes the formation of a "Society of Outsiders." Her proposal counteracts precisely that eugenic obsession with determining and codifying the superior qualities of the "insider." Rather than scurrying to establish their qualifications for membership in the racial elite of the nation, her society's members would insist on nonmembership in any national body. The Outsider would "bind herself to take no share in patriotic demonstrations; to assent to no form of national self-praise; to make no part of any claque or audience that encourages war; to absent herself from military displays, tournaments, tattoos, prize-givings and all such ceremonies as encourage the desire to impose 'our' civilization or 'our' dominion over other people."[1] This Outsider would stand at a great distance from proud claims that "we have bred more than sixty millions of the finest people the world has ever seen. . . . Therefore any race that we admit to our body social is certain to be more or less inferior."[2]

In fact, Woolf formulates her proposal in explicit resistance to the racial and sexual discourses of her day. Turning her gaze to Nazi Germany, Woolf highlights the correspondence between hierarchies of race and the circumscription of women's roles. She notes, especially in Germany but also in England, Italy, and the United States, the encroachment of "tyrants" who are more and more openly "making distinctions not merely between the sexes, but between the races" (102). Without spelling out the way in which distinctions between the sexes make possible distinctions between the races, she tellingly points out that such tyrants decree a return to the division of sex roles. She quotes German and English writers who consider the sexual division of labor the only system appropriate to the national agenda, claiming that "there are two worlds in the life of the nation, the world of men and the world of women. Nature has done well to entrust the man with the care of his family and the nation. The woman's world is her family, her husband, her children, and her home" (102). Such statements, Woolf observes with alarm, seem increasingly ubiquitous; just open the daily newspaper, she tells her reader. Her comments testify to the widespread presence of positive eugenics, with its racialized national agenda for motherhood.

Woolf appeals especially to women in her call for an Outsider society, arguing most forcefully that women are always already outsiders to their societies and that they should make a virtue of this alienation. Woolf recognizes, of course, that an English woman, like an English man, "will have imbibed, even from the governess, some romantic notion that Englishmen, those fathers and grandfathers whom she sees marching in the picture of history, are 'superior' to the men of other countries" (108). And yet a woman has grounds for questioning whether that "picture of history" and that superiority include her. In 1938, as thousands of men were in fact marching to protect (even while ostensibly resisting) this racialized version of history, Woolf imagines that the Outsider woman would engage in a dialogue with the patriotic Englishman that would go something like this:

> If he says he is fighting to protect England from foreign rule, she will reflect that for her there are no "foreigners," since by law she becomes a foreigner if she marries a foreigner. . . . "Our country," she will say, "throughout the greater part of its history has treated me as a slave; it has denied me education or any share in its possessions. 'Our' country still ceases to be mine if I marry a foreigner. 'Our' country denies me the means of protecting myself, forces me to pay others a very large sum annually to protect me, and is so little able, even so, to protect me that Air Raid precautions are written on the wall. . . . Therefore if you insist upon fighting to protect me, or 'our' country, let it be understood, soberly and rationally between us, that you are fighting to gratify a sex instinct which I cannot share; to procure benefits which I have not shared and probably will not share; but not to gratify my instincts, or to protect myself or my country. For . . . in fact, as a woman, I have no country. As a woman I want no country. As a woman my country is the whole world." (109)

Woolf clearly understood that racialized national boundaries are patriarchal boundaries, and that these boundaries paradoxically circumscribe, exclude, and depend on women. In her first novel Woolf dramatizes the extreme difficulty of positioning oneself without reference to these boundaries—of voyaging beyond them. Rachel Vinrace fails to do so in her life. She voyages beyond racial–patriarchal boundaries only by crossing that phenomenological boundary between life and death. In *To the Lighthouse* Woolf recharts the voyage so as to discover and clear those spaces among the living and between the dead and the living where the outsider can at times travel unencumbered.

Melymbrosia: *The Body Below the Surface*

In *The Voyage Out,* as in *To the Lighthouse,* Woolf uses the trope of the voyage to explore the economic and the metaphysical meanings of the daughter's journey "out" from both a national–patriarchal and a maternal origin. Woolf avidly read voyage narratives, especially enjoying those of the Elizabethan Richard Hakluyt and the Victorian Charles Darwin.[3] She cherished her copy of *The Voyage of the "Beagle,"* a gift from her father, and admired Darwin's descriptive style.[4] But Woolf also understood how these voyages were a core activity in the boundary-drawing economy of her culture—how even as the English expanded their commercial and geographic borders, they defined their racial borders ever more sharply and narrowly *against* the different races encompassed by those expanded commercial frontiers, and how at the same time Englishmen called ever more insistently for women's participation in this project as reproducers of boundaries.[5]

In this novel about the voyage of a young woman on her father's commercial ship, and even more clearly in the draft version, on which I focus here, Woolf implicitly contrasts the late Victorian woman's experience of colonial voyaging with the Victorian man's.[6] Behind this difference in experiences lies a divergence in ways of being a body in the world. As they voyage out together, Helen Ambrose represents the woman's way of being in the world for Rachel Vinrace, but at the same time Helen leads Rachel to confine her journey to the coordinates of the ship of Empire. Woolf's treatment of the mother–daughter relationship in this novel identifies for us the social coordinates that compel her transgressive remapping of the daughter figure's voyage in *To the Lighthouse.*

For all her gullibility and timidity, Rachel Vinrace in *Melymbrosia* champions a radically affiliative relationship to things in the world which resembles Mrs. Ramsay's "secret knowledge" in *To the Lighthouse.* Moreover, she does so self-consciously, imagining herself engaged in a "Great War" with her culture's compulsion to codify and master the organic world (Woolf's choice of phrase is eerily identical with that which would soon be used to describe World War I). We learn early on in *Melymbrosia* (drafted around 1910) that

> [Rachel's] quarrel with the living was that they did not realise the existence of drowned statues, undiscovered places, the birth of the world, the final darkness, and death. . . . Since she had been conscious at all, she had been conscious of what with her love of vague phrases, she called, "The Great War." It was a war waged on behalf of things like stones, jars, wreckage at the bottom of the sea, trees stars and music, against the people who believe in what they see.[7]

Rachel's "war waged on behalf of things" compares to the war Woolf fought as a writer. It is a war fought with mothers as well as fathers, and yet it is also a cause usually inherited from mothers in their struggles with fathers, however much mothers might deny it. In her essay "Professions for Women" Woolf explicitly describes how as a writer she has fought two battles: one with a mother figure, and a second on behalf of something she shares with such mothers—her female body. Her reflections in that essay provide a framework for understanding Rachel's fate.

In a now famous passage of "Professions" Woolf recalls that when she began writing, the phantom of the "Angel in the House"—the self-sacrificing mother figure—whispered in her ear, "My dear, you are a young woman. . . . Be sympathetic; be tender; flatter; deceive; use all the arts and wiles of our sex. Never let anybody guess that you have a mind of your own. Above all, be pure."[8] This angel would train her writer–daughter to keep the same limits and sacrifices she herself has lived—of mind and body, which must remain "pure," a word with both sexual and blood or racial connotations. Ever so sympathetic, the angel is nonetheless deadly to the daughter with a mind and body of her own. The angel–mother's demand for "purity" actually entails her own and her daughter's prostitution: they must "flatter; deceive." Therefore, Woolf confesses, "I turned upon her and caught her by the throat. . . . Had I not killed her she would have killed me. She would have plucked the heart out of my writing" (59). In *To the Lighthouse* Woolf reenacts this killing of the Angel in the House as she simultaneously generates a body-centered narration grounded in a materiality coextensive with but also at odds with the mother's "pure" and prostituted body.

Nonetheless, in *Melymbrosia* and other novels, as in "Professions," Woolf succeeds in trespassing only so far outside the motherly circumscription of the daughter's body. In the essay Woolf records her experience (in a passage that compares strikingly with the beadle scene in *A Room of One's Own*) of being in a dream state while at her writing desk, like a "fisherman lying sunk in dreams on the verge of a deep lake with a rod held out over the water" (61). She asks her audience to "figure to yourselves a girl sitting with a pen in her hand" whose figurative fishing line "sought the pools, the depths, the dark places where the largest fish slumber" (61). Her imagery of submersion and watery depths recalls the underwater world of "wreckage at the bottom of the sea" which Rachel fights to protect. As in the novel (and in the beadle passage in *A Room*), this world gets invaded and shattered. Suddenly "the line raced through the girl's fingers. . . . And then there was a smash. There was an explosion. The imagination had dashed itself against something hard. The girl was roused from her dream" (61). Woolf explains that the girl "had thought of something, something about the body, about the passions which it was unfitting for her as a woman to say" (61).

Although Woolf here "speak[s] without figure" in explaining the girl's taboo subject, she nonetheless stops short of fully violating that taboo, of specifying the "something" in her sentence.

Through Rachel in *Melymbrosia* we just glimpse that submerged realm of embodiment. Like Mrs. Ramsay, Rachel celebrates the objects of the world among which the body takes its place—jars, stones, trees, stars, and music. To Rachel "trees and flowers are friends" (130) in much the same way that in *To the Lighthouse* Mrs. Ramsay feels that "trees, streams, flowers . . . knew one."[9] On one of her walks alone, Rachel bends to the flowers and shrubs and performs "the rite which shame would have prevented in company. 'I've loved you. I've loved you' she repeated" (130). In addition to the word "rite" here (with its pagan connotations), the novel's elaborate network of allusions to the Sabrina figure in John Milton's *Comus*[10] as well as to the Egyptian goddess Isis[11] hints that Woolf aimed to align Rachel with an older female-oriented tradition of affiliation with the world of things in contrast to the Judaeo-Christian tradition which proclaims of things, in effect, "I've named you, I've named you."

Not surprisingly, then, Rachel's relationship to the material world is pointedly contrasted with that of her entrepreneurial father, that of the Flushings, and that of the British Empire. Both her father and the Flushings travel to South America to acquire material goods which they will sell for profit back in England, keeping in motion the wheels of Empire. With its repeated references to Elizabethan voyages, such as the "Elizabethan barque" on which Mrs. Flushing "might have been an heroic figure head,"[12] together with allusions to Darwin's *Voyage of the "Beagle,"*[13] the novel situates its heroine's journey within a long history of entre-preneurial journeying by which England expanded its access to and naming of material resources. Rachel's Great War "on behalf" of materiality is explicitly politicized by being thus situated. Her war is fought from within the empire; she wages it from inside the dominant community, as one of its "own" daughters.

And yet Rachel scarcely knows she is aboard her enemy's ship. Once in South America she lives in the "English camp," oblivious to her position (133). Her inland journey upriver and into intimacy with Terence Hewet is guided and underwritten by the Flushings' procurement of native South American women's unused ritual clothing. Rachel is thus implicated in the appropriative mechanisms of Empire despite her lack of a mastering disposition toward the material world. Moreover, because the only sanctioned form of "experience" open to her is that which is shaped and coded by the structures and members of Empire, she finally embraces that experience. And she dies of fever shortly afterward.

Many critics have read Rachel's death as her fearful retreat from sexuality.[14] But it is important to emphasize that Rachel retreats specifically from a sexuality supported and regulated by Empire[15]—and from a sexuality which, moreover, requires her to make two substitutions: of a man for a mother, and of a conquering for an affiliative relation to materiality. This novel about Rachel's "voyage out" into sexuality on the ship of Empire originates in the separation of children from mothers. In other words, it foregrounds the crucial transitional moment within the familiar Western narrative of development, in which the self becomes a self only in leaving behind the mother. Not only does the absence of Rachel's dead mother form a condition of Rachel's travels on her father's boat, but the novel opens dramatically with a scene of mother–child separation.

We turn back the cover of *Melymbrosia* to find Helen Ambrose weeping as she leaves her children to journey to her brother's villa in South America. She grieves over the fact that "her arms no longer closed upon the bodies of two small children" (3). Once Helen boards the *Euphrosyne*, the ship is made to symbolize the reverse separation—that of a daughter leaving home to become a wife and mother. In making the ship a daughter who will soon be a bride and mother, the narrative hints at the story behind Helen's scene of departure, of Helen herself having been a daughter separated from her mother. The scene takes on the mythical quality of one infinitely repeated through the lives of mothers and daughters.

> [The ship] travelled all day across an empty universe, with veils drawn before her and behind. She was more lonely than the caravan crossing the desert; she was infinitely more mysterious, moving by her own power and sustained by her own resources. The sea might give her death, or some unexampled joy, and none would know of it. . . . Her state was far more wondrous than the state of England. She was a bride going forth to her husband unattended. (19)

Woolf implies that the bride's "state" symbolizes and regenerates the "state of England," while at the same time she subverts that equation by attributing a power to the bride that surpasses that of England and furthermore derives from "her own resources." All veiled in, however, this bride is variously named and denigrated by onlookers: the *Euphrosyne* is "alternately called a Tramp, a cattle boat, a cargo boat," while "of the love and reason on board no one recked" (68).

When the boat–bride finally reaches its port in South America, Helen herself is figured as the daughter who, now become a mother herself, leaves behind and overlooks *her* mother's grief at separation: "Absorbed in her letters [from her children] she did not notice that she had left the Euphrosyne; she felt no sadness when the ship lifted up her voice and bellowed thrice like a cow separated from its calf" (69). Helen is herself caught up in the economy in which daughters separate from their mothers and substitute men for them, while also acting as substitute mothers in the lives of their men.

In a passage just preceding Helen's departure from the *Euphrosyne*, the text places Helen's heterosexual substitutions within the context of a larger colonial economy of substitutions. Her group has been discussing a recent near-catastrophe—the dangerous birth of a child aboard a ship without proper attendants—and Helen can only comment, "How people love the chance of a scene!" (68). Woolf's narrator explains Helen's superficial response to this "scene" as in keeping with her country's cold colonial exchanges, which generate in Helen an "economy of emotion": "She was content that half the population of England should be lifted to the African shore, and the void filled by negroes as she was content to mix her coffee with milk. This *economy of emotion* left her with strong passions for the objects she selected" (69; emphasis added). Likewise does Helen's short-circuited attachment to her mother (figured as the *Euphrosyne*) enable her to channel all the emotion proper to that separation into tears over her own children rather than over any one else's childbirth or over herself as separated child.

In short, the colonial economy (which allows Helen to "mix her coffee with milk") sets up the Helens of the world comfortably enough so that they can practice an "economy of emotion" which complements this colonial economy of milk and coffee. Such mothers economically limit their "passions" to their own culture and, especially, their own children. And yet such mothers also always eventually get left behind as children separate from them to become adults (either as members of Empire or as wives of the members of Empire). This narrative of separation from the mother helps to maintain the mother as an instrumental and subservient figure in the colonial economy.

And yet from Rachel's point of view Helen represents the mother from whom—until she meets Terence—Rachel has not separated. As Rachel remarks: "My mother was the person I cared for. . . . And now Helen. When she speaks it's like the beginning of a song" (197). Helen, Rachel later muses, "fills me with pleasure" (215). Rachel does not fully realize the equivocal role played by most mothers in a colonial and racial–patriarchal economy. For even while Helen accepts and returns Rachel's affection, she positions Rachel for marriage and displays a deep ambivalence toward Rachel's sexuality. Just after Rachel's engagement to Terence, as the journeyers set off on foot for the village where the Flushings will trade, the two women run on ahead of the others. Water imagery fills the passage in which their bodies meet.

> [Rachel] went ahead, and called back over her shoulder to Helen, "It's like wading out to sea!"
> She left behind her a trail of whitened grass, like a track in water. Without thinking of her forty years, Helen cried "Spring on! I'm after you!" whereupon Rachel took longer leaps and at last ran. Helen pursued her. . . . Suddenly Rachel stopped and opened her arms so that Helen rushed into them and tumbled her over onto the ground. "Oh Helen Helen!" she could hear Rachel

> gasping as she rolled her, "Don't! For God's sake! Stop! I'll tell you a secret! I'm going to be married!"
>
> Helen paused with one hand on Rachel's throat holding her head down among the grasses.
>
> "You think I didn't know that!" she cried.
>
> For some seconds she did nothing but roll Rachel over and over, knocking her down when she tried to get up; stuffing grass into her mouth; finally laying her absolutely flat on the ground, her arms out on either side of her, her hat off, her hair down.
>
> "Own yourself beaten" she panted. "Beg my pardon, and say you worship me!" (209)

In this moment of Rachel's "going forth like a bride" toward a man, a movement which Helen has fostered, Helen suddenly "pursues" Rachel and pins her. Helen fondly rolls Rachel in the grass but also holds Rachel's "head down among the grasses," which, in the context of the water imagery, becomes a figurative drowning. If the water were real, Rachel's body would become one of those "drowned statues," part of the "wreckage at the bottom of the sea" which others never see. (The imagery of drowning in fact permeates Rachel's final experience of dying, and this passage implies that the engagement to Terence is the beginning of the submersion of Rachel's body, which occurs at the hand of the mother.)

Similarly, when Helen stuffs grass into Rachel's mouth, the image is both sexual and suffocating. The doubleness of this imagery points to the sublimation of female desire in the mother–daughter relationship through sacrifice of the daughter's body to a husband. Woolf's revision of this scene in the published version of the novel suggests that she, as self-censoring author, plays out this same substitution, in particular by adding Terence to the chase and muting the sexual undertones of the mother–daughter embrace.[16] In both versions desire and domination, triumph and defeat mingle in the mother's and the daughter's gestures.

In other words, Helen acts as mother goddess (think again of the Isis and Sabrina allusions) brought into the service of patriarchy; she channels her desire *for* the daughter into a conquest *of* the daughter. When Helen demands, "Own yourself beaten," she simultaneously means that she dominates Rachel's love more than Terence and that she dominates Rachel's love as an ally of Terence. Rachel responds, "I love Terence better," which again is both a triumph and a defeat for the kin–patriarchal mother, who wins only by losing her child to a man. This is why, when Helen at first senses that Terence and Rachel are engaged, "the pain which she had felt as the Euphrosyne moved up the Thames, returned; as the steamer slipt steadily down the water she felt as if her children were drawn from her" (206). This mother figure who casually mixes coffee with milk must take the bitter with the sweet. Her loss of children is her only triumph.

Forced, at the hands of a mother, across the border between the female homoerotic and the heteroerotic which will fix her in her place as boundary marker and reproducer, Rachel enters the South American village to find herself faced with an impenetrable boundary—between her and the women of another "race." Fresh from her intimacy with Terence and Helen, Rachel half expects to feel a rapport with the South American women: "Rachel tried to understand their faces, for she had thought that her own happiness would have made it easy for her" (211). But the intimacy she has achieved with Terence does not effect this identification with the foreign women. The conditions of her visit in fact preclude it. Rachel's journey, during which she becomes engaged, is after all undertaken mainly as an economic voyage for the Flushings, benefiting the English at the expense of the South Americans, in which it is understood that only Mr. Flushing will speak directly to the women, and only for purposes of business.

Moreover, as an affiliate of the "English camp"—especially since her engagement—Rachel internalizes her "camp's" dichotomized gender mythologies, which turn out to be implicitly racialized, for the South American women do not fit them. Woolf makes clear that the South American women's "faces" are ill matched to English types and particularly to the oppositions between good and bad supposedly legible in women's bodies: "Their faces were an oily brown and this perhaps explained why they did not look like faces; they seemed neither old nor young, neither clever malicious women, or sweet sympathetic women.
. . . She owned that she knew nothing about them" (212). Just as Rachel remains naively oblivious to the underlying economics of her life, so she continues to believe in the value of these dichotomies of women even when, as we have just seen, she might instead note the hidden fusion of the "malicious" and the "sympathetic" in Helen and in all racial–patriarchal mothers who must "educate" and then hand over their daughters.

Thus does Woolf's narrative trace Rachel's substitution of a man for a mother and of the corresponding sense of racial difference for gender solidarity. Woolf juxtaposes these two substitutions in a way that suggests a connection between them. That connection is best understood as one endemic to Western racial patriarchy, in which a woman's marriage signifies her deepened bond to an ingroup over and against another group, especially a colonized group. Woolf's sequencing reflects her consciousness of such mechanisms in her culture. At the same time, *Melymbrosia* aligns these two substitutions on Rachel's part with yet another, in which Rachel's affiliative or honoring relation to materiality is superseded, briefly before her death, by a Romantic sacrificing relation. For if Rachel is to operate within Empire's "economy of emotion," she must subordinate her love for jars, stones, and trees to that for the bodies of men and children. The text represents Rachel's ambivalent and ultimately unsuccessful attempt to make this corollary substitution.

On the walk during which Rachel discovers her feelings for Terence (before the journey upriver), she carries St. John Hirst's copy of Gibbon's *Rise and Fall of the Roman Empire* under her arm. Mimicking the history of empires in her ascent up the mountain, she follows "a rise in the ground, a fall over a tuft of grass, because thus the mind was silenced" (132). Finally, "the summit attained, she stood erect, and asked out loud of the sky and the mountains, 'Am I in love?'" (132). She does not stoop to ask the flowers if she loves Terence but addresses her question and her answer to the mountains, leaving behind Hirst's idea (131) that trees, rooted in earth, are what really matter: "'I love you! I love you!' This was addressed to the mountains. Something in the speed with which they rushed up into the sky falling here rising there, rejoiced her, because she was for rushing too, up and up" (132). Hirst has apparently given Rachel his Gibbon to heighten her understanding of her own political situation; the uneducated, uncritical Rachel, however, makes of it only a prop in her imitative rise to the "summit" through the conventions of heterosexuality.

This closure to chapter 16 marks Rachel's final substitution. Addressing the Romantic explorer's mountains rather than single flowers, her twice-repeated "I love you!" replaces her earlier twice-repeated "I've loved you!" She chooses a love that destines her for marriage and motherhood and, as her clutching of Gibbon has implied, to these as they function for Empire. Her love for flowers becomes love for men, who she has confessed frighten and inhibit her. As she says to Terence: "If you could strip off my skin now you would see all my nerves gone white with fear of you" (150), for he to some degree represents all men (in a description that anticipates those of *Three Guineas*): "How cruel they are at home, how they believe in ranks and ceremonies, how they want praise and management," and how, because of men, women "are forbidden to walk down Bond Street alone." She concludes "I shall never have all the feelings I might have because of you" (151).

Hence, as the narrative now subtly hints, this "rise" in Rachel's attachments marks the beginning of her—and her community's—fall. Even as Rachel rises to address her cry to the mountains, she sees "how the sun had crossed to the opposite range of mountains" (132). Woolf emphasizes this shift from high sun to setting sun by opening the next chapter with a restatement of it: "The sun had crossed over to the other range of mountains, and after illuminating the forlorn English camp for perhaps the three hundred and eighty seventh time, had dropped to the other side of the world" (133). On this other side of the world, opposite the "English camp," the material world is not yet overcome by the social world, and one can still see clearly to the bottom of the sea: "The pools and forests there flashed blue and green; whereas in the hotel at Santa Rosa dinner had just been cleared from the tables. . . . Lethargy marked most of the figures who were now sipping coffee" (133). Though they comfortably sip the coffee of Empire, they suffer the ennui of postconquest satiety.

At the close of the novel, after Rachel's death (rendered as a drowning embrace with things), Hirst dozily witnesses the end of a chess game between Mr. Pepper and Mr. Elliot. Mr. Pepper, whose very name bespeaks the import of profitable goods and whose fantasies of Elizabethan voyages and Roman roads mark him as a loyal representative of Empire (11, 69), usually dominates his compatriots at the aristocratic and strategic game of chess. But finally he has been beaten. To what does his opponent attribute his long-sought subversion of Pepper's dominance? "It was just that move with your Queen that gave it away, Pepper," exclaimed Mr. Elliot triumphantly (244). Even as Helen, queen of this little English camp and guardian of Rachel, unwittingly "gives away" the maneuvers of Empire in her equivocal handling of Rachel, so too has Pepper's incautious use of his queen unveiled the position of his king. Both Helen and Pepper have pushed the game, and the positioning of the queen, a step too far. The daughter who was meant to die a figurative death dies a real one. The empire's loss is at her expense. Its sun sets on her fall, although Woolf implies that Rachel's fall will also hasten the end of Empire. The king depends on the vassalage of his queen, and with Rachel's death the empire loses one of its potential queens.

To the Lighthouse:
Circumventing the Mother

Whereas in *Melymbrosia* Woolf explores the way a mother figure's "protection" effects the sacrifice of daughters and the suppression of their filiative kinship with the things of the world, in *To the Lighthouse* she pushes further into the mother's own submerged attachment to the world of "stones, jars, trees." We might playfully imagine that Mrs. Ramsay is the woman Rachel would have become had she lived, married Terence, and raised several children. Rachel might thus have played strategic "queen" to her scholar–king in a nation of pepper and coffee procurers; she might have managed continually to convert her love for outdoor things into an indoor love for children and husbands; but she might also have sat at windows, gazing out to sea, feeling beckoned by that distant world as if by an old lover.

By burrowing into the mother figure's submerged attachment to the world of things through a narrator who mediates between the mother and those things,

Woolf attempts to circumvent the conditional access to a mother-imprisoned intercorporeal knowledge.[17] Through Woolf's narrator we see trees, tables, hedges from their backsides, so to speak, where they obtrude beyond the codes and categories continually imposed on them, where they lull even the racial–patriarchal mother into indifference to the social codes that, ironically, keep her in close contact with things. In effect, by making her narrator quietly privy to the mother's extrapatriarchal knowledge of intercorporeality, Woolf is able to transfer that knowledge from mother to daughter without subjecting the daughter to the mother's code of self-sacrifice.

Woolf first establishes a kinship with things shared by the mother figure Mrs. Ramsay and the daughter figure Lily Briscoe and interrupted by the father figure Mr. Ramsay; and yet she also exposes and ironizes the mother's and daughter's shared tendency to mythologize or constrict that kinship under the influence of the father's presence. Beginning in "The Window," the first section of the novel, Woolf continually gives her narrator an access to things which surpasses and demythologizes both Mrs. Ramsay's and Lily's and so allows the narrator to use the material world to generate the temporal and spatial maneuvers of her narrative. Woolf's narrator infiltrates the intercorporeal material world most fully in the "Time Passes" interlude, where she throws into relief from her "in-between" position the Romantic mythology that has created Mr. and Mrs. Ramsay's opposed relations to the material world, at the same time foregrounding the colonized figures who tend that world. Finally, Woolf depicts art itself as an intercorporeal means of moving beyond that mythology and its colonizing practices.

Mrs. Ramsay's position near the window, like her wish to open windows, signals her desire to connect the feminized indoor world with the masculine outdoor world, to dissolve oppositions into the overlapping spaces "in between" one self, one sex, one realm and another. Moreover, sitting at the border of a split world, Mrs. Ramsay engages in a disagreement with her husband about the future of the outdoor world—about tomorrow's weather. As the novel opens, Mrs. Ramsay risks a suggestion about the weather without any reference to barometers: "Yes, of course, if it's fine tomorrow" (9). In making a promise involving the outdoor world of weather, Mrs. Ramsay, like the Fisherman's Wife in the tale she reads to James, strays across a border into her husband's supposed realm of authority. She transgresses the cultural segregation of indoors and outdoors. By calling this section of her novel "The Window," Woolf establishes a world strictly divided by a border which Mrs. Ramsay both guards and peers across. Mrs. Ramsay, in short, is that necessary but unsettling bodyworker lurking among the brainworkers, of which her husband is eminently one.

Mrs. Ramsay, of course, appears the image of placidity, the image with "a semblance of serving" (193). With her son cradled in her lap, she assumes the classic posture of the protective mother. Both the artist Lily Briscoe and Woolf herself paint her in this pose. She promises her son a pleasing adventure in the outdoor world, protecting him from his father's dominating pessimism. At moments she extends the same protection and promise to her husband. But even as she serves her son and husband by constructing a place of physical and existential comfort for them, by sustaining the bordered world in which her body serves their minds (in this scene she imagines James becoming a lawyer), Mrs. Ramsay to some degree also protects that realm of physical and existential phenomenality *from* them. She hoards it for herself. She is allowed her orientation within the world of bodies because through it she supports the dominant-class world of minds. But Mrs. Ramsay feels an allegiance to the sphere of things and bodies, an allegiance which sometimes distracts her from her subordinate handworker role. Thus, her position as border figure—one who sustains the dominant world by drawing on resources denigrated or denied by that world—paradoxically makes her a threat, almost against her own will, to her husband's realm.

Like Rachel Vinrace, Mrs. Ramsay loves the "inanimate" world and knows herself through it: "It was odd, she thought, how if one was alone, one leant to inanimate things; trees, streams, flowers; felt they expressed one; felt they became one; felt they knew one, in a sense were one" (97–98). Alone with things, Mrs. Ramsay feels no Sartrean nausea at their "in-itselfness"; things do not ooze or cloy with an overheavy substantiality, dragging on her as a conscious being-for-itself. Nor do things merely "decorate the processes of thought" as the red geraniums along the garden path do for Mr. Ramsay (67). For Mrs. Ramsay phenomenal things ground and generate the "processes of thought": "One helped oneself out of solitude reluctantly by laying hold of some little odd or end, some sound, some sight" (99). Mrs. Ramsay "leans" toward things, in a sense of kinship with them. If she spoke out loud on such matters, Mrs. Ramsay might claim with the phenomenologist that "the thickness of my body, far from rivalling that of the world, is on the contrary the sole means I have to go unto the heart of things."[18]

For Mrs. Ramsay the object world is a bridge, a lever, a hinge joining this to that, here to there, her to him, now to then. When at the end of the day she mounts the stairs to her children's nursery, she thinks how it is through the objects of their world that others will "come back to this night; this moon; this wind; this house: and to her, too" (170). She passes her mother's sofa and her father's rocking chair, and she imagines that Paul Rayley and his fiancée, Minta, will "carry it on" once they have wed—will carry on these links to others through the things that surround them. Her awareness of a world of houses and trees which human bodies inhabit together gives her "that community of feeling with other people . . . as if the walls of partition had become so thin that practically . . . it was all one stream, and chairs, and table maps, were hers, were theirs, it did not matter whose, and Paul and Minta would carry it on when she was dead" (170–171). In Mrs. Ramsay's sensibility chairs, walls, and table maps are the observable traces of a physical past, with which one has a relationship that constitutes oneself, one's community, and one's future.

And yet Woolf's text quietly deconstructs and casts irony on Mrs. Ramsay's fantasy; key details point toward Mrs. Ramsay's colonially situated heterosexuality as the channel through which things are able to be "carried on." Note the reference to table maps—and, implicitly, once again to the long English tradition of "voyages out" and colonial expansion. These maps do indeed "carry it on," though not strictly in the lovely way Mrs. Ramsay fantasizes, certainly not in the form of any *global* "community of feeling with other people." Mrs. Ramsay's kinship with the world of things buoys her temporal existence and deeply informs her ideal of social relations, but that buoyancy and that ideal are, at the same time, supported and restricted by an economy in which she is at once colonized and colonizer. Such hints of an underlying economy of dominance haunt even Mrs. Ramsay's most ecstatic moments of intercorporeality. Tropes of tyranny and dominance invade her attraction to the lighthouse light, just as they shape Rachel's engagement in a "war waged on behalf of things," and as they not only invade but dominate Darwin's descriptions of co-adaptation. The rhetorical orientations of Hegel and Darwin filter perceptibly into the intercorporeal reflections of Woolf's Victorian mother figure.

The narrator explicitly sexualizes Mrs. Ramsay's response to the rhythm of the lighthouse searchlight. Given the eroticism of the description, the light might well be read as the pulse of the "unflagging, intoxicating, unappeasable search for love" which Hélène Cixous understands to be the chief impulse passed on in the mother's nurturing relation to others, especially the daughter.[19] According to Cixous, it is the mother's milk that feeds the "white ink" of the radical woman writer's text. To some extent Woolf's text bears out Cixous's celebrations; but at the same time *To the Lighthouse* suggests that the "milk" connecting mother and daughter or self and world is never pure.

Here, as in *Melymbrosia*, Woolf mixes the mother's milk, so to speak, with the coffee of colonialism. She begins by mimicking the Romantic and Victorian rhetoric of mists and brides which so effectively veils this mixture: "There rose, and she looked and looked with her needles suspended, there curled up off the floor of the mind, rose from the lake of one's being, a mist, a bride to meet her lover" (98). We then learn that Mrs. Ramsay meets the third stroke of the light as she meets a "pitiless" and "remorseless" lover. Just as when Mr. and Mrs. Ramsay's "two notes struck together" (62) but left a lingering dissonance, her response to this lover, whom she meets in the spirit of the proper Nature–bride of Romantic poetry, rushes to a sexual climax in a flow not wholly without snags and threats:

> With some irony in her interrogation, for when one woke at all, one's relations changed, she looked at the steady light, the pitiless, the remorseless, which was so much her, yet so little her, which had her at its beck and call (she woke in the night and saw it bent across their bed, stroking the floor), but for all that she thought, watching it with fascination, hypnotised, as if it were stroking with its silver fingers some sealed vessel in her brain whose bursting would flood her with delight, she had known happiness, exquisite happiness, intense happiness, and it silvered the rough waves a little more brightly, as daylight faded, and the blue went out of the sea and it rolled in waves of pure lemon which curled and swelled and broke upon the beach and the ecstasy burst in her eyes and the waves of pure delight raced over the floor of her mind and she felt, It is enough! It is enough! (99–100)

Woolf casts Mrs. Ramsay's relations to this "stroking" outer world in the language of a familiarly Romantic and ecstatic yet problematic heterosexuality, revealing how fully the culture's gendered rhetoric of materiality pervades Mrs. Ramsay's sentient being in the world and determines her subservient "postural schema." Even in such an orgasmic moment, sensual embeddedness in the flesh of the world does not escape heterosexual narratives and struggles. Rather, for this mother figure of the Anglo-Saxon educated class, encouraged to preside over an empire at home parallel to her male compatriots' empire abroad, and yet expected always to be at the beck and call of that outdoor empire, intercorporeal sensuality and oppositional struggle interpenetrate each other. Although Mrs. Ramsay is ostensibly removed from her husband's pacing and fretting over the fate of the Light Brigade (sent into a doomed battle as the result of a blunder of miscommunication), she in fact reenacts that embattled mode of existence in her sexualized, power-inflected relations with materiality and in the lies she must tell her husband, "for instance, about the greenhouse roof" (62). The lighthouse passage actually implies a certain knowingness on Mrs. Ramsay's part about such disparities, for she feels some "irony" at this moment.

Yet the description also *affirms*, in its lyrical eroticism, Mrs. Ramsay's sexual pleasure in her way of living—a pleasure suggestively clitoral, remarkably orgasmic. The light strokes the floor of her bedroom "as if it were stroking with its silver fingers some sealed vessel." This stroking "silvered the rough waves a little," eventually "bursting" the vessel and provoking memories of "exquisite happiness, intense happiness," so that she exclaims, "It is enough!" In making this orgasmic image the redeeming and defining moment in the intercorporeal sensibility of Mrs. Ramsay, Woolf eroticizes the mother's material embeddedness of being and sexualizes the intercourse of body and world which engenders her own language, thus moving in the spirit of Cixous's celebratory meditations on woman's relation to that world. Woolf's text represents Mrs. Ramsay's channeling of bodily intercorporeality into racial–patriarchal heterosexuality as in some measure successful, unlike Rachel's.

In fact, Woolf might be faulted for too lyrically embracing this channeling, especially when that success comes only within a colonial "economy of emotion" which deprives other women and men of the basic conditions for intercorporeality precisely in order to offer superior conditions to Mrs. Ramsay. After all, the dominant-class mother figure must be allowed to feed her body upon that aura of power even if the power ultimately is not hers. It is possible, as decades of Woolf criticism have made clear, to read such passages in Woolf's text and feel the ecstasy of her prose without fully registering the critique so subtly embedded in it. Woolf herself may thus be said to walk a dangerously uncertain line between sympathy with Mrs. Ramsay's romance and irony toward that romance.[20]

I walk this same line as a reader of Woolf. I philosophically embrace her lyrical embrace of Mrs. Ramsay's erotic lighthouse embrace. It seems to me that one *must* allow this embrace and walk this dangerous line between revision and Romantic reinscription if one is to do revisionary work within the Western tradition. One must mingle radical critique with recovery of what is submerged but viable in the cultures we inherit. One must embrace, in particular, this ecstatic romance with things, with bodies, with certain lyrical texts, which, as we saw in chapter 3, infused even dominant nineteenth-century discourses of materiality. One must acknowledge the cultural hoarding and cannibalizing of that ecstatic relation while at the same time laboring to resituate it, to redistribute it, to open access to it in the process of decodifying it. One must, finally, as Woolf and Morrison do in contrast to Toomer and Joyce, dematerialize it.

Although racial patriarchy as represented in *Melymbrosia* and *To the Lighthouse* systematically channels the energy of intercorporeality into its own economy, Woolf suggests in this scene that an intercorporeal engagement in the world can nevertheless become a force of resistance to that economy. She hints, that is, that one can recover material resources and orientations from the culture that hoards them and one can turn them into alternative channels. At the close of Mrs. Ramsay's lighthouse reverie the narrative suggests that the sexual energy released in intensely felt, even if heterosexually delimited, intercorporeality may sometimes forestall the colonial–patriarchal appropriation of it. When Mr. Ramsay turns and sees his wife at this moment, he notices her "rapture" and wants her attention. "But he could not speak to her. He could not interrupt her. He wanted urgently to speak to her now that James was gone and she was alone at last. But he resolved, no; he would not interrupt her" (100). Mrs. Ramsay's intercorporeal sexual rapture works here as a force that overpowers the masculine will. Once it does so, Mrs. Ramsay can with dignity give her husband "of her own free will what she knew he would never ask, and called him and [took] the green shawl off the picture frame, and [went] to him" (100). She affirms their turning toward each other most fully when he does not demand it of her, and she thus rescues her sexualized intercorporeal fluency from complete service to his dominance.

But again this current of intercorporeality is problematized by the relation to it of the daughter figure Lily Briscoe, interestingly a single woman with features described as foreign, in particular her "Chinese eyes." For Lily Briscoe's posture within the sensuous (or sensual—the two meanings merge in Woolf) is restless and shifting. On the one hand, like William Bankes she appreciates Mrs. Ramsay's feeling that the physical world draws one out of oneself, "out of solitude reluctantly by laying hold of some little odd or end, some sound, some sight" (99). Bankes and Lily share certain sensations evoked by that physical world. When they walk out together to look at the bay, "it was as if the water floated off and set sailing thoughts which had grown stagnant on dry land, and gave to their bodies even some sort of physical relief. . . . The pulse of color flooded the bay with blue, and the heart expanded with it and the body swam" (33). Lily and Bankes form a relation (and Woolf narrates it) by means of the things they see and touch in common.

And yet Lily resents the intermediating codes that transfigure this intercorporeal world. She resists Mrs. Ramsay's easy enfolding of materiality into married heterosexuality or subordinated femininity, and searches for alternate images of materiality (of which her painting, as we shall see, is one). In reaction to her frustration with the feminine need to socialize all impulses of intercorporeality, Lily is attracted to Mr. Ramsay's "subjectless" view of the world. The image Andrew gives her of the topics of Mr. Ramsay's books intrigues her: they are like "a kitchen table . . . when you're not there" (38). This unpeopled object world seemingly has the virtue of liberation from the social world's demands and from social subordinations of the material world.

But, as the narrative hints, someone has hewn and built and smoothed that table. It is one of those "scrubbed board tables, grained and knotted, whose virtue seems to have been laid bare by years of muscular integrity" (38). Muscled arms make a knotty tree into a scrubbed kitchen table. The world is not simply a collection of unconnected objects. The image of the table cannot remain single and without context, despite Lily's attraction to its unencumbered state. Against her will she sees it "lodged" upside down "in the fork" of the pear tree at which she gazes during her reverie about Mr. Ramsay's books. The table returns to the tree from whence it came; Lily lodges it in its site of material origin. Only with difficulty does she see the table in place of the tree: "With a painful effort of concentration, she focused her mind not upon the silver-bossed bark of the tree, or upon its fish-shaped leaves but upon the phantom kitchen table" (38). Equally painful is her inability to express in words or paint her metaphysical predicament, her conflicting attractions to the phantom table and to the rough-barked tree: "To follow her thought was like following a voice which speaks too quickly to be taken down by one's pencil, and the voice was her own voice saying without prompting undeniable, everlasting, contradictory things, so that even the fissures and humps on the bark of the pear tree were irrevocably fixed there for eternity" (40).

Thus, Lily also finds herself caught between her different relations to materiality; she feels held and calmed, like Mrs. Ramsay, by an embedding materiality that, with all its humps and fissures, connects one in body to others and the world; and she feels drawn, like Mr. Ramsay, to a subjectless vision of materiality that strains toward a "heroic" (39) "muscular integrity" which "scrubs" down all signs of a co-adaptive life—a war-riven world in which one is, as Mr. Ramsay imagines, "stormed at with shot and shell" (29, 49) yet can still march on, bravely and alone.

OBJECTS AS NARRATIVE PIVOTS

The narrative's own tropes and transitions encompass this complexity of attachments by pivoting on imaged objects as well as on words themselves as textual objects. Often those images that express the characters' aloneness or distance from one another harbor within themselves that same physical world that also connects the characters to one another, as the image of the table in the pear tree connects Woolf's two most autonomous characters, Lily Briscoe and Mr. Ramsay. Lily thinks of Mr. Ramsay "through" the table in the pear tree even if only to name or represent the distance between them.

More important, Woolf's narrator uses the objects on which the characters focus in common—such as the urn of geraniums or the break in the hedge—as vehicles for moving from the consciousness of one character to that of another and from one time frame to another. In this intercorporeal narrative practice objects in the world serve as points of intersection carrying the narrator between character and character or past, present, and future. These intersections create the irony in the narrative.

These ironic narrative maneuvers are fully dramatized in the passage spelling out Lily's feelings for Mrs. Ramsay. Around the pivot of Lily's painting the narrative not only moves from the present to the past and back to the present but also, by way of the painting as object, juxtaposes an incomplete moment of past intimacy between Lily and Mrs. Ramsay against a present instant of complete intimacy between Lily and Bankes. And yet the narrative simultaneously uses the painting to hint that, insofar as Mrs. Ramsay is the subject of the painting over which Lily and Bankes meet, Lily achieves intimacy with Bankes through Mrs. Ramsay and with Mrs. Ramsay through Bankes; and all of these relations escape the universal law of marriage which Mrs. Ramsay explicitly enforces.

In "The Window," as Lily stands before her canvas, she recalls one of her late-night conversations with Mrs. Ramsay. They are discussing marriage, and Lily pleads for "her own exemption from the universal law," until finally Mrs. Ramsay falls silent "with every trace of willfulness abolished, and in its stead, something clear as the space which the clouds at last uncover—the little space of sky which sleeps beside the moon" (78). Mrs. Ramsay momentarily lets go her "willful" enforcement of the "universal law" of marriage, an implicitly "natural law" governed, in Romantic thought, by the moon. "In its stead" there opens a "space of sky" next to the moon. Lily, with her head in Mrs. Ramsay's lap, presses close to Mrs. Ramsay's knees, as if pressing her way into that moon-juxtaposed space.

Standing before her painting, Lily recalls this momentary lapse of "willfulness" in Mrs. Ramsay; but she also recalls how she could do nothing more than exert a pressure on Mrs. Ramsay's knees "that Mrs. Ramsay would never know the reason of" (79). She fails to "press through into those secret chambers" so as to achieve "intimacy itself" with Mrs. Ramsay, or to "make her and Mrs. Ramsay one" (70). Therefore on that night, of course, "nothing happened. Nothing! Nothing!" (79). In their late-night meeting Mrs. Ramsay leaves room for, but still has no understanding of, Lily's difference from her ("she liked to be alone; she liked to be herself" [77]). All of these complexities of relationship inform Lily's painting, which she describes as the "residue of her thirty-three years, the deposit of each day's living mixed with something more secret than she had ever spoken or shown in the course of all those days" (81). The painting serves as a repository for Lily's contradictory mixture of emotions toward Mrs. Ramsay, and the process of painting enacts the engagement with the material world which Mrs. Ramsay represents (despite her racial–patriarchal limiting of it). The painting is the object manifesting both Lily's desire for and her failure of intimacy with Mrs. Ramsay.

But the painting also becomes, in the present moment of the text, the vehicle for Lily's intimacy with William Bankes. Even as Lily fails to enter Mrs. Ramsay's heart in this *remembered* moment, Bankes has been studying Lily's painting and has entered her heart in the *present* moment as he stands on the lawn next to her. Lily suddenly realizes that "it had been seen; it had been taken from her. This man had shared with her something profoundly intimate" (83). Lily's immersion in her past memory and her despair over the missed intimacy with Mrs. Ramsay leave her vulnerable to this sudden, unexpected intimacy with Bankes. The painting serves to ground us as readers, in our movement from past to present and from internal monologue to external dialogue, and Lily as character in her shift from alienation to intimacy, from past longing to present affiliation. Through the painting as a visible object in the material world and as a repeated, readable image in the textual world, Woolf plays a kind of narrative joke on Lily, ironizing Lily's attempts at secrecy. Such effects deserve special notice in light of Woolf criticism and feminist criticism in general which emphasize the fusion of women writers' narrators with their characters.[21] On the contrary, at least in Woolf's case, the narrator stations herself *between* characters, within the materiality they share, however unexpectedly or unwillingly, so as to capture the complex multidimensionality of intercorporeal relations.

The irony achieved by the use of objects as narrative pivots also deflates the ideals of motherhood. Lily's painting, her objective correlative for mother and child, provides the basis for an intimacy which surpasses that achieved by the traditional mother and child in a racial–patriarchal culture, just as Woolf's story about a very traditional mother extends and radicalizes what English narrative had so far been able to say about mothers and children, about self and Other. Through Lily's painting Woolf reveals the limits that historically enclose the mother even as she makes the mother figure of Mrs. Ramsay the catalyst for Lily's surpassing those limits. Lily, too, now feels a hint of that complex "common feeling [that] held the whole":

> And, thanking Mr. Ramsay for it and Mrs. Ramsay for it and the hour and the place, crediting the world with a power she had not suspected—that one could walk away down that long gallery not alone anymore but arm in arm with somebody—the strangest feeling in the world, and the most exhilarating—she nicked the catch of her paint-box to, more firmly than was necessary, and the nick seemed to surround in a circle forever the paint-box, the lawn, Mr. Bankes, and that wild villain, Cam, dashing past. (83)

Lily thanks the man and the woman, the problematic heterosexual pair who have nonetheless spawned the subject of her painting and, in turn, catalyzed her relationship with Bankes. She also thanks "the hour and the place," that is, the temporal and spatial realms structuring both the ironies and the intimacies of same-sex and dual-sex intercorporeality. These elements define the whole or the "circle" surrounding the paint box, the lawn, Mr. Bankes, and the dashing Cam. In a similar way Woolf's narrative maneuvering "nicks to" her character's dissonances and contradictions and makes inclusive the material atmosphere enclosing them.

Just as the turns of the narrative cast irony on Lily's skepticism about mutual intercorporeality, they also treat ironically Mrs. Ramsay's idealistic fantasies about it. After her triumphant *boeuf en daube* dinner party she ascends to the nursery and thinks, as we have seen, how the others who are present will "come back to this night; this moon; this wind; this house: and to her, too." But Woolf inserts a narrative detail into the peroration of Mrs. Ramsay's reflections which affords Woolf a means of expressing her critique: "And she felt, *with her hand on the nursery door,* that community of feeling with other people which emotion gives as if the walls of partition had become so thin that practically . . . it was all one stream, and chairs, and table maps, were hers, were theirs, it did not matter whose, and Paul and Minta would carry it on when she was dead" (171; emphasis added).

When Mrs. Ramsay turns the handle of the nursery door on which her hand rests throughout this reverie, the narrative turns with it. And this double "turn" deflates Mrs. Ramsay's heterosexual idealizations, for with it she enters a scene that annoys her by upsetting the "stream of life." Cam is not asleep but is sitting "bolt upright" (already adopting her mother's posture when she faces her antagonists, "suffering, death, the poor" [92]) and arguing with James over "that horrid skull" (171). James, who will inherit his father's idea that "we perish, each alone" (70, 253), "screamed if she touched it" while Cam "couldn't go to sleep with it in the room" (171). James and Cam are indeed carrying on what went before—the antagonism between their parents over the terms of life and death and the external world, represented here in the boar's skull nailed to the nursery wall.

But this implication, astoundingly, both ironizes Mrs. Ramsay's position by exposing her "community of feeling" as a "sequence of struggle"[22] and simultaneously bears out her own sense of life and death: that things will carry on when she is dead; that human connections persist, even if they involve struggles; that we do not "perish, each alone." By sublimely using objects such as the handle to open the door between characters' worlds while also throwing into relief and ironizing the differences between their perceptions, Woolf herself materially "carries on," in her narrative practice, the Janus-faced possibilities of intercorporeality.

So we see that the characters' shared materiality serves as the ground for their struggles with one another, and that these struggles are often patriarchally coded—as with the framing dialogue between Mr. and Mrs. Ramsay about whether tomorrow will or will not be fine. Mrs. Ramsay makes a mutinous claim to the outside world of sea voyages and to a future carried forward by the materiality of that world. Shadowing Mrs. Ramsay's usurpation, the narrator appropriates the objects and gestures within the story so that they structure the temporal and spatial turns of the narrative. She thus recapitulates Mrs. Ramsay's phenomenological mode of being but at the same time extends that mode beyond racial–patriarchal codes in a way that ironizes those codes.

Intercorporeal representation in this way implicitly critiques and dislodges our metaphysical orientation toward objects whereby language encloses objects, and objects in turn serve as vehicles, metaphors, or settings for transcendent human expression. In the nursery scene the door handle is neither merely metaphor nor metonymy; it is enfolded into the scene as a material element of the house of an English Victorian middle-class family. A nursery room with a door and a handle at the top of a house along the stairs of which are hung maps of distant lands: these are material things and spaces that determine the development of Mrs. Ramsay's fantasy at least as much as they project or reflect or symbolize her fantasies.

Moreover, as Woolf shows, such objects may always slip free of the fantasies they help to determine. They may break loose from their function of upholding neat Victorian compartmentalizations, giving way to strife and division. That the physical objects of the social world are continually recoded and recategorized reflects their inherent code-eluding nature. In their substantiality objects both determine and serve our mythologies, but in their autonomy they supersede any one mythology or use. A metal-headed hammer might be made by a culture that builds wooden houses and pounds in nails, but in the hands of another culture it might be used on a gong, or its back end used to peel bark from a tree. Or it might fall to the bottom of the sea, along with drowned statues, all the while remaining a thing that eyes can see and hands pick up, if only to throw it back down. To destroy the hammer—its visibility, its weight—will require labor.

The intercorporeal text works to retrieve such visible, touchable objects from their service to social mythologies, making them trespass on and reconstruct those mythologies. In *To the Lighthouse* Woolf positions her narrator at the point of slippage, of autonomy, or of reversal—at the turn of the door handle, where objects escape their containment within a single universal law or code. She thus recuperates the world of things from the racial–patriarchal mother's and father's mythologies of them. Like Toni Morrison's narrator in *Beloved*, Woolf's intercorporeal narrators make objects and bodies their favored site of narration, the ground of their alternative realism.

But this is not all. Woolf (like other writers of intercorporeality) pushes her narrative another step beyond the racial–patriarchal metaphysics which splits words from things when she makes words themselves act as objects in the world. Words are not simply names for things that fix those things within a logical system, or even sacrifice those things to the coded system. Words are themselves things, as palpable and as subject to material struggle as physical objects, a struggle theorized by Mikhail Bakhtin.[23] Language often functions in Woolf's fiction not to defer or constrict or remove us from "presence," as deconstruction suggests, but to arrange, extend, and multiply the folds of self-presence and of intercorporeality. Mr. Ramsay's repeated exclamation that, "Some one had blundered" (31, 48, 52) intrudes from time to time to interrupt the thoughts of Lily, Bankes, or Mrs. Ramsay and simultaneously to redirect the focus of the narrative, so that we move into their reflections on him. Mr. Ramsay's words become a physical presence to which Lily and Bankes respond; he in turn feels a sudden awareness of himself provoked by their awareness of him through his spoken words. The phrase makes felt the auditory space they share while it also marks the space of their divergence. Its repetition in the text likewise binds together narrative moments even as it accomplishes narrative turning points. Woolf uses this technique again and again to move *between* her characters, and to move them *toward* one another even as they resist or criticize one another, as in the dialogue about the weather or the phrases of the fairy tale which surface now and then. These phrases heard in common by the characters externalize, ironize, and advance the struggles not only between Mr. and Mrs. Ramsay but also between this text and the Romantic, racial–patriarchal narratives of materiality which it revises.

As with objects such as the door handle, these phrases serve to generate a nondeterministic vision of temporality in particular. This re-vision bears most significantly on the question of how social and intercorporeal relations may change, may be transformed over time—clearly a hope on Woolf's part—but without entailing a defensive denial of the continuity of the present and future with the past and without repeating that transcendental narrative which catapults the conscious self beyond the mother-inhabited object-grounded past. In Woolf's narrative structure these spoken phrases constitute moments at which past, present, and future converge to reveal ironies in the characters' connections, ironies which however become levers prying open a transformed future which promises alternative terms of connection. First of all, as we saw with the device of Lily's painting, they draw the characters, and especially the reader, back from the past into which the characters' thought has plunged, resituate them in the present of the text and the world, and therein reorient them to the future toward which both text and world are moving. Just as the characters will "come back to this night; this moon; this house," so too is the reader made to "come back" to the narrative present through these spoken phrases or objects which operate as our main points of orientation in the text. Thus, when Mrs. Ramsay says irritably, "It's too short" (45), as she ends her silent recollection of the Swedish maid's dying father, not only does this phrase carry the reader from "inner" to "outer" worlds by referring both to "life" and to the brown stocking she is knitting; nor does it act only as a sound object by intruding into James's world with its impatient tone; it also strenuously pulls the reader out of the past of Mrs. Ramsay's reverie, pushes us into the present narrative moment in which she measures the stocking against James's leg, and propels us forward toward the end of Mrs. Ramsay's "too short" life.

Through its pivotal place in the text's narrative syntax, this phrase makes us feel *physically* the force of an ongoing temporal movement toward the future, and thus makes us direct participants in the text's dialogue about whether or not it will be fine, whether or not there will be a voyage to the lighthouse, whether materiality will be met or be conquered. We find ourselves caught up in the tangled current moving from past reverie to present activity to future possibility, the stream that joins things gone, things here, things to come—and, more deeply, as this example emphasizes, the current between the dead and the living. This simple phrase makes us fleetingly feel the text that we hold in our hands as the fragile bridge between the writing of it in the past and the reading of it in the present, evoking sensations that will both *pass* in the future and pass *into* the future—all of which may well make us feel, irritably, that "it's too short."

The degree to which the text "lives" and, more generally, to which the dead are dead and the living are inheritors or transgressors is the key question in the rest of the text—not to mention in many of Woolf's novels. The narrative use of objects and phrases as points of continuity, however burdened with stress and ambivalence, seems to suggest that the dead live on, and the living inherit through materiality even as they break the codes that have long enclosed that materiality, a suggestion borne out, as we shall see, by the final section of the novel.

It is true that, in the closing moments of "The Window," Mrs. Ramsay acquiesces in Mr. Ramsay's insistence that "it won't be fine," and this acquiescence precipitates the temporal interruption—of Mrs. Ramsay's life and the characters' interactions—which constitutes the middle section of the book. As with Rachel Vinrace, Mrs. Ramsay's hopeful investment in the possibility of a female-defined voyage meets an abrupt collapse. In that middle section, "Time Passes," Woolf explores how the transcendental flight from materiality results in a tyranny of time that eats away at object-grounded continuity. But just before that rupture Woolf gives one last demonstration of the ways in which materially grounded continuity sustains what has gone before even while exposing the problematic encoding of that materially manifested past.

As he sits with his wife in the drawing room at the end of the day, having relished the pleasures of a novel by none other than that high-Romantic novelist Sir Walter Scott, Mr. Ramsay longs for a romantic declaration of love from *his* Rowena, Mrs. Ramsay, for an affirmation of the order of things like that which he finds in the pages of Scott's novels. But Mrs. Ramsay resists naming their love in his terms, that is, by simply saying "I love you." Instead, she expresses her love in a way that includes the physical world as the mediating term of their connection to each other and puts her declaration back within the context of their continuing struggle over ways of naming that world. She implicitly indicates that theirs is a relationship in which "he could say things—she never could" (185).

Though on the surface a defeat both of her way of naming and of the promise of future human connection (they won't now visit the lonely lighthouse men), Mrs. Ramsay's final admission that "it's going to be wet" signifies within the current of Mr. Ramsay's denial of her relationship to the material world, and so exposes that denial even while it "carries on" the current of their relationship. That is, even as the phrase denies Mrs. Ramsay's desired future, it sustains the contiguousness of past, present, and future which the dialogue of these phrases sets up in the text and thereby upholds her knowledge and challenges his. In turning language "toward others" in this double way, as the narrator tells us, Mrs. Ramsay had "triumphed again. She had not said it: yet he knew" (186).

Furthermore, this "not saying" is enfolded within a physical turning toward each other that reinforces its quiet impact: "Knowing that he was watching her, instead of saying anything she turned, holding her stocking, and looked at him. And as she looked at him she began to smile, for though she had not said a word, he knew, of course he knew, that she loved him. He could not deny it" (185). It is in the next moment that she agrees with him about tomorrow's weather. Although Mrs. Ramsay finally capitulates to Mr. Ramsay's scientific opinion, and thus appears to affirm his claim to higher authority in the material realm, she has used her embeddedness in materiality to limit his claim and to indicate that her handiwork gives her access to uses of materiality that surpass his, leaving *her* triumphant.

The dynamic here remains one of battle, of a "war" waged over things and by means of things and bodies. It will take the mother's death, the father's diminished voyage, and the daughter figure's act of redefining artistic brainwork to extend the nonoppositional intercorporeality of Woolf's narrative structure into the lives of all her characters.

WHEN TIME CONQUERS SPACE

In "Time Passes" the sequences of human intercorporeality are interrupted and, "with all the lamps put out, the moon sunk, and a thin rain drumming on the roof a downpouring of immense darkness began" (189). The pelting of hail in Mr. and Mrs. Ramsay's relationship becomes a steady downpour. The rays of light are extinguished, the moon they were all to "come back to" disappears. It won't be fine, after all. With the rupture of Mrs. Ramsay's plans for a voyage, the narrator drowns us in the dark sea Mrs. Ramsay loves and which, by way of colonial voyaging, buoys her maternal sensibility.

Situated in this underworld of materiality, Woolf's narrator reconfirms, first of all, how the effects of the imbalance in Mr. and Mrs. Ramsay's inter-corporeality—of Mr. Ramsay's "mind like a hand raised shadowing her mind" (184)—linger finally in a way that is fatal to her corporeal existence. For in winning his point about the barometer and the weather, Mr. Ramsay loses Mrs. Ramsay, and this loss provides a virtual allegory for the losses incurred by the scientific view of materiality. In the well-known bracketed passage and subordinate clause, the narrator lets slip news of Mrs. Ramsay's death: "[Mr. Ramsay, stumbling along a passage one dark morning, stretched his arms out, but Mrs. Ramsay having died rather suddenly the night before, his arms, though stretched out, remained empty.]" (194). The narrative syntax sneaks in from behind to snatch the body of Mrs. Ramsay and hold it as ransom, to be returned only with the initiation of a more balanced but also more transgressive intercorporeality.

Like Mr. Ramsay, the first-time reader feels completely unprepared for this death. And yet the paragraph just preceding this one hints—especially after a rereading—at how Western assumptions about the serving role of nature set the scene for Mrs. Ramsay's death:

> The sea tosses itself and breaks itself, and should any sleeper fancying that he might find on the beach an answer to his doubts, a sharer of his solitude, throw off his bedclothes and go down by himself to walk on the sand, no image with semblance of serving and divine promptitude comes readily to hand bringing the night to order and reflecting the compass of his soul. The hand dwindles in his hand; the voice bellows in his ear. Almost it would appear that it is useless in such confusion to ask the night those questions as to what, and why, and wherefore, which tempt the sleeper from his bed to seek an answer. (193)

We might easily interpret this passage according to the formula in which woman equals the physical world; Mrs. Ramsay (a woman) dies, so Mr. Ramsay and the reader lose touch with the order of the physical world. Certainly it seems that the sleeper and Mr. Ramsay might be identified with each other, since, for instance, Mr. Ramsay's hand remains "empty" though "stretched out," and in the sleeper's hand the other's "hand dwindles."

But the narrator's wording does not simply reiterate and uphold this metaphysical and Romantic–patriarchal equation of women with nature and of women's death with men's loss. She deconstructs that equation. She expresses this searcher's flight to the sea as a turning away from bodily human relationships: the sleeper "throws off his bedclothes"; he is tempted "from his bed" to walk by himself and to ask "in solitude" the philosophical questions of "what, and why, and wherefore." This is the traditional transcendental tendency of Western Romantic thought, as depicted, for instance, in Stephen Dedalus, who "turned away" from the girl whose "image had passed into his soul forever," leaving him free to walk the beach in solitude, in "the holy silence of his ecstasy."[24] But the questions of the dreamer, the "sleeper," make no sense, as Stephen discovers, when asked "in such confusion"—so removed, that is, from the "bed," or the place of our bodily entanglement and conception.

In light of this understanding of the bed-abandoning sleeper, we note that it is not nature that fails to answer the sleeper on this night of Mrs. Ramsay's death but an "image with semblance of serving." Likewise, a little further on the narrator concludes that "the *dream* of finding *in solitude* on the beach an answer, was then but a reflection in a mirror, and the mirror itself was but the surface glassiness which forms in quiescence when the nobler powers sleep beneath" (202; emphasis added). Mrs. Ramsay—like the "Angel in the House," like Jean Toomer's Karintha—has been a quiescent mirror for others, especially for Mr. Ramsay; she has buoyed their journeys while their journeys have buoyed her ability to mirror.

And yet all the while her "nobler powers" have "slept beneath," so that when she dies the mirror becomes empty, revealing the deconstructibility and sterility of the aggrandizing mirror in the first place. The vision of the material world as a vehicle for imaging the autonomous self rather than as intimately of a piece with the self makes of it a mirror that can only collapse us narcissistically into ourselves, so that the other's hand dwindles in our hand—especially when we push our moves with the protecting "queen" too far, as Mr. Pepper, Helen Ambrose, and Mr. Ramsay do. In recording the failure of the sleeper in his search for "something alien to the processes of domestic life" (199), Woolf records the failure, and deconstructs the fallacies, of the heroic yet narcissistic and Other-submerging voyage on the sea.

Within the vacuum created by this failure, the Ramsays' house remains empty, confusion multiplies, and "certain airs, detached from the body of the wind (the house was ramshackle after all) crept round corners and ventured indoors" (190). The airs, detached like Mr. Ramsay from the body, echo his questions, asking, "Will you fade? Will you perish?" (195). If, in a cultural world that assigns to the mother all responsibility for nonmastering intercorporeality, the mother dies, the intercorporeal substratum breaks down, and space and time meet as adversaries in a Hegelian contest of opposites. In other words, when the embodied interconnections sustained by Mrs. Ramsay stall, temporality overpowers the cumulative continuity afforded by the spatial and material properties of objects. Here Woolf's narrator stands as witness to the temporal nosings of death, as J. Hillis Miller suggests.[25] With the removal of the mother-centered web of materiality, a disembodied time intrudes "nosily" into the spaces of the house.[26]

The narrator, however, also records the resistance and responses of objects to the pressures of those detached temporal airs. At one point the narrator speaks of a "rupture" that occurs, "as after centuries of quiescence, a rock rends itself from the mountain and hurtles crashing into the valley." This is the moment at which "one fold of the shawl," which has covered the skull that hangs in the nursery, "loosened and swung to and fro" (196). Time is inexorable and immense in its rupturing effects. Death rears its head. Yet the narrator remains stationed within those objects it threatens, swinging with their sway. This simple swinging of Mrs. Ramsay's shawl, recorded as a cataclysmic event by the narrator, thus becomes a narrative antidote to Mrs. Ramsay's quiescence and death. Likewise, when the narrator records that the mirrors in the house, which "had held a world hollowed out in which a figure turned, a hand flashed, the door opened," become "solitary like a pool at evening, far distant," she reincarnates the flash of the hand, the turning figure, even as she registers their immersion under a surface of stillness. The narrator here draws us into a world like Rachel Vinrace's underwater realm of things and spaces, jars and drowned statues, and makes us measure time's erosions and unfoldings from within those things rather than arranging these objects for and within a transcendent temporality. The narrator speaks, as she sometimes does for Mrs. Ramsay in "The Window," from within what seems quiescent.

The full recovery and de-quiescence of this world, however, depends on the labor of a working-class woman of Irish descent. With the figure of Mrs. McNab, Woolf refers again to the sustaining colonialism that keeps in play the energies of intercorporeality. Mrs. MacNab comes from time to time to see to the house and stir up the still pool. She looks into those mirrors in which an Anglo-Saxon hand had turned, a dress had flashed, and she dredges up and parodically mirrors their movements.

What Mrs. McNab sees in the mirror deflates the aggrandizing hopes of those who go alone to the sea in search of final answers as well as of those who imagine ideal marriages between men and women. When she stops to look into the bedroom mirror, Mrs. MacNab sees no grand visions of "absolute good" (199), but only the image of herself "toothless, bonneted. . . . [She] stood and gaped in the glass, aimlessly smiling, and began again the old amble and hobble . . . looking sideways in the glass, as if, after all, she had her consolation, as if indeed there twined about her dirge some incorrigible hope" (196–197). This "dirge" she sings as she works is the "voice of . . . persistency itself, trodden down but springing up again" (196). With Mrs. Ramsay gone, the *other* mother's labor behind her labor becomes visible, unembellished, in the mirror.

The stolid, colonized body that labors in the world of objects without any ennobling myths or human absolutes marks a crucial site of intersection between the physical and the social. That is, the conditions of Mrs. McNab's existence are at once determined by and powerfully resistant to social hierarchies. The foreigner Mrs. McNab, like other such women in Woolf's fiction, embodies a de-mystified and overburdened yet constructive intercorporeality. This is a figure who resists submergence in temporality and death. She labors in a rhythm that reshapes the flat, ceaseless, conquering flow of time. As an agent of continuity and an unromantic body in the world, she somehow heroically counteracts the racial–patriarchal order that would master her and the world she cares for.

Just as Joyce's concern is above all with his Irish-Catholic protagonist, Woolf's is finally with her middle-class Englishwomen. Although the hint of foreignness in Lily's Chinese eyes hints at what Woolf makes explicit in *Three Guineas*—that women really have no country, are always outsiders—still she focuses less fully on women who are lower class and not English. This fact is hardly grounds for critique in itself, since most authors write from their own positions; but the question is whether Woolf makes appropriative use of such figures.

One could argue that her pivotal privileging of non-English, working-class female figures also objectifies them and makes them merely supplements to the main characters. And yet I would qualify that judgment. First of all, in striving to reconfigure materiality and intersubjectivity, Woolf not only ironizes the dominant-class mother figure but also dethrones her by means of the non-English working-class mother figure. Woolf's narrators, moreover, emulate and identify their "in-between" intercorporeal activities with such figures more fully than with middle-class mothers, who are treated with strong irony. Such figures, like Woolf's narrators, come between the dominant-class mothers and their mythologies, like the woman Clarissa Dalloway sees by accident in a window she approaches as if it were a mirror.

One might be led to criticize this identity as well, comparing Woolf's practice to Joyce's in *Ulysses* of modeling his criss-crossing, coincidence-registering narrative after his other-racial character Leopold Bloom. One could suggest that in turning her identification toward these figures of otherness Woolf, like Joyce, generates some of the energy for her transgressing or difference-bridging narrative, and thus makes appropriative use of them. And yet I would call attention to the differences in practice between Joyce and Woolf. Woolf's narrative moves finally beyond all mother figures, English and otherwise, to a daughter whose art resists transcendence of the phenomenal world and instead implicitly politicizes artistic practices insofar as they are of that world. Her strenuous narrative and syntactic reconstructions, extending both Lily's and Mrs. McNab's anonymous voices "of persistency itself" (196), express a shared agency among narrator, middle-class English "daughters," and non-English working-class women.

Certainly "Time Passes" turns from Mrs. McNab to the figure of Lily Briscoe, who, the narrator tells us, "said no"—unlike the earlier sleeper—to "the night flowing down, in purple, his head crowned . . . [said] that it was vapour, this splendour of his, and the dew had more power than he, and [she] preferred sleeping" (214). Woolf's rhetoric of night and purple splendor hints that to resist the lure of self-referential philosophy, so coveted by night-roaming sleepers, is to resist the promise of crowns and kingly power. Tempted though she is by such noble and solitary visions, Lily remains on this night in the house in bed. At dawn she "clutched at her blankets as a faller clutches at the turf on the edge of a cliff. Her eyes opened wide. Here she was again, she thought, sitting bolt upright in bed" (214).

POLITICS IN THE SPACE OF PAINTING

When Lily again sets up her easel on the lawn ten years after Mrs. Ramsay's death, she adopts a posture of readiness, for she faces the same "immense pressure" (228), in the form of Mr. Ramsay, that Mrs. Ramsay did. But she does not feel herself float off, under this pressure, "upon some wave of sympathetic expansion," as Mrs. Ramsay might have (225). She feels herself instead in a house "full of unrelated passions" (221), and with which she has "no relations" (218). Without the bound and binding mother figure to hold it in place, the universe appears fragmented. Lily declines to draw all of the pieces together in Mrs. Ramsay's stead. In returning to the picture she began ten years earlier, she stations her easel like a "barrier" against Mr. Ramsay (223), turning away from him "as if any interruption would break the frail shape she was building" (220). Lily works to tunnel her way into that in-between space the narrator and Mrs. McNab have occupied all along. She does so by means of a movement between nearby simple objects and the open horizon of the bay.

When Mr. Ramsay approaches the space of her painting activity, the physical world appears to empty to Lily, its power drained away: "The whole horizon seemed swept bare of objects to talk about." But then she notices Mr. Ramsay's boots; and here she finds the "little odd or end" in the material world which will help both of them out of themselves, allowing them to move on, and eventually enabling Lily to shape the "relation *between* those *masses*" in her painting (221; emphasis added). In response to her admiring his boots, such a trivial detail, Lily expects from Mr. Ramsay "one of his sudden roars of ill-temper, complete annihilation" (229). But Mr. Ramsay smiles. He delights in his boots. And Lily sees in him something "which was new," as if he had passed into "that final phase . . . as if he had shed worries and ambitions, and the hope for sympathy and the desire for praise, had entered some other region, was drawn on, as if by curiousity, in dumb colloquy, whether with himself or another" (233). Lily, too, enters that final phase and "other region" in this last section of the novel.

Lily's "colloquy" with Mr. Carmichael, Mr. Ramsay, and Mrs. Ramsay represents her own discovery of Woolf's method, an orientation from within objects that includes the work of art as one of those objects. The narrator–painter must discover her art as a thing which is subject to the world and which at the same time has a role in making the world to which it is subject. Such a self-present positioning gives the artist a three-dimensional open space within which to move against the collapsing of space into racial patriarchy's two-dimensional oppositions. From within that space the artist can carve something that exerts its own pressure in the hierarchy-imprisoned world of objects.

Thus, Lily's act of painting is a visceral one which flows in a rhythm between Other and self, nearness and distance. She makes her first "stroke" of the paintbrush "with a curious physical sensation, as if she were urged forward and at the same time must hold herself back" (235). And then begins "the dancing rhythmical movement, as if the pauses were one part of the rhythm and the strokes another, and all were related" (236). This is the rhythm of momentarily unbridled, un-Hegelian intercorporeality, in which one is urged out toward the other through the materiality one shares with another, and yet one inhabits a space different from the other's; indeed, this shared physicality with the Other is the very source of one's separateness from the Other, and one's attempts at expression are a kind of "stroking" of the Other. All of this creates "a curious physical sensation," which recalls Mrs. Ramsay's sexual reverie as she watches the "strokes" of the lighthouse: "Her mind kept throwing up from its depths, scenes, and names, and sayings, and memories and ideas, like a fountain spurting over that glaring hideously difficult white space, while she modeled it with greens and blues" (238). We might wonder if Woolf's choice of the word "mind" both here and in Mrs. Ramsay's earlier reverie evades the sexuality she taps; or it may work to sexualize the secretions of the intellect, to imply that "the mind" moves in physical channels rather than in purely abstract ones or to collapse the distinction between mind and body altogether.

In this scene for Lily, as for Woolf, the intercorporeal intersections of body and world extend to the experience of making art, are even epitomized in the experience of making art. Art is not a metaphysically generated "decoration for the processes of thought" (66), as Mr. Ramsay suggests. Even as it reimagines bodies such as Mrs. Ramsay's as abstractions, as points in a triangle, art also redefines thought as embodied and the making of art as physical sensation rather than, say, the means to Stephen Dedalus's impalpable, imperishable being. Art herein "takes its place among the things it touches" (*VI*, 133), and in this way, more than any other, Woolf and Lily render art political.

This self-referential or reversible immersion in the processes of art and in the "thing itself" does not, then, reflect a withdrawal from history by Woolf and other modern novelists. Art, as Woolf would fully explore in *Between the Acts*, plays its part in history, and not merely in an ethereal realm of "culture." With Lily's painting Woolf goes so far as to imply that art objects themselves, whether texts or paintings, may offer the means for thrusting oneself beyond that which binds one to the object codings of the past. The artist who builds and interacts in a material medium simultaneously takes the world as it is and hurls herself, the audience, and the world itself forward into a future different from what has been. Through such bodily situated art modern novelists attempt to intervene in history, especially in that political history which ranks and appropriates things and bodies.

As she paints, all the while feeling "a curious physical sensation . . . as if some juice necessary for the lubrication of her faculties were squirted" (235), Lily begins to consider this function of art to provide continuity yet transformation. She begins to review Mr. Carmichael's conviction that "nothing stays; all changes; but not words, not paint"—and not "what they attempted" (268). As she considers this function of art, Lily begins to weep. Her crying, like the art precipitating it, both recognizes and ruptures the past bequeathed by Mrs. Ramsay. Her tears, like her art, "rent the surface pool" and disrupt that quiescence which had earlier slept beneath the surface, in the form of Mrs. Ramsay:

> One might say, even of this scrawl, not of the actual picture, perhaps, but of what it attempted, that it "remained forever," she was going to say . . . when looking at the picture, she was surprised to find that she could not see it. Her eyes were full of a hot liquid. . . . She addressed old Carmichael again. What was it then? What did it mean? Could things thrust up their hands and grip one . . . ? For one moment she felt if they both got up, here, now on the lawn, and demanded an explanation, why was it so short, why was it so inexplicable . . . then, beauty would roll itself up; the space would fill; those empty flourishes would form into shape. (268)

As she did earlier, Lily appeals to the spatial and temporal dimensions of the present—"here, now on the lawn"—for an understanding of the past and its ability to act like the "things" that "thrust up their hands and grip one." At first, as earlier, "nothing happened." But in the next moment Lily feels stirred by "the sense of someone there, of Mrs. Ramsay, relieved for a moment of the weight the world had put on her, staying lightly by her side . . . raising to her forehead a wreath of white flowers" (269). With this inkling of a present past, of Mrs. Ramsay returned without her "willfulness" because she is "relieved for a moment of the weight the world had put on her," Lily pauses in her painting rhythm and walks out to look at the bay—"moved as she was by some instinctive need of distance and blue" (270).

In creating her painting, Lily paces the space between the bay and her easel, creating a measure of distance that will enable her to fill in, on her own terms, the space in her painting: to see Mr. Ramsay's boat as one among others and make her own separate voyage out. Like the "space" of sky beside the moon which the absence of Mrs. Ramsay's willfulness earlier made accessible for a moment, so this return, provoked by Lily's painting, of an unwillful Mrs. Ramsay makes possible Lily's filling in of the "glaring" space in her picture.

At one point Lily comments on the "extraordinary power" (279) of distance: "So much depends, she thought, upon distance: whether people are near or far from us; her feeling for Mr. Ramsay changed as he sailed further and further across the bay" (284). Her involvement with Mr. Ramsay is changed but not dissolved by distance. As far as he might go, the distance always spins out her feelings for him, and those feelings exert their pressure on what she creates. In other words, it is not the case that distance, whether of time or of space, drains away the power of feeling; rather, the spaces and objects filling the distance define the contours of what Lily calls "these emotions of the body" (265). Distance is the space between us which is opened by our movement away from the past into the future and shaped by the objects that endure in the future.

Likewise Cam, looking back from the boat at the summer house on its island, comments on the power of distance (280, 284); and the very overlap of Cam's and Lily's reciprocal distances suggests that distance is the space in-between two reversible bodies, which arises out of those bodies' positions in the world and allows them to move forward into a future which both "carries on" the struggles and keeps open the possibility of transforming those struggles. Distance is thus the "half-transparent envelope" (272) which "holds the whole" (286), across which things manifest their co-adaptation to and transformation of one another. It is the net of intimacy, thrown wide. It is the space of imagination, of "nonsense," of the leap "from the pinnacle of a tower into the air" (121) into the world of the Other: the shore of the lighthouse island.

"They will have landed," says Mr. Carmichael, watching the distant boat, and Lily feels "that she had been right. . . . They had been thinking the same things and he had answered her without her asking him anything" (309). The space between her and Carmichael has also been "full" though silent. And so through the "centre of emptiness" Lily draws "a line there, in the centre" (310), thus marking the invisible as the matrix of the visible, a matrix no longer holding and held in place by the mother.

If a kin–patriarchal metaphysics, for purposes of conquest, divides the multi-dimensional horizontal world along an oppositional, hierarchical boundary between indoors and outdoors or insider and outsider, colonizing space for the maneuvers of mind, Woolf's opening of a "full" space between Cam and Lily retrieves from under the surface of the quiescent pool the submerged "birth of the world," to borrow Rachel Vinrace's phrase. Lily and the narrator have succeeded in swimming in this watery medium which Rachel had to die to enter. In such a narrative world the journey of father and children to the lighthouse—their voyage out—becomes one small object in the field of vision rather than the beginning and end of all vision and all voyaging. Lily can finally make boats—even boats carrying the kin–patriarchal mother's "kin"—serve her own "vision." Immersed in her voyage among things, Lily finally marvels at how "one glided, one shook one's sails (there was a good deal of movement in the bay, boats were starting off) between things, beyond things. Empty it was not, but full to the brim" (285).

In *To the Lighthouse* the characters, especially Lily, struggle with the possibility of recovering by repeating the mother's intercorporeal mode of being, but also aim to avoid adopting the patriarchal code within which the mother's intercorporeality has been delimited. The narrator traces this struggle by situating herself within the seen objects and by orienting the reader around the heard phrases that connect the characters to the mother. The narrator in this way carries on within the current of physical connections and spaces traditionally attributed to and sustained by the mother, even when the mother figure herself balks at the end toward which they might carry her, indeed, even after such currents have dashed the mother against the rocks. Woolf extends the intercorporeality of persons and things beyond the realm of the racialized colonial mother, breaking up the tradition that both supports and burdens such mothers.

It is necessary to emphasize that neither Woolf's nor Lily's "common feeling" is a naive humanist "fantasy of totality" of the kind against which Julia Kristeva warns feminists.[27] Woolf renders "all sorts of waifs and strays of things. . . . A washer-woman with her basket; a rook; a red-hot poker; the purples and grey-greens of flowers" to get at what Lily Briscoe calls "the common feeling that held the whole" (286). Yet within that "common feeling" Woolf evokes ironies and antipathies; she insinuates the presence of violations, as with the suggestive red-hot poker inserted into the preceding series of images. Woolf's prose moves into the "in-between" of her characters' fleshly being, discovers its folds and ruptures, embraces its curves and arabesques. Likewise, far from maintaining the snobbery, prudery, or ethereality with which Woolf has often been associated, her narratives sensualize the processes of thought and speech, of painting and writing. Woolf thereby transgresses those divisions between sensation and knowledge, mother and adult, mind and world so complicit in the kin–patriarchal boundaries of race, nation, and sex.

7

Burning Down the House:
Interruptive Narrative in *Invisible Man*

It should be clear by now—especially if we also think of novels such as William Faulkner's *Sound and the Fury* or *Absalom! Absalom!*, Jean Rhys's *Good Morning, Midnight,* or Marcel Proust's *Remembrance of Things Past*—that to be a white modernist novelist is not a matter of being a race-neutral writer whose work takes shape free from considerations of race and grows out of autonomous and self-originating white traditions. The identities, settings, and fates of white characters in modern novels involve racial or racialized colonial questions; meanwhile, the traditions behind these novels themselves took shape in contexts permeated by race, including not only slavery and imperialism but also racialized class transformations. Since at least the eighteenth century, Western aesthetic traditions, especially those that invoke notions of transcendence, formed as racial traditions; they work with race-inflected and therefore also gender-inflected aesthetic terms. I consider Romanticism a crystallizing moment for the formation of these terms, although James Joyce points as far back as Shakespeare and even implicates the whole of Judaeo-Christian thought. Modernism distinguishes itself in part by highlighting these terms—and by challenging, through narrative form, the metaphysical values that underlie them.

In this context we can see more clearly than ever the falseness of the question whether the novels of Jean Toomer and Ralph Ellison are best read with an eye to questions of race, which presumably are specific to the black tradition, or with an eye to universals, which presumably align these authors with white traditions. Rather, race itself should be understood as a universal that shapes the interests of both traditions.[1] Since black and white literary practices form in dialogue and confrontation with each other over questions of race and transcendence, a full understanding of these authors must attend to both traditions. I am referring not to any mere borrowing or appropriation of literary strategies on either side but rather to an underlying logic whereby the racial elements of the one tradition (strategically implicit in white tradition and strategically explicit in black) depend on the presence of the other; and those racial configurations derive, in turn, from a logic of gender in which feminized matter generates a masculinized, race-bounded art. What I call the *interruptive* narrative of *Invisible Man* attempts to scuttle these boundaries, not only in its miscegenation, so to speak, of the bordering traditions,[2] but also in its exposure of the gender and metaphysical logic that structures those traditions.

INTERRUPTING RACIAL–PATRIARCHAL METAPHYSICS

In *Cane* and *Ulysses* races intermarry and mothers transgress the boundaries they should reproduce, and yet the narratives remain beholden to the eugenic and Romantic connection between race mothers and cultural production. The texts' endings contrive to call on the very logic of race culture which their beginnings and middles have thoroughly problematized, subsuming female embodiment in their winged, son-enabling endings. Whereas authors such as Woolf labor to avoid this contradiction by writing their way through and then past the race mother, other authors, whose novels I call *interruptive*, consider any return to this figure unacceptable. But how, if one inherits a race–cultural aesthetic, can one create a text without recreating the race mother who has been instrumental to the culture's text-making practice?

Ralph Ellison's protagonist in *Invisible Man* undertakes to sidestep the matrix wherein text-needs-race-needs-mother. He pursues the possibility of "being more than a member of a race," guided in his pursuit by a revision of Stephen Dedalus's ambition in *Portrait.* "Stephen's problem," the narrator recalls a college teacher saying, "was not actually one of creating the uncreated conscience of his race, but of creating the uncreated features of his face. Our task is that of making ourselves individuals."[3] Likewise would the invisible man leave behind all enabling racial mythologies and in so doing avoid dependence on and reattachment to the race mother. He would speak as an "individual," not as a race brother or race son.

But he encounters difficulties in this undertaking. First, a certain amount of excision and abridgment is required by the project to disentangle the self from the race. History, memory, and embodiment work against such a project. One must closet oneself, de-temporalize oneself, disembody oneself. And by embracing a present without a past, or speaking in a voice without a body, or living in a room without a door, one risks becoming as invisible as racial patriarchy might wish.

But if one can determine one's own invisibility, if one is born not of a flesh-and-blood mother but of one's own scribbling, invisible hand, can one speak a story undetermined by racial patriarchy? By writing free of a body (as culturally authorized writers presume to do), can one follow to its extreme the metaphysical logic of racial patriarchy and turn that logic against itself by generating discourse from those it would silence? And in the process can one make silenced bodies speak their own erasure, thus radically putting in question the logic which assumes a rupture between body and discourse?[4]

This is what Ellison's narrator and all interruptive narrators succeed in doing: they make discourse speak the cultural invisibility of their bodies and therein reveal how the body comes to shape the terms of even the most body-erasing speech. Interruptive narrators do indeed put discourse in the place of the speaker's temporally cumulative body; but they meanwhile ironically reconstitute the place occupied by the past and the body, pointing to the impossibility of total effacement. In Samuel Beckett's interruptive novel *Molloy* the narrator exposes his story as mere writing and willful fabrication, continually revising and unfixing its details, explicitly conceding, "Perhaps I'm inventing a little, perhaps embellishing."[5] Meanwhile he hints that these unreliable, embellished stories (for instance of "A or C, I can't remember") displace other stories of "other things calling me" such as "my hand on my knee . . . the heavily veined back, the pallid row of knuckles. But that is not . . . what I wish to speak of now" (11). In these narratives, as this "now" hints, the story is continually reconstituted in the form of a present that paradoxically registers by explicitly deferring the narration of an embodied (reversible, self-touching) self originating in the past.

In particular, interruptive narratives displace the mother figure who epitomizes conventionally the bodily origin of the self in the past; and yet the narrators' displacement of her also reflects their identity with her. As Molloy says of his mother, "I have taken her place. I must resemble her more and more" (7). He further hints at the way his self-negating use of language originates in his negating relation to his body-affiliated mother: "I called her Mag because for me, without my knowing why, the letter g abolished the syllable Ma, and as it were spat on it. . . . And at the same time I satisfied a deep and doubtless unacknowledged need to have a Ma, that is a mother, and to proclaim it, audibly. For before you say Mag you say Ma, inevitably" (17). Before you erase the mother and "take her place," you acknowledge her presence; before you use speech to spit upon, as it were, the body, you inevitably speak from and of the body. Thus do interruptive narratives replace the very body whose history they ostensibly erase. Likewise does Sasha in *Good Morning, Midnight* adopt the present tense to write and unwrite her past as a hostile Other would write it for her—seeming to empty herself of past and of voice yet all the while speaking, and speaking of the past.[6]

The visibility and readability—the presence—of these interruptive narratives extend the visibility of their narrators' bodies into the present even if this discursive presence also substitutes for their bodies. To write of an invisible body returns it to the visible in another form, that is, in the same discursive form a racial–patriarchal metaphysics would deny it. Interruptive writing circuitously extends the disenfranchised body's presence into the discursive realm which had been occupied hegemonically by other bodies. In this sense interruptive narratives follow the logic of a body–discourse split to subvert the intentions of that splitting and finally to expose its untenability. In *Good Morning, Midnight* and *Molloy*, as in Ellison's text, the narrators construct visible narratives of invisibility, and they do so from within enclosed spaces, in a past-displacing present, so as to escape the determinations of the embodying mother figure with whom the body–discourse split has been made to originate.

I have suggested that the will to avoid a late-Romantic recuperation of the mother figure, or even an appearance of such recuperation, motivates the writing of interruptive narrative. Such narratives rightly pinpoint the mother figure's systemic function and work toward an excision of her that would free narrative of her conservative influence. For although intercorporeal narratives vigilantly resist recuperation and replace the mother with a body-coordinating narrator, they may still be misunderstood within the culture of racial patriarchy as celebrating the mother figure, and may perhaps be dismissed for this reason as "too sentimental," a designation Woolf anticipated for *To the Lighthouse*.[7]

And yet in writing interruptive narrative authors not only avoid the misreading or reappropriations to which intercorporeal narrative is vulnerable; they also choose to make felt in their narrative structure the forces that resist a nontranscendental reconfiguration of body and language which works through and past the mother figure. We may note here an important difference in the interruptive problematics of male and female protagonists. Whereas for the female protagonist the need to undertake a circuitous, interruptive strategy for reinscribing the displaced body seems to arise mainly from woman–woman, often daughter–mother, hostilities, for the male protagonist the need arises in the context of male–male peer group hostilities. Women's struggle to escape the role of border-reproducing mother plays itself out in encounters with other women—as, for instance, in the ambivalent relation between Anna and Molly in Doris Lessing's *Golden Notebook* or in Ursa's distancing herself from the lesbianism of Cat in Gayl Jones's *Corregidora*.

It becomes clear, by contrast, in the narrative of *Invisible Man* that the male protagonist might reconstitute his relation to the mother figure and shape another kind of narrative if his approach to her did not always bring the threat of violence from other men, as we shall see it continually does. (This threat of black male–male violence in Ellison's novel should also be read in light of the increasing unrest within some urban African American communities.)[8] That is, not only does the general threat of cultural reappropriation of any story involving the race mother discourage intercorporeal narrative, but also the more specific threat of reaction against those who would challenge the boundaries of male identity upheld by the mother figure militates against the adoption of intercorporeal narrative.

In *Invisible Man* Ellison self-consciously represents this male resistance to mother-reconfiguring, nonmetaphysical speech. At the same time, however, Ellison's revisions of the "Mary" section of the novel suggest that his own narrative is delimited by this resistance, at the extratextual, cultural level. That is, Ellison to some extent internalizes the culture's censoring of intercorporeal narrative possibilities. Let us turn first, however, to the text's explicit framing of the forces of male–male resistance.

THE RACE MOTHER'S SONS

The invisible man's reefer-induced dream in the prologue serves as an allegory of the confrontations with both mothers and other men that the invisible man, and Ellison through him, would "interrupt" and avoid. Descending into a "break" in time created by the music of Louis Armstrong, the narrator enters a world specifically of black mothers. The passage is one of only three that are italicized in the entire novel, all of them containing references to mothers.

> *And beneath the swiftness of the hot tempo there was a slower tempo and a cave and I entered it and looked around and heard an old woman singing a spiritual . . . and beneath that lay a still lower level on which I saw a beautiful girl the color of ivory pleading in a voice like my mother's as she stood before a group of slaveowners who bid for her naked body.* (9)

Underneath the music of Louis Armstrong lies the music of old black women and beneath this music there unfolds the drama of ownership of the black mother's body—a mother whose skin color suggests the master's sexual ownership of her own mother and whose voice recalls the invisible narrator's mother. We glimpse the slave history which reaches forward, through the narrator's mother, to his own story. But the glimpse comes in an italicized "break" in time which the narrator soon closes. He determines to leave behind this world of mothers so as to free himself from the history she embodies.[9]

Before he manages to do so in this sequence, however, this submerged vision of the black mother opens up even more fully to reveal the intraracial, homosocial battle that takes shape around the subordinate-race mother. Following the passage just quoted, another old mother's voice suddenly interrupts the *"more rapid tempo"* of a black preacher's (recalling the women's interruption of the preacher which so unsettled Kabnis in *Cane*). She moans to the narrator who has entered this world, *"Go curse your God, boy, and die,"* and then she goes on to tell the story of her mothering of sons by a white master, how she *"hates"* the master and yet *"loves"* him because she loves her sons. In response the narrator tells her, *"I too have become acquainted with ambivalence. That's why I'm here"* (10). The ambivalence which connects them here, however, also spawns a force that separates them, in the form of other black men resisting ambivalence.

In this reverie those men are literally the black mother's sons. Her difficulties of ambivalence develop in relation to them as well as to her master: she stands between the white man and the black men. She loved the master because of her sons, yet the sons forced her to kill the master before they cut him to pieces, as they threatened. One of these sons now appears in the reverie, punches the narrator, and leads him away from the woman. His gesture ostensibly is one of protecting the mother (*"You made Ma cry!"*), but it also serves as self-protection against the awful fact of the story she has to tell: that her rape and the son's conception are one thing, that the son's birth by her and his dispossession through her are one thing. Her pivotal position as link to white culture—as matrix of biracialism and as stolen maternal and sexual origin (historically arranged) of bodily identity—makes her not just a victim but the apparent *cause* of ambivalence, as is also the case for Jean Toomer's Kabnis. This motherly predicament engages the narrator's empathy, but it also pits him against his black brothers, sons of a raped mother for whom they fight even as they silence her speech, a mother to whom the narrator would speak and listen if he could only sidestep the fight with her sons.

But if he cannot sidestep that fight without also drawing away from the mother, he will draw away from her so as to sidestep the fight, for that fight threatens his life. At the close of this reverie the narrator lurches away from the sons and out into the street. His leg is scraped by a car, suggesting the risk of life and perhaps also of phallic injury connected with "hearing" the raped black mother. (It is interesting to note that Beckett's Molloy also suffers from a collision-induced leg injury, which is what initially keeps him from visiting his mother and yet also leads to his "taking her place.") Emerging from italics, the narrator announces: "I had discovered unrecognized compulsions of my being— even though I could not answer "yes" to their promptings. I haven't smoked reefer since, however . . . because to see around corners is enough. . . . But to hear around them is too much; it inhibits action" (13). This reverie sequence reiterates the link, dramatized in *Cane,* between ambivalence toward the dispossessed race mother and competition with black brothers: in both instances black brothers struggle to censor the black mother's story by adapting it. To avoid this old drama in which one becomes a speaking man by silencing a race mother, the

179

narrator formulates his resolve to say no to what he understands as the "unrecognized compulsions" of his being and excise, or at least set aside in italics, these connections to the race mother.

Critics have argued persuasively for a distinction between the limited knowledge of Ellison's protagonist, who naively lives the events between college and the riot, and the superior knowledge of Ellison's narrator, who speaks in this prologue and arranges the entire narrative. Nonetheless, it appears from this passage that the narrator shares his youthful self's hesitation to "hear around those corners" from which mother figures speak. In fact, as I will show, Ellison's excision of an earlier version of the protagonist's first meeting with Mary, the book's main mother figure, suggests that he himself shares this hesitation with his protagonist and his narrator.

Protagonist, narrator, and author all find it difficult to avoid the battle of racial patriarchy, both within and between races. Much as the protagonist works to substitute unencumbered "action" and peacemaking speech for competition, he repeatedly gets pushed back into the ring, so to speak, by other characters and, indirectly, by Ellison. And yet once in the ring Ellison's narrator and protagonist (and by implication Ellison himself) step inside the opponent's sense of time only to inhabit once more the gap where black mothers' stories are closeted, creating textual moments in which the pressures of history and motherly hand are exerted within the interruptive story, although quickly brushed off.

To this extent Ellison, like Toomer and Joyce, exposes the limits of his own narrative practice. The fractured narrative structure of *Invisible Man* represents both the interruptions by which the protagonist attempts to avoid this overdetermined racial–patriarchal battle and the mother-inhabited breaks into which he repeatedly falls, and within which the author hints at the impossibility of silencing the body's mother-associated past or of disembodying the narrative's discursive maneuvers.

A NARRATIVE BATTLE ROYAL

Ellison's battle metaphor for his protagonist's predicament indicates his self-consciousness about the conditions of narrative self-interruption, especially insofar as his narrative's rhythm reenacts the dynamics of battle, including a series of knockout falls into temporal gaps or "nodes." In the prologue the narrator openly employs a boxing metaphor for his situation,[10] and he describes how the fight creates the conditions for his slippage in time. Like an amateur boxer in a ring with a prizefighter, the narrator explains, nothing is expected from an invisible—or subordinate-race—man; he is a mere surface for the "amazingly scientific" blows of a prizefighter. (Science figures again later in the text as a force antagonizing the protagonist's body and constricting his history—in the scientific doctors and the scientific Brotherhood.) But the amateur may surprise his opponent with a knockout punch if he suddenly steps into the "ebb" in the prizefighter's "violent flow of rapid rhythmic action" (8). Likewise, an invisible man sees and hears without being seen or heard so that "instead of the swift and imperceptible flowing of time, you are aware of its nodes, those points where time stands still or from which it leaps ahead. And you slip into the breaks and look around" (8). In the prologue it is within one of these "nodes" where "time stands still" that the narrator has encountered the ambi-valent slave mother and her boxing sons.

In the youth of the protagonist the boxing-match metaphor for the conditions of racial patriarchy—including mother-harboring "breaks"—finds literal, if surreal, expression first of all in the battle royal. Here the white men parade before the black boys the supreme evidence of their racial–patriarchal ascendancy: an owned, naked, shapely white woman. Although the protagonist does not desire the white woman strictly as a white woman (though her womanly body attracts him), he does desire the male power she represents. All of the humiliations of exposed desire and blind battle are worth the moment when he will have an audience with powerful white men: "I wanted to deliver my speech more than anything else in the world, because I felt that only these men could judge truly my ability. . . . I began fighting carefully now" (25). He even murmurs to himself the words of his speech as he swings at the other, invisible black fighters. So as to win a share of dominance, a share of the right to speak, the narrator engages fully in the homosocial "battle" set up for him by the dominant men.

In the process, as prescribed in racial–patriarchal metaphysics, he is reduced to a body without a head. The invisible man's blindfolded state intensifies his sense of visceral invisibility. He becomes highly aware, for instance, of his saliva "like hot bitter glue," and even the blindfold itself is like an emanation from his own body, "a thick skin-puckering scab" (22). His blindness has now become part of his body rather than evidence of its incompleteness, even as Ellison's narrative makes his protagonist's body felt by describing its ruptured self-presence. His unseeing head meets its appropriate knockout end by way of a blow which "sent my right eye popping like a jack-in-the-box" (25). The battle royal caricatures the competition against white men and between black men which keeps the young black man invisible and blinded; at the same time Ellison hints at how the invisible body (invisible but still implicitly present, like the a priori sound of "Ma" in "Mag") becomes a condition for the protagonist's and narrator's speech.

The battle royal scene just hints that these racial–patriarchal conditions of homosocial competition and invisible embodiment circle around the mother. Left alone in the ring with the biggest of the fighters, Tatlock, the protagonist attempts to substitute alliance for competition. As they lock arms momentarily, he whispers the suggestion that one of them fake a knockout so they may stop fighting and split the prize. But, in a dynamic magnified in the culture at large, the white men's entertainment has become the other black man's fight. Tatlock whispers back that he'll break the protagonist's behind not for them but "for *me*, sonofabitch!" (24). In a second pause in their fighting rhythm, the invisible man again attempts to bribe Tatlock into withdrawing from the competitive battle, but Tatlock hisses, "'Give it to your ma,'" meanwhile "ripping me beneath the heart" (25). In response to this heart blow, he then acts out the only possible remaining attachment, one that is sustained *through* the battle and in opposition to mother attachment: "And while I still held him I butted him and moved away" (25).

The protagonist will be in a position to repeat this contradictory butting embrace with other black men throughout the book—with men who, like Tatlock, run the "race race" for themselves against (and yet for) white men: with Bledsoe, with Lucius Brockway, with Ras, and even psychologically with his grandfather. Repeatedly, these butting embraces with other men stun the protagonist and slip him against his will into a node in time where a mother figure lurks. That is, the invisible man keeps stepping, unwittingly and unintentionally, inside his opponents' sense of time and finding there the sexual ownership of women on which the entire male world of time and competition rests.

Having arranged this framing battle metaphor for the first public speech of the invisible man, chapter 3 then frames its own "speech" similarly by creating a *narrative* "battle royal" which likewise slips the protagonist, even more explicitly and disturbingly, into the underworld of black mothers' abused bodies. The chapter intertwines and stakes against one another opposing men's narratives of the material world, all of which frame women's sexuality within racial–patriarchal mythologies: the invisible man's narrative of the feminized college campus against Norton's narrative of the feminized college campus, the protagonist's half-formed narrative of fate against Norton's narrative of fate, and finally the collision of all of these with Trueblood's whitewashed narrative of his rape of his daughter.

The narrator (not simply the protagonist) prefigures the dynamic between Norton's and the protagonist's narratives in a cynical retrospective narrative of the college which contrasts with Norton's later story about it. At the opening of the chapter the narrator's recollections of the college move in a downward, de-naturalizing trajectory from the beautiful to the barren, thus reflecting his desire to dematernalize his story. At first the narrator remembers that "honeysuckle and wisteria hung heavy from the trees and white magnolias mixed with their scents in the bee-humming air" (34). His narrative of nature originally partakes of the Romantic conflation of materiality and female sexuality, as he reimagines how he "walked along the forbidden road that winds past the girls' dormitories" until he reached a "dry riverbed, tangled with brush and clinging vines." The bridge over the riverbed was made "for trysting," although here at this school it remains "virginal and untested" (35).

But as the narrator approaches, in memory, the "southern verandas half-a-city block long," which seem to stand for white women's elaborately housed sexuality, there is a "sudden forking, barren of buildings, birds, or grass, where the road turned off to the insane asylum" (35). This sexualized narrative of nature ruptures at the forking of, or opposition between, white women's and black women's sexuality: "I always come this far and open my eyes" (35). The season abruptly changes to winter; we enter the "quietness" between the notes (recalling the pauses in Lous Armstrong's music) of a Christmas carol, and the pause between notes expresses "an ache as though all the world were loneliness" (35). Within this pause or node in time, within a song, the narrator has a vision of stifled black womanhood, as he did in the prologue while listening to Louis Armstrong. He tells us how he stands still "as for an answer" until he sees in his mind's eye "a river, sluggish and covered with algae more yellow than green in its stagnant stillness," from beyond which he hears "the drunken laughter of sad, sad whores" (35). All of these, he imagines, exist in the field beyond the asylum, at the end of the road opposite that other fork edged with elaborate verandas—precisely where he has balked in his fertile narrative of the college campus. This narrative rupture proceeds from the racialization of sexuality.

Following this vision of sad black women the narrator again breaks off. He stands suddenly at the monument of the "college Founder, the cold father symbol" wondering "what was real, what solid, what more than a pleasant *time-killing* dream? For how could it have been real if I am now invisible?" (36; emphasis added). Faced with this paradox of, on the one hand, the acute materiality of his past, leading backward to tropes of pained black womanhood, and, on the other hand, the invisible materiality of his present, lived in the shadow of the "time-killing," white-friendly patriarch, the narrator concludes that the myth of fertile origins is the illusion that prepares the road to barren disillusion.

With this conclusion the narrator not only rejects the problematic Romantic mythology of nature and women partly upheld by Toomer's narrators, but also eclipses the possibility of an alternative, nonoppositional narrative of materiality of the kind written by Virginia Woolf and Toni Morrison. The Romantic and the cynical appear as the only two possibilities: this appearance of an either-or choice between disbelief and Romantic belief, with no viable alternative, operates as the grounding assumption of an interruptive narrative. The college's beauty is merely "the product of a subtle magic"—a magic which turns out to consist of the "sizable checks" left each spring by the millionaires from the North (37).

The myth of the fertile woman as origin supports and mystifies what is actually an economy, as the narrator here recognizes. Therefore, the narrator wills a rewriting of his feminized memories of materiality: "I recall, instead of the odor of seed bursting in springtime, only the yellow contents of the cistern spread over the lawn's dead grass" (36). Not only does the denigration of black women complicate the storyteller's need to build a cultural mythology around her, as we saw with Jean Toomer's Kabnis; but also, for this narrator, that denigration sends him ricocheting away from materiality and from black women altogether, leaving unabsorbable any narratives about them. Again, it is noteworthy that the narrator, to whom these memories belong (and not simply the naive protagonist), defensively blocks out those stories, suggesting that Ellison himself must do the same. The general absence in *Invisible Man* of black women who are peers or even potential lovers of the protagonist does after all seem to recapitulate this excising of the stories of black women.

And yet mother narratives keep returning to engulf the protagonist (and perhaps the narrator) against his will. The most dramatic illustration is in the Trueblood encounter. In fact, the more the protagonist attempts to stay within the boundaries of white cultural norms and narratives, the more disruptively the stories of black women break into those narratives, subverting both the white men's master narrative and the narrator's censoring, interrupted narrative which reduces materiality to "sizable checks." In direct contrast to the narrator's demystified narrative of the material world of the college, which moves from fertility to barrenness, Mr. Norton begins his heroic, naturalized history by explaining to the narrator that he first came to the campus when it was "barren ground. There were no trees, no flowers, no fertile farmland. That was years ago before you were born" (38). This story, which begins before the narrator was born, at first seems to encapsulate or explain him. Cast as smaller than the story Norton has to tell, the narrator strains his imagination; he "listened with fascination . . . as my thoughts attempted to sweep back to the times of which he spoke" (39). Reversing the narrator's account of the college, Norton tells how the great founder transformed the campus from "barren clay to fertile soil" (45). To play a part in this story, muses Norton, "has been a pleasant fate, indeed" (39).

Perched complacently on this climactic "node" in his progressive narrative, Norton pauses—a fateful pause, for it becomes one of those breaks in time into which the narrator steps, only to come upon Trueblood's house and story. But just as Trueblood enters his daughter in the plot through the dream of a white woman, so the protagonist must move through the white man Norton's dream story of his daughter to arrive at the black woman's story. Even so, the latter story remains caught within the father's frame. The black father's narrative keeps partially unheard the painful history of black women's violated sexuality. And while Ellison's text reveals this problem, it offers no narrative means for moving beyond it.[11]

But let us trace more closely how in this chapter Ellison makes the temporal node his narrator describes in the prologue into a structure for discovering the problem. At the pause marked by the momentary culminating point of Norton's narrative, the invisible narrator flows into his own current of thought. At first, his thoughts follow in the wake of Norton's narrative, encouraged by "the car leaping leisurely beneath the pressure of my foot" (39). His images run like a movie—a white man's movie—before his eyes: "Faded and yellowed pictures of the school's early days . . . flashed across the screen of my mind, coming fitfully and fragmentarily to life" (39). In this movielike gallery of photographs black folks are "people who seemed almost without individuality, a black mob that seemed to be waiting" while the highly evolved white folks are "clear of features, striking, elegant, and confident" (39). But as Norton musingly repeats the words "pleasant fate," the narrator realizes that "at the same time I was puzzled. . . . How could anyone's fate be *pleasant?* I had always thought of it as something painful" (40).

And just at this moment when the narrator realizes that Norton's progressive narrative stands at odds with the stories he knows, he "suddenly decided to turn off the highway, down a road that seemed unfamiliar" (40). Norton remarks that he doesn't "remember this section." This "section" has been left out of his story, but the break in his story has led his listener right to it. As they leave behind the paved highway of Norton's narrative and progress along the clay road of the protagonist's (following that fork the narrator had earlier balked at), the protagonist sees a series of figures invisible to Norton—a shadowy man who looks up from his hoe to wave at the car, a sleeping man with a "lean, hungry" face who "was the kind of white man I feared," and finally a vibrating and intercorporeal physical universe: "The brown fields swept out to the horizon. A flock of birds dipped down, circled, swung up and out as though linked by invisible strings. Waves of heat danced above the engine hood. The tires sang over the highway" (41). This sudden expansion of perspective and intensified vision of the material world emboldens the invisible man to "overcome my timidity" and ask the telling question. When he asks, "Sir, why did you become interested in the school?" (41), he is asking Norton for the origins of his progressive and nature-authorized narrative. Norton at first speaks abstractly of racial destiny—"that your people were somehow closely connected with my destiny" (41)—and then turns revealingly concrete.

The positioning of Norton's story of white womanhood at the origin of a narrative of racial destiny both displays the sexual–racial logic of racial patriarchy and pointedly clarifies the inextricability of white and black storytelling traditions which Ellison's novel manifests, and which I highlighted at the opening of this

185

chapter. At the origin of the narrative of the white American man's "destiny" is "a girl, [his] daughter . . . a being more rare, more beautiful, purer, more perfect and more delicate" (she's got it all) "than the wildest dream of a poet" (42). A Romantic poet's dream indeed, which, when forced to be a reality in the form of a sailing tour around the world with her daddy—"just she and I"—kills the girl in question. And yet, even so, the dream doesn't die. Instead it lies at the foundation of a college, and at the crossing of two cultures. For, although Norton implicates himself in his daughter's death, saying he has "never forgiven" himself, he proudly concludes that "everything I've done since her passing has been a monument to her memory." And so, he tells, the narrator, "you are bound to a great dream and to a beautiful monument" (43). This is the mythical—feminine and white—origin of the master narrative.

But even as Norton reveals this most "sacred" (42) origin of his compelling narrative, the narrator has been negotiating a cross-current of dissenting questions ("But you don't even know my name, I thought, wondering what it was all about" [45]). When he asks Norton, seemingly innocently, "Shall I continue in this direction, sir?" (45), Norton is too buoyant on the current of his grand narrative to realize that his listener is, only half intentionally, about to entangle him in its undertow. For they are about to arrive at the house of Jim Trueblood, the man whose daughter, unlike Norton's daughter, survived her father's sexual consumption of her.

Within the racial patriarchy of the modern West, the "founding fathers" most commonly cast white women as either pure or promiscuous, while often black women are cast conveniently as both—mammies and whores and little girls, too—multifunctional, serving many culturally liminal purposes at once. Trueblood's male gaze, like that of the men who look at Toomer's Karintha, repeats this conflation. He begins to diminish his rape of his daughter Matty Lou by emphasizing that he did it in his sleep, but then he qualifies that dismissal, saying, "Although maybe sometimes a man can look at a little ole pigtail gal and see him a whore" (59). No doubt he can when that girl belongs to a subordinated race in a racial–patriarchal society. Such a girl upholds no "higher" racial boundaries; she only embodies transgressions of boundaries. That this doubled image of the black girl serves a veiled narrative function in white men's history is indicated not only by the white men's monetary support of Trueblood and their desire to "hear about the gal lots of times" (53) but even more specifically by the image of the clock in Trueblood's dream.

As Trueblood dozes next to his daughter on the "fateful" night, he floats from thoughts of the young boy who pursues his daughter, and who makes him feel possessive of her, to the dream of a white woman, all of which inspires his erection and his forced entry into the body of his black daughter. Note that Trueblood's sense of sexual competition over his daughter gives rise to the image of a white woman—the figure around whom white men organize the larger cultural competition between themselves and black men. In the dream Trueblood finds himself trapped in a white woman's bedroom in a white man's house. As he looks for a means of escape, the dreaming Trueblood encounters a white lady who steps out of a tall grandfather clock. Her nightgown, made of "soft white silky stuff" (57), recalls Norton's daughter's "flowing costume of soft, flimsy material" (43).

In both cases the white-clothed white woman stands at the origin of temporality, of the white father figure's grandfather clock narrative. She is the bodiless yet sexualized—and dead—figure who, for Norton, explains the destiny of his relation to black Americans. But her presence—in Norton's narrative and in Trueblood's dream, as in the narrator's memory which stopped at the elaborate verandas—veils a rupture, both of black women's sexuality and of those black male narratives that might otherwise be compelled by that sexuality. In Trueblood's story her presence tricks him into abuse of the women of his own community, even his own family.

In other words, whereas white men's containment of the white woman (in a clock in a house) generates white men's destiny in relation to other races, including their usage of black women, the black man's entrapment within this culture grounded in control of white womanhood leads him to repeat the white man's sexual consumption of black women through a "silky" dream of white women. Trueblood wakes to find that, in entering the white man's grandfather clock to escape the white woman, he has in effect fully entered the white man's master narrative, for he has repeated the white man's rape of the black woman.

Critical interpretation of the Trueblood scene sometimes continues to veil this narrative of rape enacted at the sexual matrix of white and black cultures. In celebrating Trueblood as black storyteller, critics often elide the fact that his story is one of daughter rape, some of them misrepresenting or oversimplifying Mattie Lou's response, especially by neglecting to cite the passage in which Trueblood awakens to Matty Lou "beatin' me and scratchin' and tremblin' and shakin' and cryin' all at the same time . . . she was tryin' to push me away" (58–59).[12] If Trueblood is, as critics often argue, the storyteller after whom Ellison models his narration, we have further ground for considering Ellison complicit in the submergence of the story of the black mother figure's rape, a submergence dramatized in the prologue. As Michael Awkward has shown, the intertextual references in Toni Morrison's revisions in *The Bluest Eye* of the scene of rape by the father and of the scene of *telling* that rape indicate her awareness of the problems in Ellison's novel.[13] And yet Ellison's narrative framing of the Trueblood story, as well as his framing of the entire novel by the mother reverie of the prologue, indicate a complex self-consciousness on Ellison's part.

White culture has set up Trueblood, and all other citizens of the United States (including perhaps Ellison and some of his critics, with the important exceptions of Hortense Spillers and Houston Baker), to enact this slippage (from attention to the mythology of white women, tripping past the rape of black women, to the storytelling of black men) as if in a dream. It has structured the opposed but mutually enabling positions of white and black women: to desire one is to rape the other, on several levels.[14] In some sense the universalization by white feminists of the white woman's experience of oppression has shown itself, owing to the critiques of black women, to be seduced by this same desire. Such a dynamic repeats itself throughout a history presided over by grandfather clock time.

Thus, in pursuing the story hidden in the pause of Mr. Norton's white patriarchal narrative, a pursuit metaphorically expressed as a turning off from the main road, the narrator drives straight to this story of the rape of a black woman, this time perpetrated by her own father. As with the slave woman's battling sons in the prologue, black men's desire to possess "their own" women mingles with a denigrating perception of black women (as whores in pigtails), finally playing into the hands of white men (who are happy to have black men battle one another or who pay to have the rape of black women told again and again). As audience to this story the daughter-consuming Norton can pay Trueblood (he hands him a hundred-dollar bill) to reenact, as displaced onto black women, his own sexual consumption of his daughter.

Meanwhile, as the narrator listens to this story of forced and violated black motherhood, he is "torn," as he is repeatedly in the text, "between humiliation and fascination" (68). He hovers between identification with the black woman and with the white man. As he announces in the preface, the narrator is ambivalent. His ambivalence stems in part from his existence among white men who "described to us the limitations of our lives" even while black men see "upon their lips the curdled milk of a million black slave mammies' withered dugs" (112). White men thus inveigle from black men "a treacherous and fluid knowledge of our being, imbibed at our source and now regurgitated foul upon us" (112). In other words, white men usurp black men's relation to black women, within the context of a mythology that makes women the source or origin of identity, and then put black men in a position where they can only repeat the usage of black women. Under these conditions black men have little opportunity to create their own racial–patriarchal mythology of black women and even less socially empowered basis for a genuine intimacy with black women.

And yet, perhaps not surprisingly, this traumatic collision with the history that disables such a mythology and such an intimacy provokes in the protagonist a sudden intense desire to create a speech-enabling late Romantic mythology around the black mother figure. At the same time, Ellison's revisions of the role of Mary in the novel reveal his own vacillating movement, embedded in the structure of his fiction, between attachment to and reticence about the history of this mother figure.[15]

MANAGING MARY

In the wake of Trueblood's story and Norton's collapse (which entangles the protagonist in another racially charged brawl), the invisible man becomes inspired with a late-Romantic desire to hear and subsume the voices of black mothers. In his seat at the chapel, awaiting his expulsion, he fantasizes that he will wrest back his claim on black motherhood by speaking the speech of black women. In the chapel, as with his later harangue in Harlem on behalf of the evicted "black mammy," a meditation on the black mother's presence and history moves him to speech. Abandoning what he identifies as the preacher's negative content of *"suns having hemorrhages,"* he calls upon *"the gray-haired matron in the final row"* (113) as the *"old connoisseur of voice sounds"* to hear his *"words that were no words, counterfeit notes singing achievements yet unachieved, riding upon the wings of my voice out to you, old matron"* (114). In imagination the protagonist substitutes the college preacher's imagery with words "hurled to the trees of a wilderness, or into a well of slate-gray water; more sound than sense" (113). Our hero recognizes that this matron who engenders *"voice sounds"* is a *"relic of slavery whom the campus loved but did not understand, aged, of slavery, yet bearer of something warm and vital and all-enduring"* (114). Note that the protagonist, in a move reminiscent of *Cane*'s male narrators, stakes his transformation of the mother's speech *against* the speech of other black men, who only imperfectly understand her.

Yet it is uncertain whether the invisible man understands whereof he speaks any better than other sons of the matron. In fact, he may well be another "hemorrhaging" son, birthing himself in the mother's "voice sounds" and (like *Cane*'s male speakers), displacing, even as he attempts to honor, the voice of the mother. Starting with the protagonist's imagined speech as he sits in the chapel, continuing through his speech at the eviction, and indeed implicit in the narrator's entire novelistic speech act, which opens with a slave mother's speech, these speaking men borrow inspiration from black mothers to become the spokespersons for a black community (although the narrator's ambivalence about being such a spokesperson—his desire to be "more than a member of a race"—stems in part from the instability of his position as son of such a mother). In the chapel scene the narrator refers to "voice sounds" but never renders them, as elsewhere we hear of the power and effects of his speeches, also inspired by mothers, but we never know what he says. Avoiding the contradictions of celebrating that source while containing it, the invisible narrator repeatedly submerges that maternal origin. The narrator's narrative, in effect, substitutes for those mother-sublimating speeches.

At the same time the text explains this displacement of the mother, as was noted earlier; for this approaching of the threshold of black women's lives and speech precipitates a struggle with other black men, thus transforming these approaches into "interruptions"—and sudden usurpations. In the prologue, for instance, the mother's sons punch the narrator backwards into the street and out of his reverie, which he then attributes to reefer and vows not to repeat. In the battle royal, after his offer of alliance which Tatlock considers more properly made to "your Ma," Tatlock knocks him out, and he awakens to give his excellent humble address. In the Norton incident he takes Norton down an unfamiliar road as part of a mental wrestling match with his grandfather and ends up expelled from the college. In the chapel ceremony the narrator's imagined "rush of sound" is interrupted by the processional entrance of Bledsoe, Barbee, and the white trustees, the same men who, in a later dream, castrate him.

The narrator's struggle with Lucius Brockway constitutes another example of this dynamic. And yet the encounter with Brockway, guardian of an underground world of generating machines, momentarily catapults both the protagonist and Ellison's book over male-constructed barriers and lands them in the lap of Mary. In the "Mary" sections the mother acts on the man, rather than vice versa, recuperating *his* embodiment and counteracting white mutilation and indifference. As we shall see, first in the factory scene and then in Ellison's early and published versions of the hospital scene, both Ellison and the protagonist restlessly draw strength from Mary, but then wriggle their way out of this black mother's arms to speak their stories, not hers.

If Liberty Paints is a comic allegory for white culture, with its secret formula using drops of black paint to make the "purest white that can be found" (202), then Lucius Brockway certainly embodies the narrator's grandfather's advice to "live with your head in the lion's mouth" (16). Indeed, he lives in the lion's bowels. As mastermind not simply of the color but of the "veehicle" of all Liberty paint, he works underground keeping the machines under control by releasing pressure at the right moments. Referred to as "she" and "her" by Brockway, the underground machines of this paint factory both recall the female-sexualized "engines droning earth-shaking rhythms in the dark" (34–35)[16] at the narrator's college and share the labyrinthine underground terrain of many other female-associated settings in the novel: of the hospital basement (from which the protagonist escapes in an early version of the novel), of the sewers (by way of which the protagonist escapes from the riot, hoping somehow to "get to Mary's" [560]), and of the narrator's "hole" from which he speaks his story. All of these underground worlds are worlds of hidden corporeality, in particular a vexed, mother-associated, racially burdened corporeality shaped by the history hidden in the "underground" rhythm of Louis Armstrong's music, a slave history wherein the mother's sons are also the master's sons, both literally in blood and socially as competitors in a racial–patriarchal system. In the case of Lucius Brockway's underground generator room, a scene of man-to-man combat explodes the pressure inside the underground feminized machinery.

That is, when Brockway and the protagonist wrestle for position inside the "lion's mouth," this struggle between black men interrupts the vigilant containment of the body-making (or "veehicle"-making) feminine engine at the base of both white and black men's identities. Brockway's "feminine" fighting (by biting), together with the fact that even those biting teeth are false teeth, suggest that when an aging black man loses his position to younger black men, his dependence on feminine resources is exposed. The whole game bares its cooptative aspect.

Hence, as Brockway and the protagonist sheepishly face each other after their no-win battle, the generative engines shatter their containment, sending the protagonist flying into the arms of a black mother more literally than in any other encounter so far. As he falls unconscious, he feels himself "sink to the center of a lake of heavy water and pause, transfixed and numb with the sense that I had lost irrevocably an important victory" (230). This latest abortive battle with other black men creates another "pause" within which the protagonist collapses, finally, into the hands of the feminine. The fall into "the center of a lake of heavy water" (recalling the stagnant water opposite the elaborate verandas) initially provokes a sense of physical numbness and emotional defeat.

In an early version of *Invisible Man* the fall into the feminine is quite direct. In a long passage which Ellison later replaced with the white doctors and shock therapy of chapters 11 and 12, the protagonist awakens to the countenance of Mary. It is she who frees him, in this version, from the glass and metal machine in which he finds himself encaged. But her body, her manipulations of his body, and her power to liberate his body all provoke deep ambivalence in him. This ambivalence repeats itself in the author, for Ellison excised this encounter from the published novel and then a decade later published it in a collection of African American fiction, commenting that more attention to Mary would have made *Invisible Man* "a better book." Let us now explore the excised section at length, comparing it to chapters 11 and 12 of the published novel, to demonstrate how Ellison's book, as a written production, repeats that "running" in the "race race," especially insofar as that race is run in part *away from* the subordinate-race mother.

In the earlier version of the invisible man's hospital experience, as Mary peers at him through glass (he lies prone in a coffinlike container with a glass lid) and tries "seriously to communicate" with him, he wonders at his feeling that he "had known her for a long time."[17] He emphasizes that she seems "strangely familiar," but when she manages to loosen some bolts and slightly open the lid to his enclosure, "suddenly I no longer wanted to be freed. . . . For though I wanted release, I was frightened lest it should come through this ignorant, unscientific old woman. Where was the doctor? Why didn't somebody come?" (245). If only male birth or "release" did not depend on some old female body! The protagonist finds that he actually would prefer the intrusions of white "scientific" doctors to this "strangely familiar" old woman. He is most comfortable putting his body in the hands of white men's medical science, while opposing the hold of science on the body to that of the older brown-skinned woman, whose body and herbal cures modern science and the protagonist distrust.

His ambivalence toward Mary manifests itself in alternating revulsion toward and fixation on her body—especially as her body "labors" for his release. He feels "an irrational desire to retch as I watched [her fingers] strain with the heavy lid" (246); her fingers are like the struggling "legs of an obscene insect," and he is "seized by a savage impulse to bite them" (246). Yet his "eyes were drawn to their scarred leather-brown texture, the smooth polish of the knuckles" (245). When Mary's fingers become caught, "a mixture of relief and despair flooded over me as I saw an expression of pain grip her features" (246).

Mary eventually lifts the lid and feeds the protagonist, smilingly slipping food into his mouth with her fingers, "as though actually feeding a baby" (249). Her patient "didn't like the idea" (249). Later she brings him a strengthening herb— "something I got from my mama"—which the protagonist "wanted both to reject and accept. . . . I distrusted it, yet I had to draw strength from some source. . . . Fearfully, I put it into my mouth and bit it in half, swallowing part and holding the rest between my teeth" (261). He distrusts her folk cure which her own mother has taught her, fearing the "unscientific" African American heritage of herbal healing as well as the "old woman" aspect of Mary, to which he repeatedly refers. Nonetheless, he eats (some of) her herbs and feels strength return to his "impotent arms and legs" (259). His body sweats and flames, making him uncomfortable yet enabling him to escape safely, in this version, from the hospital doctors in a wild chase. Thus, the mother's body makes "potent" the son's body, fostering his escape; but this escape only reengages him once again in the homosocial "race race," which entails running away from Mary.

All of this mothering and midwifery on Mary's part, preparing his escape from the hospital and arousing ambivalence in the protagonist, contrasts sharply with the scenes that replace them in the published version of the novel. In the earlier version the protagonist concludes that "for all my resentment, I wished for

[Mary]." And yet even there it is not exactly Mary he wishes for: "I imagined her returning subtly transformed into a young pink nurse. . . . Yes, she'd come and open the case and my impotent arms and legs would be strong and well and I would take her away with me" (259).

In the published version the invisible man awakens to the faces of the white doctor and pink nurses for whom, in the excised section, he wished. The symbolism of this revised version, read alone, places him more absolutely at the mercy of white doctors, and thus appears more bleak, perhaps more "realistic": no mediating mother intervenes between black men and white culture—only shock therapy. If one considers the excised section side by side with the published version, however, one sees that such mediating black mother figures actually represent a threat that is closer to home than that of the white doctors and nurses, who are therefore preferred by the earlier protagonist as safer than the black mother. The black mother evokes attachment, enacted and felt in the body, and for this reason threatens the narrator with, as the speaker in *Cane*'s "Harvest Song" says, "knowledge of [his] hunger."[18]

In his revision Ellison indulges his protagonist's wish to avoid this uncomfortable knowledge. The whites mother him in place of Mary. In the published version the white doctor murmurs "something encouraging, as though I were a child," and then gives him a pill, saying, "It's good for you" (231). In effect the white doctor is a more acceptable mother, as one to whom the protagonist feels no attachment, and a more powerful mother, whose power has been proven precisely by his appropriation of the black mother's body and of her power to heal. But the doctor's simultaneously maternal and "scientific" treatment quickly escalates into the shock therapy which only recapitulates the ambivalence the protagonist wants to leave behind. In the shock therapy the invisible man's bodily sensations of revulsion and fascination for Mary's body are replaced by "two forces" which "tore savagely" at his stomach and back (232). With shock therapy, it seems science has created a finely tuned objective, or bodily, correlative for the protagonist's emotional ambivalence. Ellison's book implicitly links the scientific interaction with (or tearing up of) the body to the ambivalence that tears up the emotions felt toward mothers, even as this scene more obliquely reveals, when read against the earlier version, how that ambivalence also shapes Ellison's narrative representation of the mother.

Once again, in the midst of these forces that tear him in two the protagonist hears a music which evokes a sensual or "naked" southern past, alludes to the songs of mother figures, and finally surfaces a "wail of female pain." First, the electric current recalls for the protagonist the rhythm of Beethoven's Fifth Symphony, which "racks" him until he reaches an undercurrent where "voices droned harmoniously" (234). These voices recall for him a past of southern sensuousness, the images of which he uses to interrogate the doctor's current, to step inside his opponent's "violent flow of rapid rhythmic action": "Oh, doctor, I thought drowsily, did you ever wade in a brook before breakfast? Ever chew on a sugar cane?" (234). Next he recollects songs sung by his grandmother, until finally "the music became," like the underground strains he hears in the prologue, "a distinct wail of female pain" (235).

But with the kind of sudden shift to which the reader of this text has become accustomed—the sudden shutdown which epitomizes interruptive narratives when they encounter mother figures—the doctor's voice returns abruptly. In response to this white voice, the wail of female pain gives way, in a repetition of the familiar pattern, to the first words spoken by the narrator since he fell into the "lake of heavy water." These first words—"I don't have enough room"—express the protagonist's wedged-in position between the ambivalence-provoking mother figure and the intelligence-rating doctors. (This sensation of a lack of space also resonates, as we shall see, with Morrison's characters' predicament in *Beloved.*)

The doctor's response—another dose of electricity—moves the protagonist to his most complete state of disembodiment: "I was beyond anger. I was only bewildered. . . . All my limbs seemed amputated. . . . My eyes were swimming with tears. Why, I didn't know. . . . I seemed to have lost all sense of proportion. Where did my body end and the crystal white world begin?" (238). Abandoned completely to this white world, with all black mother figures excised and silenced, the protagonist loses himself in the "violent flow." The book as a whole, spoken by an invisible narrator, consciously mimics this condition of the character, as when it subjects him again and again to violent "forces" which "tear savagely" at his body. In order to expose these "savage" forces, the interruptive text represents them.

Ironically, having got the narrator to this disembodied state, the doctors then put to him the very questions—about the mother—which their treatment has rendered him unable to answer. They ask, "What is your name?" "Who are you?" And finally, "What is your mother's name?" "Who is your mother?" (241). The white men displace the black cultural mother; then they make invisible the body which, under racial patriarchy, connects the black man to a mother; and finally they "tear" him up by asking him to identify himself by way of the displaced, appropriated, and disconnected mother figure.

The doctors continue their verbal "tearing up" of the narrator with the loaded question, "Who was Brer Rabbit?"—touching, probably unwittingly, on a piece of cultural lore that precisely expresses the equivocal relation to the mother engendered by the black man's "torn" position. In asking this question of the protagonist, the doctors may well display that "treacherous and fluid knowledge of our being" stolen from black men through "black slave mammies" (112) such as

Mary—the "mammy" these white doctors replace in Ellison's novel. Certainly the recollections inspired by this question reveal the protagonist's will to regain a hold on the mother's body. He recalls that as a child he particularly identified with "Buckeye Rabbit," behind which hid the sexy trickster identity of Brer Rabbit. As "your mother's backdoor man" (242), Brer Rabbit has a special connection to the sexuality of the mother; he knows her other side. He secretly maintains intimate relations with her—and this is indeed what our narrator does throughout *Invisible Man*, as does Ellison, although by excluding the "Mary" section, he keeps the secret fairly well concealed.

The invisible man bemusedly thinks to himself that in receiving the doctors' questions and silently answering them, "I was really playing a game with myself and . . . they were taking part. A kind of combat. . . . I imagined myself whirling about in my mind like an old man attempting to catch a small boy in some mischief" (242). Similarly, in displacing Mary's birthing of the protagonist with the white doctor's construction of his identity ("I felt a tug at my belly and looked down to see one of the physicians pull the cord which was attached to the stomach node" [243]), Ellison plays a substitution game with his protagonist's identity—a game in which we take part. The white father displaces the black mother; meanwhile the "small boy" of the past, who fools behind the older man's back, knows the invisible man's secret "identity" with the mother.

We might imagine that Ellison is likewise playing an elaborate game with white culture, fully cognizant of the ironies of mother excision and homosocial "combat" in his novel, which might be read as absolute parody. But such a view is complicated by the fact that when he finally publishes the displaced "Mary" passage sixteen years later, Ellison appears unconsciously to reenact this "game." In the 1968 collection *Soon, One Morning* he introduces the original "Mary" section with these comments, worth quoting in full:

> The following narrative formed a part of the original version of a novel called
> *Invisible Man*, and it marked an attempt to get the hero of that memoir out of
> the hospital and into the world of Harlem. It was Mary's world, the world of the
> urbanized (or partially urbanized), Negro folk, and I found it quite pleasurable
> to discover, during those expansive days of composition before the necessities
> of publication became a reality, that it was Mary, a woman of the folk, who
> helped release the hero from the machine. I was quite sorry that considerations
> of space made it necessary that I reconceive the development.
>
> I am pleased for Mary's sake to see this version in print. She deserved more
> space in the novel and would, I think, have made it a better book. (243)

The description here of "those expansive days of composition before the necessities of publication [become] a reality" recalls a familiar narrative of development, in which the mother figure presides over an innocent, embodied, and naive past which the mental maneuvers of sophisticated language must necessarily surpass.[19] The "expansive days" before the pressure of "necessities" are the days of childhood, the days when the small boy remained connected to the mother behind the old man's back. In other words, Mary's centrality shapes the "childhood" of the novel but is significantly excised when the novel enters adult "reality." The author finds it "necessary" to "reconceive the development" of his narrative. Indeed. So did Freud, and many men before him, in order to establish their origins and legitimize themselves as not subject to but speaking in the place of the feminine. Like his narrator, then, Ellison "draws strength" from the figure of Mary in order to move his hero "out of the hospital and into the world," but then reabsorbs this strength into his own power as author when he cuts this section and "reconceives" the development of his hero. This substitution mirrors the interruptive patterns of his novel—its repeated swerving away from the very mother figures who engender the characters and impel them "into the world." In his framing remarks for the excised section, Ellison further on invites his readers to "take this proffered middle, this agon, this passion, and supply their own beginning and . . . ending" (244). If this "Mary" section is a middle that has been left out, then what we have here is indeed an "absent center," where the mother figure invisibly gives birth to a creation that absents her originary role because of the ambivalence that the subordinate-race mother, in particular, provokes.

And yet it is important to register, again, the way in which the mother figure is herself partly responsible for this ambivalence. Having been nourished back to health by Mary, the protagonist in the published novel expresses the same ambivalence toward her that the protagonist in the earlier version did. His comments throw light on the mother figure's complicity in the "torn" position he occupies. He realizes that Mary is "something more" than a friend to him. She is

> a force, a stable, familiar force like something out of my past which kept me from whirling off into some unknown which I dared not face. It was a most painful position, for at the same time, Mary reminded me constantly that something was expected of me, some act of leadership . . . and I was torn between resenting her for it and loving her for the nebulous hope she kept alive. (258)

Again, the invisible man associates Mary with "something" from his past, although here his ambivalence toward this aspect of her is expressed less graphically, less as a response merely to her physical body. Rather (in addition to reiterating the link between mother figures and the past of the self), this comment spells out in psychological terms Mary's active part in the contradictions and ambivalences of the protagonist's existence as a black man. Even as she revives his body and recalls him to his past, she also urges him to "lead and fight and move us all on a little higher" (255). Ironically, her expectation of "some act of leadership" from him sends him back into the streets from which her home had rescued him. He asks, "Why should it be this way, that the very job which might make it possible for me to do some of the things which she expected of me required that I leave her?" (315). The invisible man himself questions the logic of the racial–patriarchal rending of mother and man.

Mary displays here the doubleness inherent in the racial–patriarchal mother: she is at once a subversive and conservative voice. She abides by the rending of mother and man, street and home, when she accepts an order in which she must feed and he must fight. Her combination of unconditional and expectation-filled mothering issues from her assumption of the reality of this rending. Necessary as her assumption may be, the protagonist feels irritated and implicitly betrayed by it—by its confusing mix of maternal and masculine heroic values.

In the excised section, where the protagonist's ambivalence toward Mary is more graphic, Mary's contradictory relation to the protagonist is more starkly dramatized: Mary begins to trust and help the invisible man *only* when he concocts a past in which he violently confronted a white man; she mothers him only after he evidences his potential for street-fighting black manhood. In this light we can read Ellison's novel as addressed *to* the black mother figure, as a kind of plea for closer scrutiny of the contradictions she embodies—even as we should also consider black women's novels like *The Bluest Eye* as pleas addressed to black father figures such as Trueblood (and Ellison), urging closer scrutiny of their male competitive, mother-sublimating storytelling practices.

FROM MOTHERS TO BROTHERS

The protagonist's move from Mary's home to the Brotherhood repeats the irony he identifies in his relation to Mary: bodily associations that recall him to his past at the same time, within a competitive homosocial world, catapult him into a future removed from that past. Two catalyzing, memory-provoking experiences of food move the narrator into the Brotherhood. First, eating yams leads him to accept and celebrate his southern black past and prepares him to give the speech that wins the admiration of Brother Jack; later the smell of cabbage cooking at Mary's house reminds him of the "leaner years of [his] childhood" (296) and makes him realize that he cannot realistically refuse the offer of a job. Between these body-inspired yet body-abandoning moves away from his past, there is nested a crucial scene of mother-evoking, mother-displacing speech which impels him toward his past-excising future.

After enjoying at length the "stab of swift nostalgia" (262) and the "intense feeling of freedom" inspired by eating yams, the narrator's sense of the need for upward progression emerges to overshadow these pleasures. For pleasure only on the "yam level" of life was "far less than I had expected upon coming to the city. An unpleasant taste bloomed in my mouth now as I bit the end of the yam and threw it into the street" (267). This return of ambition, of the desire to compete and succeed, intersects tellingly with a memory of his mother which threatens further to disable the protagonist's ambition but which, almost without his willing it, actually ends up making those ambitions possible—to a point. It is exactly his sublimation, in his speech, of his unsettling attachment to his own mother that gives him an entry into the realm of white speech making.

Coming upon a "motherly-looking old woman" being carried out of her home in a chair by two white men; noticing knocking bones, a curling iron, an old faded lace fan, and her "free papers"; and hearing "the old female, mind-plunging crying" of the evicted woman, the narrator stumbles inward to a vision of his own mother. The vision is associated with the slave mother passage in the prologue by its rendering in italics and the suggestion that what he sees forces him to look "around a corner" into the past.

> I turned and stared again at the jumble, no longer looking at what was before my eyes, but inwardly-outwardly, around a corner and into the dark, far-away-and-long-ago, not so much of my own memory as of remembered words, of linked verbal echoes, images, heard even when not listening at home. And it was as if I myself was being dispossessed of some painful yet precious thing which I could not bear to lose; something confounding, like a rotten tooth that one would rather suffer indefinitely than endure the short, violent eruption of pain that would mark its removal. . . . This junk, these shabby chairs, these heavy old-fashioned pressing irons, zinc wash tubs with dented bottoms—all throbbed within me with more meaning than there should have been: *And why did I, standing in the crowd, see like a vision my mother hanging wash on a cold windy day, so cold that the warm clothes froze even before the vapor thinned and hung stiff on the line, and her hands white and raw in the skirt-swirling wind and her gray head bare to the darkened sky—why were they causing me discomfort so far beyond their intrinsic meaning as objects? And why did I see them now, as behind a veil that threatened to lift, stirred by the cold wind in the narrow street?* (273)

In an image of a rotten tooth which Morrison would later evoke in *The Bluest Eye*, this old woman's past, recalling the protagonist's past, is infected, like a tooth, with slavery and racism; but it also marks the common root of the community. It is something no one can "bear to lose." At the center of this past, in a sudden narrative leap backward to a place earlier in the protagonist's past than the story has yet taken us, stands the protagonist's mother, in her only appearance in the novel (the earlier reverie "recalled" her voice). The mother's bared head and raw hands bespeak a realm of exposed embodiment which causes the narrator extreme "discomfort." Ambivalence remains his response to the bodily complications the mother represents—in *her* body: the veil sheathing the mother "threatens" rather than promises to lift.

Like the narrative-generating phenomenality of objects in *To the Lighthouse* and in Morrison's novels, here too the objects—the tubs and the irons and the wind—transport the past into the present and become pivotal in the character's individual, communal, and temporal consciousness. As is the case for Sethe in *Beloved,* these objects create "more meaning than there should have been." This surplus of painful meaning keeps the characters, as Sethe would say, "working hard to remember as close to nothing as was safe."[20] But whereas Morrison's novel, despite Sethe's efforts, burrows its way inside the objects and the painful past they contain, Ellison's novel springboards off these objects and away from the past, using their phenomenality to inspire a speech that pushes his protagonist beyond the "yam level" of life—ultimately into a well-paid career as a "Brother."[21]

Moreover, even as the protagonist channels the agitation that these objects cause him into the speech that will make him a Brother, he insists on the inherent neutrality of objects. Or perhaps he must insist on their neutrality in order to effect the sublimation that will energize his speech. The pressing iron, the free papers, and his mother's raw hands cause the narrator "discomfort," he says, "beyond their intrinsic meaning as objects." It seems that anything more than a strictly scientific account and neutral presence of the "objects" here baffles and discomfits the protagonist. Like the earlier longing for scientific doctors when faced with Mary, here when confronted with a vision of his mother the protagonist clings to the "objective" view of objects as having neutral meaning. In this way he protects himself from answering the question of his mother's role.

The invisible man's squeamishness about objects' potential for "meaning" recalls Ellison's condescension to readers of the excised "Mary" section who "hunger and thirst for meaning" and "desire more than the sheer narrative ride" (243). He invites his readers, if they must, to "supply their own" beginning, ending, and if necessary a "moral or perception" for the excised section. Ellison, however, distinguishes himself from such readers, saying, "For me, of course, the narrative *is* the meaning." Even as he presents the excised section and encourages readers to consider "what this country would be without its Marys," he dissociates himself from her "meaning" by limiting his interest to the "sheer narrative ride."[22]

Ellison's characterization of Mary as a kind of content for his form, or as the ground from which his narrative takes flight, compares with—and perhaps underlies—the invisible man's pivot from the past into a neutral, scientific future through the sensations of eating and the experience of seeing pressing irons, zinc washtubs, and a vision of his mother's body. It is finally the "odor of Mary's cabbage," indicating her need for his rent money, that "changed my mind" in favor of joining the Brotherhood (296). Ironically, immersion in a world of things and bodies draws the protagonist toward visions and decisions that neutralize the "meaning" of objects, empty the narrator's body of his past identity, and keep that body "running." For Ellison's protagonist intercorporeality is a veiled dynamic and a contained force channeled into his transcendence of the "yam level" of life.

The philosophy of the Brotherhood epitomizes this neutralization and use of material conditions, for it prides itself above all on being "scientific." Its approach to the redistribution of material resources is "scientific." The narrator's leaving behind his old name, residence, and life follows from the Brotherhood's "scientific" approach—a top-down uniformity bequeathed from above. In the protagonist's development, then, as in modern Western racial–patriarchal culture at large, an economic "science" of resource distribution (whether Marxist or capitalist) makes use of the mothering body even as it reduces the "meaning" of that body.

The protagonist's speech making for the Brotherhood fully realizes this covert use of the powers of the black mother. In the midst of one of the narrator's ambitious fantasies about climbing his way up the ladder of power in the Brotherhood, he reveals that he will use the "magic of words" to get to "the very top" (355, 380): "For now I had begun to believe, despite all the talk of science around me, that there was a magic in spoken words" (381). This is a magic he has earlier associated with the mother figures in the "back row," as one of those "old connoisseurs of word sounds" (113). Of course, even as he is using these motherly word sounds, the Brotherhood is using them through him. Justly, then, the scientific Brotherhood will "use" his unscientific speeches in the same way his speeches "use" the unscientific old mothers. In short his desire to use mother words yet stand at one remove from the claims of the mother, to neutralize her meaning, predisposes him to the Brotherhood's offer of scientism and allows the Brotherhood to use him.

Ras the Exhorter explicitly identifies the mother sacrifice at the heart of the protagonist's adoption of the scientific method and provokes the protagonist's open expression of the metaphysics underlying that method. The invisible man responds to Ras's insistence that "we sons of Mama Africa" and his question "What kind of black mahn is that who betray his own mama?" (371) with metaphysical paternalism. He believes, as he explains later, that the "scientific approach" of the Brotherhood "channelizes" emotion. Parroting white culture's gendered, late-Romantic, scientific logic, he concedes that "the emotion is there; but it's actually our scientific approach that releases it" (413). So he advises Ras to "start thinking with your mind and not your emotions," to which Ras responds. "I ask both of you, are you awake or sleeping? What is your pahst and where are you going? Never mind, take your corrupt ideology and eat out your own guts like a laughing hyena" (375).

Ras implies that this split between thinking and feeling originates in a disassociation from the mother-affiliated past and a covert cannibalistic relation to one's body. When one aims for transcendence of a "southern backwardness" epitomized in the embodied, chitterling-eating mother and at the same time one draws on the resources of that "backwardness" to gain "forward" position and power, then one survives by degrading and violating the body through which one survives.

The invisible man later twice refers to himself as having been asleep and thus implicitly hints at the accuracy of Ras's account (although a closer reading of Ras would reveal his *own* brand of late-Romantic mythologizing of "Mama Africa"). After the announcement of Tod Clifton's disappearance and the event of his death, the protagonist thinks, "It was as though I had been suddenly awakened from a deep sleep" (422), and then more emphatically after Tod's death, "I'd been asleep, dreaming" (444). He begins to apprehend that, for all his good intentions, his work in the Brotherhood has repeated the work of the college founder, whose inspiration for his cultural achievement flows from the "matron in the back row" whom he "loved but did not understand" (114).

"THE NEED TO REAFFIRM IT ALL"

The nightmare riot in Harlem near the end of the book reaches its climax through a series of gendered scenes that suggest, once more, how the black mother becomes the sacrificial victim in black men's attempt to run the race—and speak the narrative—of invisible embodiment. Ellison's creation of these scenes, as we shall see, indicates his consciousness of a problem, while his catastrophic and blocked ending indicates that he sees no viable solutions. His ending can be contrasted with Joyce's ending in *Ulysses*. Whereas, after his characters' descent into the chaos of Nighttown, Joyce creates an anticlimactic street scuffle and then a recuperative mother's monologue, Ellison's narrator, following his chaotic nighttime descent into chaos, attempts to "return to Mary's" but fails. (A similar contrast can be made between Toomer and Ellison.) Ellison rejects the late-Romantic movement toward recuperation; instead, in the epilogue, his narrator expresses a need for an alternative path back to his past, though confessing himself unable to map one out.

In the midst of his dazed wandering through the Harlem riot, the narrator comes upon a group of men acting out a farcical circus scene: "a crowd of men running up pulling a Borden's milk wagon, on top of which, surrounded by a row of railroad flares, a huge woman in a gingham pinafore sat drinking beer from a barrel which sat before her" (544). In self-parody of the black mammy figure, the woman holds a dipper "like a gravy spoon" while she reaches "nonchalantly with her free hand to send quart after quart of milk crashing into the street. And all the time the men running with the wagon over the debris" (545). No longer giving away *her* milk to the white folks as she serves up gravy, instead the large black woman in a pinafore uses her "free" hand to waste *their* milk.

Of course, this is also the black community's morning milk; they will suffer from its absence even if the whites suffer economically from its loss. But the marauding group's undertaking of this self-sacrifice as a gesture of destructiveness toward the white patriarchal community emblematizes the role of the black mother's subordination in the black community's dispossession. Her act of insubordination is likewise their gesture of insubordination. This scene reflects the same will that underlies the writing of interruptive narrative: the will to demystify the serving mother's role. The group's gesture crucially involves a mocking demystification of the mother—here as also in *Molloy, The Golden Notebook,* and *Good Morning, Midnight*—because of her association with the body as site of oppression and origin of invisible corporeality.

But from a feminist point of view the liberatory status of this gesture depends in part on the mother's degree of agency. Here that agency is unclear. At least in the comments of the onlooking men the woman is constructed as ridiculous rather than cleverly vengeful in her milk-destroying act. They ask, "How they going to get her down from there after she gits fulla beer?" implying that she is pathetically a pawn the men's hands, their effigy, not her own. They scorn her waste of "all that good milk" (545). Painfully the group's demystifying gesture, far from liberating the mother, turns back upon her, making her the scapegoat for the men rather than the agent of their defiance.

And yet the protagonist apprehends without understanding something of the import of her actions. As he watches, he feels both "sad" and "unnerved," his typically mixed feelings reflecting the contradictory status of the woman as both upsetting agent of her own undoing and pitiful expression of the men's desperation: "The big woman left me unnerved. Milk and beer—I felt sad. . . . How much has happened? Why was I torn?" (545). Again the protagonist moves toward a questioning of his feelings about the mother figure but leaves his questions to linger and multiply in the mind of the reader. Torn from a mother? Torn between sadness for the mother and fear of being "unnerved" by her? Torn between a wish to follow the mother and a need to follow the group of mother-mocking, house-burning men?

Like Kabnis, the invisible man is torn between his need for men and his need for a mother, between the homosocial and the heterosocial, and he is torn *because* these two have been pitted against each other, defined in mutual exclusion of each other: to be a man one must leave behind, denigrate, and subordinate a mother. Lost and torn in this scene, as in most others, he follows in the train of the men who head off to reenact what they have just witnessed and disapproved of: they will burn the house of the mother as the other men have made an effigy of the mother. Foreshadowing this repetition, as the narrator's group walks on, their kerosene, like the other men's beer, "splashed into the pale spilt milk" (545).

At the tenement maternal claims meet more direct, less farcical subordination. The wife of the man who has organized the burning of his own tenement house emerges from the building, fully pregnant, and pleads with her husband not to burn down the house because "you know my time's almost here . . . you *know* it is" (546). Her husband, Dupre, "pulled away and rose to a higher step," telling his wife to "git on out the way" and then flashing a revolver to challenge the men's potential arguments as well (547). Poised like the protagonist between men and a mother, Dupre adopts a battle stance toward them both.

Impressed with these scenes, tempted to intervene in them on behalf of mothers, and yet threatened once again with male violence in the form, ironically, of Ras the Exhorter, the invisible man eventually slips underground to escape the cataclysmic, mother-sacrificing riot in Harlem. And yet he thinks longingly of the mother figure as he goes. He tells himself, "Mary, I should have gone to Mary's. I would go now to Mary's in the only way I could. . . . I moved off over the black water, floating sighing . . . sleeping invisibly (428). In the next breath, however, the invisible man reminds himself that the late-Romantic return to the mother cannot work since, as we have seen here and in *Cane* and *Ulysses*, the recovery of the mother only returns the man (sometimes with the mother's complicity) to the dynamic of male competition over the mother as cultural resource, either covertly or explicitly. He acknowledges again that he can never "return to Mary's, or to any part of my old life" (571). He highlights the extent to which his past, his "old life," is held captive within a mythology of mothers, a mythology he by now knows enough to reject, but which rejection also cuts him off from his past and the possibility of renarrating it.

In the epilogue the invisible man expresses the frustration of this situation, weaving in and out of a "passion" to reclaim his past: "Sometimes I feel the need to reaffirm it all, the whole unhappy territory and all the things loved and unlovable in it, for it is all a part of me" (579). Yet he sees no way to do so: "Till now, however, this is as far as I've gotten, for all life seen from the hole of invisibility is absurd" (579). And so Ellison leaves interrupted his narrator's impulse toward a story that would integrate the past and "all the things loved and unlovable in it." In *Beloved* Toni Morrison narrates this same risky "passion" for and of the mother-associated, slavery-haunted past of the embodied African American self.

Before turning to Morrison's novel, however, let us recall Ellison's closing narrative gesture, in which the opposition between black and white, visible and invisible, self and other promises to metamorphose—although it "is this which frightens" the narrator—into a reversible "identity without superposition," to borrow Merleau-Ponty's phrase. The narrator wonders if perhaps "on the lower frequencies, I speak for you?" (581). On the one hand, if his question is understood to be addressed to a brotherhood of men, it may reinscribe that dialogue between men across the body of the silenced mother figure.

On the other hand, if we note that the narrator considers this identity of narrator and audience unsettling, and if we correlate these "lower frequencies" with the musical undercurrents in which the mother's voice can be heard, we can read the narrator's question as signaling (without pursuing) the possibility of intercorporeal narration in two ways. First, the fact that it is on the "lower," mother-registering frequencies that "I" can speak for "you" suggests that this speaking in identity with the other might create an intercorporeality which extends and surpasses that relation originally promised (or threatened) by the mother. Second, and more important for an understanding of the nonmetaphysical underpinnings of Ellison's interruptive novel, it signals how the narrator has been speaking from an invisibility that depends on visibility and reversibility, for the word "*in*visible" is predicated on the word "visible" in the same way that the *g* in "Mag" that spits on "Ma" also requires a *ma*. The narrator's invisibility forms the condition of the audience's visibility, and vice versa. The "you" and the "I" speak through each other. Likewise, texts that erase the body, including both Western scientific discourses and Ellison's novel, actually continually refer to it, make a touchstone of it, by moving against it, by "re-placing" it in both of the mutually contradictory senses of that word.

This contradictory "re-placement" of the body by speech explains the repetitive, frenetic rhythm of interruptive narratives: just as they bring to a culmination the other-body–erasing logic of Western metaphysics, so do they invert it, flip it over so that the very tool of other-bodily erasure—language—becomes an instrument of that other body's presence. In the interruptive narrative this dynamic repeats itself endlessly, the mother's body being the site at which the inversion continually and abruptly occurs.

The interruptive narrative's inversion of the metaphysics of language (wherein language's displacement of presence is made to betray the pressure of presence) points toward the intercorporeal embeddedness of language even as it expressly resists that embeddedness. The invisibility that marks the absence of the speaking body is also the space of its possibility—its entry point, its medium of existence. To posit absence is to posit presence; to emphasize the half-empty glass of water is to acknowledge its being half full. The two are intertwined;

neither can fully usurp or elide the other, for then they would no longer "be" at all, even in opposition to each other. Their intertwining depends on their mutual dehiscence.

And so it is with language and bodies: the domain of sense encompasses, always exists inherently in, the domain of speech, even if speech can simultaneously refer to the domain of sense as if it stood outside it. Speech and sense, like the presence of a body to itself and of one body to another, fold over on each other. They meet at the time and place of their difference and differ at the time and place of their entanglement, just as *here* inflects *there*, and *then* inflects *now*, while the inflection also presumes a distinction.

Interruptive narrative makes a story of the *denial* of these reversals and intertwinings but in the process must trace them. In contrast, intercorporeal narrative more openly traces the reversibility of bodies, things, and speech, although in the process it must register and override the bodily inscribed denial of that reversibility. In this sense, interruptive and intercorporeal narratives display a reversibility in their relation to one another.

8

"To Get to a Place": Intercorporeality in *Beloved*

From *The Bluest Eye* through *Beloved,* Toni Morrison surfaces and reconstructs Ellison's submerged story of black motherhood. In *The Bluest Eye*, as Michael Awkward has noted, Morrison removes the father's rape of the daughter from its status as a framed, disowned story within a story instead positioning it as the central event in her novel.[1] At the same time, in all of her novels she reconfigures the violation and abuse of black motherhood in part by transforming the storytelling techniques that speak it. In *The Bluest Eye* this means that she echoes Ellison's imagery yet changes it from a veiled symbology of the motherly past to a body-embedded phenomenology of that past. Furthermore, in all of her fiction, but especially in *Beloved*, Morrison creates an intercorporeal narrative that conforms to neither the Romantic subsumption of objects and nature typical of Mr. Norton's master narrative in *Invisible Man* nor the deconstructive purging of objects and "meaning" typical of Ellison's interruptive narrative. Her narrators, like Virginia Woolf's, make bodies and objects the favored level of the real, a narrative medium and a narrative locale.

But whereas Woolf's narrator tends to move from body to body through the objects and spaces between them, Morrison's narrator lingers in bodies, at the horizons of their flesh, positioning herself where bodies touch and in touching remember pain or joy. The dead mother figure who returns to haunt Lily Briscoe's act of painting in *To the Lighthouse* takes on flesh in *Beloved* and becomes a literal body pregnant with the history of motherly and daughterly violations. History returns in the flesh.[2] In short, while Morrison engages in dialogue with Ralph Ellison over the cultural and slave heritage of the black mother, she also engages in dialogue with Virginia Woolf over the intercorporeal narrative strategies for transforming such a heritage.[3]

TRUEBLOOD, BREEDLOVE, AND THE LOST TOOTH

Just before the narrator's second vision of his mother in *Invisible Man*, he stands at the site of the old folks' eviction in Harlem and finds himself looking "inwardly-outwardly, around a corner into the dark, far-away-and-long-ago, not so much of my own memories as of remembered words, of linked verbal echoes, images, heard when not even listening at home."[4] Words and spoken rhythms act as verbal echoes that link present to past. Recalling these word sounds, he feels a sudden sense of "dispossession" of "something painful yet precious." He compares that something to a rotten tooth "that one would rather suffer indefinitely than endure the short, violent eruption of pain that would mark its removal" (273). Paradoxically, the invisible man clings covertly to his past in resisting its pain and curtailing its place in his narrative.

In *The Bluest Eye* Pauline Breedlove moves north, her memories of the South grow dim, and she develops a rotten front tooth, the literal equivalent of the invisible man's metaphorical image. Pauline loses her tooth one day as she bites into a candy bar, a food without sustenance, a far cry from the fish fries of the South which her neighbor Marie remembers: "The weakened roots . . . responded one day to severe pressure, and the tooth fell free, leaving a ragged stump behind."[5] Like Ellison, Morrison elaborates on the tooth as a metaphor for the uprooting of her character from a southern community and past. And yet in Morrison the tooth is also real, and it actually falls out; Morrison inflicts on her character the "short, violent eruption of pain" which Ellison allows his character to avoid, ironically by silencing the echoes of the past. In Morrison's novel Pauline's loss of a past is sudden and complete; it entails a loss in body; it amounts to a literal subtraction of herself. In depicting this loss as one of the body, Morrison faces its full pain head on, ironically freeing her to return to the "old territory" and work through its legacy. Pauline's loss of a tooth has bodily and life consequences which Morrison carefully traces. The loss ushers in a new era in Pauline's history in which white people's "word sounds" supplant the "verbal echoes" of her past. She increases her attendance at movies about happy white people, and these in turn further heighten her alienation from her own and her daughter's brown bodies. Pauline's physical transformation plays its part in her husband Cholly's disaffection and his rape of their daughter Pecola, as Morrison implies when Pecola awakens from her rape to encounter the hovering figure of her mother and then connects that figure, not the father, with the pain between her legs.

In short, the difference between symbolic metaphor and bodily fact in these representations of the rotten tooth signals a larger difference between Ellison's and Morrison's confrontations with a mother-inhabited past. The invisible man says that "with this sense of dispossession came a pang of vague recognition," and the vagueness of the recognition immediately comes into focus as a "vision" of his mother "hanging wash on a cold windy day . . . her hands white and raw in the skirt-swirling wind and her gray head bare to the darkened sky." Thus, the tooth symbolizes not only the South but specifically his mother as a figure in that past place, who appears to him from behind a veil "that threatened to lift" (273).

In the last section of *The Bluest Eye* Claudia MacTeer likewise describes a recurring vision she has of her mother in the midst of a storm. The imagery recalls Ellison's: "Biting the strawberry, thinking of storms, I see her. A slim young girl in a pink crepe dress. . . . The wind swoops her up, high above the houses, but she is still standing, hand on hip. . . . She is strong, smiling, and relaxed while the world falls down about her" (146). Both protagonists imagine the mother as a strongly embodied figure exposed to bad weather, to an antagonistic materiality (a figure who at the same time, in her role as buffer, implicitly "feeds" them their respective yams and strawberries). But the remembered mother image from which Claudia draws strength causes the invisible man "discomfort" (273). Claudia brings her narrative to closure through this vision of her windswept mother, just as she had opened her narrative with a memory of her mother as "somebody with hands who does not want me to die" (14). Claudia thus frames her supplement to Pecola's story—as Morrison frames her revision of Ellison's story—with an open sense of debt to that mother who causes the invisible man so much ambivalence and discomfort. That which is veiled, those "unrecognized compulsions" repressed in Ellison's narrative, emerge into the open in Morrison's novel. With them comes a closer involvement—and acknowledgment, even by Claudia, of complicity—in the story of the black father's rape of a beloved daughter.

These differences reflect Morrison's attempt to move from metaphorical, protected renderings of the body and the history it "carries on" to an intercorporeal tasting and touching of that bodily history, in which the physical world of rotten teeth and misguided lovemaking bodies provides material facts and narrative causes rather than just symbols and motifs operating from behind a veil. In substituting symbolic and interruptive strategies of narration with intercorporeal ones, Morrison moves from submersion of the race mother's story to full exposure and foregrounding of that story. By the time she writes *Beloved*, Morrison is ready to unveil that story more fully in order to work her way past it into a narrative of the living and the dead, the past and the present, which no longer depends on the mother's presence.

PLACES AND THINGS

In *Beloved* Morrison details a phenomenological mode of being, an intercorporeal world of bodily labor, bodily "joy,"[6] and bodily disorientation which is made to bear especially heavily on the mother figure, driving her to kill the child's body she loves. And yet the novel as I read it continually shifts the tasks of embodiment out of the hands, or off the back, of Sethe, the mother. It labors in its narrative maneuvers to put Sethe's corporeality back within a world of other-beckoning, weighted being; and so it labors to invert that order (to which Sethe herself implicitly subscribes) which traces the world of corporeal being to the mothering belly and places the world's corporeal weight on a mother's back.

Thus in *Beloved* Morrison intervenes against the racial–patriarchal story in two ways: she exposes the self–displacing, mother-appropriating effects of a hierarchical metaphysics as institutionalized and lived in slavery; and she uncovers another extramaternal phenomenology by which to retrieve and find strength in the painful slave past. William Andrews has discussed how dialogues in slave narrative expose the limit of white hegemony over speech.[7] Morrison clarifies the limit of white hegemony over black history, bodies, and narrative, especially as these require an ontological "place" in the world of objects.

Several critics have noted the importance of place in Morrison's fiction, linking her representations of place to those in African, African American, and women's traditions.[8] I too foreground place as an element of Morrison's vision, but I analyze place, in the vocabulary of phenomenology, as an ontological ground circumscribed in *Beloved* by the conditions and legacy of slavery. I situate Morrison's depiction of place within that ongoing Western dialogue over the nature and status of materiality which in turn takes shape within the context of American slavery. The ex-slave characters in *Beloved* struggle together to situate themselves in history, both personal and communal, by attempting to gain a place in the world of space and objects. They must reorient themselves not only *toward* objects and bodies but also *within* the medium of space which they inhabit together with objects, that medium into which they and others and objects are "thrown" together, to use Heidegger's term.[9] Furthermore, they must negotiate the gender ideologies that work in tandem with those of race and slavery to disrupt the black American's emplacement in the world. To reenter history, to have a future and the capacity to make "plans," the characters must transform the ontology determined for them by slavery.

In slavery the situating capacity of objects and space is withheld from the slave. From the experience of the Middle Passage, during which African persons found themselves stored like cargo, to one-room cabins on plantations, to hideouts such as Harriet Jacobs's nine-by-seven-by-three-foot "loophole" of space above her grandmother's shed, slaves experienced a constriction of space that left little opportunity for bodily self-projection into the world of things, persons, and places. As Paul D reflects, being a slave meant "listening to the doves in Alfred, Georgia, and having neither the right nor the permission to enjoy it because in that place mist, doves, sunlight, copper dirt, moon—everything belonged to the men who had the guns."[10] Not only do the men with guns deprive Paul D of the situating presence of doves and copper dirt, but they inhabit in his place the invisible envelopes of being that secrete those things—the mist, the sunlight, the moonlight.

As Paul D consequently realizes, freedom does not mean, first of all, the freedom to control or, as Sartre has it, to form projects in the world; rather it begins with one's ability "to get to a place where you could love anything you chose . . . well, now *that* was freedom" (162). One "gets to a place" of freedom. Freedom and the loving it entails require, first of all, a "place." If slavery usually generates a natal alienation by removing one from one's geographic and social place, then freedom means the ability to be where one wishes, to choose what will be "here" and what "there." Freedom thus starts with a form of voluntary situatedness in the "thrown" world. Only from such a chosen, situated position can a person choose what to gaze at and when, whom to touch and when, who will touch one and when, for only then does a person fully *inhabit* space (or Merleau-Ponty's "invisible") along with other persons and things. A free person can, to paraphrase Merleau-Ponty, take her place among the things she touches. But the occupation of a place depends on the situating presence (instead of the dominating or violating presence) of another, in most cultures beginning with a mother.

THE MOTHER NEITHER HERE NOR THERE

Ideally the human sense of situatedness originates in an intimate relation with and orientation toward the body of another—another, as Claudia says in *The Bluest Eye,* "with hands who does not want [us] to die." Another with hands. The first "place" we inhabit is, so to speak, a pair of hands. We are held in space by hands, by cradling arms, by bent backs. Place begins here, and typically those suspending, supporting, emplacing hands have been a mother's or female mother figure's. (I emphasize again that these hands or this body might be a man's, but typically have not been, and so the cultural symbolism of this phenomenological first "place" is, in many cultures, female and maternal.) Morrison details, like many ex-slave narrators before her, the deprivation in slave life of such an originary phenomenological-ontological place.

Slave narratives typically begin with a story of separation from parents, in particular a mother. Frederick Douglass recalls at the outset of his narrative that "my mother and I were separated when I was but an infant."[11] J. W. C. Pennington opens his story by bemoaning the "evil of slavery" which left his parents unable "to give any attention to their children during the day" so that he, like all slave children, was "a helpless human being thrown upon the world" or, he emphasizes, "thrown into the world without a social circle to flee to."[12] In the first paragraph of his memoir William Craft recalls that because his wife was white-skinned and looked like the master, her mistress "separated my wife from her mother."[13] Writing the story of ex-slaves in the late twentieth century, Morrison carefully describes this ontology without a horizon, this being born without a "social circle" formed around one. Her account traces the ever-elusive over-thereness" of the slave mother in relation to the slave child—that is, her position outside the child's circle of being, which makes of space a void to be crossed or a challenge to be met. This being out of reach of the mother figure leaves the space between "here" and "there" haunted by the absence of the mother's, or another's, situating body. For Sethe, the haunted space she experienced in her childhood returns for her in her motherhood.

Sethe's mother explicitly occupies an unreachable "over there," and this maternal displacement conditions Sethe's every act, including her most momen-tous motherly one. Her first accessible memory of her mother is of seeing her "pointed out as the one among many backs turned away from her, stooping in a watery field" (30). Sethe's mother—half submerged in the watery field, half drowned perhaps in the sea she crossed with her friend Nan—stands out of reach, scarcely visible, only her back in sight. Sethe distinguishes her "ma'am" from the other women by way of "a cloth hat as opposed to a straw one" (31). This, Sethe's first vision of her mother, as Sethe remembers it, represents the inadequate postural schema, or the uncaught thrownness, which Sethe tries to overcome in killing her children. She tries to make a "here" out of "there" by bringing together herself, her children, and her ma'am. Instead, she makes a ghost.

For when the master's hat graphically replaces the mother's on the horizon of Sethe's vision—that is, when Sethe "recognized schoolteacher's hat" entering the yard at 124—she "collected every bit of life she had made . . . and carried, pushed, dragged them through the veil, out, away, over there where no one could hurt them" (163). In moving her children "over there," she moves them into the position of her ma'am, into that place where from afar Sethe views and desires her. Sethe puts the point more clearly when she explains her act to Beloved: "My plan was to take us all to the other side where my own ma'am is" (203). Recogniz-ing that her act fails and instead reimposes the "overthere" relation between mother and daughter, Sethe praises Beloved, who "came right on back like a good girl, like a daughter which is what I wanted to be and would have been if my ma'am had been let out of the rice long enough before they hanged her and let me be one" (203). Yet the return of Beloved to 124 can neither bridge the uncrossable distance between Sethe and her own mother nor substitute for the world outside 124 which is the rich phenomenal realm that lies always between one person and another, which they must cross to meet each other. Beloved requires no crossing from Sethe; she only extends and encourages Sethe's absence from the free person's world of crossable things. It is Paul D and Denver, as we shall see, who return Sethe to things so that she can once again walk across and among them.

Before schoolteacher's hat enters the horizon of Sethe's vision and approaches in the way not he but her mother ought to, before she is forced to a crisis, Sethe compensates for the forever-over-there position of her mother with her own abundant mothering. As an infant Sethe nursed at "another woman's tit that never had enough for all" (203), but Sethe by contrast declares when she arrives at 124 that she has "milk enough for all" (100). Sethe at first must also feed more than one child, but she is free to luxuriate in her capacity. If her mother-in-law Baby Suggs is right, however, there is something worrying about the fervor of Sethe's love, as if now that she has "got to a place" where she may love what she chooses, and how much, her love becomes an argument as well as an emotion: see, she could love all she liked and plenty; see, she had milk enough for all. See, though she never got enough milk, she had plenty to give.

The return of this phrase "milk enough for all" into Sethe's life gives the sharpest warning that what looks like the securing of Sethe's and Paul D's future is actually an oncoming crisis. As she plans supper for him after her visit to the clearing, Sethe thinks suddenly that "sure enough, she had milk enough for all" (100). But she doesn't, and shouldn't, for a ghost is still one of her children—herself as a child, whom she has always carried with her—and that child can never be sated. She can only be held, wept over, then purged.

THE TREE BETWEEN THEM

In the first part of the novel Paul D and Sethe inch toward a mutual healing of their ruptured ontology in the world of things. But that healing is hindered by the clash of their respective gender complexes, which Sethe's claim to have "milk enough for all" signals. Paul D's attraction to Sethe precisely as a woman with milk enough for all and who thus promises a future finds its match in her attraction to him as a man who might lift away the past by sharing it with her. He wants a tree to sit under, and she wants a clear space to move in. He wants her house; she wants his legs. But both of them, despite the appearance of easy and abundant maleness and femaleness, quake with fear at their own and the other's gender inadequacies. Both his tobacco tin and her house are sealed tight against what they want but do not have and therefore cannot give away.

The opening scenes between Paul D and Sethe, in the kitchen and the bedroom, circle around trees as markers of the displacement that undercuts their relation to each other. Like Pauline's tooth in *The Bluest Eye*, trees function throughout *Beloved* as more than metaphors. They manifest the phenomenal effects of the history of slavery, such as with those "most beautiful sycamores in the world" from which Sethe can remember seeing "boys hanging" (6). At the same time trees and the material world to which they belong hold out the promise of an ontological "clearing" into which the intercorporeal self can step and speak.

At first Paul D seems capable of anything, even the carving out of a clearing, of a suspending space. He holds Sethe's breasts and hugs her scar-dead back. Although she cannot feel him trace her tree-shaped scar with his lips, his embrace makes her feel that perhaps she can for the first time "trust things and remember things because the last of the Sweet Home men was there to catch her if she sank" (18). Perhaps, she thinks, she will finally be "caught" within this world of things into which she is thrown, in which she might otherwise sink. Perhaps someone from "there" has appeared "here" to encircle her. Not surprisingly, this hope involves a lightening of her mothering history: as Paul D kisses her back, all she can feel is that he also cups her breasts, so "the responsibility for her breasts, at last, was in somebody else's hands" (18). He "catches" both her daughterhood and her motherhood when he cradles her breasts. Both the inadequate and the abundant mothering she has survived lift away, and this leaves Sethe pondering whether there might finally be "a little space . . . a little time" (78)—in other words, a reconstituted ontology—in which to be, and to be free. Perhaps that haunted space will relax and she will cross it as she pleases. She will "get to a place" she can love freely, not as proof or compensation.

But not yet. Our first hint that Sethe's readiness to trust Paul D's hands is premature appears in the way he must return her to the tree on her back—the scar shaped like a chokecherry tree. What is to her invisible and impalpable serves for him as a point of orientation. She strays from the story of the whipping and the scar and speaks instead of her mothering and her children: "what it's like to send your children off when your breasts are full" (16). Paul D reminds her, "We was talking 'bout a tree, Sethe" (16). But Sethe cannot feel the tree, and she cannot see it. She tells Paul D she has "never seen it and never will" and knows about it only through the "whitegirl" (16). The tree is invisible to her because it is her.

A tree should be an object around which Sethe orients herself and with which she shares space but this one cleaves to her from behind, collapsing the distinction between her and the world she inhabits. The dehumanizing act of whipping has left its ontological mark on her back: she lacks positionality; she can occupy no "place," see no things because she has been reduced to one of the objects of a white gaze. She says: "I got a tree on my back and a haint in my house, and nothing in between but the daughter I am holding in my arms" (15). The "nothing in between" is the daughter she holds: where Sethe has no place she inserts a daughter; she inserts her mothering. Her mothering fills the space that yawns open before her—originally, between her and her own mother—but which she cannot occupy as a free, mobile body. Never having been "held" herself, she "holds" another in her own place. But such a condition precipitates the return of herself in the form of another daughter, a hungry, ghostly one: the "haint" in her house. In effect Sethe is surrounded by traces of herself clamoring for a space she can occupy. It is these traces of herself that will eventually displace Paul D.

Although Sethe can speak only of mothering and feel only her breasts while Paul D traces a tree, it still looks at first as if Paul D has cleared the space Sethe needs when he chases out the ghost: "[he] broke up the place, making room, shifting it, moving it over to someplace else, then standing in the place he had made" (39). Once he makes of the house "a place," Sethe notices that "things became what they were: drabness looked drab; heat was hot. Windows suddenly had view" (39). In a glimpse Sethe sees the world outside a window like that through which Mrs. Ramsay in *To the Lighthouse* steadily gazes to absorb the phenomenal world, even colonizing it for her own history. Much as Morrison makes her fictional houses into powerful places for women and reveals black women such as Eva Peace changing the meanings of houses, she also registers the way houses become for some women a defensive barracks (as for Nel's mother in *Sula* or Geraldine in *The Bluest Eye*) against the politically invaded phenomenological universe. Yet for a moment Sethe sees things outside the house—and she experiences a fresh impulse toward the "over there." In consequence she is temporarily, tentatively returned to the dimension of time as well: "The notion of a future . . . was beginning to stroke her mind" (42). Within this space opened by Paul D time becomes a hand that strokes the mind, that circles Sethe back to her presence in the world, that does not want her to die.

But, as the lovemaking scene reveals, the tree has oddly lodged itself not only between Sethe and herself but also between Paul D and Sethe and between them and their future. Trees have functioned in Paul D's life the way daughters have in Sethe's: to fill an emptied space, to counter his displacement. Sethe followed her nursing daughter north, and Paul D has taken the Cherokees' advice to "follow the tree flowers. . . . Only the tree flowers. As they go, you go. You will be where you want to be when they are gone" (112). The flowering trees have drawn him closer to that place of freedom "where you could love anything you chose" (162), as Sethe's children have drawn her. Trees have provisionally positioned Paul D in the world. But Sethe's tree cannot do so.

After they make love, Paul D compares the tree on Sethe's back to other trees and finds Sethe's tree unfit to be called a tree: "maybe shaped like one" but still "nothing like any tree he knew because trees were inviting; things you could trust and be near; talk to if you wanted to" (21). Trees give Paul D a place; they occupy the "near" for him. In giving "the near" substantiality, trees put his body in a state of trust. Sethe's tree, however, recalls his knowledge of the opposite condition: it marks a site of bodily displacement, the primal trauma of the "over there" parent, the missing horizon, the violating world that "takes" a person's "milk." In reaction, Paul D remembers Brother: "Now *that* was a tree."

If the tree on Sethe's back is the physical trace of her experience of the out-of-reach mother, a symptom of slavery's collapse of positionality, Paul D's favorite tree Brother may be understood as a similar marker. He, too, orients toward a tree, as positioning Other, in the traditional place of the mother. But, as his nickname for his favorite tree at Sweet Home suggests, Paul D has also always had something more than a tree which he could substitute for a mother: a "Brother," which is to say other men. He implies that for him the meaning of a tree is bound up with the manhood of his friends, specifically the perfect manhood of Sixo: *"There* was a man and *that* was a tree" (22). Instead of a mother, Sixo and a tree called Brother stand for that which one "can trust and be near" (21). Sethe has never had a surrogate mother, whether male, female, or tree. She recalls how she knew nothing about children and had to turn to her mistress Mrs. Garner for support.

Not only is Sethe without means for making such a substitution of another for a mother, but she also represents that which the men's substitutions replace. She recalls that when she used to bring the men their midday food, "they never took it from her hands. They stood back and waited for her to put it on the ground (at the foot of a tree) and leave" (23). Sethe holds out for them the one hope of a female figure coming "near," approaching them from the horizon; but the hope is too dim and too intense at the same time, so they enact a ritual substitution whereby the foot of a tree replaces her hand. Her participation in their ritual substitution— they replace the "here" of the nurturing mother with the nearness of the tree— leaves her isolated while it draws them together around the presence and sign of a "Brother." On those occasions when she lingers and watches them covertly, she notices "how different they were without her, how they laughed and played and urinated and sang" (23).

In *Invisible Man* we saw that homosocial connections among men, while including them in a "Brotherhood," also blocked their transformation of the mother relation. Those same homosocial conditions emerge here as an even more absolute barrier to Sethe's healing of her m/other deprivation. When alone, Sethe recalls, she had tried her own form of this substitution of plant for emplacing other: "A few yellow flowers on the table, some myrtle tied around the handle of the flatiron holding the door open for a breeze calmed her . . . she felt fine" (22). And yet, witnessed alone, such substitutions fall short. In bed now next to Paul D, she laughs at her feeble attempts to make herself a place in the world: "As though a handful of myrtle stuck in the handle of a pressing iron propped against the door in a whitewoman's kitchen could make it hers. As though mint sprig in the mouth changed the breath as well as its odor. A bigger fool never lived" (23–24). Not knowing her husband Halle's story yet, she associates this naïveté about the power of a plant with the failure of Halle to reach 124. Just as she had once thought a handful of myrtle could rescue her from her displacement, so she thought Halle could do the same, or at least could join her and so confirm her escape from that condition of displacement. But just as, in the absence of an emplacing Other, myrtle can do nothing to change her condition of being, so in a world in which men do not show up her attempts at intercorporeal salvation abort. No, she now concludes, "a man ain't nothing but a man" (23).

And yet as he lies beside Sethe, Paul D likewise faces a loss of faith both in the other sex and in his own gendered logic of phenomenal substitution. He questions the substitution organized around Brother. For even Brother can only partially amend the fact that, just as for Sethe the master's hat rather than Halle's came to occupy the place of the mother's, Paul D's positionality depends finally not on the tree, not on the Brother or brothers, but on the master, Mr. Garner, who "garners" space—the farm, the "sweet home," the here and the near—for himself: "Garner called and announced them men—but only on Sweet Home and only by his leave" (220), for "one step off that ground and they were trespassers on the human race. Watchdogs without teeth; steer bulls without horns; gelded workhorses" (125). So, Paul D wonders, does manhood lie in "the naming done by a whiteman who was supposed to know?" (125). Paul D has no doubt about Sixo: "It was always clear to Paul D" that Sixo was a man "whether Garner said so or not" (220). But "it troubled him that, concerning his own manhood, he could not satisfy himself on that point" (220). Thus, lying next to Sethe and studying her back, he thinks about Sixo and Brother and concludes that "himself lying in the bed and the 'tree' lying next to him didn't compare" (22). As Sethe's back-cloven tree falls short of the autonomous "treeness" of Brother, so Paul D's contingent manhood falls short of Sixo's seemingly absolute manhood, and Sethe's tree thus marks the displacement that Paul D and Sethe have in common.

Sethe's and Paul D's meditations indicate the intersection of gender and ontology in the racialized slave world. Myrtle ain't nothing but myrtle and a man ain't nothing but a man. Like husbands, and like the calves the Sweet Home men substitute for women, things in the slave world stand radically apart, never fully giving you back to yourself, never giving themselves and their worlds to you. The ex-slaves' gender trouble forms as an extension of their phenomenological crises. Whereas typically the adult romantic relationship may become a substitute for or even a healing of the parent–child relationship, in slavery that adult relationship threatens most of all to repeat the child's trauma, specifically the inability to "get to a place" where one can love.[14] So the belief in the other sex's capacity to enrich one's experience of intercorporeal being appears as an illusion.

The Narrative Tree

And yet herein lies the irony with which Morrison works; herein lies her supplement of the critique of history with the recovery of its resources, especially as embedded in the body. For, despite the deadness of Sethe's tree and despite Paul D's doubts about whether he can stand up next to any tree anymore, much less a woman with a dead one on her back, the bodies about which Sethe and Paul D have so much doubt serve, in the narrative sequencing of the bedroom scene, as the medium through which they orient themselves toward each other and through which they enter the past together, and thereby progress (albeit haltingly) toward a future together. The tissue between them, numb as it is, is the terrain on which they must meet, and is, more important, the terrain on which the text forces us to meet them and their history.

Although Sethe's and Paul D's full encounter will entail further bodily separation and displacement, here in this second chapter Morrison signals that the recovery of the past and the ground of another future lies in the numb but still present phenomenality they share. In the same scene in which they reflect on their gendered alienation from each other, both characters remember their pasts and discover their alienation *because* they lie together in a room, in a bed, touching each other: during a pause in his reflections "Paul D looked through the window and folded his hands behind his head. An elbow grazed Sethe's shoulder. The touch of cloth on her skin startled her. She had forgotten he had not taken off his shirt" (22). This touch provides the pivot on which the narrative turns from Paul D's memories to Sethe's. When Paul D shifts his suddenly uncomfortable body, involuntarily touching the woman with whom he shares a past, his past touches hers in the narrative—for his touching Sethe recalls her past for her, and the narrative moves into *her* recollections of Sweet Home.

After musing a while, Sethe likewise pauses, shifts her body unconsciously, and draws the attention of Paul D. We exit Sethe's memories and enter Paul D's

217

when "Sethe started to turn over on her stomach but changed her mind. She did not want to call Paul D's attention back to her, so she settled for crossing her ankles" (24). But "Paul D noticed the movement as well as the change in her breathing" (24). And because he sees her movements, the narrative can complete its turn from Sethe's past to this present moment of their lovemaking back into the parallel past embedded in Paul D's body. Morrison thus makes their bodies in her story achieve the very phenomenological positioning of present in relation to past, of self in relation to Other, of man in relation to woman which they at this moment doubt the possibility of, precisely because of their bodily histories.

Morrison's narrator makes their flesh her narrative bridge, her conduit not only between their two subjectivities and their two pasts but also between the African American slave past and "free" present, and so implicitly between the history she tells and the audience to whom she tells it. In other words, the touching of Sethe's and Paul D's resisting bodies, which liberates their histories, also liberates Morrison's story, which strives continually to connect the past with the present in the form of touching bodies. Her use of these moments of physical contact places us in between her two characters, allowing us to see the shared history (both theirs and ours along with theirs) accumulated in that involuntary touching, a history the characters themselves cannot recall in common. Their bodies are in bed together, each moving with the other's movements, involuntarily, unknowingly remembering the other's memories and generating Morrison's story.

In staging this drama, Morrison first of all carries out her critique of oppression by showing how her characters are blind to their own common ground because of its having become numb scar tissue. Furthermore, she retrieves history and writes the story of another future by putting us as readers in the narrative position of orientation around their common phenomenal ground. She makes the narrative body revive the phenomenological function of which slavery had stripped the slave body; and she simultaneously makes that phenomenological body the site at which the slave history intersects with contemporary history in the form of her story.

Again and again in the novel physical phenomena, while surfacing memories for the characters, by the same token make space for the recovery of history in the narrative. In the opening moments of the novel, for example, we learn that Sethe would be doing her housework with "nothing else in her mind" but then suddenly some small thing or sensation would bring back her past: "Then something. The plash of water, the sight of her shoes and stocking awry on the path were she had flung them; or Here Boy lapping in the puddle near her feet and suddenly there was Sweet Home rolling, rolling, rolling out before her eyes" (6). In the passages that follow, Morrison's readers glimpse their first view of that history at Sweet

Home. As in Virginia Woolf's fiction, the past materializes both for the character and for the reader through "something"—some touch or sight or sound.

In this opening scene Morrison gives that past an intercorporeal or physically interactive presence through the character of Paul D, who appears at this moment "as if to punish [Sethe] further for her terrible memory" (6). Morrison reinforces the point here that for each of us the embodied Other rematerializes our past, even as the plash of water might, and she further hints, as the drama of Beloved, Paul D, Sethe, and Denver unfolds, that the embodied world and the embodied Other insert past into present interactively, bringing their own pasts to bear upon our bearing upon them.

Thus, the shifting between past and present and between points of view in the novel by way of the things and bodies of the phenomenal world models for the reader a structure of the phenomenal intertwining of histories and bodies. The doubleness of mutual attraction and resistance in this intertwining determines Morrison's circuitous narrative structure, for her narrative follows the self-protective rhythms of her characters' Other-entangled bodies, pursuing tenaciously the histories they (like the invisible man) repress.

And so, as the novel makes evident, only these bodies will save them and us, their inheritors. But first these bodies, represented in Paul D and Sethe, will move apart, playing out the gender anxiety suppressed and yet expressed in their touching bodies—like that of the two turtles Beloved later sees coupling just before Paul D leaves 124: "The gravity of their shields, clashing, countered and mocked the floating heads touching" (105). They resist even as they touch; their memories are opposed even as they constitute a shared history and a single story.

BELOVED'S PLACE

Paul D's and Beloved's relations replay and exacerbate this shifting and ironic intercorporeal history. Shortly after Beloved's arrival we learn abruptly and emphatically that "SHE MOVED HIM" (114). "Whenever she turned her behind up, the calves of his youth (was that it?) cracked his resolve" (126). What are these "calves of youth"? More than desire in his muscles, these calves also refer to the logic of phenomenal substitution to which a slave or ex-slave is forced and yet which finally fails him. The "calves" of Paul D's youth signify the history of sexual deprivation which sometimes drove him and the other men to substitute a calf for a woman. Lying with Sethe in bed that first morning, Paul D considers that "the jump . . . from a calf to a girl wasn't all that mighty" (26). This substitution recalls those other substitutions, of a tree for a brother, a brother for a mother, a calf for a woman, and now, in bed with Sethe, a woman for a calf. It is in part this logic of substitution that makes him wonder if "schoolteacher was right" about the slaves not being men.

In effect, Paul D's inability "to satisfy himself on that point" (220) leaves him vulnerable to Beloved's approaches and makes her capable of "moving" him. She renews and extends for him, as schoolteacher's arrival at 124 did for Sethe, his youthful displacement. As he explains, what most humiliates him is "being moved, *placed* where she wanted him, and there was nothing he was able to do about it" (114; emphasis added). His removal begins with his impulse to substitute the rocking chair for the bed he shares with Sethe, and he follows the impulse because after sleeping in the chair he recalls other "good-sleep places" such as "the base of certain trees here and there" (114). The detail hints at how this first move reenacts the substitutional emplacement trees perform for Paul D; it is a kind of movement he knows, and therefore initially he cooperates with it. In short, Paul D has lived a logic of substitutions—of trees for brothers, of calves for women, of loving small things in the place of big (162). This logic, however, puts him in doubt about his manhood; it reminds him of how the simple substitution of one master for another makes him no longer a man; it suggests that perhaps if he can love a calf in the place of a woman, he is not a man but an animal. It reminds him of Sixo, who refused substitution—wouldn't substitute English for his African language or substitute a nearby woman or a calf for a woman thirty miles away. What substitution would Paul D refuse? In the life of Sethe he substitutes for Halle. Who is he then? And is he a man?

With this gender doubt as Beloved's lever "she moved him. Just when doubt, regret and every single unasked question was packed away, long after he believed he had willed himself into being, at the very time and place he wanted to take root—she moved him. From room to room. Like a rag doll" (221). Paul D is about to leave off the life of substitutions; he is about to take up a position in this "very time and place." But Beloved reopens the doubts that were only "packed away" and not extinguished. And she forces to its extreme his gender-anxious accommodation to displacement, until he inhabits neither the shade of a tree nor the warmth of a bed but only a pallet in the cold shed and finally the frozen steps of a church. Beloved's last removal of Paul D comes when she precipitates, at least in his perception, his break with Sethe: "'Your love is too thick,' he said, thinking, That bitch is looking at me; she is right over my head looking down through the floor at me" (164). He blames his cutting words to Sethe on Beloved.

On the one hand, Paul D has a point about Sethe's love and about Beloved's part in his departure. He is right that Sethe's problem, as revealed in her killing of her baby, is that she "didn't know where the world stopped and she began" (164). In addition, as he seems to sense, Beloved's supposed ability to look through floors is a mirror image of Sethe's blindness to boundaries between herself and the world. The mother and daughter transgress boundaries, penetrate boundaries, sabotaging their prescribed cultural function to create and reproduce boundaries. And Paul D is right to resist both Sethe's and Beloved's tendency toward radical boundary collapse, their tendency to close the horizon because it always holds "over there" what you most want near: so the one or two things you hold (your daughters or mother) you hold tight.

On the other hand, none of this changes or accounts for the fact that Paul D *receives* Beloved's transgressive gaze and Sethe's transgressive act with such involuntary shame: he instinctively feels compelled to remark, "You got two feet, Sethe, not four," though "later he would wonder what had made him say it? the calves of his youth? or the conviction that he was being observed through the ceiling? How fast he moved from his shame to hers. From his cold-house secret to her too-thick love" (165). He moves fast because both he and Sethe struggle with different forms, as we have seen, of the same displaced condition, a condition created by the master's enforcement of an opposition between master and slave, man and animal, wherein the latter only marks the horizon of the master's field, and rarely is the center around which a horizon forms its circle.

Thus, if Beloved precipitates Paul D's offense against Sethe, this means only that Beloved engages and forces to a crisis, through Sethe, Paul D's gender anxiety about that boundary between two feet and four—between a calf and a woman, a man and an animal, between "here" and "there." And in forcing it to a crisis in Paul D, in precipitating his words and his removal, Beloved also forces this anxiety over the distinction between human and animal to a crisis in Sethe. For it is after Paul D leaves that Sethe returns in memory to the moment when she heard schoolteacher authoring the catalogue of her animal and human characteristics.

Moreover, it is after Paul D leaves that Sethe takes Beloved and Denver out skating—to reenact, again and again, the tragic phenomenology of "falling" where there is no one to see you, and thereby of feeling forced to kneel on all fours: "Making a circle or a line, the three of them could not stay upright for one whole minute, but nobody saw them falling" (174). When Sethe determines suddenly to take the girls out skating, with only three skates among them, distributed so that the girls share three and Sethe gets none, she thinks how "anybody feeling sorry for her, anybody wandering by to peep in and see how she was getting on (including Paul D) would discover that the woman junkheaped for the third time because she loved her children—that woman was sailing happily on a frozen creek" (174). But she slips rather than sails on the frozen creek, which is her own frozen history; and anyway, nobody wanders by and "nobody saw them falling."

This repeated line structures the scene like a choral chant, even as the scene itself symbolically repeats the trauma of "thrownness" where no one sees or catches you. The three desperate women "fought gravity for each other's hands. Their skirts flew like wings and their skin turned pewter in the cold and dying light. Nobody saw them falling" (174). After Denver falls comically and the three lie down laughing hysterically, Sethe rises "to her hands and knees. . . . She stayed that way for a while, on all fours" (175). The narrator's phrase echoes Paul D's accusation. Sethe's laughter becomes a flow of tears, and in the posture of an animal with four legs, not two, she weeps. Once again "junkheaped," once again moving within a field in which she falls and gazes at the m/other, the m/other who with back bent and turned cannot see her falling, Sethe once more becomes that which other humans define themselves against. Here Morrison explores the real import, for being, of what gets figured as a distinction between two feet and four, human and beast, mind and body in nineteenth- and twentieth-century discourses of the body. What makes one feel like a "mere" beast is a state in which no one catches one and no one sees one fall. (The image recalls Sasha Jansens's in Jean Rhys's *Good Morning, Midnight* of "the struggle and the drowning . . . when there are no willing and eager friends around, and you sink.")[15]

At the close of the scene in which no one has seen them fall, Sethe reciprocally has lost her desire to see. Beloved asks, "You finished with your eyes?" and Sethe answers, "Yes, I'm finished with my eyes" (175). Just following this shutting down of the reversible visible and Sethe's removal from human intercorporeality, which, as she feels it, marks the recovery of her dream to join with her daughter and mother directly, to go "over there," Sethe hears Beloved sing the song only Sethe's children know and "the click came . . . the settling of pieces into places designed and made especially for them" (175). A regressive emplacement is fixed in position. At this moment Sethe thinks of Baby Suggs, who remembers not her daughter's hands but only that the daughter loved burned bread; she thinks of her ma'am showing the brand under her breast and saying, "Here. Look here. This is your ma'am. If you can't tell me by my face, look here" (176). Even as her ma'am must sutstitute the mark of her owner for the features of her face, and Baby Suggs must substitute burned bread for "little hands," so Sethe must substitute Beloved for herself; she must agree with Beloved to be finished with her eyes.

In such a moment "the peace of winter stars seemed permanent" (176), but it was not. For although the next morning Sethe finds herself "smiling, smiling at the things she would not have to remember now" (182), on that day and many to follow "her mind was busy with the things she could forget" (191)—*could* forget but does not. Instead of being freed of the past, Sethe obsessively repeats it, both in her ongoing deeds of self-displacement and in her words. Although she thinks, "Thank God I don't have to rememory or say a thing because you know it," she goes on to explain it all to Beloved, over and over: "You know I never would have left you. . . . It was all I could think of to do," and so on (191).

The fixedness of the three women clicked into their places, which forbids their free movement from place to place—house to street, street to other house—climaxes with the round of monologues they speak to one another. They repeat and repeat their possessive, self-collapsing identity, and repeat moreover a whole people's history in which the space around one collapses and there remains no common ground outside of each through which each is oriented toward the other. It is this collapsed space that Baby Suggs had earlier labored to open, to clear out, in her sermons at the Clearing.

CLEARING THE SPACE FOR INTERCORPOREALITY

As prelude to a discussion of the Clearing, let us recall the notion that Morrison labors, especially through a rhetoric of tree-oriented bodies, to open up an inter-corporeal space within her text. This rhetoric informs the scene in which Sethe and Paul D separate and prompts us to interpret their parting in light of Baby Suggs's sermons in the Clearing—that space among trees.

Paul D's reminder to Sethe that she has two feet not four abandons Sethe to the discursive order in which two feet stand always opposed to four. It returns her, and him, to a Darwinian world in which being is ranked and antagonistic. It forces them both down on all fours and leaves them, finally, to fold in on themselves. But in closing the scene in which Paul D accuses Sethe of animality, and in preparing an undercurrent for the skating chapter in which Sethe, Denver, and Beloved fall together and no one sees them, Morrison again makes the division between Paul D and Sethe into a tree-filled space of possibility. "'You got two feet, Sethe, not four,' he said, and right then a forest sprang up between them; trackless and quiet" (165). Here the numbed tree between them—the visible that for Sethe is invisible—grows into an unexplored forest. This forest "lock[s] the distance between them, giving it shape and heft" (165). It expands the impasse between them. But just as the tree in their first lovemaking moment marked not only the site of their numbness but also their point of contact, now this forest opens up and gives shape to the scary, quiet place where they can explore their gendered and phenomenological trouble with place, time, and each other. Sethe must play out all the way her experience of falling where there is no one to see or catch her. Paul D must breathe the smell leaking from his tobacco tin heart. Beloved must force a new distance between Paul D and Sethe into place, but it is the very same distance into which she herself will finally disappear when Paul D and Sethe have tracked their ways across it.

In the form of a rhetoric of trees Morrison generates a narrative from Paul D and Sethe's locked stasis; she clears a space for their future. In other words, Morrison keeps in play, unbeknownst to her characters, a narrative phenomenology wherein the material world that is the field of their oppositional, human–animal orientation also serves as the potential field of their reencounter and as the text's rhetorical field for establishing a narrative intercorporeality. For only in a forest can one find a "clearing." Only in the midst of things, of trees, can one "get to the place" Baby Suggs would take them to if she were alive and well.

In this context it is no surprise that, when she speaks in the Clearing, Baby Suggs calls out the people from among the trees. In the novel's short life, the Clearing scene has been quoted many times, a reflection of its attunement to contemporary cultural—and, I would add, phenomenological and revisionary—preoccupations.[16] Now the scene must take its explicitly prominent place in this reading of *Beloved,* for in the Clearing Baby Suggs speaks from the kind of intercorporeal "place" that Paul D, Sethe, and Denver need to get to—"a wide-open place cut deep in the woods nobody knew what for"—and yet where everybody came, saw, and was seen (87).

In the Clearing trees participate in and echo the convergence of bodies; they yield persons to the space in which they interact: the folks "waited among the trees" until Baby Suggs calls them out, first the children who "ran from the trees toward her," then the men who "stepped out one by one from among the ringing trees" (87). The trees "ring" both visually, in a circle around the people, and aurally, for the "woods rang" with children's laughter. Within this ring of trees the gendered direction of the gaze is reversed as Baby Suggs invites the men to "let your wives and your children see you dance," and when they do "the ground-life shuddered under their feet" (87). A further crossing of gender and parent–child divisions occurs as "women stopped crying and danced; men sat down and cried; children danced, women laughed, children cried until, exhausted and riven, all and each lay about the Clearing damp and gasping for breath" (88).

When Baby Suggs then speaks in the aural space of "the silence that followed," she begins with the word "here" and she repeats it. "'Here,' she said, 'in this here place, we flesh'" (88). The emphatic "here" of her sentence gives place to "flesh." In this place she pieces the parts of the unloved body back together, from eyes to mouths to necks to livers to hands to feet, until finally she stands up to dance them into one cohering movement "while the others," forming an emplacing world for Baby Suggs as she has for them, "opened their mouths and gave her the music" (89).

Baby Suggs has moved toward this recognition of "flesh" and her power to name it for herself from the day she left the South and entered free territory. At the moment when Baby Suggs crosses that border, not expecting to feel anything, wondering why she is leaving her life behind, two kinds of freedom, bodily and linguistic, intersect and surprise her: "Suddenly she saw her hands and thought with a clarity as simple as it was dazzling, 'These hands belong to me. These *my* hands'" (141). In the same instant in which Baby Suggs's flesh enters a free space, her speech crosses a linguistic border into the vernacular: from "these hands belong to me" to "these my hands." Morrison makes Baby Suggs's hands the lever of her self-transformative speech even as she makes the bodies of Paul D and Sethe the hinges of the narrative's swing from past into present and from one point of view to another. It is at this narrational level that Morrison realizes Baby Suggs's call to worship the flesh.

But Baby Suggs "collapses." Morrison repeats her reference to "Baby Suggs' collapse" (89, 90). And around her collapses the space of intercorporeality, so that for her last days Baby Suggs merely "lay in the keeping-room bed roused once in a while by a craving for color and not for another *thing*" (89; emphasis added). And, likewise for Sethe, although she returns many years later in the hope of inhabiting a clearing in which the flesh might find a place, she discovers instead that even the Clearing is for her haunted—violated by the very hands that never did hold her as a child and now strangle her in the form of her own child. Twenty-eight days of Baby Suggs's flesh love were not enough to undo the history in which schoolteacher's hat replaced her mother's on the horizon of her vision. Her ghostly daughter, who is also her ghostly and daughterly self, turns the hands of flesh–love into the hands locking around an emptiness, fixing it in place. Baby Suggs's call to "love your neck; put a hand on it, grace it, stroke it and hold it up" (88) seems at first to be carried out by Baby Suggs herself as Sethe sits on the rock; but the caressing fingers soon become the daughterly fingers that have "a grip on [Sethe] that would not let her breathe" (96).

And yet again we must keep in mind how Morrison smuggles in the past and the body exactly through these moments of bodily betrayal. Sethe's return to the physical space of the Clearing not only precipitates her return to the memory of her long-ago arrival at 124 and of her embrace by Baby Suggs's free hands but also provides the vehicle for the text's enfolding of that history. The fictional return to the Clearing, in other words, creates a secondary narrative opening into which Morrison inserts a history. Sethe returns because she wants "to listen to the spaces that the long-ago singing had left behind" (89), and Morrison inserts a history into that ringing space: "Followed by the two girls, down a bright green corridor of oak and horse chestnut, Sethe began to sweat a sweat just like the other one when she woke, mud-caked, on the banks of the Ohio" (90). In this Clearing a birth is recalled, literally of Denver, implicitly of the novel's inter-corporeal intertwining of history, bodies, and words.

THE PLACE OF DENVER

The convergence of these two laborious births—the text's and Denver's—occurs because Denver is the daughter who actively manipulates the world and the past so as to create the future. It is the unghostly daughter, whom Sethe did not manage to send "over there," who must carry on the body-embedded temporality the text seeks to represent. Because Paul D is involuntarily "moved" by the ghost of Sethe's daughterhood which also invokes the ghost of his substitutional manhood, he alone cannot enact the proper return and purge of Sethe's bodily, daughterly history. Only Denver, the living daughter, can begin a new daughterly history that will both reembody and surpass the old. Denver is she who drank her sister's blood with her mother's milk, which I understand to mean that in nursing from her mother's bloody breast after the murder of her sister, Denver drinks in the ghost of her mother's displaced daugherly self, for it is that displaced self, as we have seen, that drives Sethe to murder. Or, to put it differently, the ghost is both milk sister and blood mother to Denver, the latter insofar as the ghost is a reembodiment of her mother as a child. Denver interacts with this ghost in making her own future out of her mother's bloodied past. If Paul D is "moved" and displaced by Beloved, then behind Beloved stands the "charmed" mover, Denver.

Denver has a special relation to the baby ghost. She can hear the ghost when no one else can and when she herself can hear nothing else. She sees her kneeling beside her mother in the keeping room when her mother is unaware of any other presence. She knows the ghost has "plans." But in fact it is Denver's future at least as much as Sethe's that the ghost's plans bear on. For Denver's sensitivity to the ghost begins when she loses the future promised by the lessons at Lady Jones's house. After the loss of that promise, manipulations effected *through* the ghost—that is, through indirect interaction with her mother's past as embodied in the displaced ghost—become Denver's only means to a future. After Nelson Lord's question about her mother and jail, Denver shifts her energy from book learning to thinking about the ghost: "The monstrous and unmanageable dreams about Sethe found release in the concentration Denver began to fix on the baby ghost" (103). We learn that "before Nelson Lord, she had been barely interested in its antics" but after his question the ghost "held for her all the anger, love and fear she didn't know what to do with" (103). The ghost, originally the object and the vehicle of all of the anger, love, and fear which Sethe does not know what to do with, thus becomes a similar vehicle for Denver, for those emotions provoked by and inherited from her mother. The ghost is the physical effect of that unchanneled, "uncaught" set of emotions which constrict Sethe and Denver in time and place.

Denver's alternative connection to the future through this ghost of the past is more painful than the common path of learning to read and write. And yet it is necessary because Denver cannot after all embrace another future without confronting and purging the ghost of her mother's past. That Denver's future rests fragilely upon her mother's traumatic past appears in the fact that Denver encourages her mother to make the story of her, Denver's, birth into Sethe's only "told story," the sum of all the stories of Sethe's past.

When in this light we think of the ghost as the material link between Sethe's daughterly past and Denver's daughterly future, we further understand Morrison's phenomenological imagination. Through Beloved she grounds the cumulative temporal flow from past to present to future in a phenomenal presence, in the presence of a "pregnant" body—which is not after all a mother's body but the pregnancy of embodiment itself as an enfolding of the breathing invisible within the visible. Morrison gives us a phenomenology of the "supernatural." Beloved is the supremely intercorporeal expression of the supernatural, the surreal, which turns out simply to be the reversible side of the "real," the invisible enfolded within, and giving place to, the visible. For the characters the ghostly Beloved is all of that ghostly, stolen-away-by-whites-but-always-there-waiting-for-you time and place of the slave past; for the novel she is that ghostly, invisible time and place rendered visible, turned inside out, and revealed as interactive, enabling, necessary. For Denver she is the one remaining point of physical leverage into the spatiotemporal world which includes but transforms a painful slave past.

Therefore, when Paul D comes and exorcises the ghost from the house, Denver faces a crisis not only of run-of-the-mill loneliness and jealousy but also of a deeply ontological order. Her instrument of insertion (the ghost with plans, the past harboring a future) into a temporal ongoingness, into her own future, has been taken. If somehow Sethe, in the arms of Paul D, can leave behind a past that cruelly keeps her daughter from her own future, Denver faces an ontological annihilation, a repetition of her mother's displacement. After the exorcism, when Paul D, Sethe, and Denver hold hands walking to the carnival, it appears as if they might manage to bring her with them into another future. But despite the impressiveness of Paul D's initial exorcism, he too walks only one step in front of a locked-away past (the calves of his youth). Like Sethe's, his past will return to haunt him—through the "antics" of Beloved.

I suggest that Denver instigates the return of the past for her mother, herself, and Paul D. Through Beloved, Denver forces to the surface not only her mother's murderous boundary-violating act but also her mother's deeper hurt and anger and fear over her own mother. Put in a desperate position, she moves her mother and Paul D, through the antics of Beloved, past the story of her birth to the untold stories of her mother's "miscarriage" and act of murder. It is Denver who initially provokes the ghost to break up the first embrace of Paul D and Sethe. Sensing the attraction between them, Denver "wished for the baby ghost." A moment later the ghost rocks the house and throws Paul D to the floor. Furthermore, as Sethe explains to Paul D, the companionship Beloved provides for Denver makes Sethe tolerant of and even tender toward Beloved. Beloved arrives and is allowed to remain *because* of Denver; Beloved then does the work of bringing to the surface both Paul D's and Sethe's pasts so that Denver can move beyond them, out of the house, into her own future.

I do not mean to suggest that Denver catalyzes this transformation consciously. On the contrary, the process involves a painful experience of exclusion for Denver. In the process of transposition her mother and Beloved must pair off against Denver. And yet here again a division becomes an expanded site of future possibilities, as the division of cells engenders growth, and as the dividing tree on Sethe's back becomes the forest holding the future of Sethe and Paul D.

The space created around Denver by the pairing of Beloved and Sethe becomes the opening through which Denver finally sees her mother for herself. She sees that her mother's body is starving, her mother's fleshly self-presence, epitomized in the connection between touching fingers, is thinning—"Denver saw the flesh between her mother's forefinger and thumb fade"—and suddenly she knows that "the job she started out with, protecting Beloved from Sethe, changed to protecting her mother from Beloved" (243). She sees her own positionality between them, which is also her positionality between her mother's past and her and her mother's future. So Denver moves out into that other outdoor space which has awaited her all along. She can now pursue her future once again, as she had long ago begun to do, with the aid of Lady Jones rather than the ghost.

And with the guidance of Baby Suggs. It is Baby Suggs's words, urging her to "go on out the yard" (244), that move Denver off the front porch steps and into the street, just as it was Baby Suggs who earlier told Denver "her things," called her "charmed," and reminded her to "always listen to my body and love it" (209).[17] Denver prides herself on "knowing the things behind things" (37). She creates her own private "clearing" in the dome of boxwood bushes, where "protected by the live green walls, she felt ripe and clear" (29). And so Denver becomes the daughter who will carry on Baby Suggs's and Morrison's enactment of an emplacing, ongoing intercorporeality.

Her entry into the larger world of things and persons catalyzes a reenactment by the women of the community of the nurturing role performed—at one remove—by Sethe for the Sweet Home men. Two days after her visit to Lady Jones, Denver notices "something lying on the tree stump at the edge of the yard"—"a sack of white beans" (248–49). As Sethe once placed food for the men, and in the process supplemented their attempts at emplacement, so here the women begin to supplement Denver's attempt to reposition herself and her mother in the world, begun by Denver's confronting the world of places outside her house.

This process of reemplacement of Denver and Sethe climaxes when the community women come directly to Sethe's door, see her daughterly ghost, and sing. "For Sethe it was as though the Clearing had come to her with all its heat and shimmering leaves" (261). Through the women, and through the daughter who engages them, Sethe finally occupies a place. The leaves of the trees other than the one on her back come alive for her as she sees "not one touch of death in the definite green of the leaves" (261). Although Morrison makes clear through Sethe's attempted attack on her neighbor Mr. Bodwin that any seeming reappearance of the black hat on her horizon would quickly send her right back to her daughterly fear and rage, she also shows how that regression can be forestalled by a ring of emplacing others who catch her as she falls.

THE PAST PASSED

When Paul D traces his steps back to 124, his presence evokes for Sethe the memory that "her ma'am had hurt her feelings and she couldn't find her hat anywhere" (272). When at this moment she begins to cry and mumbles, "She left me. . . . She was my best thing" (272), we know how fully the ghost of Beloved has enacted for her the loss of her own mother. Her own gendered mother–daughter condition is named. Paul D meanwhile thinks of Sixo and his thirty-mile woman; that is, *his* gendered condition is likewise recalled. He remembers that Sixo called his woman a "friend of my mind. . . . The pieces I am, she gather them and give them back to me." Paul D then thinks how Sethe always "left him his manhood" so that now he thinks of her as a "friend of his mind" and finds "he wants to put his story next to hers" (273). Their two gendered stories of traumatized being—of "time that didn't stay put" (272) and stars that aren't theirs to look at—can now embrace without a clash of shields. Paul D and Sethe are finally in a position to put side by side those stories that Morrison has put side by side, in the form of their touching bodies and of a rhetoric of trees, throughout the novel. When Paul D tells Sethe that "we got more yesterday than anybody. We need some kind of tomorrow," he begins to place them in a shared future-oriented temporality (273). When he tells Sethe that she is her own "best thing" while "his holding fingers were holding hers" (273), he initiates between them a renewed intercorporeality that lets them "take their place among the things they touch" (*VI*, 133) and lets readers take their places beside these written and fictional yet nonetheless phenomenal bodies.

The closing lines of *Beloved* acknowledge the paradox it has narrated. If *Invisible Man* covertly clings to and repeats a painful history by partially repressing it, *Beloved* purges and heals (for a time) that painful history by fully embracing it. Thus the novel passes on a story that is not to be passed on. The story of transgressive time and constricted space, of ruptured intercorporeality, is a story to pass through and beyond in time and place, so as to enter the here and now and tomorrow—for, as the narrator tells us, after the ghosts that people the world of things, and after the people who become a world of ghosts, "the rest is weather" (275). Or, as Virginia Woolf's narrator concludes in *The Waves*, after all is said and done, "the waves broke on the shore."[18] Only these bodies, here and now, turned toward one another in gesture, word, and deed, will create a future worth living in that vaster world of waves and weather, the world against which the storm-racked bodies of the Mrs. McNabs and Mrs. MacTeers have, until now, served as buffers.

Conclusion

If phenomenologists and modern novelists bring to the surface the subversive undercurrents of Romantic and scientific discourses of the body, further converging and crisscrossing words and bodies, mixing mothers and authors, those undercurrents have hardly yet succeeded in redirecting the main current of racial–patriarchal history. It seemed at first that, with the demise of Nazi Germany and the exposure of its genocidal crimes, the sexual–racial mythologies so loudly expressed in eugenics would meet their demise as well. In the disciplines of sociology, psychology, history, and anthropology, the ascendant biological frameworks of analysis, in particular racial and sexual determinism, began to be supplanted by cultural frameworks of analysis. But in hindsight it is clear that the "war against matter," and against those affiliated with it, simply took new forms and moved to other terrains.

Not only did science shift its ground to the still racially and sexually biased notions of "gene pools" and the mastery-driven pursuit of atom-splitting devices, and not only did sociologists and anthropologists adopt functionalist and sociobiological frameworks in the place of biological ones, and not only did the mass media merely assimilate a few exceptional Others' faces into barely changed models of the same stratified economy, but the old, starkly violent activities enacted at the street-level borders of race and sex and of speech and body have continued on doggedly. We need only think of Los Angeles, Detroit, the increasingly terrorist pro-life movement, the unabated tide of domestic violence; we need only ponder Ireland, the Middle East, Bosnia.

In the midst of these scenes of violence, and in the face of their long, even ancient history, modern novels (not to mention studies of modern novels such as this one) seem to arm us only inadequately against a sea of troubles. The undercurrents they ride might well appear slight within this tidal wave of violent politics. But the violence and the shifting vocabularies reflect the felt presence of resistance, not least of all "the Resistance" or, earlier, the Underground Railroad. And even this model of resistance may be inadequate to describe the limits of political hegemony. The "flesh" may predate or surpass the conception of it as this or that kind of "body."[1] What we too readily think of as the countervoice may either predate and provoke the "voice" or cooriginate with this mastering voice, so that we need to speak always of at least two voices. Against experimental books and unassimilated speech the dominant voice holds forth, but its work is endless, for it is in the grip of the thing it seeks to master: a speaking body. In other words, the undercurrent deflects and shapes the speech flow of the main current from within.

In this book I have sought not only to speak at odds with racial patriarchy but also to expose its central myth of the division of words from bodies. When we emphasize how political torture and violence break the body away from its power to speak, as Elaine Scarry does in her study *The Body in Pain*,[2] we might well consider this fact—namely, that such extreme bodily means are required to make the body speechless—as testimony to the depth of the body's entanglement in speech. If a master class must enter the domain of the body to subdue speech, then discourse must share the body's realm. And so it follows that other discourses may also speak from within the domain of sense, but so as to embellish rather than usurp the body's place.

In this light, to speak of the "mere" texts of modern novelists or modern intellectuals is to swallow all over again this myth that modern racial patriarchy feeds us even as it rejects it for itself. For racial patriarchy authorizes *through words* its military maneuvers and its economic programs, its distribution of material goods and its differential treatment of bodies, through curfews, ads, laws, speeches, songs, ceremonies, and treaties. It capitalizes on that connection between words and acts, bodies and texts, while denigrating the words of those who protest.

Literary critics, especially politically concerned critics, sometimes succumb to this pressure to divide words from acts when they deride the project of literary theory. I believe theories of all kinds are fruitful, for they generate a critical mass of vocabularies to pick from and to engage with the semiotic and rhetorical maneuvers of everything from Disney films to ad copy to news shows to Wordsworthian poetics. At the same time, theories are most effective if they are conceived of not merely as words but as integral to the various worlds we move in—personal, domestic, social, political, and, not least, phenomenal. The open inclusion of one's own subject position is a useful way of grounding one's theory and referring to these worlds, especially the personal, the social, and the political. But this by itself is inadequate. I feel the absence in literary criticism of attention to the world of phenomena, of trees and stars, of words as things, of bodies as contra–dictions.

In her depiction of Paul D chained to the bodies of other men in one long line, Toni Morrison renders the phenomenal as a site of contradictory possibilities, a matrix susceptible to the shapes of both the beautiful and the political. As Paul D perceives each day, his chains do not erase the beauty of the morning dew; rather,

232

they share a material plane of being with it. To be chainable is also to have eyes that see the sparkle of dew. Or, again, the materiality of his chains simultaneously puts them and him within the grip of a master and yet constitutes a means of resistance to the master. By tugging rhythmically on their chains one morning, the men in the ditch signal to one another and so effect their escape: the very phenomenality that serves the will to power thus also frees Paul D of tyranny's grasp. Chains may both imprison and liberate, just as the invisible distance between us both separates and joins us. All things of the world are reversible, metamorphic, powerful in their susceptibility to manifold uses—including their paradoxical adherence to and surpassing of the words we speak.

The more we as critics delineate the discursive realm as it intertwines with the material; the more we understand bodies, words, and things as both invaded by ideology and resistant to it; the more we resist the tendency to circumscribe the phenomenal within the ideological—the more we will have subverted and converged the positions racial patriarchy puts us in. I am white and female, of Irish-Catholic heritage, an assistant professor and a parent of two boys; but I am also a person who has typed this book sitting in a chair, sometimes gazing through the window at the sky, working with hands that are like yours. If we met, we could touch, but we needn't meet to speak and listen and see anew together: our words extend across the space between us, our writing bodies transgress the borders constructed among us. A community of scholars can achieve this phenomenal encounter, and our words should bear testimony to its phenomenality.

Notes

Preface

1. James Joyce, "Ireland, Isle of Saints and Sages," in *The Critical Writings of James Joyce*, ed. Ellsworth Mason and Richard Ellman (New York: Viking, 1959), 165.

Introduction

1. For feminist and womanist literary scholarship focused on maternal models of authorship and on literary foremothers, see Virginia Woolf, *A Room of One's Own* (New York: Harcourt Brace Jovanovich, 1929); Alice Walker, *In Search of Our Mothers' Gardens* (New York: Harcourt Brace Jovanovich, 1984); Claudia Tate, "Allegories of Black Female Desire; or, Rereading Nineteenth-Century Sentimental Narratives of Black Female Authority," in *Changing Our Own Words*, ed. Cheryl Wall (New Brunswick, N.J.: Rutgers University Press, 1989), 98–126; Dianne F. Sadoff, "Black Matrilineage: The Case of Alice Walker and Zora Neale Hurston," in *Black Women in America*, ed. Micheline R. Malson et al. (Chicago: University of Chicago Press, 1990), 197–219; Judith Kegan Gardiner, "On Female Identity and Writing by Women," in *Writing and Sexual Difference*, ed. Elizabeth Abel (Chicago: University of Chicago Press, 1982), 177–92; and see the essays in Shirley Nelson Garner, Claire Kahane, and Madelon Sprengnether, eds. *The (M)other Tongue* (Ithaca, N.Y.: Cornell University Press, 1985), as well as in Ruth Perry and Martine Watson Brownley, eds., *Mothering the Mind* (New York: Holmes and Meier, 1984). On specifically modern images of or texts involving the mother figure, see Marianne Hirsch, *The Mother-Daughter Plot* (Bloomington: Indiana University Press, 1989); Jane Silverman Van Buren, *The Modernist Madonna: Semiotics of the Maternal Metaphor* (Bloomington: Indiana University Press, 1989); E. Ann Kaplan, *Motherhood and Representation: The Mother in Popular Culture and Melodrama* (New York: Routledge, 1992); Ellen Bayuk Rosenman, *The Invisible Presence: Virginia Woolf and the Mother–Daughter Relationship* (Baton Rouge: Louisiana State University Press, 1986); and Deborah Kelly Kloepfer, *The Unspeakable Mother: Forbidden Discourse in Jean Rhys and H.D.* (Ithaca, N.Y.: Cornell University Press, 1989). See also the essays by Annette Van Dyke and Rosemary Curb in *Lesbian Texts and Contexts*, ed. Karla Jay and Joanne Glasgow (New York: New York University Press, 1990); the essays by Dorothy Allison and Molly Hite in *Reading Black, Reading Feminist*, ed. Henry Louis Gates, Jr. (New York: Meridian-Penguin Books, 1990); and the essays by Susan Rubin Suleiman, Julia Kristeva, and Nancy Huston in *The Female Body in Western Culture*, ed. Susan Rubin Suleiman (Cambridge, Mass.: Harvard University Press, 1985). See also, of course, the work of theorists such as Hélène Cixous, especially "The Laugh of the Medusa," in *New French Feminisms*,

ed. Elaine Marks and Isabelle de Courtivron (New York: Schocken, 1981), 239–56, and Julia Kristeva, especially "Stabat Mater," in *The Kristeva Reader*, ed. Toril Moi (Oxford: Basil Blackwell, 1986), 160–87.

2. Alice Jardine, *Gynesis: Configurations of Woman and Modernity* (Ithaca, N.Y.: Cornell University Press, 1985); Hirsch, *The Mother-Daughter Plot*.

3. See S. P. Fullenwider, "Jean Toomer: Lost Generation, or Negro Renaissance," in *Studies in Cane*, ed. Frank Durham (Columbus, Ohio: Charles E. Merrill, 1971), 66–75; Bernard W. Bell, "Jean Toomer's 'Blue Meridian': The Poet as Prophet of a New Order of Man" (343–52), and William J. Goede, "Jean Toomer's Ralph Kabnis: Portrait of the Negro Artist as a Young Man" (359–75), both in *Jean Toomer: A Critical Evaluation*, ed. Therman B. O'Daniel (Washington, D.C.: Howard University Press, 1988). Analogous questions have been raised about Ralph Ellison. See Valerie Smith, "The Meaning of Narration in *Invisible Man*," in *New Essays on "Invisible Man*,*"* ed. Robert O'Meally (New York: Cambridge University Press, 1988), 25–53; and Houston Baker, "To Move Without Moving," in *Black Literature and Literary Theory*, ed. Henry Louis Gates, Jr. (New York: Methuen, 1984), 221–48.

4. James Joyce, *Ulysses* (New York: Vintage, 1986), 15.1817.

5. Doris Lessing, *Martha Quest* (New York: Vintage, 1952), 10–11.

6. Samuel Beckett, *Molloy* (New York: Grove Press, 1955), 113.

7. Orlando Patterson, *Slavery and Social Death* (Cambridge, Mass.: Harvard University Press, 1982), 172–79. See chapter 1 in this volume for fuller development of this point.

8. V. G. Kiernan, *Lords of Humankind: Black Man, Yellow Man, and White Man in an Age of Empire* (Boston: Little, Brown, 1969), 229.

9. On race and Romanticism, see Mary Jacobus, *Romanticism, Writing, and Sexual Difference: Essays on "The Prelude"* (New York: Oxford University Press, 1989); Alan Richardson, "Colonialism, Race, and Lyric Irony in Blake's "The Little Black Boy," *Papers in Language and Literature*, 26 (1990): 233–48; and Richardson, "Romantic Voodoo: Obeah and British Culture, 1797–1807," *Studies in Romanticism*, 32 (Spring 1993): 3–28. On nationalism and Romanticism, see especially Marlon Ross, "Romancing the Nation State: The Poetics of Romantic Nationalism," in *Macropolitics of Nineteenth-Century Literature: Nationalism, Exoticism, Imperialism*, ed. Jonathan Arac and Harriet Ritvo (Philadelphia: University of Pennsylvania Press, 1991), 56–85. Ross comes very close to a reading of race without ever using the word; he notes kinship and blood metaphors in passing, but he reads these metaphors only within the context of nationalism.

10. bell hooks was among the first scholars to begin formulating the interconnection of American racism and images of white and black womanhood; she does so beginning with *ain't i a woman?* (Boston: South End Press, 1981). Paula Giddings, *When and Where I Enter: The Impact of Black Women on Race and Sex in America* (New York: Bantam, 1984), and Hazel Carby, *Reconstructing Womanhood: The Emergence of the Afro-American Woman Novelist* (New York: Oxford University Press, 1987), extend bell hooks's pioneering work, and yet neither of these has as its focus the examination of the *structural* meeting points of racial and sexual ideology. See also Ronald Tataki, *Iron Cages: Race and Culture in Nineteenth-Century America* (New York: Oxford University Press, 1990); Elizabeth Fox-Genovese, *Within the Plantation Household;* and Jean Fegen Yellin, *Women and Sisters: The Anti-Slavery Feminists in American Culture* (New Haven: Yale University Press, 1989). More than any of these, Ann Laura Stoler has theorized the interdependence of sexuality and race, specifically in the imperialist context; see her "Carnal Knowledge and Imperial

Power: Gender, Race, and Morality in Colonial Asia," in *Gender at the Crossroads of Knowledge: Feminist Anthropology in the Postmodern Era*, ed. Micaela de Leonardo (Berkeley: University of California Press, 1991), 51–101.

11. Caleb Saleeby, *Parenthood and Race Culture: An Outline of Eugenics* (New York: Moffat, Yard, 1911), xv.

12. Terry Eagleton, *The Ideology of the Aesthetic* (Oxford: Basil Blackwell, 1990), 28.

13. Ralph Ellison, *Invisible Man* (New York: Vintage, 1989, 1947), 581. For a fuller reading of the invisible narrator's closing suggestion that perhaps "on the lower frequencies, I speak for you," see chapter 7 in this volume, especially the final pages.

Chapter 1

1. Quoted in Magnus Hirschfeld's early study of racial ideologies in Nazi Germany entitled *Racism*, trans. and ed. Eden and Cedar Paul (New York: Kennikat Press, 1938), 298. Hirschfeld, a prominent and respected "sexologist" in Berlin from about 1910 to 1930, was concerned, among other things, about removing the stigma from homosexuality. He founded the Institute of Sexual Science, which eventually housed a library totaling ten thousand volumes. The Nazis hounded him out of Germany in 1933 and subsequently burned all of the institute's books. Hirschfeld wrote this book while in exile in 1934; it includes many useful primary sources, offers keen insights into racism, and —especially for my purposes—forges links between sexual and racial discrimination.

2. Eugenics was, in fact, an international movement in the early twentieth century. See Mark B. Adams, ed., *The Well-Born Science: Eugenics in Germany, France, Brazil, and Russia* (New York: Oxford University Press, 1990). See also Nancy Stepan's full-length study of eugenics in Latin America, *The Hour of Eugenics: Race, Gender, and Nation in Latin America* (Ithaca, N.Y.: Cornell University Press, 1991).

3. James Joyce, *Ulysses* (New York: Vintage, 1986), 14.1284–85. Also see 14.832 and 14.1250.

4. *F. Scott Fitzgerald in His Own Time: A Miscellany*, ed. Matthew J. Bruccoli and Jackson R. Bryer (Kent, Ohio: Kent State University Press, 1971), 18.

5. Benjamin Kidd, *The Control of the Tropics* (New York: Macmillan, 1898), 2.

6. Quoted in Donald A. MacKenzie, *Statistics in Britain, 1865–1930: The Social Construction of Scientific Knowledge* (Edinburgh: Edinburgh University Press, 1981), 34.

7. S. D. Porteus and Marjorie Babcock, *Temperament and Race* (Boston: Richardo G. Badger, 1926), 327.

8. Quoted in MacKenzie, *Statistics in Britain*, 88.

9. Ibid., 86.

10. Henry H. Goddard, *Human Efficiency and Levels of Intelligence* (Princeton, N.J.: Princeton University Press, 1920), 1.

11. Karl Pearson, "Darwinism, Medical Progress and Eugenics" [1912], in *Eugenics Laboratory Lecture Series*, ed. Charles Rosenberg (New York: Garland, 1985), 23.

12. George Bernard Shaw, *Man and Superman* (New York: Penguin Books, 1977), 25.

13. Quoted in Kevles, *In the Name of Eugenics: Genetics and the Uses of Human Heredity* (New York: Knopf, 1985), 88, 90, 64. The essays in Adams, *The Well-Born Science*, further demonstrate the diverse uses and voices of eugenics. Nancy Stepan notices that eugenics "as a theme, seems to have that porous quality that makes it open to many interpretations" (personal correspondence, August 25, 1992).

14. For an account of dissenting voices in the racialist debate, see Carl Degler, *In Search of Human Nature: The Decline and Revival of Darwinism in American Social Thought* (New York: Oxford University Press, 1991); and for an interesting analysis of the various degrees and strategies of dissent, see Nancy Leys Stepan and Sander Gilman, "Appropriating the Idioms of Science: The Rejection of Scientific Racism," in *The Bounds of Race: Perspectives on Hegemony and Resistance*, ed. Dominick LaCapra (Ithaca, N.Y.: Cornell University Press, 1991), 72–103. I am inclined to question Degler's picture of a dissenting faction nearly equal in authority and influence to the scientific–racialist voice (14, 109, 187, and throughout). My view is closer to that of Stepan, Gilman, Kevles, and others who highlight the degree to which the tradition of racialist and deterministic science set the terms of the discussion.

15. Francis Galton, *Inquiries into Human Faculty and Its Development* (London: Macmillan, 1883), 25–26, 29.

16. In Searle, *Eugenics and Politics in Britain*, 27.

17. Raymond B. Cattell, *The Fight for Our National Intelligence* (London: P. S. King & Son, 1937), 5, v. Cattell's book is among many that mingle the class, racial, and gender fears characteristic of the mainstream eugenics movement (see, e.g., 1–5, 61–62, 104–5). Cattell also writes explicitly in the rhetoric of battle, beginning with his book title, continuing through chapters and sections with headings such as "Sharper Definition of the Field of Campaign" and "Perspectives on Measures in a First Attack," and ending with the judgment that the "struggle" to reverse "dysgenic" trends "will not be won by firing a long-range gun. . . . It will be won by men and women fit for the hand-to-hand fighting of communities" (164). For eye-opening and insightful documentation of the intensification of such rhetoric in the late nineteenth and early twentieth centuries, see Cecil Degrotte Eby, *The Road to Armageddon: The Martial Spirit in English Popular Literature, 1870–1914* (Durham: Duke University Press, 1987). See also H. Bruce Franklin, *War Stars* (New York: Oxford University Press, 1988).

18. As described by Havelock Ellis, *Little Essays of Love and Virtue* (New York: George H. Doran, 1922), 151. Although Ellis argued against the presence of any serious "racial degradation" (152) and dissociated himself from the eugenic panic, he nonetheless considered one of the highest ends of marriage to be procreation in the service of the race. After a series of chapters on the special erotic intimacy that may be achieved between men and women, Ellis turns in his last chapter, "The Individual and the Race," to "the most intimate of all relations" (134). In other books, such as *Man and Woman*, Ellis similarly seems to defend women's needs and strengths ("the advantages of women's affectability," for example) while at the same time he holds in place a model in which women are instruments to "higher ends." See Havelock Ellis, *Man and Woman: A Study of Human Secondary Sexual Characteristics*, 6th ed. (London: A & C Black, 1926), xxii.

19. Quoted in Darwin, *The Origin of Species and the Descent of Man* (New York: Modern Library, 1936), 505.

20. Sidney Webb, *The Decline in the Birth Rate*, Fabian Tract No. 131 (London: The Fabian Society, 1907), 16–17.

21. Cattell, *The Fight for Our National Intelligence*, 124.

22. Quoted in Kidd, *Control of the Tropics*, 76.

23. Quoted in Leon Poliakov, *The Aryan Myth: A History of Racist and Nationalist Ideas in Europe*, trans. Edmund Howard (London: Chatto Heinemann, 1974), 268.

24. Cattell, *The Fight for Our National Intelligence*, 1. For a similar argument about the

fall of empire owing to "racial deterioration," see W. E. Castle, *Genetics and Eugenics* (Cambridge, Mass.: Harvard University Press, 1916). This popular textbook went through four editions in fifteen years.

25. Kenneth M. Ludmerer, *Genetics and American Society* (Baltimore: Johns Hopkins University Press, 1972), 99.

26. Quoted in Mark Haller, *Eugenics: Hereditarian Attitudes in American Thought* (1963; rpt. New Brunswick, N.J.: Rutgers University Press, 1984), 146, 147. Edward A. Ross, *The Old World in the New* (New York: The Century Co., 1914), 113. See also Prescott F. Hall, *Immigration and Its Effects Upon the United States* (New York: Henry Holt, 1906).

27. Degler, *In Search of Human Nature*, 18–19.

28. Quoted in Ludmerer, *Genetics and American Society*, 101.

29. Quoted in ibid., 104.

30. Madison Grant, *The Passing of the Great Race* (New York: Charles Scribner's Sons, 1916), 56.

31. Quoted in Haller, *Eugenics*, 148.

32. Grant, *The Passing of the Great Race*, 15–16.

33. Haller, *Eugenics*, 152.

34. Kevles, *In the Name of Eugenics*, 83.

35. Haller, *Eugenics*, 137.

36. See Harry Laughlin, *The Legal Status of Eugenical Sterilization*, Supplement to the Annual Report of the Municipal Court of Chicago (Chicago, 1930), 52.

37. Kevles, *In the Name of Eugenics*, 168.

38. Haller, *Eugenics*, 138.

39. Ibid., 138.

40. Kevles, *In the Name of Eugenics*, 107.

41. Ibid., 108. Such practices lingered even after the sterilization laws were revoked. In 1976, for instance, it came to light that the Indiana Health Service had ignored federal regulations and sterilized over a thousand women without their consent (ibid., 275).

42. Goddard, *Human Efficiency*, 1.

43. Aristotle, as a founding father of Western metaphysics, himself sets a precedent for this usage when he describes it as "natural and expedient for the body to be ruled by the soul, and for the emotional part of our natures to be ruled by the mind." See Aristotle, *The Politics*, trans. T. A. Sinclair (New York: Penguin, 1981), 68.

44. Quoted in Kevles, *In the Name of Eugenics*, 107.

45. Ibid., 108.

46. Quoted in ibid., 53.

47. Quoted in ibid., 116.

48. Ibid., 89.

49. Castle, *Genetics and Eugenics*, 263.

50. F. P. Armitage, "Introduction," in Cattell, *Fight for Our National Intelligence*, xiii.

51. Quoted in Joan Burstyn, "The Medical Case Against Higher Education for Women in England, 1870–1900," in *Proceedings of the American Philosophical Society*, 117, no. 2 (April 1973): 87.

52. For the persistence of such arguments in contemporary politics, see, for example, Geraldine Heng and Janadas Devan, "State Fatherhood: The Politics of Nationalism, Sexuality, and Race in Singapore," in *Nationalisms and Sexualities*, ed. Andrew Parker et

al. (New York: Routledge, 1992), 343–65. Susan Faludi's book *Backlash* (New York: Crown, 1991), might also be read as an exposure of lingering eugenic pressures on women in the United States.

53. Caleb Saleeby, *Parenthood and Race Culture: An Outline of Eugenics* (New York: Moffat, Yard, 1911), 182, xv, xiii–xiv.

54. Ibid., xv.

55. See note 18.

56. Stepan and Gilman, "Appropriating the Idioms of Science," 92.

57. Cattell, *Fight for Our National Intelligence*, 151, 152, 154. Though too mercurial a figure to analyze adequately here, Sigmund Freud deserves fuller study for his participation in a discourse in which sexual and racial assumptions intertwine. Sander Gilman has approached Freud from this direction, but much work remains to be done.

58. Quoted in Kevles, *In the Name of Eugenics*, 57.

59. For work on the interchangeability and overlaying of sexual and racial tropes, see Edward Said, *Orientalism* (New York: Pantheon, 1978); Sander Gilman, "Black Bodies, White Bodies: Toward an Iconography of Female Sexuality in Late Nineteenth-Century Art, Medicine, and Literature," in *"Race," Writing, and Difference*, ed. Henry Louis Gates, Jr. (Chicago: University of Chicago Press, 1985), 223–61; Satya P. Mohanty, "Drawing the Color Line: Kipling and the Culture of Colonial Rule," in LaCapra, *The Bounds of Race*, 311–43; and Henry Louis Gates, Jr., *Figures in Black* (New York: Oxford University Press, 1987), where Gates speaks, for instance, of the "metaphorical substitution of sex for race" in *Cane* (221). Black feminist criticism, in particular, improves on such models as well as on merely "additive" models in focusing on what Barbara Smith has described as the "crucially interlocking factors" of race, sex, and class. See her seminal essay "Toward a Black Feminist Criticism," reprinted in *The New Feminist Criticism*, ed. Elaine Showalter (New York: Pantheon, 1985), 170. And yet the project to "suspend," in the words of Valerie Smith, "the variables of race, class, and gender in mutually interrogative relation" ("Black Feminist Theory and the Representation of the 'Other,'" in *Changing Our Own Words* [New Brunswick, N.J.: Rutgers University Press, 1989], 48) still tends to leave unformulated the underlying logic and interlocked economy that determine these variables' relations to one another. I would not substitute one project for the other, since the "mutually interrogative" method allows for a fluidity of analysis which the attempt to surface "a" logic or "an" economy tends to limit. But I believe that at this point we sorely lack the latter kind of analysis. The only other scholar I am aware of who takes the structural approach is Ann Laura Stoler; as I do here, she also emphasizes the ways in which "sexual control has figured in the fixing of racial boundaries per se"; see her "Carnal Knowledge and Imperial Power: Gender, Race, and Morality in Colonial Asia," in *Gender at the Crossroads of Knowledge: Feminist Anthropology in the Postmodern Era*, ed. Micaela di Leonardo (Berkeley: University of California, Press, 1991), 55.

60. I use the term *compounded* to suggest that such an approach analyzes the exchanges and special pressures that result from intersections of racial, sexual, and class oppressions, though without making an analysis of the structures underlying these exchanges and pressures. Historians such as Ronald Tataki and Jacqueline Jones seem to me to make excellent use of this compounding methodology.

61. See Louise Lamphere, "Foreword" to di Leonardo, *Gender at the Crossroads of Knowledge*, ix.

62. Anne McClintock, "'No Longer in a Future Heaven': Women and Nationalism in South Africa," *Transition*, 51 (1991): 120.

63. Some feminist anthropologists prefer to use the word *patriarchy* only to describe those cultures in which inheritance is patrilineal, which is not the case in many non-Western societies, as well as in most modern Western societies. I am using it not in this strict sense but in effect as a synonym for male gender hierarchy.

64. See MacKenzie, *Statistics in Britain*, 86.

65. Igor Kopytoff, ed., *The African Frontier: The Reproduction of Traditional African Societies* (Bloomington: Indiana University Press, 1987), 122; emphasis added.

66. Lila Abu-Lughod, *Veiled Sentiments: Honor and Poetry in Bedouin Society* (Berkeley: University of California Press, 1986), 56.

67. Ivan Brady, *Transactions in Kinship: Adoption and Fosterage in Oceania* (Honolulu: University of Hawaii Press, 1976), x.

68. For an interesting case of the uses of spiritual kinship, see Bernard Vernier, "Putting Kin and Kinship to Good Use: The Circulation of Goods, Labour, and Names on Karpathos (Greece)," in *Interest and Emotion: Essays on the Study of Family and Kinship*, ed. Hans Medick and David Warren Sabean (Cambridge: Cambridge University Press, 1984), 28–76. The collection also contains two thought-provoking essays on "the clash of interests between mother and child."

69. Jack Goody, *The Development of the Family and Marriage in Europe* (Cambridge: Cambridge University Press, 1983), chap. 9.

70. David M. Schneider is prominent among those who question the vocabulary of kinship altogether, asserting that "'kinship' is an artifact of the anthropologists' analytical apparatus" and "does not exist in any culture known to man"; see his *Critique of the Study of Kinship* (Ann Arbor: University of Michigan Press, 1984), vii.

71. See the introduction in Jane Fishburne Collier and Sylvia Junko Yanagisako, eds., *Gender and Kinship: Essays Toward a Unified Analysis* (Stanford: Stanford University Press, 1987), 3–8. Most of the essays in this collection either explicitly or implicitly underwrite this view. See also the essays in di Leonardo, *Gender at the Crossroads of Knowledge*, including Harold W. Scheffler, "Sexism and Naturalism in the Study of Kinship," 361–82. Scheffler defends kinship studies and considers Collier and Yanagisako too narrow in their view of how kinship and gender studies might best be combined. In my understanding of Collier and Yanagisako, Scheffler has less of a disagreement with them than he seems to think.

72. See, for instance, the dialogues in Gates, *"Race," Writing, and Difference*, and Judith Butler, *Gender Trouble: Feminism and the Subversion of Identity* (New York: Routledge, 1990).

73. Collier and Yanagisako, *Gender and Kinship*, 13. Also see the introduction to di Leonardo, *Gender at the Crossroads of Knowledge*.

74. Gayle Rubin, "The Traffic in Women: Notes on the 'Political Economy' of Sex," in *Toward an Anthropology of Women*, ed. Rayna Reiter (New York: Monthly Review Press, 1975), 157–211. In her full and cogent essay Rubin gives a critical edge to Claude Lévi-Strauss's insight in *The Elementary Structures of Kinship* (Boston: Beacon, 1969) that "the reciprocal bond basic to marriage is not set up between men and women, but between men and men by means of women, who are only the principal occasion for it" (6). What for Lévi-Strauss is a culture-building bond for Rubin and many other women is a culture-

inhibiting subjection. Rubin's insight does not apply to all societies. In some cultures—including, to a certain degree, earlier aristocratic European societies—it appears that men have been "trafficked" in as much as women, insofar as older men have a general "rights-in-persons" that allows them to determine marriage arrangements for younger men as well as women. On the social model of "rights-in-persons," see Suzanne Miers and Igor Kopytoff, eds., *Slavery in Africa: Historical and Anthropological Perspectives* (Madison: University of Wisconsin Press, 1977), 7–11. See also Polly Hill, "Comparative West African Farm-Slavery Systems," in *Slaves and Slavery in Muslim Africa*, ed. John Ralph Willis (London: Frank Cass and Company, 1985), 2:33–51; Jean-Paul Olivier de Sardan, "Marriage Among the Wogo," in *Relations of Production: Marxist Approaches to Economic Anthropology*, ed. David Seddon, trans. Helen Lackner (London: Frank Cass and Company, 1978); and Kopytoff, *African Frontier* (see Kopytoff's opening essay, 44–46). Also relevant are essays by Chet S. Lancaster, William P. Murphy and Caroline Bledsoe, and Randall M. Packard in *African Frontier*. In some societies female elders have a say in all social matters, including marriage arrangements. See, for example, Judith K. Brown, "Iroquois Women: An Ethnohistoric Note," in Reiter, *Toward an Anthropology of Women*, 235–52. For distinctions between economic systems of woman exchange, especially those of dowry and brideprice, see Jack Goody, "Inheritance, Property and Women," in *Family and Inheritance: Rural Society in Western Europe, 1200–1800*, ed. Jack Goody, Joan Thirsk, and E. P. Thompson (Cambridge: Cambridge University Press, 1976), 10–37. See also J. L. Comaroff, ed., *The Meaning of Marriage Payments* (New York: Academic Press, 1980).

75. A number of anthropologists have studied the links between the cultural arrangements of kinship and economy, including Claude Meillassoux, Kathleen Gough, and Jack Goody.

76. Jack Goody develops these correlations most extensively in *Technology, Tradition, and the State in Africa* (Cambridge: Cambridge University Press, 1971). On exogamous extension of "people resources," see Kopytoff, *African Frontier*, 41–43. See also James L. Watson's distinction between "open" and "closed" kinship and slave systems in his introduction to *Asian and African Systems of Slavery*, ed. James L. Watson (Berkeley: University of California Press, 1980), 1–15.

77. Kidd, *Control of the Tropics*, 2.

78. William P. Murphy and Caroline Bledsoe, "Kinship and Territory in the History of a Kpelle Chiefdom," in Kopytoff, *African Frontier*, 121–48.

79. Ibid., 140. On matrilateral ties, see also Kathleen Gough, "Nuer Kinship: A Reexamination," in *The Translation of Culture: Essays to E. E. Evans-Pritchard*, ed. T. O. Beidelman (London: Tavistock, 1971), 70–121; and Edmund R. Leach, "The Structural Implications of Matrilateral Cross-Cousin Marriage," in *Rethinking Anthropology* (London: Athlone Press, 1961), 54–104.

80. See essays in Goody, Thirsk, and Thompson, *Family and Inheritance*, esp. Joan Thirsk, "The European Debate on Customs of Inheritance, 1500–1700," 177–92. See also Goody, *Development*.

81. Ralph Ellison, *Invisible Man* (New York: Vintage, 1989), 112.

82. See, for example, *The Second Sex* (trans. H. M. Parshley [New York: Knopf, 1953]), in which Simone de Beauvoir clarifies how women serve existentially as a marginalized Other through whom men construct a centered self.

83. Quoted in Kevles, *In the Name of Eugenics*, 84, 107.

84. Aristotle, *Politics*, 68.

85. The terms are Karl Pearson's, quoted in MacKenzie, 86.

86. Quoted in Henry Louis Gates, Jr., *Figures in Black* (New York: Oxford University Press, 1987), xix.

87. Aristotle, *Politics*, 68.

88. Yvon Garlan, *Slavery in Ancient Greece*, trans. Janet Lloyd, rev. ed. (Ithaca, N.Y.: Cornell University Press, 1988), 62.

89. Paul Virgil McCracken Flesher, *Oxen, Women, or Citizens: Slaves in the System of the Mishnah* (Atlanta: Scholars Press, 1988), ix.

90. On the Chinese usage, see Gerda Lerner, *The Creation of Patriarchy* (New York: Oxford University Press, 1986), 94. Later in this chapter I return to Lerner's exploration of the historical gendering of slavery.

91. For this account of slavery I am indebted to Lerner; see esp. ibid., chap. 4. For an example of the recognition of but also the deemphasis on women's status as the first slaves, see David Brion Davis, *Slavery and Human Progress* (New York: Oxford University Press, 1984), 54–55.

92. Slave practices under Islam represent a partial exception insofar as slaves were usually women (concubines), often serving to provide additional heirs. See Orlando Patterson, *Slavery and Social Death* (Cambridge, Mass.: Harvard University Press, 1982).

93. M. I. Finley, "Slavery," in *Encyclopedia of the Social Sciences* (New York: Free Press, 1968), 14:307–13.

94. Garlan, *Slavery in Ancient Greece*, 46.

95. Aristotle, *Politics*, 57.

96. On the derivation of the word *slave*, see Davis, *Slavery and Human Progress*, 32.

97. Patterson, *Slavery and Social Death*, 172–79.

98. Henri Lévy-Bruhl, "Théorie de l'esclavage," in *Slavery in Classical Antiquity*, ed. M. I. Finley (Cambridge, Eng.: W. Heffer and Sons, 1960), 151–70.

99. See Lionel Kaplan, in Watson, *Asian and African Systems of Slavery;* and for further discussion of the applicability of categories of race and class to India's caste system, see Harold A. Gould, *The Hindu Caste System* (Delhi: Chanakya Publications, 1987), chaps. 1 and 3.

100. See Patterson, *Slavery and Social Death*, 133–34.

101. Ibid., chap. 5.

102. Jordan, *White over Black;* Tataki, *Iron Cages.*

103. Quoted in David Brion Davis, *The Problem of Slavery in Western Culture* (1966; rpt. New York: Oxford University Press, 1988), 455, 463, 461.

104. G. W. F. Hegel, *The Philosophy of History*, trans. J. Sibree (New York: Dover, 1956), 93, 98, 99.

105. Quoted in Poliakov, *The Aryan Myth*, 239–40.

106. Quoted in Patrick Brantlinger, *Rule of Darkness: British Literature and Imperialism, 1830–1914* (Ithaca, N.Y.: Cornell University Press, 1988), 183.

107. Quoted in MacKenzie, *Statistics in Britain*, 185.

108. Quoted in ibid., 86.

109. Ibid., 33.

110. James Hunt tells this story in his preface to Carl Vogt, *Lectures on Man* (London: Longman, Green, Longman, and Roberts, 1864). For accounts of women's entry into professional science, see Londa Schiebinger, *The Mind Has No Sex? Women in the Origins of Modern Science* (Cambridge, Mass.: Harvard University Press, 1989). And on the

resistance to women's progress in education and the professions see Joan N. Burstyn, "Education and Sex: The Medical Case Against Higher Education for Women in England, 1870–1900," *Proceedings of the American Philosophical Society*, 117 (April 1973), 79–89.

111. Galton, *Inquiries*, 29.

112. MacKenzie, *Statistics in Britain*, 42.

113. For discussions of the ways in which motherhood is both spiritualized and/or corporealized in Victorian culture, see Gillian Brown, *Domestic Individualism: Imagining Self in Nineteenth-Century America* (Berkeley: University of California Press, 1990); and Nicholas Bromell, *By the Sweat of the Brow: Literature and Labor in Antebellum America* (Chicago: University of Chicago Press, 1993).

Chapter 2

1. James Joyce, *A Portrait of the Artist as a Young Man*, in *The Portable James Joyce*, ed. Harry Levin (New York: Viking, 1947), 525. All subsequent references are cited in the text.

2. On race and Romanticism, see Mary Jacobus, *Romanticism, Writing, and Sexual Difference: Essays on "The Prelude"* (New York: Oxford University Press, 1989); Alan Richardson, "Colonialism, Race, and Lyric Irony in Blake's 'The Little Black Boy,'" *Papers in Language and Literature*, 26 (1990), 233–48; idem, "Romantic Voodoo: Obeah and British Culture, 1797–1807," *Studies in Romanticism*, 32 (Spring 1993), 3–28. See also the work of Nigel Leask, Marilyn Butler, and Sara Suleri.

3. Martin Bernal, *Black Athena: The Afro-Asiatic Roots of Classical Civilization* (New Brunswick, N.J.: Rutgers University Press, 1987), 1:204–11.

4. See Alan Richardson, "Romanticism and the Colonization of the Feminine," in *Romanticism and Feminism*, ed. Anne K. Mellor (Bloomington: Indiana University Press, 1988), 15.

5. William Wordsworth, *Selected Prose Writings*, ed. John O. Hayden (New York: Penguin, 1988), 289. All subsequent references to Wordsworth's prose writings are from this volume and are cited in the text as *SP*.

6. In addition to Richardson, see Barbara A. Schapiro, *The Romantic Mother: Narcissistic Patterns in Romantic Poetry* (Baltimore, Md.: The Johns Hopkins University Press, 1983). Schapiro makes many assumptions with which I disagree; for example, that maturity in a poet can be measured by his degree of separation from mother figures in the poems. She does, however, thoroughly detail the deep ambivalence in Romantic poetry toward its recurring mother figures.

7. William Wordsworth, *The Prelude*, 1799, 1805, 1850, ed. Jonathan Wordsworth, M. H. Abrams, and Stephen Gill (New York: W. W. Norton, 1979), 79.

8. On nationalism and Romanticism, see especially Marlon Ross, "Romancing the Nation State: The Poetics of Romantic Nationalism," in *Macropolitics of Nineteenth-Century Literature: Nationalism, Exoticism, Imperialism*, ed. Jonathan Arac and Harriet Ritvo (Philadelphia: University of Pennsylvania Press, 1991), 56–85. Ross comes very close to a reading of race without ever using the word; he notes kinship and blood metaphors in passing, but he reads these metaphors only within the context of nationalism. See also Anne Janowitz, *England's Ruins: Poetic Purpose and the National Landscape* (Cambridge, Mass.: Basil Blackwell, 1990).

9 See Marlon B. Ross, *The Contours of Masculine Desire: Romanticism and the Rise of Women's Poetry* (New York: Oxford University Press, 1989).

10. Quoted in Leon Poliakov, *The Aryan Myth: A History of Racist and Nationalist Ideas in Europe*, trans. Edmund Howard (London: Chatto Heinemann, 1974). See also Hannah Arendt, *The Origins of Totalitarianism* (New York: Harcourt Brace Jovanovich, 1948); and Jacques Barzun, *The French Race: Theories of Its Origins and Their Social and Political Implications, Prior to the Revolution* (New York: Columbia University Press, 1932). Poliakov's is the most thorough and careful treatment of the subject. Also pertinent are Christopher Hill's discussions of the "Norman yoke" in *Puritanism and Revolution* (New York: Schocken, 1958), and discussions throughout his *Collected Essays*, vols. 1 and 2 (Amherst: University of Massachusetts Press, 1985–86). See also V. G. Kiernan's discussion of race and class in Europe in *Lords of Humankind* (Boston: Little, Brown, 1969).

11. Kiernan, *Lords of Humankind*, 229.

12. In *The Origins of Totalitarianism* Arendt emphasizes the weakening of the aristocracy as a cause of its increased articulation of racial and conqueror mythologies (165). But she underemphasizes the revolutionaries' use of these same mythologies and therefore partly misses the channels of transmission of the ideologies. Arendt's account of the emergent European racial mythologies of hierarchy loosely aligns with more recent ones such as Poliakov's and those of historians such as George Stocking and Nancy Stepan; it remains an important contribution to the subject. Yet by now Arendt's account is less authoritative and possibly inaccurate in some of its details; see, for instance, her impressionistic discussion of polygenism in England (178), which is thrown into question by more recent historical accounts such as Nancy Stepan's in *The Idea of Race in Science* (Hamden, Conn.: Archon, 1982), 29–35.

13. Quoted in Poliakov, *The Aryan Myth*, 24.

14. Quoted in ibid., 22.

15. Montesquieu's remark is from his *Esprit des Lois* and is quoted by Poliakov, *The Aryan Myth*, 26.

16. Quoted in ibid., 29.

17. Quoted in ibid., 30. For another account of Thierry's influence in both scientific and political debates, see Claude Blanckaert, "On the Origins of French Ethnology: William Edwards and the Doctrine of Race," in *Bones, Bodies, Behavior: Essays on Biological Anthropology*, ed. George W. Stocking, Jr. (Madison: University of Wisconsin Press, 1988), 24–28.

18. Quoted in Poliakov, *The Aryan Myth*, 31. See also Thierry's book *The Third Estate in France*, trans. Rev. Frances B. Wells (London: Thomas Bosworth, 1855). For an extremely suggestive account of gender in French revolutionary propaganda, see Lynn Hunt, *The Family Romance of the French Revolution* (Berkeley: University of California Press, 1992), especially the chapter titled "The Bad Mother."

19. Poliakov, *The Aryan Myth*, 53.

20. See discussions in Antonio Gramsci, *Selections from the Prison Notebooks*, ed. Q. Hoare and G. Nowell Smith (London, 1971); and Terry Eagleton, *The Ideology of the Aesthetic* (Cambridge, Mass.: Basil Blackwell, 1990), especially pp. 62, 123. Following Gramsci, Eagleton stresses the "hybrid" nature of class ideologies in England.

21. Quoted in Poliakov, *The Aryan Myth*, 48.

22. Quoted in ibid.

23. Quoted in Hill, *Collected Essays*, 2:215.

24. Hill, "The Norman Yoke," in *Puritanism and Revolution;* and *Collected Essays*, esp. vols. 1 and 2.

25. Poliakov, *The Aryan Myth*, 47; emphasis added.

26. Jonathan Swift, "An Abstract of the History of England" in *Prose Works*, 12 vols. (London: George Bell and Sons, 1902), 10:225.

27. David Hume, *The History of England from the Invasion of Julius Caesar*, 8 vols. (London: Wm. Pickering, 1826), 1:177.

28. Nancy Stepan, *The Idea of Race in Science* (Hamden, Conn.: Archon Books, 1982), esp. chap. 1, "Race and the Return of the Great Chain of Being," 1–19.

29. Gramsci, *Prison Notebooks*, ed. Joseph A. Buttigieg, trans. Joseph A. Buttigieg and Antonio Callari (New York: Columbia University Press, 1992).

30. This point is reinforced by Marlon Ross's analysis of how Scott used the profits of his writing (read by a middle-class readership) to buy a title and land—in other words, to join the aristocracy. See Ross, "Romancing the Nation State."

31. Sir Walter Scott, *Ivanhoe* (New York: Viking Penguin, 1986), 8. All subsequent references are cited in the text.

32. See especially Georg Lukács, *The Historical Novel*, trans. M. and S. Mitchell (London: Merlin Press, 1962).

33. See a related discussion of this novel in Alide Cagidemetrio, "A Plea for Fictional Histories and Old-Time Jewesses," in *Inventing Ethnicity*, ed. Werner Sollors (New York: Oxford University Press, 1989), 14–43.

34. William Wordsworth, *The Poems*, ed. John O. Hayden (New York: Penguin, 1990), 1:370. All subsequent references are cited in the text.

35. Evidence of the gendering of race can be found in many statements and sources, especially during and after the Romantic period. F. W. Schelling speaks of a virile "Japhetic, Promethean, Caucasian race," and Ludwig Feuerbach theorizes (using gender and metaphysical distinctions together) that "the heart—the feminine principle, the sense of the finite, the seat of materialism—is French; the head—the masculine principle, the seat of idealism—is German" (quoted in Poliakov, *The Aryan Myth*, 364). Similarly, Bismarck referred to Slavs, Celts, and Latins as "womanly" races that were "passive, unproductive" (quoted in Poliakov, *The Aryan Myth*, 253). Increasingly throughout the nineteenth century, theories that feminized subjugated races gained authority (see the discussion of paedomorphism in chapter 3).

36. Marlon B. Ross, *The Contours of Masculine Desire and the Rise of Women's Poetry* (New York: Oxford University Press, 1989).

37. Quoted in ibid., 53.

38. G. W. F. Hegel, *Phenomenology of Spirit*, trans. A. V. Miller (New York: Oxford University Press, 1979), 113.

39. Edmund Burke, *Reflections on the Revolution in France* (Harmondsworth, Eng.: Penguin, 1968).

40. Herbert Spencer, "The Gospel of Relaxation," in *Land and Labour in the United States*, ed. William Godwin Moody (New York: Charles Scribner's Sons, 1883), 281.

41. Marlon Ross makes similar suggestions about the common interest (in a double sense) of science and Romantic poetry in the material world. See Ross, *Contours*, 105, and chap. 1.

42. T. H. Huxley as quoted in a creative, scholarly study of the quest motif in evolu-

tionary discourse by Misia Landau, *Narratives of Human Evolution* (New Haven, Conn.: Yale University Press, 1991), 26. In *The Descent of Man* Charles Darwin prefaces his discussion of reason with the statement that "of all the faculties of the human mind, it will, I presume, be admitted that Reason stands at the summit." He also holds that the European races "immeasurably surpass their former savage progenitors, and stand at the summit of civilization." *The Origin of Species and The Descent of Man* (New York: Modern Library, 1936), 453, 507.

Chapter 3

1. See Jack Morrell and Arnold Thackerary, *Gentlemen of Science: Early Years of the British Association for the Advancement of Science* (New York: Oxford University Press, 1981); Bruce Haley, *The Healthy Body and Victorian Culture* (Cambridge, Mass.: Harvard University Press, 1978).

2. See Michel Foucault, *The History of Sexuality*, vol. 1, *An Introduction*, trans. Robert Hurley (New York: Vintage, 1980).

3. See Nancy Stepan and Sander Gilman, "Appropriating the Idioms of Science: The Rejection of Scientific Racism," in *The Bounds of Race: Perspectives on Hegemony and Resistance*, ed. Dominick LaCapra (Ithaca, N.Y.: Cornell University Press, 1991), 72–103.

4. Terry Eagleton, *The Aesthetic of Ideology* (Oxford: Basil Blackwell, 1990), 104.

5. J. G. Spurzheim, *Phrenology, or the Doctrine of the Mental Phenomena* (Boston: Marsh Capen and Lyon, 1832), 1:17.

6. Karl Pearson, *The Grammar of Science* (London: J. M. Dent and Sons, 1892), 20.

7. See Morrell and Thackeray, *Gentleman of Science;* Carolyn Merchant, *The Death of Nature: Women, Ecology, and the Scientific Revolution* (San Francisco: Harper and Row, 1980); Londa Schiebinger, *The Mind Has No Sex? Women in the Origins of Modern Science* (Cambridge, Mass.: Harvard University Press, 1989). The influence of science had already begun to expand in the seventeenth century, as reflected in the founding of the Royal Society in London about 1645; but not until the early nineteenth century did science threaten to usurp the claims of other domains, including religion.

8. G. W. F. Hegel, *Phenomenology of Spirit*, trans. A. V. Miller (New York: Oxford University Press, 1979), 3.

9. Ibid., 21.

10. Ibid., 14.

11. Spurzheim, *Phrenology*, 15.

12. William Wordsworth, *Selected Prose Writings*, ed. John O. Hayden (New York: Penguin, 1988), 292.

13. Ibid., 293.

14. Quoted in Marlon Ross, *The Contours of Masculine Desire and the Rise of Women's Poetry* (New York: Oxford University Press, 1989), 41.

15. Wordsworth, *Selected Prose*, 388.

16. T. H. Huxley, "Science and Art," in *The World's Great Speeches*, ed. L. Copeland and L. W. Lamm (New York: Dover, 1973), 682.

17. See Lynn Hunt on masculinized mother figures in revolutionary rhetoric, *The Family Romance of the French Revolution* (Berkeley: University of California Press, 1992); on monstrous mother imagery in Victorian domestic tracts see Sally Shuttleworth,

"Demonic Mothers," in *Rewriting the Victorians: Theory, History, and the Politics of Gender*, ed. Linda Shires (New York: Routledge, 1992); see Mark Seltzer on machines made to figure as masculinized engines of reproduction in his book *Bodies and Machines* (New York: Routledge, 1992).

18. Huxley, "Science and Art," 682.

19. Ibid.

20. In chapter 1; and see my discussion in the next section of this chapter.

21. T. H. Huxley, *Collected Essays* (London: Macmillan, 1894), 3:407.

22. Although spokespersons for science such as Huxley are often considered popularizers and not true practitioners, this distinction too often veils the way in which such writers often simply made crudely explicit what "real" scientists left implicit. The implicit and the explicit work as two channels of transmission—at "higher" and "lower" cultural levels—of what are, in their political aspects, the same hierarchical ideas. Even though practitioners and popularizers might distance themselves from one another, they frequently serve one another's interests by securing a cultural foothold for scientific ideologies, thereby securing high-status employment for a range of scientific men.

23. Huxley, *Collected Essays*, 408.

24. See Schiebinger, *The Mind Has No Sex?*; Merchant, *Death of Nature*; and Ludmilla Jordanova, *Sexual Visions: Images of Gender in Science Between the Eighteenth and Twentieth Centuries* (Madison: University of Wisconsin Press, 1989).

25. See the sources cited in note 17.

26. Spurzheim, *Phrenology*, 20.

27. Herbert Spencer, *Principles of Sociology* (Westport, Conn.: Greenwood Press, 1975), 3:172.

28. See Gillian Beer, *Darwin's Plots: Evolutionary Narrative in Darwin, George Eliot, and Nineteenth-Century Fiction* (London: Routledge & Kegan Paul, 1983); Michel Foucault, *The Order of Things* (New York: Vintage, 1973), 251; Bruce Haley, *The Healthy Body and Victorian Culture* (Cambridge, Mass.: Harvard University Press, 1978). Foucault argues that the notion of a great hidden force reveals discourse working at the limits of representation; I would note, however, that a close reading of Herbert Spencer, Edward Carpenter, and others who speak of these forces shows that they equate them with the powers of reason, such as when Carpenter speaks of "Nerve force" as the highest form of energy in the physical universe. I also would suggest that these concepts of force represent further attempts to masculinize the realm of nature once it was recognized as "active."

29. Christopher Herbert, *Culture and Anomie: The Ethnographic Imagination in the Nineteenth Century* (Chicago: University of Chicago Press, 1991), 28.

30. See Nancy Stepan, *The Idea of Race in Science* (Hamden, Conn.: Archon Books, 1982).

31. George Combe, *A System of Phrenology* (New York: Wm. H. Colyer, 1841), 52.

32. Ibid., 2.

33. Ibid., 59.

34. Ibid., 52–56.

35. Spurzheim, *Phrenology*, 36.

36. Combe, *System of Phrenology*, 114.

37. Although phrenology itself was not sufficiently long-lived as an authoritative science to become the established basis for such arguments, it certainly provided the materials. Later in the nineteenth-century, studies first of pelvic structures, then of repro-

ductive organs, would be used to prove that women's destiny was childbearing. See Schiebinger, *The Mind Has No Sex?;* Joan N. Burstyn, "Education and Sex," in *Proceedings of the American Philosophical Society*, 117 (April 1973), 79–89; Thomas Laqueur, "Orgasm, Generation, and the Politics of Reproductive Biology," in *The Making of the Modern Body*, ed. Catherine Gallagher and Thomas Laqueur (Berkeley: University of California Press, 1987), 133–65; and Flavia Alaya, "Victorian Science and the 'Genius' of Women," in *Journal of the History of Ideas*, 38 (1977): 261–80.

38. J. G. Spurzheim, *The Physiognomical Systems of Drs Gall and Spurzheim, Founded on an Anatomical and Physiological Examination of the Nervous System in General and of the Brain in Particular; and Indicating the Dispositions and Manifestations of the Mind* (London: Baldwin, Cranbock, and Joy, 1815), 105.

39. Quoted in Stepan, *Idea of Race*, 25–26; emphasis added.

40. Combe, *System of Phrenology*, 485.

41. See Haley, *The Healthy Body and Victorian Culture.*

42. For these phrases, in their respective order, see ibid., 35; Robert Knox, *The Races of Men: A Fragment* (Philadelphia: Lea and Blanchard, 1850), 34; Geroge Stocking, Jr., ed., *Bones, Bodies, and Behavior: Essays on Biological Anthropology* (Madison: University of Wisconsin Press, 1988), 23; and S. D. Porteus and Marjorie Babcock, *Temperament and Race* (Boston: Richardo G. Badger, 1926), 327.

43. Robert Knox, *The Races of Men*, 7. All subsequent references are cited in the text.

44. Charles Darwin, *The Descent of Man* (New York: Modern Library, 1958), 418.

45. Francis Galton, *Inquiries into Human Faculty and Its Development* (London: Macmillan, 1883), 332.

46. Darwin, *Descent*, 507.

47. Ibid., 502.

48. Saint-Simon, quoted in Leon Poliakov, *The Aryan Myth: A History of Racist and Nationalist Ideas in Europe* (London: Chatto and Heinemann, 1974), 217; emphasis added.

49. Porteus and Babcock, *Temperament and Race*, 169, 172.

50. Alaya, "Victorian Science," 266.

51. Quoted ibid., 267.

52. Francis Galton, *Hereditary Genius* (New York, 1870), 38.

53. Cesare Lombroso quoted in Alaya, "Victorian Science," 267.

54. Darwin, *Descent*, 907.

55. See Haley, *Healthy Body*, 60–68 and passim.

56. Quoted in Alaya, "Victorian Science," 265.

57. G. Stanley Hall, quoted in Stephen Jay Gould, *Ontogeny and Phylogeny* (Cambridge, Mass.: Harvard University Press, 1977), 130; Benjamin Kidd, *The Control of the Tropics* (New York: Macmillan, 1898), 52.

58. Francis Galton, "Hereditary Talent and Character," in *Images of Race*, ed. Michael Biddis (New York: Holmes and Meier, 1979), 69.

59. Carl Vogt, *Lectures on Man*, ed. James Hunt (London: Longman, Green, Longman and Roberts, 1864), 192 and 81. See also Nancy Stepan, "The Use of Analogy in Science: Race and Sex" *Isis*, 77 (1986): 261–77.

60. Quoted in Gould, *Ontogeny and Phylogeny*, 131.

61. Porteus and Babcock, *Temperament and Race*, 162.

62. Friedrich Schiller, *On the Aesthetic Education of Man*, ed. Elizabeth M. Wilkinson and L. A. Willoghby (Oxford: Oxford University Press, 1967), 163, 169, 217.

63. Terry Eagleton, *The Ideology of the Aesthetic* (Oxford: Basil Blackwell, 1990), 28, 13.

64. Schiebinger, *The Mind Has No Sex?;* Jordanova, *Sexual Visions.*

65. Charles Darwin, *Origin of Species and The Descent of Man* (New York: Modern Library, 1936), 51. All subsequent references are cited in the text.

66. For an early refutation of biological science's reduction of all relationships to "struggle," see Peter Kropotkin, *Mutual Aid* [1902], as excerpted in *Darwin: The Norton Critical Edition,* ed. Philip Appleman, 2d ed. (New York: Norton, 1979), 405–15. Kropotkin to some degree exempts Darwin from his critique in ways I would not.

67. See Beer, *Darwin's Plots,* especially the chapter titled "Darwin's Language."

68. Maurice Merleau-Ponty, *The Visible and the Invisible* (Evanston, Ill.: Northwestern University Press, 1968), 133. All subsequent references are cited in the text as *VI.*

69. For a pertinent essay on the relation of Merleau-Ponty's thought to Hegel's, see Joseph C. Flay, "Merleau-Ponty and Hegel: Radical Essentialism," in *Ontology and Alterity in Merleau-Ponty,* ed. Galen A. Johnson and Michael B. Smith (Evanston, Ill.: Northwestern University Press, 1990), 142–57. Flay's argument about Hegel is loosely similar to mine in that he finds a deep radicalism in his thought, though I consider that radicalism to be buried (alive, one might say) in Hegel's thought. I also consider "essentialism" an inadequate word for describing Merleau-Ponty's thinking.

70. Here again my view of the relation between Hegel and Merleau-Ponty differs significantly from Flay's.

71. G. W. F. Hegel, *The Philosophy of History,* trans. John Sibree (New York: Dover, 1956), 93, 90.

72. Herbert, *Culture and Anomie,* 67.

73. Edmund Husserl, *The Crisis of European Sciences and Transcendental Phenomenology,* trans. David Carr (Evanston, Ill.: Northwestern University Press, 1970), 51–52.

74. Maurice Merleau-Ponty, *Phenomenology of Perception,* trans. Colin Smith (New York: Routledge & Kegan Paul, 1981), viii. All subsequent references are cited in the text as *PP.*

75. Hélène Cixous, "The Laugh of the Medusa," in *New French Feminisms,* ed. Elaine Marks and Isabelle de Courtivron (New York: Schocken Books, 1981), 254.

76. Husserl, *Crisis of European Sciences,* 106–7, 217.

77. Martin Heidegger, *Being and Time,* trans. John Macquarrie and Edward Robinson (New York: Harper & Row, 1962), 88.

78. Ibid., 88.

79. See Jacques Derrida, *Speech and Phenomena,* trans. David B. Allison (Evanston, Ill.: Northwestern University Press, 1973).

80. Maurice Merleau-Ponty, *The Structure of Behavior,* trans. Alden Fisher (Boston: Beacon Press, 1963), 148.

81. Notwithstanding Elaine Scarry's argument about Christianity as an ideological embrace of the corporeal world; see Elaine Scarry, *The Body in Pain* (New York: Oxford University Press, 1985).

82. Darwin, *Descent of Man,* 502.

83. See Sigmund Freud, *Introductory Lectures on Psychoanalysis,* trans. James Strachey (New York: Norton, 1966), 285.

84. Stan Draenos, *Freud's Odyssey: Psychoanalysis and the End of Metaphysics* (New Haven: Yale University Press, 1982).

85. For discussion of Freud's Jewish identity as a source of complications for his attitudes toward sexuality and the body, see John Murray Cuddihy, *The Ordeal of Civility: Freud, Marx, Lévi-Strauss, and the Jewish Struggle with Modernity* (New York: Basic Books, 1974). For a reading that complicates Freud's analysis of sexuality and the body more generally, see Leo Bersani, *The Freudian Body: Psychoanalysis and Art* (New York: Columbia University Press, 1986).

86. Herbert Marcuse, *Eros and Civilization* (Boston: Beacon, 1955); and Bersani, *The Freudian Body*.

87. See Michael David Levin, "Visions of Narcissism: Intersubjectivity and the Reversals of Reflection," in *Merleau-Ponty Vivant*, ed. M. C. Dillon (Albany: State University of New York Press, 1991), 47–90.

88. See *The World of Henri Wallon*, ed. Gilbert Voyat (New York: Jason Aronson, 1984).

89. Carol Gilligan, *In a Different Voice* (Cambridge, Mass.: Harvard University Press, 1982); Sara Ruddick contributes two essays related to this point, "Maternal Thinking" and "Preservative Love and Military Destruction," in *Mothering*, ed. Joyce Trebilcot (Totowa, N.J.: Rowman and Allanheld, 1983), 213–30 and 231–62.

90. Maurice Merleau-Ponty, "The Child's Relations with Others," trans. William Cobb, in *The Primacy of Perception*, ed. James M. Edie (Evanston, Ill.: Northwestern University Press, 1964), 96–155.

91. Virginia Woolf, *To the Lighthouse* (New York: Harcourt Brace Jovanovich, 1926), 9.

92. Daniel Stern, *The Interpersonal World of the Human Infant* (New York: Basic Books, 1985), esp. 47–53, 86–87. Stern unfortunately retains a partially metaphysical model when he speaks of "amodal" perception and of the functions of language.

93. See Jacques Lacan, "The Mirror Stage as Formative of the Function of the 'I'" and "The Function and Field of Speech and Language in Psychoanalysis," in *Écrits*, trans. Alan Sheridan (New York: Norton, 1977), 1–8, 30–113. Although Lacan's ideas have helped to make some important links between the complexes of inhabitants of kin–patriarchal cultures as understood by Freud and the functions of language, his phallic determinism closes off as many possibilities as his critique opens up. His determinism stems from his assumption about the infant's lack of existential capacities, which leaves a vacuumlike set of needs that the phallic Law fills. When Lacan speaks of the "primordial discord" (4) of the infant's world; when he pities infants' "motor incapacity and nursling dependence" and postulates a "specific prematurity of birth" in human infants (4); and when he imagines a mirror as the only source of the infant's bodily self-consciousness, he toes the kin–patriarchal metaphysical line on embodiment and "lack," and above all reveals his own lack of observation of or involvement with infants. This lack may explain Lacan's defensiveness toward the "matriarchal air" of female psychoanalysts, and his dismissal of object relations psychology, "to which our analyst-nurses are so attached" (37).

94. See Julia Kristeva, *Revolution in Poetic Language*, trans. Margaret Waller (New York: Columbia University Press, 1984).

95. Quoted in Thomas Langan, *Merleau-Ponty's Critique of Reason* (New Haven: Yale University Press, 1966), 125.

96. See William Andrews, *To Tell a Free Story: The First Century of Afro-American Autobiography* (Urbana: University of Illinois Press, 1986), and Mikhail Bakhtin, *The Dialogic Imagination: Four Essays*, trans. Caryl Emerson and Michael Holquist (Austin:

University of Texas Press, 1981). Also see Lev Vygotsky, *Thought and Language,* ed. and trans. Alex Kozulin (Cambridge, Mass.: MIT Press, 1986), and Michael Holquist, "The Politics of Representation," in *Allegory and Representation,* ed. S. J. Greenblatt (Baltimore: Johns Hopkins University Press, 1982), 163–83.

97. For evidence that Merleau-Ponty himself had glimpsed the symbolic role of the mother, see Merleau-Ponty, *Visible and Invisible,* 267.

Chapter 4

1. Critics have noted the way in which male–female boundaries substitute for and overlap with black–white boundaries in *Cane.* Following Robert Bone, Henry Louis Gates, Jr., speaks of the "metaphorical substitution of sex for race" in this book; see his *Figures in Black: Words, Signs, and the Racial Self* (New York: Oxford University Press, 1987), 221. While I agree that the interconnectedness of race and sex sometimes takes the form of metaphorical substitutions, it seems to me—with respect to *Cane* and in general—that the relationship between the imagery of race and sex is more than metaphorical. That is, boundaries of race and of sex work together as interlocked elements in a system of economic hierarchy and competitive male homosociality. The imagery of sex and race in *Cane* serves to delineate, acutely and critically, this structural relationship between sex and race, not merely to set up echoes between them.

2. Eve Kosofsky Sedgwick, *Between Men: English Literature and Male Homosocial Desire* (New York: Columbia University Press, 1985).

3. Jean Toomer, *Cane* (New York: Liveright, 1975). All subsequent references are cited in the text.

4. I am indebted to Karen Prager's senior thesis at Harvard University, "Destroying the White Baby Doll" (1991) for the placement of Toomer's poem within the blazon tradition of poetry.

5. See John Mbiti, *African Religions and Philosophy* (New York: Praeger, 1969), for an account of nonmetaphysical African views of the universe which may have carried into African American culture. For evidence of such carryover, see Melville J. Herskovits, *The Myth of the Negro Past* (1941; rpt. Boston: Beacon Press, 1958); Lawrence Levine, *Black Culture and Black Consciousness* (New York: Oxford University Press, 1977); and Joseph E. Holloway, *Africanisms in American Culture* (Bloomington: Indiana University Press, 1990).

6. For feminist readings of the blazon tradition in Renaissance poetry, see Nancy Vickers, "Diana Described: Scattered Women and Scattered Rhyme," in *Writing and Sexual Difference,* ed. Elizabeth Abel (Chicago: University of Chicago Press, 1982); and Vickers, "This Heraldry in Lucrece' Face," in *The Female Body in Western Culture,* ed. Susan Rubin Suleimen (Cambridge, Mass.: Harvard University Press, 1986).

7. On song in American slave culture, see Levine, *Black Culture and Black Consciousness,* 5–19, 190–297.

8. Critics likewise show a mixture of pity and admiration for the alienation of the women in *Cane,* such as when Houston Baker, Jr., describes *Cane* as "a book in which Afro-American women are beautifully and tragically mute in their own repressed spirituality"; see his "There Is No More Beautiful Way," in *Afro-American Literary Study in the 1990s,* ed. Houston A. Baker, Jr., and Patricia Redmond (Chicago: University of Chicago Press, 1989), 149. Patricia Chase's discussion, "The Women in Cane," in *Jean Toomer: A*

Critical Evaluation, ed. Therman B. O'Daniel (Washington, D.C.; Howard University Press, 1988), 389, recognizes but sees no need to critique the fact that Toomer's women are "rare and sensual" just like "the form" of his book and that they serve as instruments of his fictional vision.

9. See Nicholas Bromell, *By the Sweat of Our Brow* (Chicago: University of Chicago Press, 1993), for a provocative discussion of the relationship between labor, freedom, and song in Afro-American slave narratives.

10. For a parallel discussion of Romanticism in relation to *Cane,* see Barbara E. Bowen, "Untroubled Voice: Call and Response in *Cane,"* in *Black Literature and Literary Theory,* ed. Henry Louis Gates, Jr. (New York: Methuen, 1984), 187–205. Bowen suggests that *Cane* "enacts the confrontation of Romanticism and Afro-American culture" (202) but contrasts the Romantic search for an "unfallen continuity of language and nature" to *Cane*'s attempt to recover an "Unexiled continuity of speaker and listener" (194). In my view *Cane,* in the Romantic tradition, desires union with nature as well as with a listener. And for *Cane,* as for the Romantic, both of these Others are problematically gendered. Similarly, although my assessment comes very close to Bowen's that in *Cane* there is a "meeting of self-consciousness with nostalgia for an untroubled voice" (188), I locate much of the "trouble" in this meeting to gender, an aspect of Toomer's text to which Bowen pays little attention.

11. For discussions of *Cane* in terms of its favoring of body over mind, see Bernard Bell, "A Key to the Poems in *Cane,"* and Udo O. H. Jung, "Spirit-Torsos of Exquisite Strength," both in O'Daniel, *Jean Toomer,* 321–27, 293–96.

12. Toomer himself commented that "we are hypnotized by literacy," revealing his consciousness that the power of writing can become writing's power *over* those objects it represents. Quoted in Gates, *Figures in Black,* 196.

13. In *Specifying* (Madison: University of Wisconsin Press, 1987), Susan Willis reads Paule Marshall's character "Avey" in *Praisesong* as a critical gloss on Toomer's portrayal of Avey in *Cane.* Willis understands Toomer's Avey as "the embodiment of her creator's own conflicted relationship to race" (82). Although I agree with Willis, I would suggest, as in note 1, that such women are not merely projections of or substitutes for the men's racial conflicts, but are part and parcel of those conflicts insofar as a male racial identity requires a subordinate female identity. See the closing paragraphs of this chapter for a further comment on this point.

14. Elisabeth Bronfen, *Over Her Dead Body: Death, Femininity, and the Aesthetic* (New York: Routledge, 1992).

15. Significantly, in Toomer's own account the homosocial call-and-response poem "Harvest Song" forms the "spiritual" climax and end point of his book: "From the point of view of the spiritual entity behind the work, the curve really starts with Bona and Paul (awakening), plunges into Kaabnis, emerges in Karintha, etc., swings upward into Theater and Box Seat, and ends (pauses) in Harvest Song." Quoted in Bowen, "Untroubled Voice," 195.

16. For a loose comparison of *Cane* to James Joyce's *Portrait,* see William J. Goede, "Jean Toomer's Kabnis: Portrait of the Negro Artist as a Young Man," in O'Daniel, *Jean Toomer* (359–75); and for the association of Toomer's work with white modernism, see Bernard Bell, "Blue Meridian: The Poet as Prophet of a New Order of Man," in O'Daniel, *Jean Toomer* (343–52). These essays indirectly support my comparison of Toomer and Joyce, but my analysis has little in common with theirs.

17. For a full discussion of the blocked access of racially subordinate men to culture-building through women (thus feminizing the men), see chapter 1.

18. A line from "November Cotton Flower" (Toomer, *Cane*, 4) which implicitly alludes to Karintha.

19. See Susan Blake, "The Spectatorial Artist and the Structure of Cane," in O'Daniel, *Jean Toomer* (198–211) for an insightful analysis of the narrative distances created in *Cane* and problematized in the character of Kabnis.

20. Toomer laments: "With Negroes also the trend was toward the small town and then the city—and industry and commerce and machines. The folk-spirit was walking in to die on the modern desert. That spirit was so beautiful. Its death was so tragic. . . . And this was the feeling I put into *Cane*. *Cane* was a swan-song. It was a song of an end" (quoted in Bowen, "Untroubled Voice," 196). Given Toomer's Romantic gendering of that folk landscape and spirit ("so beautiful"), we may well read his book as an "end" ("so tragic") to a certain kind of male–female relation in the making of cultural artifacts, as I do here.

21. For discussions of Toomer's turnabout in racial identity, see Gates, *Figures in Black*, chap. 7; Darwin Turner, "Introduction," in Toomer, *Cane;* Nellie McKay, *Jean Toomer, Artist: A Study of His Literary Life and Work, 1894–1936* (Chapel Hill: University of North Carolina Press, 1984), chap. 6; and Alice Walker, *In Search of Our Mothers' Gardens* (New York: Harcourt Brace Jovanovich, 1984).

Chapter 5

1. James Joyce, *Ulysses*, ed. Hans Walter Gabler et al. (New York: Random House, 1986), 15.4648. All subsequent references are cited in the text.

2. A few works have begun to attend to the signs of race, or constructions of whiteness, in texts of white writers. See Aldon Lynn Nielsen, *Reading Race: White American Poets and the Racial Discourse in the Twentieth Century* (Athens: University of Georgia Press, 1988); and Toni Morrison, *Playing in the Dark* (New York: Vintage Books, 1993).

3. Harry Levin, "Introduction," in *The Portable James Joyce*, ed. Harry Levin (New York: Viking Press, 1974), 4.

4. See Ira B. Nadel, *Joyce and the Jews: Culture and Texts* (Basingstoke, Hampshire: Macmillan, 1989). For documentation of Joyce's familiarity with racial theories, see Marilyn Reizbaum, "James Joyce's Judaic Other: Texts and Contexts" (Ph.D. diss., University of Wisconsin, 1985); appendix 1 includes a list of books in Joyce's library related to Jews and racial theory.

5. For Reizbaum's argument that in *Ulysses* Joyce critiqued Otto Weininger's book *Sex and Character*, see her essay "The Jewish Connection Cont'd," in *The Seventh of Joyce*, ed. Bernard Benstock (Bloomington: Indiana University Press, 1982), 229–37.

6. Otto Weininger, *Sex and Character* (1906; rpt. New York: AMS Press, 1975), 302, 316, 329.

7. Richard Ellmann, *James Joyce* (New York: Oxford University Press, 1972), 477. See also Reizbaum, "Jewish Connection," 229–30.

8. James Joyce, "Ireland, Isle of Saints and Sages," in *The Critical Writings of James Joyce*, ed. Ellsworth Mason and Richard Ellman (New York: Viking, 1959), 165. All subsequent references are cited in the text.

9. James Joyce "Force," in *Critical Writings*, 22. All subsequent references are cited in the text.

10. Werner Sollors has explored the racial mythologies in which the story of Cain becomes entangled in his paper "The Curse of Ham," presented at Harvard University, October 1990.

11. Zoe borrows from the Song of Solomon a line that translates "I am black, but comely, O ye daughters of Jerusalem." See Don Gifford with Robert J. Seidman, *Ulysses Annotated*, 2d ed. (Berkeley: University of California Press, 1988), 470. All subsequent references are cited in the text. Vincent Cheng has also brought to my attention another meaning of jujuby—the candy which comes in the colors of the British Empire.

12. In addition to the references to horse races discussed in this essay, see Joyce, *Ulysses*, 5.526–48; 6.559; 7.385; 8.156; 8.813–45; 8.1008–19; 12.1550–65; 15.2140; 15.2936; 15.3965–90; 15.4862; 16.1242–80; 18.424–26. For an essay that pays similar attention to these references, see Vincent Cheng, "White Horse, Dark Horse: Joyce's Allhorse of Another Color," *Joyce Studies Annual*, 2 (Summer 1991): 101–28.

13. See Cecil Degrotte Eby, *The Road to Armageddon* (Durham: Duke University Press, 1987).

14. James Joyce, *A Portrait of the Artist as a Young Man*, in *The Portable James Joyce*, ed. Harry Levin (New York: Viking, 1947), 525. All subsequent references are cited in the text.

15. See annotations for the "Oxen of the Sun" chapter in Gifford, *Ulysses Annotated*.

16. See L. P. Curtis, Jr., *Apes and Angels: The Irishman in Victorian Caricature* (Washington, D.C.: Smithsonian Institution Press, 1971).

17. For another reading of Ulysses as more than merely parodic, see James McMichaels, *Ulysses and Justice* (Princeton, N.J.: Princeton University Press, 1991).

18. Several critics, however, have considered Bloom an unflattering stereotype of the Jew, including in his sensuality. For discussion of this issue and the question of whether Joyce was anti-Semitic, see Edmund L. Epstein, "Joyce and Judaism," in Benstock, *The Seventh of Joyce*, 221–24.

19. Toni Morrison, *Beloved* (New York: Knopf, 1987), 273.

20. Kimberly Devlin, "The Female Eye: Joyce's Voyeuristic Narcissists," in *New Alliances in Joyce Studies*, ed. Bonnie Kime Scott (Newark: University of Delaware Press, 1988), 135–43.

21. Maurice Merleau-Ponty, *The Visible and the Invisible* (Evanston, Ill.: Northwestern University Press, 1968), 123.

22. See, for example, Theodore Holmes, "Bloom, the Father," *Sewanee Review*, 79 (Spring 1971); 236–55; and Vladimir Nabokov's lectures on *Ulysses* in *Lectures on Literature*, ed. Fredson Bowers (New York: Harcourt Brace Jovanovich, 1980).

23. William Faulkner, *Light in August* (New York: Vintage, 1990). For instance, in Faulkner's novel bodies in motion define intersecting narrational horizons, as with Lena Grove and Armstid in the novel's opening scene; likewise the novel uses spatial organization to represent a collapse of gender and racial boundaries when its racially and sexually ambiguous characters converge on the town of Jefferson.

24. Roy K. Gottfried, *The Art of Joyce's Syntax in Ulysses* (Athens: University of Georgia Press, 1980).

25. See the essays in *Women in Joyce*, ed. Suzette Henke and Elaine Unkeless (Urbana: University of Illinois Press, 1982).

Chapter 6

1. Virginia Woolf, *Three Guineas* (New York: Harcourt Brace Jovanovich, 1938), 109. All subsequent references are cited in the text.

2. Quoted in Mark Haller, *Eugenics* (1963; rpt. New Brunswick, N.J.: Rutgers University Press, 1984), 147.

3. For Woolf's reading of and writing about Hakluyt, see Alice Fox, *Virginia Woolf and the English Renaissance* (Oxford: Clarendon Press, 1990). For a discussion of Woolf and Darwin, see Gillian Beer, "Virginia Woolf and Pre-History," in *Virginia Woolf: Centenary Essays*, ed. Eric Warner (New York: St. Martin's Press, 1984), 99–123.

4. Beer, "Virginia Woolf and Pre-History," 113.

5. For discussion of this dynamic of border expansion, see Marlon Ross, "Romancing the Nation State," in *Macro-Politics of the Nineteenth Century*, ed. Jonathan Arac and Harriet Ritvo (Philadelphia: University of Pennsylvania Press, 1991), 56–57.

6. For a discussion of the voyaging theme in Woolf, see Fox, *Virginia Woolf*; Louise DeSalvo, "Introduction," in Virginia Woolf, *Melymbrosia* (New York: New York Public Library, 1982), xxxiii–ix.

7. Woolf, *Melymbrosia*, 21. All subsequent references are cited in the text.

8. Virginia Woolf, "Professions for Women," in *Virginia Woolf: Women and Writing*, ed. Michelle Barrett (New York: Harcourt Brace Jovanovich, 1980), 59. All subsequent references are cited in the text.

9. Virginia Woolf, *To the Lighthouse* (New York: Harcourt Brace Jovanovich, 1927), 59. All subsequent references appear in the text.

10. For discussion of the Comus allusions, see Evelyn Haller, "The Anti-Madonna in the Work and Thought of Virginia Woolf," in *Virginia Woolf: Centennial Essays*, ed. Elaine K. Ginsberg and Laura Moss Gottlieb (Troy, N.Y.: Whitston, 1983).

11. For discussion of Isis and other Egyptian allusions in Woolf, see ibid., 96–97; DeSalvo, "Introduction," xxxiii; and Jane Marcus, *Virginia Woolf and the Languages of Patriarchy* (Bloomington: Indiana University Press, 1978), chap. 2.

12. For Mr. Pepper's meditations on Empire, see Woolf, *Melymbrosia*, 11, 69, 101.

13. See Beer, "Virginia Woolf and Pre-History," 108–9.

14. See George Ella Lyon, "Virginia Woolf and the Problem of the Body," in Ginsberg and Gottlieb, *Virginia Woolf*, 114–16.

15. See Ann Laura Stoler, "Carnal Knowledge and Imperial Power: Gender, Race, and Morality in Colonial Asia," in *Gender at the Crossroads of Knowledge*, ed. Micaela de Leonardo (Berkeley: University of California Press, 1991), 51–101.

16. In Virginia Woolf, *The Voyage Out* (London: Duckworth and Company, 1915), the homoerotic elements of this passage are deleted, and Helen appears as a sky god rather than an earth goddess. Her hand drops "abrupt as iron" on Rachel's shoulder; "it might have been a bolt from heaven" (283–84). Also Rachel looks up from the grass to see Helen and Terence together above her. Woolf seems to make her own substitution of male for mother in this revision.

17. For a discussion of the body as Woolf's means of locating her narrative outside history, see Jo-Ann Wallace, "Woolf's 'Spinsters': The Body and the Blank Page of His/Story," *English Studies in Canada*, 16, no. 2 (June 1990): 202. More generally, for another discussion that uses Merleau-Ponty to illuminate Woolf's treatment of the body,

see Mark Hussey, *The Singing of the Real World* (Columbus: Ohio State University Press, 1986).

18. Maurice Merleau-Ponty, *The Visible and the Invisible* (Evanston, Ill.: Northwestern University Press, 1968), 135. All subsequent references to this work appear in the text as *VI*.

19. Hélène Cixous, "The Laugh of the Medusa," in *New French Feminisms*, ed. Elaine Marks and Isabelle de Courtivron (New York: Schocken, 1981), 251.

20. For a provocative discussion of Woolf's mixed impulses of nostalgia and liberation, see John Burt, "Irreconcilable Habits of Thought in *A Room of One's Own* and *To the Lighthouse*," in *Virginia Woolf: Modern Critical Views*, ed. Harold Bloom (New York: Chelsea House, 1986), 191–206.

21. For an example of one such theory, based on the ideas of Nancy Chodorow, see Judith Kegan Gardiner, "On Female Identity and Writing by Women," in *Writing and Sexual Difference*, ed. Elizabeth Abel (Chicago: University of Chicago Press, 1982), 177–92. On Woolf, see Minow Pinckney, *Virginia Woolf and the Problem of the Subject* (Brighton, Sussex: Harvester, 1987).

22. Cixous, "The Laugh of the Medusa," 254.

23. Mikhail Bakhtin, *The Dialogic Imagination*, trans. Carly Emerson and Michael Holquist (Austin: University of Texas Press, 1981).

24. James Joyce, *A Portrait of the Artist as a Young Man*, in *The Portable James Joyce*, ed. Harry Levin (New York: Viking, 1947), 429–32.

25. See J. Hillis Miller, "Mrs. Dalloway: Repetition as the Raising of the Dead," in Bloom, *Virginia Woolf*, 169–90.

26. Some of Woolf's more cautious representations of the body might well be read as the effect of her experience of molestation by her half-brother, including not only the discussions in *A Room of One's Own* and "Professions" but also those moments in her fiction where characters' bodies hardly touch and are brought together mainly through external objects. This image of time nosing its way into the house may also resonate with that part of her experience. I would suggest that both Woolf's extreme sensitivity to bodies and her artful reticence about them derive in part from this trauma. For full discussion of Woolf as a victim of incest, see Louise DeSalvo, *Virginia Woolf: The Impact of Childhood Sexual Abuse on Her Life and Work* (New York: Ballantine Books, 1989).

27. See Julia Kristeva, "Women's Time," in *The Kristeva Reader*, ed. Toril Moi (Oxford: Basil Blackwell, 1986), 187–213.

Chapter 7

1. Ralph Ellison's attempts to avoid strict racial affiliations, like Jean Toomer's, has sometimes "jeopardized his credibility with more ideological writers and scholars," as Valerie Smith notes; see her essay "The Meaning of Narration in *Invisible Man*," in *New Essays on "Invisible Man*," ed. Robert O'Meally (New York: Cambridge University Press, 1988), 26. But once we see how white modernists engaged questions of race, we may understand Ellison's attraction to writers such as Joyce as a recognition, whether conscious or unconscious, that he shared with them the problematics of racial–patriarchal aesthetics.

2. For full treatment of Ellison's dialogical intertwining of white and black traditions, see Alan Nadel, *Invisible Criticism: Ralph Ellison and the American Canon* (Iowa City:

University of Iowa Press, 1988). See also the variety of discussions in the section titled "The Novel and Its Afro-American, American, and European Traditions," in *Approaches to Teaching Ralph Ellison's Invisible Man,* ed. Susan Resneck Parr and Pancho Savery (New York: Modern Language Association, 1989).

3. Ralph Ellison, *Invisible Man* (New York: Vintage, 1980), 354–55. All subsequent references are cited in the text.

4. For another discussion of the invisible man–visible text paradox, see Hortense Spillers, "Ellison's 'Usable Past': Toward a Theory of Myth," in *Speaking for You: The Vision of Ralph Ellison,* ed. Kimberly Benston (Washington, D.C.: Howard University Press, 1987), 144–58.

5. Samuel Beckett, *Molloy* (New York: Grove Press, 1955), 8. All subsequent references are cited in the text.

6. On Jean Rhys, see Deborah Kelly Kloepfer, *The Unspeakable Mother: Forbidden Discourse in Jean Rhys and H.D.* (Ithaca, N.Y.: Cornell University Press, 1989). See also Laura Anne Doyle, *The Body Poetic: Language and Materiality in Modern Women's Narrative* (Ann Arbor: University of Michigan Press, 1987).

7. See *The Diary of Virginia Woolf,* vol. 3, *1925–1930,* ed. Anne Olivier Bell (New York: Harcourt Brace Jovanovich, 1980), 107.

8. The period of Ellison's writing this novel coincided with that of Marcus Garvey's call to black nationalism and his organization of trade unions, and in general with a time of active unrest among the expanding populations of blacks in northern cities. As Harlem became increasingly overcrowded and for decades after the Great Depression work grew scarce for blacks, a number of "race riots" occurred, including the one in 1943 which Ellison covered for the *New York Post*. Although the discourse of eugenics had been hushed by events in Nazi Germany, the intertwined pressures of race and gender peculiar to a racial–patriarchal economy remained palpable and severe, as my reading of the novel confirms.

9. Many critics have noted the invisible man's ambivalence toward his southern past, and several have also commented on the role of women in Ellison's novel, but none that I am aware of has considered in full the relation between these two elements. As a result most critics have suggested that the narrator has come to accept that past which the young protagonist keeps trying to escape. But the narrator's bracketing of the vision of the slave mother in the prologue indicates that he still suffers from the old ambivalence. My account revises the view of the invisible man as progressing toward knowledge through storytelling; by contrast I suggest that both the narrator's and Ellison's acts of storytelling, which continue the subsumption of mother figures, repeat the problems unresolved in the protagonist's life. For consideration of women and gender in the novel, see Hortense Spillers, "'The Permanent Obliquity of an In(pha)llibly Straight': In the Time of the Daughters and the Fathers," in *Changing Our Own Words,* ed. Cheryl Wall (New Brunswick, N.J.: Rutgers University Press, 1989), 127–49; Claudia Tate, "Notes on the Invisible Women in Ralph Ellison's *Invisible Man,*" in Benston, *Speaking for You,* 163–72; and Mary Rohrberger, "'Ball the Jack': Surreality, Sexuality, and the Role of Women in *Invisible Man,*" in Parr and Savery, *Approaches,* 124–32.

10. For discussion and historicization of this battle metaphor, see John S. Wright, "The Conscious Hero and the Rites of Man: Ellison's War," in O'Meally, *New Essays on "Invisible Man,"* 157–87. Wright is among those critics who pay passing attention to the "maternal folk community" in the novel; but he is also among those who give a progressive

account of the novel in which the protagonist "ultimately reaffirms" this community and its past (161).

11. See also Spillers, "Usable Past," for a reading of the novel as offering no redemption from or solution to the problems it raises.

12. In Trueblood's account Matty Lou eventually comes to feel pleasure and does not want him to pull away from her, but it is also clear that he has forced his way into her against her will. By my definition this is rape, which is not to say rape is uncomplicated. On the contrary, one problematic aspect of child molestation and rape is that bodies sometimes respond positively to unasked-for advances, and this ambivalence puts the victim in the position of sorting through his or her own responsibility for the act. But such victims are not responsible for these acts when they have labored to resist them. Yet most critics underplay or misrepresent Trueblood's violation of his daughter. Some speak merely of Trueblood as having "slept with his daughter" (see Smith, "The Meaning of Narration," 45) while others actually suggest that Matty Lou initiated the fondling. Keith Byerman, for instance, misreads Matty Lou's whispering "Daddy" as a direct address (read invitation) to her father; but Trueblood himself recognizes that she is thinking of some other man in her dream and is using the term colloquially (Ellison, *Invisible Man*, 56). In his otherwise careful and enlightening study of black fiction, Byerman goes so far as to suggest that Matty Lou "instinctively responds to a man sleeping with her"; see Keith Byerman, *Fingering the Jagged Grain* (Athens: University of Georgia Press, 1985), 18. But more telling and more pertinent here than these accounts of the rape is the tendency to read Trueblood's storytelling and his self-made identity as a model for Ellison and his narrator. Thomas Schaub speaks for several other critics when he suggests that Trueblood, who "lives by his own tempo and tells his own story," provides the "key to Ellison's sophisticated handling of structure and language in this novel" (Thomas Schaub, "Ellison's Masks and the Novel of Reality," in O'Meally, *New Essays on "Invisible Man,"* 140). In fact, I agree with Schaub that storytelling is the "enabling instrument" by which both the narrator and Trueblood "manage to retain a sense of themselves apart from the controlling images other have of them" (150). But more attention might be paid to the use of black women's bodies and stories in the making of these stories told by the men. Hortense Spillers in "The Permanent Obliquity" and Houston Baker in his analysis of the "phallic" performance of Trueblood, are among the few scholars who bring any critical light to Trueblood's narrative. See Baker's essay "To Move Without Moving," in *Black Literature and Literary Theory*, ed. Henry Louis Gates, Jr. (New York: Methuen, 1984), 221–48.

13. Michael Awkward, "Roadblocks and Relatives: Critical Revision in Toni Morrison's *The Bluest Eye*," in *Critical Essays on Toni Morrison*, ed. Nellie McKay (Boston: G. K. Hall, 1988), 57–67.

14. We might notice a similar situation in Richard Wright's *Native Son*, in which Bigger's rape of his black girlfriend hardly figures as an event in the novel but is a moment of release for the anger, fear, and frustration Bigger feels after having been trapped (like Trueblood) in a white man's house with a white woman. See his discussion of Wright's novel in this context in Houston Baker, Jr., *The Workings of the Spirit: The Poetics of Afro-American Women's Writing* (Chicago: University of Chicago Press, 1991), 126–28.

15. See Rohrberger, "Ball the Jack," and Tate, "Notes on the Invisible Women," for discussions of Mary.

16. Trueblood, in fact, compares the "dark tunnel" he enters in his dream to "the power plant they got up to the school" (Ellison, *Invisible Man*, 58).

17. Ralph Ellison, "Out of the Hospital and Under the Bar," in *Soon One Morning: New Writing by American Negroes, 1940–1962,* ed. Herbert Hill (New York: Alfred A. Knopf, 1963), 244. All subsequent references are cited in the text.

18. Jean Toomer, *Cane* (New York: Liveright, 1975), 69.

19. In contrast to Toomer, who seems more attuned to the problematics of mind over body and less aware of the pitfalls of sexual hierarchy, Ellison seems more aware of gender complications and yet is more conventional in his view of metaphysical relations and narratives. In an interview with John O'Brien printed in *Interviews with Ten Black Writers* (New York: Liveright, 1973), Ellison speaks of the centrality of "consciousness" and remarks that "human life is a move toward the rational" (83).

20. Toni Morrison, *Beloved* (New York: Knopf, 1987), 2.

21. My point may be read as a relative one in light of Ellison's sense of kinship with Ernest Hemingway (as analyzed by Robert O'Meally) insofar as he and Hemingway both love "the things of this earth" more than any theory or ideology about them. See Robert G. O'Meally, "The Rules of Magic: Hemingway as Ellison's Ancestor," in Benston, *Speaking for You,* 245–71. However, a close reader of Hemingway might find some Ellisonian ambivalence toward and neutralizing of the meaning of "the things of this earth."

22. This reduction of Mary to a kind of folk content for Ellison's "wider" form might take on further significance in light of Houston Baker's analysis of Ellison's use of folk traditions; see "To Move Without Moving."

Chapter 8

1. Michael Awkward, "Roadblocks and Relatives: Critical Revision in Toni Morrison's *The Bluest Eye,*" in *Critical Essays on Toni Morrison,* ed. Nellie McKay (Boston: G. K. Hall, 1988), 57–67.

2. For other discussions of the body, motherhood, and history in *Beloved,* see Anne E. Goldman, "'I Made the Ink': (Literary) Production and Reproduction in *Dessa Rose* and *Beloved,*" *Feminist Studies,* 16, no. 2 (1990): 313–30; Barbara Offutt Mathieson, "Memory and Mother Love in Morrison's *Beloved,*" *American Imago,* 47, no. 1 (Spring 1990): 1–21; and David Lawrence, "Fleshly Ghosts and Ghostly Flesh: The Word and the Body in *Beloved,*" *Studies in American Fiction,* 19, no. 2 (Autumn 1991): 189–201. For a pertinent discussion of representations of the flesh and the material world in relation to history in Afro-American women's literature, see Hortense J. Spillers, "Mama's Baby, Papa's Maybe: An Annotated Grammar Book," *Diacritics,* 17 (Summer 1987): 65–83; and Houston A. Baker, Jr., *The Workings of the Spirit: The Poetics of Afro-American Women's Writing* (Chicago: University of Chicago Press, 1991).

3. Having written her master's thesis on "Virginia Woolf's and William Faulkner's Treatment of the Alienated" (Cornell University, 1955), Morrison later creates fiction which implicitly extends her reflections there.

4. Ralph Ellison, *Invisible Man* (New York: Vintage, 1980), 273. All subsequent references are cited in the text.

5. Toni Morrison, *The Bluest Eye* (New York: Washington Square Press, 1971), 92. All subsequent references are cited in the text.

6. Cornel West, "The Black Body," Ralph Waldo Emerson Lecture at Harvard University, Spring 1991.

7. William Andrews, *To Tell a Free Story* (Urbana: University of Illinois Press, 1986).

8. See Melvin Dixon, *Ride Out the Wilderness: Geography and Identity in Afro-American Literature* (Urbana: University of Illinois Press, 1987). Baker, *Workings of the Spirit*, chap. 3; and Morrison's interview with Robert Stepto, "'Intimate Things in Place': A Conversation with Toni Morrison," in *Chant of Saints: A Gathering of Afro-American Literature, Art, and Scholarship*, ed. Michael S. Harper and Robert B. Stepto (Urbana: University of Illinois Press, 1979), 213–29.

9. Martin Heidegger, *Being and Time,* trans. John Macquarrie and Edward Robinson (San Francisco: Harper & Row, 1962), 219–24.

10. Toni Morrison, *Beloved* (New York: Knopf, 1987), 162. All subsequent references are cited in the text.

11. *Narrative of the Life of Frederick Douglass, An American Slave,* ed. Houston A. Baker, Jr. (New York: Penguin, 1982), 48.

12. J. W. C. Pennington, "The Fugitive Blacksmith," in *Great Slave Narratives,* ed. Arna Bontemps (Boston: Beacon, 1969), 206.

13. William Craft, "Running a Thousand Miles for Freedom," in *Great Slave Narratives,* 271.

14. For a study of the disruption of gender relations and sexual behavior among slave youth, see Anthony S. Parent, Jr., and Susan Brown Wallace, "Childhood and Sexual Identity Under Slavery," in *American Sexual Politics: Sex, Gender, and Race Since the Civil War,* ed. John C. Fout and Maura Shaw Tantillo (Chicago: University of Chicago Press, 1993), 19–58.

15. Jean Rhys, *Good Morning, Midnight* (New York: Harper & Row, 1939), 10.

16. See, for example, Lawrence, "Fleshly Ghosts and Ghostly Flesh," 192–93; and Baker, *Workings of the Spirit*, 37.

17. Thus Morrison revives the desires of not only Sethe and Paul D through Denver but also the "collapsed" Baby Suggs. My reading of Baby Suggs contrasts on this point with that of Trudier Harris, who interprets Baby Suggs as assuming the role of victim, in *Fiction and Folklore: The Novels of Toni Morrison* (Knoxville: University of Tennessee Press, 1991), 175.

18. Virginia Woolf, *The Waves* (London: Hogarth Press, 1990), 203.

Conclusion

1. For another discussion of the flesh versus the body, see Hortense Spillers, "Mama's Baby, Papa's Maybe: An Annotated Grammar Book," *Diacritics,* 17 (Summer 1987): 65–83.

2. Elaine Scarry, *The Body in Pain* (New York: Oxford University Press, 1985).

Index

Alaya, Flavia, 64
Andrews, William, 79, 209
Anthropology, 21–23
Arendt, Hannah, 245n.12
Aristotle, 28, 31, 239n.43
 Politics, 29
Art
 competition of science with, 55–58
 intercorporeality and, 169–73, 217–19, 227
 racial patriarchy and, 35–36
Artist, subordinate group, 26–27, 33–34
Awkward, Michael, 187, 206

Baker, Houston, Jr., 188, 252n.8, 259n.12
Bakhtin, Mikhail, 79, 161
Beckett, Samuel, 8
 Molloy, 3, 4, 176, 202
Beddoe, John, 63
Beloved (Morrison)
 animal imagery in, 221, 222, 223
 Clearing scene in, 223–25
 Denver and, 226–29
 gender relations in, 212–17
 intercorporeality and, 126–27, 209–10, 223–25, 229–30, 232–33
 narrative structure in, 217–19, 221–22
 narrator in, 126–27, 161, 218
 race mother in, 209
 racial patriarchy and, 26–27, 209
 slavery and, 203, 206, 209–12, 213–14, 215–17, 221
 tree imagery in, 212–19, 220, 223, 224
Bernal, Martin, 36
Biology. *See* Eugenics; Science
Birth control, 12
Bledsoe, Caroline, 24
Body. *See also* Intercorporeality; Materiality; Maternal; Metaphysics
 in *Beloved*, 217–19, 224–26
 in *Cane*, 86–88, 91–94
 disembodiment and, 33–34, 175–76, 194
 drive for containment of, 54, 55–58
 Freud's developmental story and, 77
 in *Invisible Man*, 190–94
 male vs. female protagonists and, 177–78
 movement of, 87, 129–30, 137, 219–20, 255n.23

narrative structure and, 41–42, 82, 86–88
phenomenology and, x, 7, 70–76
science and, 61, 66–67, 231
subjectivity of, 67, 86–88
in *Ulysses*, 126, 127–28
in Woolf, 143–44
Bowen, Barbara E., 253n.10
Brigham, Carl, 16
Bronfen, Elizabeth, 100, 102
Buck v. Bell, 16
Burton, Sir Richard, 31

Camus, Albert, 3, 4
Cane (Toomer)
 artist–characters in, 100–102, 103, 109
 homosociality and, 82–85, 89, 91, 94–100
 intercorporeality and, 81–82, 85–88, 91–92, 94
 narrative structure in, 85–88
 narrators in, 84–85, 94–100, 102–3
 race mother in, 33, 81–82, 94–102, 103–8
 racial patriarchy and, 26, 82–85, 90–94, 101
 relation between sex and race and, 252n.1
 Ulysses and, 103, 105
Castle, W. E., 18–19
Cattell, Raymond B., 13–14, 20, 32, 238n.17
Chase, Patricia, 252n.8
Cheng, Vincent, 115, 255n.11
Cixous, Hélène, 72, 153
Class boundaries. *See also* Laborer
 eugenics and, 31–32
 kinship patriarchy and, 24–25
 phrenology and, 61
 racial patriarchy and, 37–40, 44–47
Co-adaptation
 in Darwin, 67–70, 73, 153
 in Merleau-Ponty, 70–71, 73–74, 77–80
Colette, 8
Collier, Jane Fishburne, 241n.71
Combe, George, 59–60, 61
Community economy, 22, 23–24
Competition
 homosocial, and race mother, 179, 180–89, 197–201
 horse race imagery in *Ulysses* and, 115–17
 natural selection and, 68–69
 notions of materiality and, 55–58

263

in *Invisible Man*, 179, 180–89, 197–201,
202–3
narrator and, 125, 126–27
race and, 125
race mother and, 82–85, 109, 178–80
racial patriarchy and, 109
hooks, bell, 236n.10
Human development, stories of, 76–80
Hume, David, 39–40
Hunt, James
Hurston, Zora Neale, 8
Husserl, Edmund, 72–73
Huxley, T. H., 52–53, 57–58

Immigration, and eugenics, 14–15
Intelligence. *See also* Metaphysics
as genetically coded, 11–12, 64
race and, 15–16, 28, 63–64
Intercorporeality. See also *Beloved; To the
Lighthouse*
concept of, 67, 70–71, 72, 73–76
disruption of racial patriarchy and, 76–80
eugenics and, 7
human development and, 76–80
interruption and, 8
language and, 79–80, 175–77, 204–5, 232–33
literary criticism and, x, 232–33
metaphysics and, 21–22, 70–71, 161, 173
narrative structure and, 110–11, 128–31,
137–38
reversibility and, 73–74, 75, 79–80
textual practice of, 94, 131, 157–64, 206,
217–19
words and, 79–80, 161–64, 232–33
Interruption, 175–78, 204–5. See also *Invisible Man*
intercorporeality and, 8
in *To the Lighthouse*, 164–67
Invisible Man (Ellison)
ambivalence in, 178–80, 186, 191–93, 196–
97, 202–4
intercorporeality and, 199, 200, 204–5
Mary sections of, 189–97
metaphysics of racial patriarchy and, 175–
78
narrative structure in, 180–89, 199
narrator in, 175–78, 204, 258n.9
objects in, 199–200, 207–8
race mother in, 33, 178–80, 191–93, 196–97
racial patriarchy and, 26, 185–88, 194–95
rape scene in, 186–89, 258n.12
riot scene in, 201–5
slavery and, 203, 230
speech in, 180–89, 197–201

Jacobus, Mary, 6
Janowitz, Anne, 37

Jardine, Alice, 3
Jennings, H. S., 15
Jones, Gayl, 8
Corregidora, 3, 4, 177
Jordanova, Ludmilla, 67
Joyce, James. See also *Ulysses*
eugenics and, 115–16, 128
A Portrait of the Artist as a Young Man, 35,
79, 118, 119, 123, 124, 175
racial patriarchy and, 26, 35–36
Judeo-Christian tradition, 76, 120–21, 121

Kevles, David, 12
Kidd, Benjamin, 11, 24, 65
Kiernan, V. G., 5, 37
Kinship patriarchy, 5, 21–23. *See also* Racial
patriarchy; theory of
Knox, Robert, 62–63
Kopytoff, Igor, 22
Kpelle of Liberia, 24–25
Kristeva, Julia, x, 79, 173

Laborer
in *To the Lighthouse*, 167–69
science and, 57–58, 63
Wordsworth and, 42–47, 57, 58
Lacan, Jacques, x, 79, 251n.93
Lamphere, Louise, 21
Language. *See* Speech
Larsen, Nella, 3
Late-Romantic text, 82, 102, 201, 203. See
also *Cane; Ulysses*
Laughlin, Harry, 10, 15
Lerner, Gerda, 29
Lessing, Doris, 4, 8, 33, 177, 202
Levin, Harry, 111
Lévi-Strauss, Claude, 23, 241n.74
Lévy-Bruhl, Henri, 30

McClintock, Anne, 21
MacKenzie, Donald, 32
Marriage
eugenics and, 15–16, 24, 26
kinship patriarchy and, 23–26
miscegenation and, 15–16
Marx, Karl, 40
Materiality. *See also* Body
co-adaptation and, 67–71
competing conceptions of, 55–58
gendered rhetoric and, 153–55
intercorporeality and, 76–80, 156–57
in *Invisible Man*, 182–84, 185
in *Melymbrosia*, 144, 145, 148–50
metaphysics of race and sex and, 58–67
narrative of human development and, 76–
80
phenomenology and, 71–76
in *To the Lighthouse*, 150–57